TECHNICAL AND VOCATIONAL EDUCATION AND TRAINING IN THE PHILIPPINES IN THE AGE OF INDUSTRY 4.0

MARCH 2021

ASIAN DEVELOPMENT BANK

 Creative Commons Attribution 3.0 IGO license (CC BY 3.0 IGO)

© 2021 Asian Development Bank
6 ADB Avenue, Mandaluyong City, 1550 Metro Manila, Philippines
Tel +63 2 8632 4444; Fax +63 2 8636 2444
www.adb.org

Some rights reserved. Published in 2021.

ISBN 978-92-9262-573-3 (print); 978-92-9262-574-0 (electronic); 978-92-9262-575-7 (ebook)
Publication Stock No. TCS210084
DOI: http://dx.doi.org/10.22617/TCS210084

The views expressed in this publication are those of the authors and do not necessarily reflect the views and policies of the Asian Development Bank (ADB) or its Board of Governors or the governments they represent.

ADB does not guarantee the accuracy of the data included in this publication and accepts no responsibility for any consequence of their use. The mention of specific companies or products of manufacturers does not imply that they are endorsed or recommended by ADB in preference to others of a similar nature that are not mentioned.

By making any designation of or reference to a particular territory or geographic area, or by using the term "country" in this document, ADB does not intend to make any judgments as to the legal or other status of any territory or area.

This work is available under the Creative Commons Attribution 3.0 IGO license (CC BY 3.0 IGO) https://creativecommons.org/licenses/by/3.0/igo/. By using the content of this publication, you agree to be bound by the terms of this license. For attribution, translations, adaptations, and permissions, please read the provisions and terms of use at https://www.adb.org/terms-use#openaccess.

This CC license does not apply to non-ADB copyright materials in this publication. If the material is attributed to another source, please contact the copyright owner or publisher of that source for permission to reproduce it. ADB cannot be held liable for any claims that arise as a result of your use of the material.

Please contact pubsmarketing@adb.org if you have questions or comments with respect to content, or if you wish to obtain copyright permission for your intended use that does not fall within these terms, or for permission to use the ADB logo.

Corrigenda to ADB publications may be found at http://www.adb.org/publications/corrigenda.

Notes:
In this publication, "$" refers to United States dollars.
ADB recognizes "China" as the People's Republic of China and "Vietnam" as Viet Nam.

Cover design by Michael Cortes.

Contents

Tables, Figures, and Boxes	iv
Foreword by the Vice-President, Asian Development Bank	ix
Foreword by the Director General, Technical Education and Skills Development Authority	x
Acknowledgments	xi
Contributors	xiii
Abbreviations	xv
Executive Summary	xvii

Part I.	**Economic and Labor Market Context**	**1**
	1. Structural Transformation in the Philippines	2
	2. Labor Market Diagnostics	21
	3. Industry 4.0 and the Changing Demand for Labor	45
	4. Impact of COVID-19 on the Labor Market	67
Part II.	**Technical and Vocational Education and Training and the Education System in the Philippines**	**85**
	5. Technical and Vocational Education and Training Provision in the Context of Industry 4.0	86
	6. Education System Reforms and the Implications for Technical and Vocational Education and Training	102
	7. Technical and Vocational Education and Training Trends Over the Last Decade	114
Part III.	**Empirical Findings for Technical and Vocational Education and Training Performance**	**133**
	8. Employment Outcomes for Technical and Vocational Education and Training Graduates	134
	9. Returns to Technical and Vocational Education and Training in the Philippines	150
	10. Measuring Training–Job Mismatch	173
	11. Impact of the Technical Education and Skills Development Authority Scholarships	186
Part IV.	**Conclusions and Recommendations**	**209**
	12. What Works for Technical and Vocational Education and Training: Review of International Experience	210
	13. Conclusions and Recommendations	222

Background Papers	233
References	234

Tables, Figures, and Boxes

Tables

2.1	Change in Key Labor Market Indicators by Demographic Group, 2008–2018	23
2.2	Regional Diagnostics and Labor Market Indicators, 2018	32
A2.1	Regional Labor Market Indicators by Demographic Groups, 2018	42
3.1	Changing Importance of Different Skills in the IT-BPO and Electronics Manufacturing Industries, 2018 and 2030	65
4.1	Unemployed Persons by Highest Grade Completed, April 2020 versus April 2019	73
4.2	Job Losses and Labor Reallocation, 2020	74
7.1	Top 10 Qualifications with Expected Occupations and Corresponding Occupational Groups, 2013–2016	123
7.2	Regional Technical and Vocational Education and Training Statistics	126
A7.1	Male and Female Share of Graduates, Employment-to-Population Rate, Unemployment Rate, and Labor Force Participation Rate by Course/Program	130
8.1	Average Treatment Effect on the Treated of Technical and Vocational Education and Training on Employment Outcomes, 2018	140
8.2	Overidentification Test for Covariate Balance	140
8.3	Wald Test for Endogeneity of the Unobservable Characteristics	140
A8.1	Summary Statistics of the Sample, 2018	146
A8.2	Employment Status by Selected Demographic Groups, 2018	146
A8.3	Underemployment Status by Selected Demographic Groups, 2018	146
A8.4	Average Marginal Employment Effects of Demographic and Program-Specific Characteristics, 2017 Graduate Tracer Study	148
9.1	Sample and Population Distribution by Education Level	153
A9.1	Heckman Selection Model, Without Controls	166
A9.2	Heckman Selection Model, With Controls	167
A9.3	Returns to Education by Level	168
A9.4	First Stage Probit Regression: Heckman Model with Labor Force Participation Selection	168
A9.5	Returns to Upper Secondary Education by Track	169
A9.6	Returns to Post-Secondary Non-Tertiary Technical and Vocational Education and Training	170
A9.7	Returns to Post-Secondary Non-Tertiary Technical and Vocational Education and Training by Field	171
A9.8	Returns to Short-Cycle Tertiary Technical and Vocational Education and Training	171
A9.9	Returns to Tertiary Education by Level	172
10.1	Types of Skills Mismatch	174
10.2	Measures of Skills Mismatch	175
10.3	Sample Identified from the Individual Graduate Tracer Surveys, 2013–2014 and 2017	179
A10.1	Coefficient Estimates from the Logit Regression, 2013–2014 and 2017 Technical and Vocational Education and Training Graduates	184
11.1	TWSP, STEP, and PESFA Distribution of Qualifications by Industry, 2018	191

Figures

1.1	Annual Average Gross Domestic Product Growth Rate, by Broad Sector	3
1.2	Gross Value Added Share of Gross Domestic Product, by Broad Sector	4
1.3	Gross Value Added Share of Gross Domestic Product, by Industry	5
1.4	Annual Average Gross Value Added Growth, by Industry	5
1.5	Annual Average Gross Value Added Growth of Manufacturing Sector, by Technology Level	6
1.6	Annual Average Growth of Manufacturing Exports, by Technology	7
1.7	Annual Average Gross Domestic Product/Gross Value Added Growth and Employment Growth, 2000–2010 and 2010–2019	9
1.8	Elasticity of Wage Employment to Gross Domestic Product/Gross Value Added Growth, by Broad Sector	10
1.9	Elasticity of Low-Paid Wage Employment to Gross Domestic Product/Gross Value Added Growth, by Broad Sector	11
1.10	Elasticity of Vulnerable Employment to Gross Domestic Product/Gross Value Added Growth, by Broad Sector	11
1.11	Elasticity of Underemployment to Gross Domestic Product/Gross Value Added Growth, by Broad Sector	12
1.12	Labor Productivity and Employment Share, 2000	15
1.13	Labor Productivity and Employment Share, 2019	15
1.14	Decomposition of Aggregate Labor Productivity Change, 2000–2010	16
1.15	Decomposition of Aggregate Labor Productivity Change, 2010–2019	16
2.1	Gross Domestic Product Growth and Employment-to-Population Ration in the Philippines and East Asia and the Pacific, 2000–2018	22
2.2	Key Labor Market Indicators, 2008–2019	23
2.3	Employment Share by Broad Sector, 1998–2019	24
2.4	Average Annual Employment Growth Rate and Net Employment Growth by Sector, 2008–2018	25
2.5	Employment by Industry, 2018 (1-digit PSIC)	26
2.6	Employment Share by Major Occupational Group and Skill Category, 2001–2019	27
2.7	Average Annual Employment Growth Rates by Major Occupational Group, 2001–2018	28
2.8	Skills Demand and Supply, 2012–2017	29
2.9	Status in Employment Distribution, 2008–2019	30
2.10	Change in Regional Labor Market Indicators, 2008–2018	31
2.11	Average Annual Employment Growth, 2008–2018	33
2.12	Poverty Incidence and Regional Labor Market Indicators, 2018	34
2.13	Employment Shift from Agriculture to Industry and Services at the Regional Level, 2008–2018	35
2.14	Regional Employment Shares by Broad Sector, 2018	36
2.15	Average Annual Growth Rate by Broad Sector and Region, 2008–2018	37
A2.1	A Snapshot of the Philippines Labor Market, 2018	39
A2.2	Change in Agriculture Share in Employment and Decline in Vulnerable Employment Rate, 2008–2018	40
A2.3	Population Growth Rates and Change in Urbanization Rates at the Regional Level, 2008–2018	40
A2.4	Poverty Incidence, Change in Poverty Incidence, and Public Share of Technical and Vocational Education and Training Enrollment by Region	41
3.1	Net Employment Growth in Manufacturing by Technology Intensity, 2010–2017	48
3.2	Average Annual Employment Growth Rate in Manufacturing by Technology Intensity, 2010–2017	48
3.3	Net Employment Growth by Labor Productivity Group, 2010–2017	49
3.4	Average Annual Employment Growth Rate in Services by Labor Productivity Group, 2010–2017	49
3.5	Workforce Composition across Global Value Chains	50
3.6	Change in Wage and Salaried Work and Precarious Employment in Manufacturing by Technology Intensity, 2010–2017	52

3.7	Change in Wage and Salaried Share and Precarious Employment Share in Services, 2010–2017	53
3.8	Change in Working Hours and Labor Productivity Growth by Industry, 2010–2017	53
3.9	Employment Distribution by Skill Level and Skills Intensity at the Aggregate Level, 2010–2018	54
3.10	Demand Share by Task Content of Occupations, 2010–2018	55
3.11	Employment Distribution by Broad Occupational Group, 2010–2018	55
3.12	Change in Occupational Demand by Skill Category, Selected Manufacturing Industries, 2010–2017	56
3.13	Basic Daily Pay by Task-Based Occupational Group, 2010 and 2018	59
3.14	Skill Premium by Sex, 2010 and 2018	59
3.15	Gender Pay Gaps and Change in Real Wages (Basic Pay), 2010 and 2018	60
3.16	Labor Substitution Risk in Key Industries	60
3.17	Industries Facing Highest Risk of Job Losses due to Automation	63
3.18	Female Share of Employment in Industries at High Risk of Automation	64
4.1	Real Gross Domestic Product Growth Rate and Employment Growth Rate, 2008–2021	68
4.2	Real Gross Value Added Growth Rate by Industry Group, Year-on-Year	69
4.3	Estimated Change in Employment by Broad Industry Group	69
4.4	Real Gross Value Added Growth Rate by Industry Sectors, Year-on-Year	70
4.5	Estimated Job Losses in the Industry Sectors	71
4.6	Real Gross Value Added Growth Rate for Most Affected Services Sectors, Year-on-Year	71
4.7	Estimated Job Losses in the Services Sectors	72
4.8	Unemployment, April 2005–July 2020	73
4.9	Working-Age Population by Labor Market Status	74
4.10	Job Losses due to COVID-19 in Selected Sectors, 2020 Preliminary versus Projections	75
4.11	COVID-19 Stringency and Mobility in the Philippines	75
4.12	Change in Employment by Working Time, Selected Sectors	76
4.13	Number of Working Poor in Select Sectors, 2020	77
4.14	Change in the Number of Poor, 2020 versus 2018, Various Approaches	78
5.1	Organizational Anchors of Technical Education and Skills Development Authority	87
5.2	Structure of Technical Education and Skills Development Authority Secretariat	87
5.3	Technical and Vocational Education and Training Institutions and their Perception of Readiness for Industry 4.0	95
6.1	Time Frame of Selected Reform Milestones	103
6.2	The Philippine Qualifications Framework	111
7.1	Technical and Vocational Education and Training Enrollment, Program Completion, Assessment, and Certification, 2008–2018	114
7.2	Technical and Vocational Education and Training Enrollment by Delivery Mode, 2009–2018	115
7.3	Enrollment in Post-Secondary Courses (2013–2017) and Senior High School (2016 and 2017)	116
7.4	Employment-to-Population Rate and Labor Force Participation Rate of Technical and Vocational Education and Training Graduates, 2012–2018	117
7.5	Unemployment Rate of Technical and Vocational Education and Training Graduates and Share of Working-Age Population, 2012–2018	117
7.6	Top Programs and Courses among Male and Female Technical and Vocational Education and Training Graduates in the Overall Population, 2016	119

7.7	Top Courses in Terms of Total Male and Female Technical and Vocational Education and Training Enrollment, 2018	120
7.8	Industry Shares of Technical and Vocational Education and Training Graduate Employment and Overall Employment, 2012 and 2018	122
7.9	Technical and Vocational Education and Training Graduates' Share in Employment by Detailed Industry, 2012–2015 and 2016–2018	124
7.10	Technical and Vocational Education and Training Enrollment by Sector, 2018	125
7.11	Technical and Vocational Education and Training Share of Working-Age Population and Annual Growth Rate of Enrollment by Region	128
A7.1	Regional Share in Technical and Vocational Education and Training Enrollment and Population Share, 2018	132
8.1	Youth and Adult Unemployment Rate, 2006–2016	135
9.1	Stepwise Regression Coefficients, Returns to Education	155
9.2	Returns to Education by Level (No Schooling As Reference)	157
9.3	Returns to Upper Secondary Education by Track (Lower High School Graduate As Reference)	158
9.4	Returns to Post-Secondary Non-Tertiary Education (Lower Secondary Graduates As Reference)	159
9.5	Returns to Technical Education and Skills Development Authority National Certificates by Field (Lower Secondary Graduates As Reference)	160
9.6	Returns to Short-Cycle Tertiary Education (Lower Secondary Graduate As Reference)	161
9.7	Returns to Short-Cycle Tertiary Education by Field (Lower Secondary Graduate As Reference)	162
9.8	Returns to Tertiary Education (Lower Secondary Graduate As Reference)	163
10.1	Mismatch Rates Using Simple Matching Technique, 2013, 2014, and 2017 Graduates	179
10.2	Share of Trainees Matched, Underqualified, or Overqualified, 2013, 2014, and 2017	180
10.3	Share of Trainees Matched with Expected Occupation, Top 10 Programs	181
10.4	Share of Trainees Unmatched with Expected Occupation and in Occupations with Higher Qualification Requirements	181
10.5	Share of Trainees Unmatched with Expected Occupation and in Occupations Requiring Lower Qualifications	182
11.1	TWSP, STEP, and PESFA Target Beneficiaries, 2014–2018	187
11.2	TWSP, STEP, and PESFA Total Budget Allocation, 2014–2018	188
11.3	TWSP, STEP, and PESFA Total Enrollment and Graduation, 2014–2018	189
11.4	Selected Labor Market Indicators for Technical and Vocational Education and Training Graduates, 2017	190
11.5	Impact of Scholarships on Completion—TWSP, STEP, and PESFA	196
11.6	Impact of Scholarships on Assessment—TWSP, STEP, and PESFA	197
11.7	Impact of Scholarships on Competency—TWSP, STEP, and PESFA	198
11.8	Impact of Scholarships on National Certification—TWSP, STEP, and PESFA	198
11.9	Employment Rates for Scholars and Non-Scholars	201
11.10	Monthly Earnings for Scholars and Non-Scholars	201

Boxes

1.1	Labor Productivity is the Main Contributor to Gross Domestic Product Per Capita Growth	8
1.2	Variations in Regional Labor Productivity	18
3.1	What is Industry 4.0?	47
3.2	Routine-Biased Technological Change and the Task Content of Occupations	57
3.3	Adoption of Industry 4.0 Technologies in the IT-BPO and Electronics Manufacturing Industries	58
3.4	Impact of Industry 4.0 on Jobs and Skills in the IT-BPO and Electronics Manufacturing Industries	62
5.1	Technical Education and Skills Development Authority Responses to the COVID-19 Pandemic	89
5.2	Relevance of the Technical Education and Skills Development Authority Online Programs to COVID-19	91
5.3	Strategies to Prepare for Industry 4.0 in the National Technical Education and Skills Development Plan 2018–2022	96
6.1	Policy Recommendations on Three Technical and Vocational Education and Training Areas As Outlined in the Philippine Education Sector Study	105
6.2	Related Recommendations by Committees under the Presidential Commission on Educational Reform on Technical and Vocational Education and Training	106
6.3	Selected Recommendations in the First Biennial Congress under the Presidential Task Force for Education	108
8.1	Employability of Technical and Vocational Education and Training Graduates—Case of the Philippines	136
9.1	Accounting for Ability Bias	151
9.2	Returns to Technical and Vocational Education and Training in Related Literature	152
10.1	Example of Simple Matching Technique versus Occupational Distance Scoring	178
11.1	Technical Education and Skills Development Authority Scholarship Targets	187
11.2	Eligibility Criteria for Beneficiaries	192
11.3	Factors Associated with Receipt of Scholarship	195
12.1	Active Employers' Engagement in German Technical and Vocational Education and Training Systems	212
12.2	Lessons Learned from ADB Projects for Industry Engagement in Technical and Vocational Education and Training	213
12.3	Incentives for Working Adults to Expand Occupational Skills in New Areas	214
12.4	Lessons Learned from ADB Projects on Lifelong Learning	215
12.5	Digital Technical and Vocational Education and Training Delivery in Hunan	216
12.6	Lessons Learned from ADB Projects around Access and Inclusion	216
12.7	Qualified Technical and Vocational Education and Training Teachers in Indonesia	218
12.8	Lessons Learned from ADB Projects on Technical and Vocational Education and Training Teacher Training	219
12.9	Lessons Learned from ADB Experience in Supporting Governance, Management, and Quality Assurance	220

Foreword

By the Vice-President, Asian Development Bank

Newly emerging industrial technologies, sometimes referred to as Industry 4.0, are rapidly changing the nature of work and, as a consequence, the demand for skills. These developments pose a particularly significant challenge for developing nations that have traditionally relied on industrialization, and its capacity to generate high-paying jobs, as a path toward economic growth and prosperity.

Recognizing this, the Asian Development Bank (ADB) was asked in 2018 by the Technical Education and Skills Development Authority (TESDA) of the Philippines to support a review of the national system of technical and vocational education and training (TVET). We have worked with the government, led by TESDA, to assess the accomplishments of, and challenges facing, the national TVET system. Our work has proceeded against the backdrop of the coronavirus disease (COVID-19) global pandemic that has disproportionately hurt those segments of the population most in need of skills upgrading.

It is not yet clear whether Industry 4.0 will have a positive or negative net impact on employment, but we do know for certain that it will have important distributional effects on industries, firms, and workers. For individuals, the quality and availability of training and skills will make an important difference in employment outcomes. And at the country level, skills policy and TVET will shape workforce and national competitiveness, affecting both growth prospects and the distribution of gains (or losses) across a population.

TESDA requested that ADB examine the organizational structure of TESDA and its role in the country's broader education ecosystem. We were also asked to reassess publicly provided training in light of the anticipated impact of Industry 4.0. Our study therefore examines whether the TVET system and TESDA are well positioned to face the challenges and meet the objectives of a competitive workforce, and social equity and inclusion as per TESDA's National Technical Education and Skills Development Plan 2018–2022.

The ADB team worked closely with TESDA colleagues during data collection, stakeholder consultations, and research. We are grateful to them for their support and collaboration. It is our hope that this research will help the country achieve the policy targets of the Philippine Development Plan 2017–2022, national education policies, industry road maps, and labor and employment policies.

We look forward to ADB's continued engagement and partnership with the Government of the Philippines on training and skills development in the country.

Ahmed M. Saeed
Vice-President for East Asia, Southeast Asia, and the Pacific
Asian Development Bank

Foreword
By the Director General, Technical Education and Skills Development Authority

The Technical Education and Skills Development Authority (TESDA) actively pursues a two-pronged strategy for technical and vocational education and training (TVET) in the Philippines. One is to support global competitiveness and workforce readiness. The other is to contribute to social equity and poverty reduction in delivering services to Filipinos through times of robust growth and even during crises. Anchored in the National Technical Education and Skills Development Plan 2018–2022 and aligned with the Philippine Development Plan 2017–2022, both prongs of the strategy firmly define the roles of TESDA and TVET in nation-building and economic development.

The TVET sector study, produced through strong partnership and collaboration between TESDA and the Asian Development Bank (ADB), provides objective, empirical, and detailed analyses of TESDA and TVET in the Philippines. In essence, it examines how well we have been performing and suggests how we can best move forward.

The study is a key part of TESDA's mission to scale up the provision of skills training opportunities for the benefit of the Filipino people and the economy, and to ensure a better-prepared and resilient TVET sector. Likewise, it provides details on the assessment of the Philippine TVET sector in the context of the Fourth Industrial Revolution and the changing demand for labor, especially with the coronavirus disease (COVID-19) pandemic, which has amplified the importance of TVET in the upskilling and reskilling of our workforce.

Just as importantly, the study provides substantive recommendations for successful TVET provision such as strengthening governance, institutionalizing communication channels between the three Philippine education agencies, boosting TVET enrollment in priority sectors, intensifying industry engagements, and leveraging TVET for the post-COVID-19 economic recovery. Further, it also presents useful bases in the development and pursuit of TVET collaborations with relevant stakeholders, both local and international, and should also be of interest to TVET policy makers, area managers, school administrators, teaching and non-teaching staff, and researchers.

On behalf of TESDA, I would like to thank the ADB staff and consultants, as well as the TESDA Deputy Directors General, Executive Directors, and the Regional Directors, for all the hard work in the development of this very significant study.

The following are also acknowledged for their critical review of the draft study report prior to publication: Sameer Khatiwada of ADB; Rosanna A. Urdaneta, Deputy Director General for Policies and Planning; Marissa G. Legaspi, Executive Director of the Planning Office; and the Project Development Division and the Policy Research and Evaluation Division Planning Office.

Isidro S. Lapeña
Director General
Technical Education and Skills Development Authority

Acknowledgments

This report was prepared by the Southeast Asia Department's Social Sector Division at the Asian Development Bank (ADB), headed by Director Ayako Inagaki. Preparation of this study was led by Sameer Khatiwada, Social Sector Specialist (ICT), with guidance and support from Shamit Chakravarti, Principal Social Sector Specialist and Lynnette Perez, Principal Education Specialist.

The report is a collective effort that brought together researchers from a diverse group and several colleagues from the Technical Education and Skills Development Authority (TESDA). The team that worked on this project shared a common belief that publicly provided training in the age of Industry 4.0 needs to reinvent itself to meet the needs of the Philippine labor market.

We are especially grateful to TESDA Secretary Isidro Lapeña for his guidance and deep interest in the project. This report would not have been possible without the support from the TESDA Deputy Director General Rosanna Urdaneta. She was deeply engaged in the study and provided useful insights to the team throughout the process. Other TESDA colleagues who provided valuable support and feedback to the technical and vocational education and training (TVET) study team include Executive Director Marissa Legaspi, Executive Director David Bungallon, Director Maria Angelina Carreon, Stephen Cezar, Charlyn Justimbaste, Pamfilo Tabu, Katherine Amor Zarsadias, and Andrei Aguilar.

We would like to thank participants during the ADB–TESDA Workshop that was held on 28 January 2020 at ADB headquarters. Participants from the regional offices of TESDA provided invaluable feedback to the preliminary findings presented by the authors of the TVET study. In particular, Regional Director Gaspar Gayona, TESDA Region VI; Regional Director Florencio Sunico, Jr., TESDA NCR; Executive Director Maria Susan Dela Rama; and Regional Director Elmer Talavera, TESDA Region V.

Several ADB colleagues have played a key role in making this study a reality. We would like to thank ADB's Sustainable Development and Climate Change Department Chief of Education Sector Group Brajesh Panth and Principal Education Specialist Shanti Jaganathan. Education specialists from the Education Sector Group Per Borjegren and Lisa-Marie J. Kreibich are core contributors to the report. Many thanks to colleagues from ADB's Economic Research and Regional Cooperation Department for taking part in the workshop, providing useful feedback, and helping with data access to the team: Senior Economist Paul Vandberg, Jade R. Laranjo, Pamela Lapitan, and Arturo Martinez, Jr.

Many thanks to ADB's Philippine Country Office Director Kelly Bird and Principal Country Specialist Cristina Lozano. Valuable support was provided by Advisor Joven Balbosa and Principal Communications Specialist Jason Rush as well as Ruchel Marie Roque-Villaroman, Luvette Ann Cauman Balite, Raquel Tabanao, and Janice Chua Alalay. We are also grateful for the team working on ADB's financial support for TESDA in 2021 who provided useful feedback and suggestions: Fook Yen Chong, Anne Mendoza, Jose Tiusonco, Friedemann Gille, Vandana Rao, Lalaine Encarnacion, and Dama Yaris.

We would like to thank our two highly respected and admired reviewers: Professor Emmanuel Esguerra, University of the Philippines Diliman and Professor Aniceto Orbeta, Philippine Institute for Development Studies. Their respective inputs were instrumental to the success and quality of the study.

The report was designed, organized, and structured by Sameer Khatiwada, with technical and editorial contributions from Souleima El Achkar Hilal, Richard Horne, Ian Nicole Generalao, Rosa Mia Arao, and Michael Cabalfin.

Ramesh Subramaniam
Director General
Southeast Asia Department
Asian Development Bank

Contributors

Souleima El Achkar Hilal is an economist and labor market information specialist, with considerable experience in skills systems and technical and vocational education and training (TVET). She holds a master's degree in economics from Concordia University, Montreal and a master's degree in international affairs from Carleton University, Ottawa. Following employment as an official for the International Labour Organization (ILO) in 2009-2010, she has worked over the past 10 years as a consultant for the ILO, the World Bank, and, most recently, Asian Development Bank (ADB).

Rosa Mia Arao is a consultant for the Southeast Asia Department of ADB. She works on development policy research using microdata. Prior to joining ADB, she was a policy consultant for the Health Policy and Development Program (HPDP), where she provided technical support for tuberculosis programs in the Philippines. She is a doctor of philosophy (PhD) candidate in economics at the University of the Philippines.

Per Börjegren is a senior education specialist at ADB. He has more than 20 years of experience in TVET reform. Before joining ADB, he worked 10 years for Deutsche Gesellschaft für Internationale Zusammenarbeit (GIZ) as technical advisor, project manager, and department head in Asia, Africa, and the Middle East. He has been supporting continental bodies, sector associations, and national and provincial governments in improving their skills development systems. He holds a master's degree in educational leadership and management from the University of Nottingham, United Kingdom.

Emily Christi Cabegin is a professor at the School of Labor and Industrial Relations, University of the Philippines. Her research works include gender inequality in labor force participation and labor market outcomes, migration and remittances, economic growth and employment, and informal employment. She obtained a master's degree in demography and PhD in economics at the University of the Philippines and was recipient of the Robert-Solow Post-Doctoral Fellowship granted by Centre Cournot pour la Recherche en Economie.

Michael Cabalfin is a consultant labor economist/econometrician at ADB. He has also consulted for the Philippine Institute for Development Studies, UNICEF, and the World Bank. He has worked on education and labor economics for over 12 years to date including on early childhood care and development, primary and secondary education, TVET, and higher education. He is a former assistant professor in economics at the University of the Philippines where he has taught human resource economics and econometrics, among others. He obtained his PhD in economics from The Australian National University.

Ann Arguelles Cortes is an independent consultant on human resource and organization development, currently engaged with a local government unit in post-COVID recovery planning and reengineering initiatives for efficient government service delivery. Previous projects related to TVET include: Assessment of Technical and Vocational Training Skills in Southern Mindanao, and Strategic Planning for a Quality Assured Technology-Based Education and Technical Education and Skills Development Investment Programming. She has a degree in organization development from SAIDI Graduate School of Organization Development and a degree in Psychology from Ateneo de Manila University.

Ian Nicole Generalao is a consultant in ADB's Southeast Asia Regional Department. His research focuses on the analyses of labor markets and policies, TVET, and higher education systems. He is also a research fellow at the University of the Philippines Center for Integrative and Development Studies. He has taught as a teaching fellow at the University of the Philippines School of Economics, where he obtained his bachelor's and master's degrees in economics.

Richard Horne is a labor market and jobs measurement specialist, with extensive experience leading flagship reports and multicountry research. He has a master's degree in macroeconomic policy and financial markets from the Barcelona Graduate School of Economics, Spain. He was previously an official for the ILO in Geneva and Bangkok and has been a consultant for a range of organizations over the past 10 years. Currently he is director of Empstat, a consultancy firm specializing in labor market analysis and research.

Sameer Khatiwada is an economist working on technology and innovation in social sectors for ADB's Southeast Asia Department. He was previously with ADB's Economic Research Department, where he contributed to the Asian Development Outlook. He has published extensively on labor market, technology and jobs, innovation, macroeconomics, and development issues. Sameer spent close to 10 years at the ILO in Geneva. He holds a PhD in economics from the Graduate Institute of International and Development Studies in Geneva and has a master's degree in public policy from Harvard University.

Lisa-Marie Kreibich works as an education specialist at ADB, contributing to design and implementation of TVET projects. Prior to joining ADB, she worked as team leader for the TVET project of the German Development Cooperation in Viet Nam. She has experience at the ILO and in the private sector. She holds a degree in international business management from the European School of Business, Germany and Reims Management School, France and a master's degree in public policy from Hertie School of Governance, Germany.

Rozanno Rufino is an education policy and reform consultant for ADB in the Philippines. Focusing on the education sector, and indigenous peoples and development, he has had broad exposure in the development field, having worked in government, civil society, and international development agencies. He was senior specialist in National Economic and Development Authority's education unit, education specialist in the World Bank in the Philippines, and led the establishment of the National Indigenous Peoples Education (IPEd) Program of the Department of Education. He is the convenor of the DO62 IPEd Partnership Initiative of De La Salle Philippines.

Abbreviations

4IR	Fourth Industrial Revolution
ADB	Asian Development Bank
ALMP	active labor market policy
AQRF	ASEAN Qualifications Reference Framework
ARMM	Autonomous Region in Muslim Mindanao
ASEAN	Association of Southeast Asian Nations
ATET	average treatment effect on the treated
BPM	business process management
BPO	business process outsourcing
CAC	competency assessment and certification
CALABARZON	Cavite, Laguna, Batangas, Rizal, and Quezon
CAR	Cordillera Administrative Region
CHED	Commission on Higher Education
COC	certificate of competency
COVID-19	coronavirus disease
DECS	Department of Education Culture and Sports
DepEd	Department of Education
DOLE	Department of Labor and Employment
DOLE-BLE	Department of Labor and Employment-Bureau of Local Employment
DTI	Department of Trade and Industry
E&E	electrical and electronics
EBT	enterprise-based training
EDCOM	Congressional Commission on Education
EPR	employment-to-population rate
FIES	Family Income and Expenditure Survey
GDP	gross domestic product
GVA	gross value added
GVC	global value chain
ICE	Inter-agency Coordination for Education
ICT	information and communication technology
IPWRA	inverse-probability weighted regression adjustment
ISCO	International Standard Classification of Occupations
ISO	International Organization for Standardization
IT	information technology
IV	instrumental variable
LEP	ladderized education program
LFPR	labor force participation rate
LFS	labor force survey
LGU	local government unit
MIMAROPA	Occidental Mindoro, Oriental Mindoro, Marinduque, Romblon, and Palawan
NC	national certificate
NCC	National Coordinating Council
NCCE	National Coordinating Council for Education
NCE	National Council for Education

Abbreviations

NCR	National Capital Region
NEDA	National Economic and Development Authority
NEET	neither in employment nor in education or training
NITESD	National Institute for Technical Education and Skills Development
NTESDP	National Technical Education and Skills Development Plan
OLS	ordinary least squares
PCER	Presidential Commission on Educational Reform
PDP	Philippine Development Plan
PESFA	Private Education Student Financial Assistance
PESS	Philippine Education Sector Study
PQF	Philippine Qualifications Framework
PSA	Philippine Statistics Authority
PSM	propensity score matching
PSOC	Philippine Standard Occupational Classification
PTFE	Presidential Task Force for Education
RIB	Recognized Industry Board
SETG	Study on Employment of TVET Graduates
SOCCSKSARGEN	South Cotabato, Cotabato, Sultan Kudarat, Sarangani and General Santos
STEP	Special Training for Employment Program
TESD	Technical Education and Skills Development
TESDA	Technical Education and Skills Development Authority
TTI	TESDA technology institution
TVET	technical and vocational education and training
TVI	technical–vocational institution
TVL	technical–vocational and livelihood
TWSP	Training for Work Scholarship Program
UAQTEA	Universal Access to Quality Tertiary Education Act
UTPRAS	Unified TVET Program Registration and Accreditation System
VER	vulnerable employment rate

Executive Summary

Prior to the coronavirus disease (COVID-19) pandemic, Industry 4.0, also known as the Fourth Industrial Revolution or 4IR, was already having a wide impact on labor markets worldwide, and the disruption is set to continue. Industry 4.0 is expected to bring about both massive job displacement and job gains and transform work tasks and occupations. The COVID-19 pandemic has had unprecedented impacts on the Philippine labor market and has exacerbated existing inequalities. It has heightened the importance of adequate and timely investment in skills—involving reskilling, upskilling, and the development of strong technical and soft skills—to help transition displaced workers into new jobs. The technical and vocational education and training (TVET) system provides an opportunity to shape labor market outcomes, and adapt and respond to anticipated changes, provided the system and its governing bodies have the necessary resources, capacity, and political will.

This study examines the Philippines' TVET system in the context of Industry 4.0 and the changing demand for labor. It seeks to answer the following questions:

- Is the TVET system and the Technical Education and Skills Development Authority (TESDA) well positioned to face the challenges and meet the objectives of competitive workforce, and social equity/inclusion as per TESDA's National Technical Education and Skills Development Plan 2018–2022?
- How can the Philippines' TVET system and TESDA be more or better prepared?

The executive summary is structured as follows:

- **Part I. Economic and labor market context:** structural transformation underway in the country and labor market trends, Industry 4.0 and the changing demand for labor, and COVID-19 impacts of the labor market.
- **Part II. TVET and the Philippine education system:** TVET provision in the context of Industry 4.0, TVET in the context of education sector reforms, and TVET trends over the last decade.
- **Part III. Empirical findings for TVET performance:** empirical analysis of the impact of TVET on employment outcomes, returns to TVET, skills mismatch, and impact of TESDA's scholarships.
- **Part IV. Conclusions and recommendations:** international and Asian Development Bank (ADB) best practices around TVET, and conclusions and recommendations going forward.

Economic and Labor Market Context

Compounding the impact of the structural transformation underway in the Philippines, technological change under Industry 4.0 is likely to correspond to further changes in the demand for jobs and skills.

High gross domestic product (GDP) growth in the last decade and until the onset of the COVID-19 pandemic has not led to net employment growth on a massive scale, but instead to major changes in the structure and quality of employment in the Philippines. Even with the rapid and accelerated pace of economic growth (from 4.8% for 2000–2010 to 6.2% for 2010–2018), net employment creation has fallen short of working-age population growth, and labor force participation remains lower than the regional average.

Notwithstanding its low employment elasticity, recent growth was accompanied by significant labor reallocation from agriculture toward services and industry, with an increasingly dominant role for the services sector in the country's output and employment. The highest growth rates have been for the tradable services of financial intermediation, information and communication, and real estate and business activities.

Although the manufacturing share in value added has remained largely unchanged for the past couple of decades, there was a shift in structure from lower technology industries to medium-high and high-technology manufacturing industries. The faster growth of the past decade was better aligned with improvements in decent work indicated by declining shares of low-paid wage employment and vulnerable employment. Despite its declining employment and share in value added, the agriculture sector continues to be important for the Philippines, and the challenge of raising the sector's productivity, including through upskilling of the agriculture workforce, remains high on TESDA's agenda.

The benefits of growth have not been equitably distributed, with large differences across the country's regions and demographic groups. The National Capital Region (Metro Manila) and adjacent regions of Cavite, Laguna, Batangas, Rizal, and Quezon (CALABARZON) and Central Luzon experienced high employment growth and the largest declines in unemployment. On the opposite end, the Cagayan Valley, the Cordillera Administrative Region (CAR), and the Autonomous Region in Muslim Mindanao (ARMM) had less positive labor market outcomes, with the ARMM in particular continuing to lag far behind other regions on many labor market indicators.

There are important differences across demographic groups as well. Despite having achieved gender parity in education and significantly narrowed the gender gap in health outcomes, the Philippines still has major gender gaps in terms of employment opportunities and labor force participation. Youth unemployment and "neither in employment nor in education or training" rates remain elevated, and recent declines are attributable to decreased labor force participation following the K to 12 reforms, rather than expanded employment opportunities.

Despite progress in terms of employment quality, work shortages persist. Although some high-productivity service and manufacturing industries have seen rapid employment growth, much of the displaced agriculture employment has been absorbed into the lower productivity wholesale and retail trade sector, hotels and restaurants and other services, as well as the construction sector, boosted by the strong "Build, Build, Build" infrastructure program. Informality remains a major challenge in the Philippines, where more than half of workers (52% in 2018, down from 57% in 2010) are estimated to be in informal employment. Underemployment is also a persistent challenge.

Despite the decline in unemployment over the past decade, the underemployment rate, defined as the share of employed wanting additional work, remained elevated at 18% in 2018. Furthermore, while the vulnerable employment rate declined from nearly 45% of employed persons in 2008 to approximately one-third of workers in 2019, the increase in wage and salaried employment has also been accompanied in many industries by a rise in precarious employment, defined as short-term, seasonal, or casual work, including fixed-term employment and workers employed through contracting or subcontracting agencies. Workers in precarious employment often do not have the benefits associated with wage and salaried work, such as stability and security in terms of job tenure, access to social protection, and other labor rights (ILO, 2017). This trend is linked to the rise of irregular or nonstandard forms of employment increasingly characterizing working arrangements in the context of Industry 4.0 and the future of work.

It is crucial for TVET to ensure a supply of graduates with in-demand technical skills as well as the soft skills required to adapt to the rapidly changing world of work.

Rapidly changing demand for skills in the Philippine labor market has underscored the importance of quality TVET. The changing economic structure is reflected in a changing labor demand. The past decade has seen a declining share of agricultural and elementary occupations (from 50% in 2008 to 38% in 2018), and an increase in demand for both high-skill and middle-skill occupations (from 19% to 23% and from 31% to 40%, respectively), along with a shift in the composition of the middle-skilled. Specifically, craft and related trades workers had negative employment growth rate from 2001 to 2008, while plant and machine operators and assemblers had positive growth rates, reflecting a restructuring from labor-intensive production toward more capital-intensive production within and across manufacturing industries. In the past decade, however, both middle-skill groups saw a rise in employment due to rapid growth in manufacturing and construction. Current trends suggest a continued demand for middle-skilled and skilled TVET graduates to support growth sectors of the Philippine economy.

Increasing globalization and the advent of Industry 4.0 bring added pressure to the workforce to reskill and upskill, changing the very nature of work and how specific tasks are performed in occupations. With skill-biased technological change, trade and technology lead to an increased demand for high-skilled workers, while the routine-biased technological change hypothesis posits that occupations with higher routine task content are more likely to be automated and offshored. These trends, which have led to rapid employment growth in the Philippines' information technology-business process outsourcing (IT-BPO) industry so far, may have a different impact in the coming years.

Recent studies have found that as many as 49% of jobs in the Philippines, including over 80% of workers in the BPO and electronics manufacturing sector, were at high risk of being substituted by technology (ILO, 2017). A recently completed ADB study estimates lower job displacement levels in the two latter sectors (at 24%), partly offset by higher productivity and scale effects (ADB, 2020). Both studies show that IT-BPO employers believe Industry 4.0 will lead to a shift from routine to nonroutine and analytical work. Some of the skills for which there would be an increase in demand are technical and IT, critical thinking and adaptive learning, and complex problem-solving. The ADB study finds that on-the job and professional training will be key for both IT-BPO and electronics sectors.

In an Industry 4.0 environment, where change is the only constant, workers must be able to move across industries and occupations, along career paths that may be nonlinear. In that regard, all levels of the education and skills supply system need to work in tandem to ensure that flexible pathways exist between different levels of formal education and for the recognition and development of skills acquired outside formal education (lifelong learning).

With respect to TVET, vocational streams and clusters should be used to impart transferable skills and prepare students not only for an entry-level job, but for careers during which they may transition between jobs with similar skill requirements. This suggests a shift away from narrowly defined competencies. Furthermore, although foundational and transversal skills need to be instilled early in the education process, emphasis on these skills must continue through to post-secondary and tertiary education.

The COVID-19 pandemic has presented TVET with both challenges and opportunities.

The COVID-19 pandemic had a devastating economic and labor market impact in the Philippines. The country's unemployment rate soared to 17.7% in April 2020—from 5.1% in the comparable period in 2019—the highest unemployment rate recorded, translating into 5 million additional unemployed workers. Low-skilled workers have been disproportionately affected due to their sectors of employment, which, in addition to being heavily affected, are characterized by lower job security.

The massive rise in unemployment is linked to the stringent lockdown measures put in place that effectively prevented labor reallocations toward lower productivity sectors and informal employment, which typically accompanies economic shocks in developing economies. Ultimately, through job losses, work stoppages, and reduction of working hours, the pandemic and associated measures to contain it have pushed many Filipino workers and their families below the poverty line.

As the country faces unprecedented levels of unemployment and job loss, the role of innovative and flexible learning programs such as TESDA's online programs play a critical role in retooling and upskilling displaced workers. TESDA has demonstrated that it can respond swiftly and relevantly to emerging needs, by expanding access to its online programs through partnership with the private sector. Moreover, immediately after the country was placed under lockdown, TESDA released "OPLAN TESDA ABOT LAHAT-TVET towards the New Normal" geared toward developing relevant policies and programs to help the country to respond to the ongoing crisis and adjust to the new normal. According to the Inter-Agency Task Force Technical Working Group for Anticipatory and Forward Planning (IATF-TWG for AFP) (2020), the new normal is characterized by the need to observe social distance and strict personal hygiene and other sanitation protocols. There may still be sporadic lockdowns, though over a smaller geographic unit. At the same time, the COVID-19 threat looms large in the minds of individuals—consumers and business alike.

Despite challenges in terms of school disruptions and closures that have affected learning at all levels, including TVET and work-based learning, the pandemic provides a unique opportunity for an intensified shift toward solutions that make use of distance learning and digital tools. However, resource constraints and infrastructure challenges posing access barriers to remote areas and disadvantaged households need to be considered, consistently with the objective of social equity and workforce inclusion. Moreover, the shift toward remote learning has also drawn attention its weaknesses in serving as a substitute for imparting technical-vocational skills acquired through learning-by-doing or hands-on experience at the workplace. Thus, the pandemic has delineated which aspects of TVET instruction can be effectively done remotely and which are best carried out in-person or in a flexible setting.

The COVID-19 pandemic has increased the urgency of Industry 4.0 preparedness by precipitating automation and the shift toward digital and technological solutions in many fields, all the while putting a strain on government resources. TESDA must meet its objectives with respect to Industry 4.0, during and beyond the recovery period, while also answering to emerging priorities like reskilling workers displaced by the pandemic.

TVET and the Philippine Education System

Recent education reforms have boosted the TVET sector's growth, but strained TESDA's already limited resources.

While recent reforms have boosted the growth of the TVET sector and its potential to contribute to improving workforce competitiveness and poverty reduction, lack of adequate resources has become a more pressing concern. The two major developments on education sector reform in the Philippines—the institutionalization of the Philippine Qualifications Framework (PQF) in 2012, and the shift to K to 12 basic education program, adding 1 year of kindergarten and 2 years of senior high school to the previous 10-year program—have had far-reaching implications for TVET. A notable development stemming from the K to 12 reform was the senior high school program with a distinct technical-vocational and livelihood (TVL) track that provides students with an opportunity to acquire a National Certificate for courses that follow TESDA's training regulations after undergoing the necessary assessment.

In 2017–2018, the TVL track had the second-biggest share of the 2.7 million total senior high school enrollees (1.03 million, or 37.5%), with females comprising almost half of the TVL students. The operationalization of the

PQF is critical in the context of Industry 4.0 and the rapidly changing world of work, allowing for pathways that facilitate transitions between different levels of education, and in line with the principles of lifelong learning. These developments have underscored the importance of coordination between TESDA, the Department of Education, and the Commission on Higher Education.

TESDA is well placed to address the skill needs of Industry 4.0; however, a range of issues hamper the organization's effectiveness and relevance, undermining this position.

While TESDA has made strides over the years, questions around its appropriate role, endemic resource constraints, and organizational capacity weigh on its ability to respond to Industry 4.0. For the last 25 years, TESDA has evolved to play a multifaceted role, providing varied technical education and skills development programs and activities, including for the marginalized sector of Philippine society. However, a range of challenges exists: there is an unsettled issue of devolution of its direct training function; resource constraints impact capital outlay, reducing its ability to provide up-to-date facilities, as well as trained staff; shortages of technology competency assessors and lengthy processes for developing standards and assessment tools undermine the ability to provide up-to-date services; and insufficient industry engagement hinders the ability to respond to changing private sector demand for skills.

TESDA's main challenge is how to redefine its role as the authority of TVET in the context of fast-changing environments and the realities of its own organizational resources. It needs to address issues of limited resources, particularly funds and personnel, as well as the issue of its direct training function. Moreover, with the new demands of emerging technology in the age of Industry 4.0, the organization needs to move beyond the confines of bureaucratic space and set the tone of a learning organization that models the 21st century skills of creativity, critical thinking, communication, and collaboration.

Enrollment in TVET is increasing; however, provision of enterprise-based training is concentrated in industrialized regions and not always available.

Enrollment in TVET is on the rise, with a greater share of female students among recent enrollees. Over 5% of the Philippines' working-age population has completed some form of TVET program, and TVET graduates are far more likely than average to participate in the labor market. TVET enrollment has increased in recent years, as has the number of assessed and certified graduates. The gender gap in TVET has been closed in the Philippines, with a larger share of females than males among TVET enrollees in recent years, but TVET enrollment remains highly gender-segregated in terms of courses. Regional TVET enrollment is generally proportional to regional population size, but particularly low in the ARMM.

Enrollment in community-based TVET has grown faster than other modalities, underscoring the importance of continued efforts to ensure high-quality training at the local level. Community-based training surpassed institution-based training in 2017 and 2018, as the modality with the highest enrollment shares. Community-based training in the Philippines is often delivered through partnerships with technical–vocational institutions (TVIs) and can be more responsive to local needs. However, concerns about it being of poorer quality and largely supply-driven due to limited resources/facilities and linkages with industry, warrant continuous monitoring efforts from TESDA, particularly as these issues may be exacerbated in the context of Industry 4.0.

Despite efforts, enterprise-based training remains low and largely concentrated in more industrialized regions. With rapid technological change, some tasks may become redundant and skills irrelevant. In this context, enterprise-based training (EBT) has an edge, as this modality delivers TVET that is more in line with rapidly evolving workplace and workshop needs. Possibly due to a misalignment between incentives and funding sources,

EBT still accounted for less than 4% of TVET enrollment at the national level in 2018. It represented relatively larger—but still limited—shares in more urban and industrialized region, but was virtually absent in some other regions. EBT generally has the highest employment rates and provides training that is most relevant to industry needs; its importance is expected to be heightened in the context of Industry 4.0 and rapid technological change.

Publicly provided TVET in the Philippines targets the poor and vulnerable population, consistent with TESDA's objectives of social equity for workforce inclusion and poverty reduction.

TVET programs run by TESDA target poor households, and the public share of TVET provision is generally higher in less industrialized regions. The distribution of those enrolled in post-secondary and TVET differs significantly between public and private schools, and this difference has increased in recent years. While the poorest income deciles' share in enrollment has increased from 2013 to 2016–2017 for public TVIs, the largest shares of enrollment in private TVIs have shifted from middle-income to the highest-income deciles. However, while public TVET targets disadvantaged segments of the population, enrollment shares in public institutions are not necessarily higher in the poorer regions. Public TVET provision in poor regions and remote areas must be focused on local needs, including agriculture and other sectors of rural economies.

Top courses in terms of TVET enrollment in recent years reflect growth sectors of the Philippine economy. But these sectors have generally been found to face a high risk of automation.

The most-availed courses in recent years, particularly among female enrollees, include many that lead to low-productivity, low-pay occupations, often involving nonroutine manual tasks. Several courses have always been among the top TVET programs in the Philippines, such as automotive and mechanics, electronics, and welding, and have remained so, particularly for male TVET graduates.

Other courses more popular among women TVET graduates (e.g., related to garments, secretarial work, and the beauty/cosmetics industry) seem to have fallen behind those geared toward growing sectors of the Philippine economy, specifically sales and services occupations in retail and wholesale trade, tourism and hospitality (hotels and restaurants), and personal services. The latter courses include food and beverage services, housekeeping, bread and pastry production, bartending, and cookery. Other popular courses in recent years include those geared toward the IT and BPO industries. These high-growth sectors, however, have also been identified as likely to be disproportionately affected by Industry 4.0, with the share of jobs at risk of automation estimated at 86% for construction, 68% for hospitality, 89% for BPO, and 81% for the electrical and electronics sector (ILO, 2017).

Awareness of Industry 4.0 has been on the policy agenda in the Philippines, including with respect to TVET. The challenge will largely be in implementation.

There is high awareness of Industry 4.0 in the Philippines, and some innovative policies are already in place, but an apparent gap in terms of implementation underscores the need to enhance and support TVI preparedness to meet Industry 4.0 challenges. A recent ADB study found strong alignment between the perceptions of training institutions and employers regarding skills requirements for the future in the BPO and electronics manufacturing industries. While 80% of surveyed TVIs believed they had a good understanding of skills needs in relation to Industry 4.0, 88% agreed or strongly agreed that they needed additional technical and financial support specifically for Industry 4.0 skills provision.

There may be a gap between awareness and implementation. For instance, although 90% of TVIs believed their graduates to be adequately prepared for the labor market, only 52% of employers in BPO and 58% in electronics manufacturing agreed. Furthermore, less than half of training institutions reported reviewing their curricula and course offerings on an annual or more frequent basis, or providing trainees with information on labor market conditions.

Empirical Findings for TVET Performance

Employment outcomes for TVET graduates are determined by demand-side factors (occupational and skills demand) and supply-side factors (quality, employability, and relevance of skills).

While there can be positive impacts of TVET on labor force participation of young individuals not in school or training, the impacts on employment are less favorable. In particular, using the inverse-probability weighted regression adjustment estimator, we found that TVET completion increases the average labor force participation rate of graduates by an average of 3.2 to 5.3 percentage points compared to the counterfactual case (i.e., had they not completed any TVET program).

Findings suggest that TVET program completion among TVET graduates does not consistently lead to employment. Further, looking at aspects of employment quality, the chapter finds that TVET does not help solve the problem of youth underemployment. The results suggest that even when TVET leads to employment, this is apparently more likely to be in occupations where workers still desire additional working hours, and look for an additional job or even a new job with longer hours.

The employers' perspective on the work performance of hired TVET graduates plays a critical role in assessing their skill level and reflects their overall employability. Using the Employers' Satisfaction Survey for 2011 and 2014, there is a slight decline over time in employers' satisfaction on the work performance of employees who underwent TVET in two out of three aspects: theoretical and practical knowledge in performing tasks and work attitudes.

The notable declines are specifically in their ability to communicate in speech and writing and in observing protocols using standard operating procedures. In terms of trainability on the relevant job skills, the mean rating of TVET graduates recorded a small uptick, with the highest increase in their ability to learn new skills. The proportion of establishments satisfied with TVET graduates' performance also decreased from 94% to 90%.

In lieu of tertiary education, which entails higher direct and indirect costs, TVET is estimated to be an economically viable alternative.

Returns to TVET differ depending on the level and the course; however, the post-secondary and tertiary levels offer largely positive returns. This study estimates returns to TVET at the upper secondary, post-secondary, and tertiary levels using the Mincer (1974) equation as benchmark, accounting for observed characteristics and correcting for selection bias using the Heckman (1979) model. It finds that returns to TVET at the upper secondary level are not significant for completion and even negative for incomplete participation, while the return to upper secondary academic track completion is 4% (the first-ever evaluation of returns to the K to 12 program). Nevertheless, returns to TVET at the post-secondary, non-tertiary level are significant.

Assuming a 1-year duration for a certificate places returns at 16%, comparable to returns to tertiary education even at post-graduate level. Moreover, given the shorter actual training durations, average returns to post-secondary TVET are even higher at 40%, with returns to TESDA national certificates at 57% and to other TVET courses at 31%. Across fields, returns are highest for services, education, and welfare and arts and humanities; lowest for engineering, manufacturing and construction, and business, administration, and law; and insignificant for agriculture, forestry, fisheries, and veterinary. While returns to short-cycle tertiary level TVET are lower due their longer durations, 10.6% for completion and 7.7% for incomplete participation, they are slightly higher than those for bachelor education: 10.5% for completion, 6% for incomplete participation.

Training–job mismatches exist between courses offered and skills in demand by employers, hindering employability.

Skill mismatches limit TVET graduates' employability and reflect an inability to keep the training curriculum, course offerings, and training equipment relevant for the job market. Chapter 10 examines the effectiveness of TVET programs as measured by the level of training–job mismatch of graduates using simple matching and occupational distance measures, and finds high mismatch rates. Using the former, TVET graduates have been recording very high mismatch rates ranging from 42%–81%. Using a task-based framework, the latter serves as a proxy and finds that only about one-third (32%–36%) are successfully matched with the expected post-training occupation of their program.

The most effective programs, in terms of training–job matching, are mostly nonroutine manual in nature. Paradoxically, these are also those identified as leading to lower productivity jobs and lower wages. Furthermore, the study finds that those who are male and less educated are less likely to experience training–job mismatch.

TESDA's scholarships are most effective for achieving higher completion and assessment rates for scholars. However, they are less effective at improving certification, employment, and productivity.

Three major scholarships offered by TESDA are evaluated: Training for Work Scholarship Program (TWSP), Special Training for Employment Program (STEP), and Private Education Student Financial Assistance (PESFA). Using the most appropriate econometric techniques for specific outcomes and scholarship interventions, Chapter 11 evaluates the impacts of scholarship programs on completion, assessment, competency, and national certification rates, as well as employment and earnings. It finds that STEP and PESFA have positive impacts on completion rates which may be attributed to the provision of training allowance. TWSP and STEP have positive impacts on assessment rates given the mandatory assessment and coverage of fees.

STEP also has a positive impact on competency certification rate, which may be attributed to shorter courses and the supplemental entrepreneurship training. However, all three scholarships have negative impacts on national certification rates as there are no incentives for obtaining certification. TWSP has a positive impact on employment but none of the scholarships has a positive impact on earnings. TWSP and PESFA scholars are generally more disadvantaged but more able than non-scholars, while STEP scholars are generally more advantaged and less able than non-scholars. The findings suggest that while the scholarships largely satisfy the objective of social equity, much improvement is needed in promoting competitiveness and productivity.

Conclusions and Recommendations

According to international evidence and ADB's experience, success in TVET systems follows several common principles that can guide TESDA moving forward.

In general, there is a need for TVET systems to reform and redefine their roles to equip various target groups with skills that meet the rapidly evolving needs of the labor market. Governments across Asia and the Pacific are increasingly recognizing the importance of skills for the continuation of the region's economic and developmental success. Improving TVET systems has high priority and these characteristics are clearly reflected in recent projects supported by ADB. International experiences, including literature and ADB's experience on projects, can inform the design of successful TVET systems.

Lessons from ADB-supported projects reinforce many of the international findings of what works in TVET systems. These include the following (Chapter 12): qualified teachers and managers are fundamental pillars of high-quality TVET, a strong link between public and private actors is fundamental for demand-driven TVET, and mutually beneficial partnerships need to be facilitated and capacities strengthened. Further, successful TVET goes beyond narrow technical skills for a specific job and takes a lifelong learning approach that includes transversal and entrepreneurial skills; coherent pathways between various education levels are needed and transitions must be supported; and standardization of workshops, equipment, and digital solutions based on international norms improve quality and cost-effectiveness.

The TVET sector study underscores the following:

- **TVET governance**
    - Adequate funding is needed for TESDA to fulfill its dual objective of a competitive workforce and social equity.
    - Settling the debate around devolving TESDA's training function, improving financial management, and optimizing use of funds would improve its organizational capacity.
- **Close collaboration between TESDA, the Department of Education, and the Commission on Higher Education for:**
    - strengthening institutional mechanisms for coordination and policy setting, particularly in the aftermath of K to 12;
    - expanding TESDA's role in the senior high school TVL track program;
    - developing and strengthening pathways between various education levels, including lifelong learning, by fast-tracking the formulation of an action plan to operationalize the PQF; and
    - imparting transferable/transversal/21st century skills/soft skills throughout the learning process.
- **Promoting TVET enrollment in priority sectors**
    - Priority sectors should include high-productivity services and higher value-added manufacturing industries, ensuring an adequate supply of skills as the Philippines moves up global and regional value-added chains.
    - While wholesale and retail trade, in particular, and also tourism have greater capacity to absorb labor, these involve mainly low-productivity, nonroutine manual jobs.
    - Enrollment in agriculture courses, which remains very low, should be increased, as this may increase the productivity of agricultural regions.
- **Seeking new and effective ways of securing industry engagement in TVET, including:**
    - anticipating skills demand, ensuring better targeting of TVET programs and greater efficiency of skills supply, limiting mismatches, and improving labor market outcomes; and
    - standardizing and improving workshops, equipment, and digital solutions to meet international norms and improve quality.
- **Enhancing Industry 4.0 preparedness, including:**
    - supporting TVIs in imparting technical and soft skills complementary to technology; and
    - making use of vocational streams and clusters to impart transferable skills for flexible workers and improved career options.
- **Strengthening the role of TVET in a post-pandemic economy, including:**
    - enhancing online training, while keeping in mind equity considerations in terms of access and infrastructure; and
    - promoting TVET as crucial component of active labor market policies throughout the recovery and beyond.

Fast-growing economy. The "Build, Build, Build" infrastructure development program has helped the Philippines achieve rapid economic growth since 2000.

PART I
ECONOMIC AND LABOR MARKET CONTEXT

Part I of the technical and vocational education and training (TVET) sector study focuses on providing the information upon which an assessment of TVET provision in the Philippines can be contextualized. Chapter 1 provides an overview of the economic and labor market context including drivers of growth, inclusiveness of growth, and sources of aggregate labor productivity. Chapter 2 outlines labor market diagnostics for the country, including key indicators for the labor market, changing occupational distributions and skills demand, as well as regional trends. Chapter 3 provides an overview of Industry 4.0 and the changing demand for labor, including an overview of technological change and employment as well as distributional impacts and the centrality of skills. Finally, Chapter 4 provides an overview of impacts of COVID-19 on the labor market, comparing estimated employment impacts with findings from labor market data of the first three quarters of 2020, and estimating the potential impact on working poverty.

1. Structural Transformation in the Philippines

Since 2000, the Philippines has exhibited high gross domestic product (GDP) growth, making it one of the fastest-growing economies in the world. GDP growth was recorded at 4.8% per annum for 2000–2010 and 6.3% between 2010 and 2019. The more rapid output growth in the recent decade was supported by the stronger gross fixed capital formation growth from an annual average of 5.7% for 2000–2010 to 9.9% for 2010–2019, even as household and government consumption spending jointly posted an accelerated growth from 4.3% in the former period to 6.4% in the latter. However, the Philippines faces downside risks with a burgeoning trade deficit as the growth in imports between 2010 and 2019 has largely outpaced that of exports.

The Philippines is the 12th-most populous country in the world, but ranks 110th in terms of GDP per capita. The Philippines' per capita GDP, adjusted for purchasing power parity, of $9,471 was only half of the world's average in 2019. The country is poorer than many of its Association of Southeast Asian Nations (ASEAN) neighbors, including Singapore, with a per capita GDP, adjusted for purchasing power parity, of around $103,000; Malaysia with $32,900; Thailand with $20,400; and Indonesia with $14,000. Although the Philippines' population growth has slowed in recent years, it remains the highest in the ASEAN region. The large population of 107 million people has weighed on the annual growth of the country's per capita GDP (at constant 2018 prices), which lagged total output growth, at 2.8% from 2000–2010 and 4.6% from 2010–2019. At the same time, poverty remains high at 21.6% in 2015, corresponding to 22 million Filipinos living below the national threshold[1] and presenting an important challenge: how to achieve a more equitable distribution of the benefits of economic growth.

The Philippines' accelerated economic growth was accompanied by structural transformation characterized by the reallocation of resources from lower-productivity to higher-productivity economic sectors. Many economists[2] assert that structural transformation is necessary for a country to sustain a high-growth trajectory. As the Philippine Development Plan 2017–2022 aims to shift the economy from a lower middle-income country to an upper middle-income country by 2022, structural change that moves resources to more productive economic activities is important to realize this vision and to speed up the transition. This chapter explores the structural change process through its growth performance, inclusiveness of growth, and sources of aggregate labor productivity growth. It concludes with policy recommendations.

---

[1] The national poverty threshold is the minimum income required to meet the food needs satisfying 100% of the recommended energy and nutrient intake for energy and protein and 80% for vitamins and minerals, and basic non-food needs (e.g., clothing, housing, fuel, light and water, health, and education).
[2] See Herrendorf, Rogerson, and Valentinyi (2013); Lewis (1954); and McMillian and Rodrik (2011).

Growth Performance and Economic Structural Transformation

Over the past 2 decades, the Philippines' structural transformation has been driven predominantly by expansion in services, and also, but to a lesser extent, industry. Real GDP growth was driven largely by the services sector for 2000–2010 and by both the services and industry sectors for 2010–2019. As agricultural growth decelerated from an annual average growth rate of 3.5% between 2000 and 2010 to 1.9% between 2010 and 2019, that of the industry sector accelerated from 4.2% to 6.3% and the services sector from 5.5% to 7.1% (Figure 1.1). This corresponded to a shrinking contribution of the agriculture sector to GDP from 15% in 2000 to 9% in 2019, which was accompanied by an increase in the share of the services sector from 53% to 61%, while the share of the industry sector posted a slight decline from 32% in 2000 to 30% in 2019 (Figure 1.2). Despite the exemplary performance of the industry sector in the past decade, the services sector remains the fastest-growing sector and continued to account for the largest share of GDP.

The accelerated growth in tradable services may be partly due to regulatory reforms. Such reforms include the enactment of the Ease of Doing Business and Efficient Government Service Delivery Act of 2018, which amended the Anti-Red Tape Act of 2007. These laws are aimed at minimizing bureaucratic red tape in government offices covering business enterprise and improving efficiency by the imposition of a shorter transaction period for business processes, automation of business licensing and certification systems, and the prescription of heavier penalties against administrative and criminal liabilities. The Philippines' ranking in the World Bank's Ease of Doing Business Index improved by 10 notches from 134th place in 2010 to 124th in 2018, and by another 29 notches to 95th place out of 190 economies in 2019.

There has also been increased diversification of services exported, reflecting a movement toward more internationally competitive and higher-productivity industries. Trade in services can cover a wide range of industries including travel and transportation; financial and insurance services; technical, professional,

Figure 1.1: Annual Average Gross Domestic Product Growth Rate, by Broad Sector

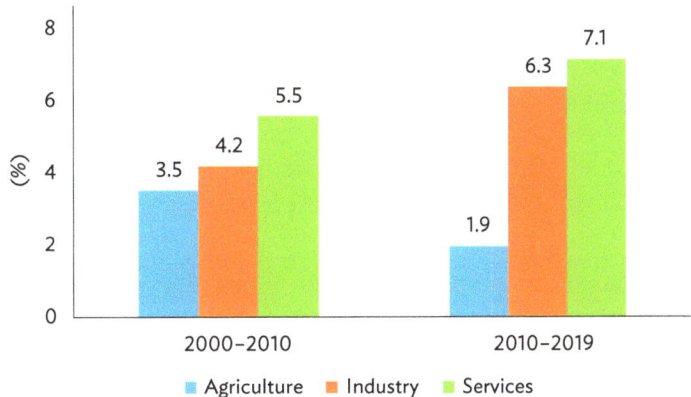

GDP = gross domestic product, GVA = gross value added.
Note: GDP/GVA at constant 2018 prices.
Sources: National Accounts, Philippine Statistics Authority; ADB estimates.

Figure 1.2: Gross Value Added Share of Gross Domestic Product, by Broad Sector

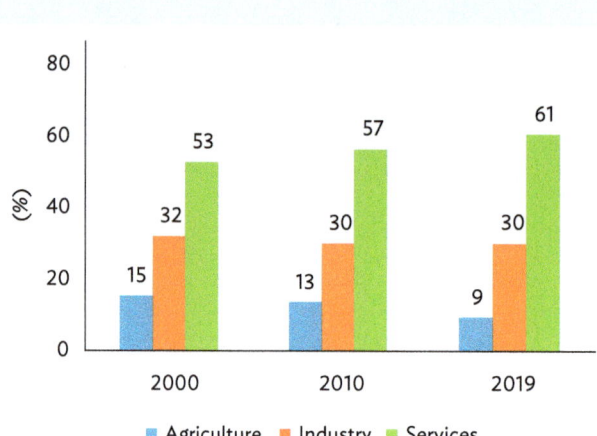

GDP = gross domestic product, GVA = gross value added.
Note: GDP/GVA at constant 2018 prices.
Sources: National Accounts, Philippine Statistics Authority; ADB estimates.

and business services; telecommunications and information services; and construction services.[3] Philippine exports of commercial services grew rapidly at an average of 14% per year between 2000 and 2010 and 8.9% per year between 2010 and 2019. The telecommunication, computer, and information services exports; and research and development, professional, technical, and other business services exports recorded elevated growth rates at 30%–31% every year for 2000–2010 and a lower but still high growth rates of 15.1% and 6.2%, respectively, for 2010–2018. With the advancement and lower costs of information technology (IT), the Philippines was transformed into a global center of business process outsourcing (BPO), leading in voice BPO and ranking second in non-voice BPO.

The manufacturing industry in the Philippines accounts for the largest share of the industry sector output, but this has diminished slightly over the last 2 decades. Manufacturing accounted for 70% of industry value added in 2000, decreasing to 62% in 2019. In terms of GDP, the share of the manufacturing sector declined from 23% in 2000 to 19% in 2019 as its average annual growth rate in the past 2 decades was also surpassed by the services industries, particularly the high-productivity tradable services (Figure 1.3). Construction growth, however, increased from 5.6% to 9.6% (Figure 1.4). The boom in the construction industry was supported by a strong "Build, Build, Build" infrastructure development program of the Duterte administration that has an estimated

---

[3] The 1995 General Agreement on Trade in Services of the World Trade Organization provides the legal framework for trade in a wide range of services industries among member countries including the Philippines. The General Agreement on Trade in Services has four modes of cross-border supply of services: (i) Cross-border (Mode 1) is the supply of a service with the supplier and consumer remaining in their respective countries. Examples of this would be remotely (i.e., by phone, email, fax, video chat) providing legal, accounting, human resources, and IT services by a company in one country to a company in another country; (ii) Consumption abroad (Mode 2) is the supply of services to a service consumer in another country such as tourist activities including visits to monuments, historical places, museums, study tours, and medical and wellness tourism or obtaining medical care and surgical treatment overseas, spa treatments, etc.; (iii) Commercial presence (Mode 3) refers to a service supplier providing services through the establishment of a business or professional affiliate or branch in the country of the consumer such as foreign bank or school subsidiary or branch; and (iv) Presence of natural persons (Mode 4) is the supply of services by a supplier who temporarily moves to the country of the consumer to do so, such as Filipino overseas contract workers working in construction sites or in households in the country of destination (United Nations, 2010).

Figure 1.3: Gross Value Added Share of Gross Domestic Product, by Industry

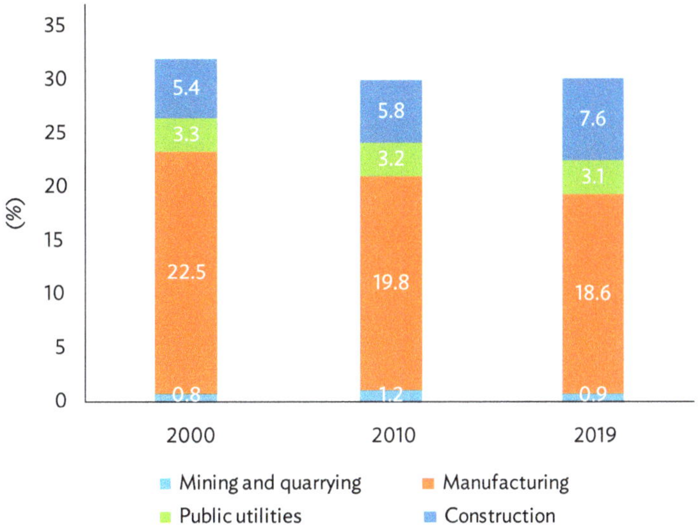

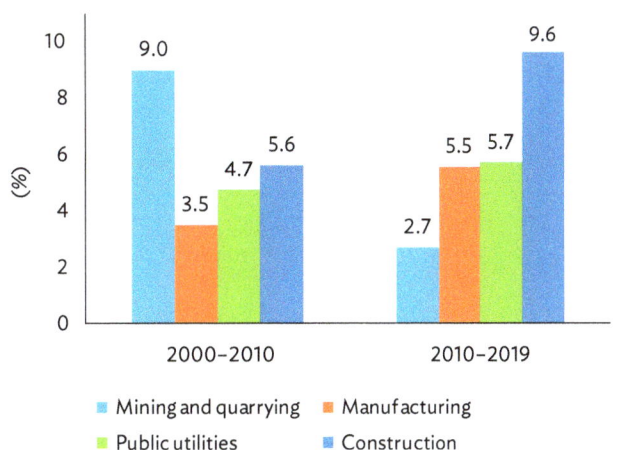

2000	2010	2019
Construction: 5.4	5.8	7.6
Public utilities: 3.3	3.2	3.1
Manufacturing: 22.5	19.8	18.6
Mining and quarrying: 0.8	1.2	0.9

GDP = gross domestic product, GVA = gross value added.
Note: GDP/GVA at constant 2018 prices.
Sources: National Accounts, Philippine Statistics Authority; ADB estimates.

Figure 1.4: Annual Average Gross Value Added Growth, by Industry

	2000–2010	2010–2019
Mining and quarrying	9.0	2.7
Manufacturing	3.5	5.5
Public utilities	4.7	5.7
Construction	5.6	9.6

GDP = gross domestic product, GVA = gross value added.
Note: GDP/GVA at constant 2018 prices.
Sources: National Accounts, Philippine Statistics Authority; ADB estimates.

fund allocation of more than ₱8 trillion from 2016 to 2022, and reflected an accelerated public infrastructure spending from 5.1% of GDP in 2016 to 7.4% in 2022.[4]

The increase in manufacturing growth was driven largely by the rapid growth of medium-high and high-technology industries.[5] As displayed in Figure 1.5, medium-high and high technology industries, increased from 5.1% per annum during 2000–2010 to 8.1% during 2010–2019. Although low-technology industries continue to dominate the manufacturing sector, their share in manufacturing value added has declined from 66% in 2000 to 60% in 2019. The share of medium-low technology industries to manufacturing value added also decreased from 14% in 2000 to 12% in 2019, while that of medium-high and high-technology industries increased from 29% to 37%, reflecting a shift of manufacturing industries from lower to higher technological intensity.

There is increased diversification of the medium-high and high-technology industries particularly with rapid growth of chemical and chemical products industries. The growth rate ion these industries increased from 6.6% in 2000–2010 to 12.8% in 2010–2019, outpacing the growth of electronics industry that was at an annual average of 4.3% in 2000–2010 and 5.3% in 2010–2019. The chemical industry supplanted the electronics industry as the dominant high-technology manufacturing industry, increasing its share of medium-high and high-technology manufacturing value added from 24% in 2000 to 41% in 2019, while that for the electronics industry diminished from 51% in 2000 to 38%. Other high-performing

Figure 1.5: Annual Average Gross Value Added Growth of Manufacturing Sector, by Technology Level

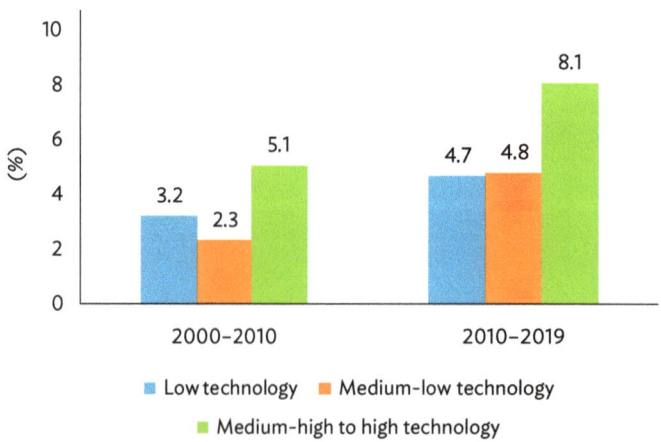

GDP = gross domestic product, GVA = gross value added.
Note: GDP/GVA at constant 2018 prices.
Source: National Accounts, Philippine Statistics Authority; ADB estimates.

---

[4] Government of the Philippines, National Economic Development Authority (NEDA). 2017. *Philippine Development Plan 2017–2022*. Pasig.
[5] Following the United Nations (1990), industries are classified based on International Standard Industrial Classification Rev.3 as follows: (i) Low-technology industries cover food and beverages; textiles and wearing apparel; leather and footwear; wood, furniture, and fixtures; paper and paper products; publishing and printing; and miscellaneous manufactures; (ii) Medium-low technology industries comprise petroleum and fuel products, rubber and plastic products, non-metallic mineral products, basic metals, and fabricated metal products; and (iii) Medium-high to high-technology industries include chemical and chemical products; machinery and equipment; electrical machinery and apparatus; office, accounting, and computing machinery; electronics and communication equipment and apparatus; and transport equipment.

Figure 1.6: Annual Average Growth of Manufacturing Exports, by Technology

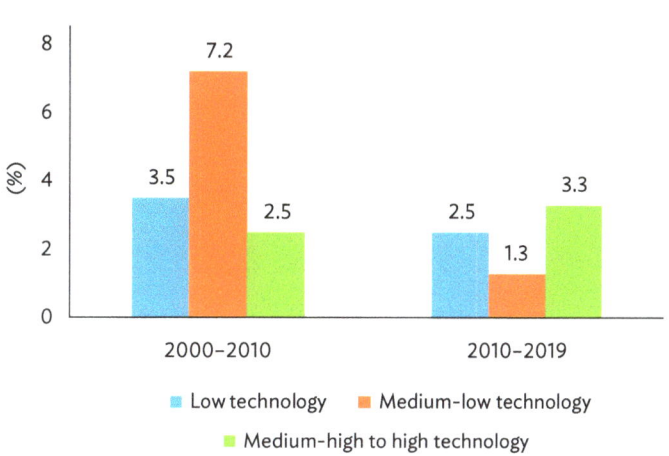

Sources: Foreign Trade, Philippine Statistics Authority; ADB estimates.

industries include electrical machinery (7.8% in 2000–2010 and 8.6% in 2010–2019) and transport equipment industry (10.6% in 2000–2010 and 5.5% in 2010–2019).

Medium-high and high-technology manufactures contributed more than 80% of manufactured exports for the past 2 decades. This has been driven in part by consistent growth in manufacturing exports for this level of technology (Figure 1.6). Meanwhile, low-technology manufactures (e.g., processed food products) contributed 16%, while medium-low technology manufactures (e.g., petroleum and basic metals) accounted for a meager 1% of manufactures exports. Electronic exports led the high-technology manufacture exports, growing at an average of 4.3% for 2000–2010 and 3.4% for 2010–2019, and contributing an increasing share of manufactures exports from 51% in 2000 to 61% in 2019.

Inclusiveness of Growth

Amid rapid economic growth, the Philippines continues to be saddled by persistent job deficiencies, emphasizing the inclusiveness of growth. For economic growth to be sustainable, it must be inclusive. This means benefiting the bulk of the workforce with decent jobs and higher standards of living,[6] and providing better access to members of society to participate in the growth process.[7] Yet, despite rapid growth, 2.3 million of the Filipino labor force were unemployed and an additional 5.9 million were underemployed in 2019.

The employment elasticity of growth is an important indicator of the capacity of the economy to generate employment across major sectors and different population groups.[8] Output growth can be attributed to a larger labor supply or rising labor productivity (Box 1.1), where there is an inverse proportionality between

---

[6] R. Balakrishnan, C. Steinberg, and M. Syed. 2013. The Elusive Quest for Inclusive Growth: Growth, Poverty and Inequality in Asia. *IMF Working Papers* 13/152. Washington, DC.

[7] I. Ali and J. Zhuang. 2007. Inclusive Growth toward a Prosperous Asia: Policy Implications. *Economics and Research RD Working Paper* No. 97. Manila: Asian Development Bank.

[8] Employment elasticity of growth is calculated as the percentage change in employment as output increases by 1 percentage point; an elasticity of 0.7 means that employment increases by 0.7 percentage point for every 1 percentage point increase in GDP.

Box 1.1: Labor Productivity is the Main Contributor to Gross Domestic Product Per Capita Growth

Per capita gross domestic product (GDP) growth can be affected by changes in population growth and demographic structure. In the past 2 decades, the slowdown in Philippine fertility rates alongside declining mortality rates resulted in an increase in working-age share of the population from 63% in 2000 to 68% in 2019, and a decline in age dependency ratio from 71% to 56%.[a] The Philippines is now in the second stage of demographic transition, where a demographic dividend for more rapid economic growth can be realized depending on the economy's ability to transition the burgeoning labor force into productive employment and decent work.

Using the Shapley decomposition approach (Appendix 1.1), we find that the acceleration in per capita GDP growth in the past 2 decades was attributed primarily to higher output per worker, which increased its share from 71% for 2000–2010 to 93% of output growth in 2010–2019 (figure).[b] Higher output per worker can lead to higher labor incomes which may reduce poverty incidence.

Decomposition of Annual Average GDP Per Capita Growth

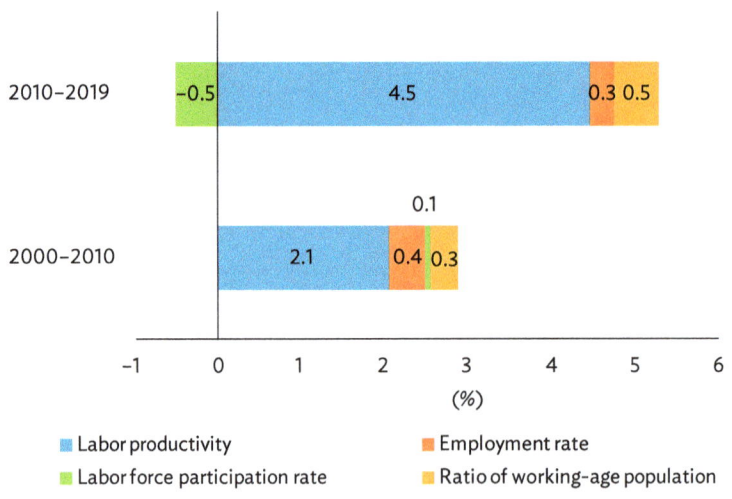

GDP = gross domestic product.
Note: GDP at constant 2018 prices.
[a] Age dependency ratio is the ratio of the number of dependents (population less than 15 years old and older than 64 years old) to the working-age population aged 15 to 64.
[b] Following the Shapley decomposition approach (Gutierrez et al. 2007), the growth rate in per capita GDP can be expressed as the sum of four growth components: (i) labor productivity; (ii) employment rate; (iii) labor force participation rate, and (iv) ratio of working-age population.
Sources: National Accounts, Philippine Statistics Authority; ADB estimates.

By region, labor productivity accounted for at least 99% of per capita output growth in all the regions except for the National Capital Region and its contiguous regions of Cavite, Laguna, Batangas, Rizal, and Quezon (CALABARZON) and Central Luzon where changes in labor productivity accounted for 60%–90% of total regional per capita output growth. For the three latter regions, changes in employment rate and working-age population ratio appeared to have relatively more substantial effect on per capita output growth, with a lower dependency ratio accounting for 8%–34% and a higher employment rate taking up 7%–12% of the growth in per capita gross regional domestic product.

Source: Authors.

employment and productivity. Hence, an employment elasticity of growth of 0.7 also means that 70% of output growth is due to an increase in employment and 30% to higher labor productivity, other things being equal. Khan (2001) asserts that a developing economy with a large workforce and high level of poverty would need to achieve an elasticity of output growth for productive employment of 0.7 to facilitate the transition to an upper middle-income economy. To provide some indication of whether output growth was associated with the absorption of remunerative employment or better-quality jobs, employment elasticities are presented by type of employment: wage employment, low-paid wage employment, vulnerable employment, and underemployment.[9]

Although the surge in economic growth in the recent decade was accompanied by a decline in employment elasticity, it was associated with increased generation of better-quality jobs compared to the previous decade. Employment growth has lagged output growth and increasingly so in 2010–2019 compared to the previous decade. While real GDP growth accelerated from an annual average of 4.8% to 6.3%, that of employment slackened from 2.8% to 1.8%, reducing the employment elasticity of growth from 0.58 to 0.29 (Figure 1.7). The rate of growth of wage employment increased slightly from 3.5% annually in 2000–2010 to 3.7% in 2010–2019, while the annual growth rate dropped sharply for low-paid employment (from 2.7% to 0.1%), vulnerable employment

Figure 1.7: Annual Average Gross Domestic Product/Gross Value Added Growth and Employment Growth, 2000–2010 and 2010–2019

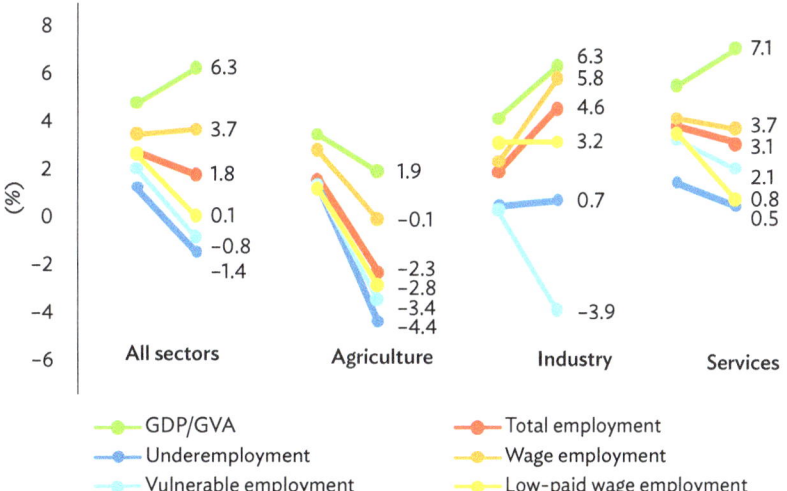

GDP = gross domestic product, GVA = gross value added.
Note: GDP/GVA at constant 2018 prices; growth rates for low-paid wage employment refer to the periods 2001–2010 and 2010–2019.
Sources: National Accounts and Labor and Employment, Philippine Statistics Authority; ADB estimates.

---

[9] A worker is in wage employment if he/she works with pay in a private household, private establishment, government institution or in a family-operated farm or business. A portion of these wage employees are low-paid or those with hourly basic pay in their primary job below two-thirds of the median hourly basic pay of total wage workers (Philippine Statistics Authority [PSA], 2019). Workers in vulnerable employment consist of unpaid family workers and own-account workers (self-employed workers without any paid employees). A worker is considered underemployed if he/she would want to work more hours.

(from 2.1% to –0.8%), and underemployment (from 1.3% to –1.4%). This indicates that the growth in employment in 2000–2010 consisted of lower-quality jobs compared to those created in 2010–2019.

Similar to low-paid wage employment, vulnerable employment and underemployment also reflect decent work deficits that are closely linked to poverty. These types of employment are associated with workers who cannot afford to be unemployed for a prolonged period or to search longer for more decent work, but instead forced to take on jobs with inadequate earnings, in poor working conditions, and lacking social security and collective representation, signifying their higher risk of poverty than the long-term unemployed who may have other sources of income or support.[10] Low-paid wage employment, vulnerable employment, and underemployment increased alongside economic growth in 2000–2010, but contracted with accelerated economic growth in 2010–2019. In terms of employment elasticities, a 1% GDP growth in 2000–2010 increased wage employment by 0.72%, but also increased low-paid wage employment by 0.54%, vulnerable employment by 0.43%, and underemployment by 0.27%. In contrast, a 1% GDP growth in 2010–2019 was accompanied by an increase in wage employment by 0.59%, an almost 0% change in low-paid wage employment, and a decline of –0.13% for vulnerable employment and –0.23% for underemployment.

Lower rates of employment growth were also associated with a diminishing marginal increase in the lower-quality types of employment across sectors. In the agriculture sector, the contraction in wage employment was accompanied by more pronounced declines in low-paid wage employment, vulnerable employment, and underemployment in the more recent decade. The employment elasticity of agriculture value-added growth in 2010–2019 was –0.04 for wage employment, –1.46 for low-paid wage employment, –1.74 for vulnerable employment, and –2.24 for underemployment (Figure 1.8 to Figure 1.11). The share of the wage

Figure 1.8: Elasticity of Wage Employment to Gross Domestic Product/Gross Value Added Growth, by Broad Sector

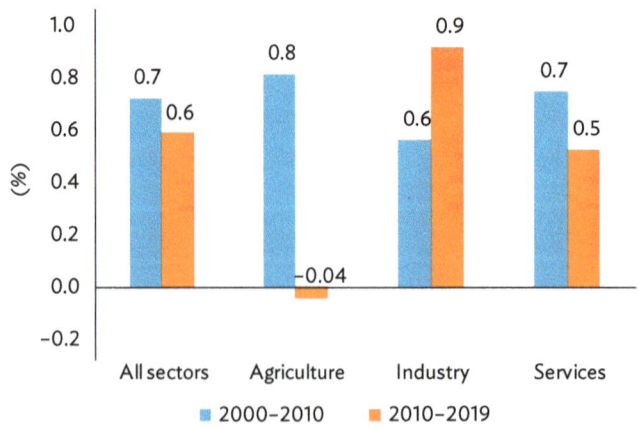

GDP = gross domestic product, GVA = gross value added.
Note: GDP/GVA at constant 2018 prices; growth rates for low-paid wage employment refer to the periods 2001–2010 and 2010–2019.
Sources: National Accounts and Labor and Employment, Philippine Statistics Authority for 2019 figures; ADB estimates.

---

[10] See Esguerra, Ogawa, and Vodopivec (2002); and Sugiyarto (2007).

Figure 1.9: Elasticity of Low-Paid Wage Employment to Gross Domestic Product/Gross Value Added Growth, by Broad Sector

GDP = gross domestic product, GVA = gross value added.
Note: GDP/GVA at constant 2018 prices; growth rates for low-paid wage employment refer to the periods 2001–2010 and 2010–2019.
Sources: National Accounts and Labor and Employment, Philippine Statistics Authority for 2019 figures; ADB estimates.

Figure 1.10: Elasticity of Vulnerable Employment to Gross Domestic Product/Gross Value Added Growth, by Broad Sector

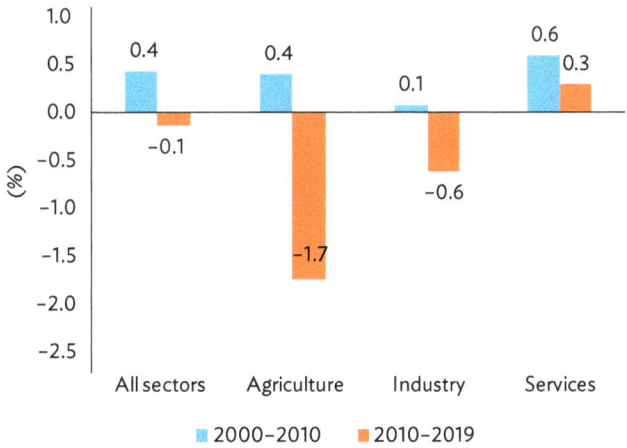

GDP = gross domestic product, GVA = gross value added.
Note: GDP/GVA at constant 2018 prices; growth rates for low-paid wage employment refer to the periods 2001–2010 and 2010–2019.
Sources: National Accounts and Labor and Employment, Philippine Statistics Authority for 2019 figures; ADB estimates.

Figure 1.11: Elasticity of Underemployment to Gross Domestic Product/Gross Value Added Growth, by Broad Sector

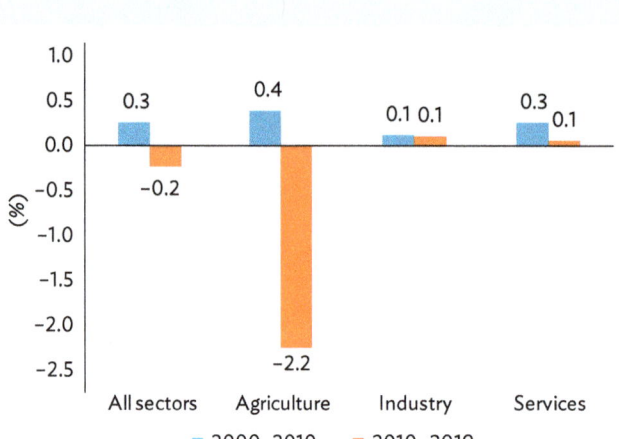

GDP = gross domestic product, GVA = gross value added.
Note: GDP/GVA at constant 2018 prices; growth rates for low-paid wage employment refer to the periods 2001–2010 and 2010–2019.
Sources: National Accounts and Labor and Employment, Philippine Statistics Authority for 2019 figures; ADB estimates.

workers in agriculture increased by 10 percentage points from 24% in 2000 to 34% in 2019, but this remains way below that of the share of wage workers in the other sectors in 2019, which was 91% in the industry sector and 67% in the services sector. The sharp decline in low-quality agricultural employment was manifested in a very marked reduction in the share of low-paid workers to total wage workers in agriculture from 60% in 2000 to 39% in 2019, while the share of vulnerable workers to total agricultural workers dropped from 67% to 59% and underemployment rate in agriculture declined from 26% to 21%.

Declines in agricultural employment may be due to rural–urban migration of better-educated rural workers. A study by the National Economic and Development Authority (NEDA)[11] attributed the decline in agricultural employment to increased education in rural areas, which spurred the migration of the younger and better-educated rural workers to urban areas with the objective of seeking to avail of better-paying employment opportunities in construction, transportation, retail trade, food services, food processing manufacturing, and household personnel services. Close to 60% of agricultural workers in 2019 were own-account workers and unpaid workers in a family farm or business compared with the corresponding shares of 7% in the industry sector and 31% in the services sector. The same study also indicated that the agriculture labor force has been an increasing source of foreign employment with the higher incidence of migration by female rural workers for overseas domestic work.

For the services sector, the employment elasticity of services value added contracted alongside improvements in employment quality indicators. All types of services sector employment grew with value-added growth, but with low-paid wage employment, vulnerable employment, and underemployment growing slower relative to

---

[11] Government of the Philippines, NEDA. 2019a. Out-migration in Agriculture: An Analysis of the Loss of Labor in Agriculture Sector in the Philippines. *R&D Policy Note 1(1)*. Pasig.

wage employment. Between 2010 and 2019, wage employment in the services sector grew at annual average of 3.7% compared with 2.1% for vulnerable employment, 0.8% for low-paid wage employment, and 0.5% for underemployment. This is reflected in the higher elasticity of services value-added growth in wage employment relative to the lower quality of employment and with wider gaps observed in the more recent period. A 1% growth in services value added was associated with a 0.62% increase in low-paid wage employment in 2000–2010 and only 0.11% increase in 2010–2019, while the corresponding increases for vulnerable employment was 0.60% in 2000–2010 and 0.29% in 2010–2019. The increase in the underemployed services sector workers for every percentage point increase in services value added also diminished from 0.27% for 2000–2010 to almost zero in 2010–2019. Improvements in labor quality for the services sector is likewise evidenced by the declining share of low-paid wage employees from 25% in 2010 to 19% in 2019, and the reduction in the share of the vulnerable workers in the services sector from 34% to 31% and of underemployed workers from 14% to 11%.

Unlike in the services and the agriculture sectors, the employment elasticity of value-added growth improved in the industry sector. The accelerated industry employment growth was largely driven by the brisk growth of wage employment at 5.8% annually for 2010–2019, which was accompanied by a positive but lower annual growth of low-paid wage employees at 3.2%. This is attributed to the very rapid employment growth in the low value-added construction sector at an annual average of 8.4% for 2010–2019 compared with the 2.3% annual growth of employment in the higher value-added manufacturing sector. The growth of underemployed workers in the industry sector has also remained meager at 0.7% in 2010–2019, while vulnerable employment growth declined sharply at −3.9%. Wage employment elasticity of value added was highest in the industry sector in 2010–2019 at 0.92, which was way above that for low-paid wage employment at 0.51, for underemployment at 0.11, and for vulnerable employment at −0.61 (Figure 1.8 to Figure 1.11). Labor quality improvement in the industry sector was indicated by a drop in the share of low-paid wage employees from 15% in 2010 to 11% in 2019, and the declining shares of vulnerable workers and underemployed workers from 16% to 7% and from 19% to 14%, respectively.

The responsiveness of employment to output growth differs between men and women as the Philippine labor market is highly gender-segregated in industry and occupation. Employment of Filipino women is clustered in the services industries and occupations, while the men tend to cluster in both the agriculture and industry sectors. With the services sector driving economic growth in 2000–2010, female employment elasticity at 0.67 was higher than that of males at 0.51. This period was also associated with higher absorption into wage employment with slightly larger effects for women. The pattern was reversed in the period 2010–2019, where the rapid growth of industry value added was driven largely by the construction industry that has a very high absorptive capacity for male labor. In the period 2010–2019, the employment elasticity for the industry sector was 0.88 for males and only 0.23 for females. The process of economic transformation that accompanies output growth can affect the gendered outcomes in employment generation and absorption; rapid growth in the construction industry generates more employment for men and a strong growth in the services value added produces larger employment gains for women.

Employment elasticity of output growth also varied by age group and lowest among the youth aged 15 to 24 compared to those in the prime adult ages of 25 to 54 or to more senior ages. Youth workers still lag far behind adult workers in reaping the gains in employment generation from more rapid economic growth. The youth employment elasticity was only about 0.44 in 2000–2010 and diminished further to 0.17 in 2010–2016. By comparison, that of workers in the prime adult ages was 0.64 for 2000–2010 and 0.34 for 2010–2016. The more recent drastic drop in youth employment elasticity in 2016–2018 may be attributed to more students staying in school longer as a result of the K to 12 basic education program extending secondary education from 4 to 6 years, and with the first batch of students in the program expected to have graduated in March 2018.

The lower and diminishing youth employment elasticity of output growth in the past 2 decades has important implications given that the unemployment in the Philippines is primarily a youth problem. The failure to transition the large youth workforce into productive employment translates to foregone gains from the demographic dividend afforded by a larger working-age population which the Philippines is currently experiencing.[12] The youth unemployment rate of 13.4% in 2018 has fallen short of the target in the Philippine Development Plan 2017–2020 of a reduction to 10.4% by 2018, which suggests it will be difficult to achieve the target of 8% by 2022. There is a need to devise more effective programs that would gainfully employ the young entrants to the workforce, reduce the massive youth unemployment, and harness more fully the Philippine demographic dividend.

Sources of Aggregate Labor Productivity Growth

Aggregate labor productivity has grown rapidly over the last decade, from an annual average of 2% for 2000–2010 to 4.4% for 2010–2019. At constant 2018 prices, aggregate labor productivity increased from P254,500 per worker in 2000 to P310,400 per worker in 2010 and P456,500 per worker in 2019. As shown in Figure 1.12 and Figure 1.13, between 2000 and 2019, there was a movement of labor from the lower-productivity agriculture sector to the higher-productivity services and industry sectors, and a within-sector increase in the labor productivity for all the sectors.

Disaggregating changes in aggregate labor productivity provides further insights into the nature of structural transformation. Changes in aggregate labor productivity can be disaggregated into three different components (Appendix 1.2): (i) intra- or within-sector labor productivity, whereby productivity changes within the sector, for instance, as a result of innovation developments or use of more productive approaches; (ii) reallocation of workers from less productive sectors to more productive sectors (or vice versa), such as from agriculture to services, known as static reallocation; and (iii) reallocation of workers to other sectors with faster growth (or vice versa), i.e., to sectors that are not necessarily more productive in levels of labor productivity, but are becoming more productive overall, such as shifting into a new and emerging industry, known as dynamic reallocation.

Within-sector productivity growth is the main driver of aggregate labor productivity growth. Although the services sector contributed the majority of aggregate labor productivity growth in the past 2 decades, this contribution has diminished from 74% in 2000–2010 to 69% in 2010–2019 as the industry sector increased its share from 21% to 31% (Figures 1.14 and 1.15). Despite the increasing role of labor reallocation in the more recent decade, aggregate labor productivity growth remains determined largely by within-sector productivity increases, which contributed close to 72.4% of aggregate productivity growth in 2010–2019.

The Philippine economy is characterized by wide inter-industry productivity gaps, which imply a large scope for increasing aggregate labor productivity through a labor shift from industries of lower productivity to higher productivity. At the high end of the productivity spectrum are industries with labor productivity levels that are more than twice that of the economy-wide labor productivity, including manufacturing and public utilities in the industry sector; and the tradable business services of financial intermediation, information and communication, and real estate and business activities in the services sector. Public utilities have very limited labor absorptive capacity and accounted for less than 1% of the total employed in 2019. Tradable business services which have higher average labor productivity than the manufacturing sector and close to three times higher average labor productivity than the national economy, accounted for 7.5% of total employment, while the share of manufacturing to total employment was 8.5%.

---

[12] See Abrigo et al. (2018) and Mapa (2015).

Figure 1.12: Labor Productivity and Employment Share, 2000

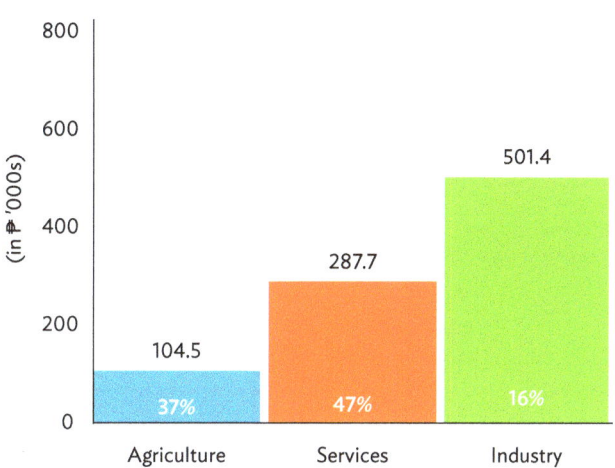

Sources: National Accounts and Labor and Employment, Philippine Statistics Authority for 2019 figures; ADB estimates.

Figure 1.13: Labor Productivity and Employment Share, 2019

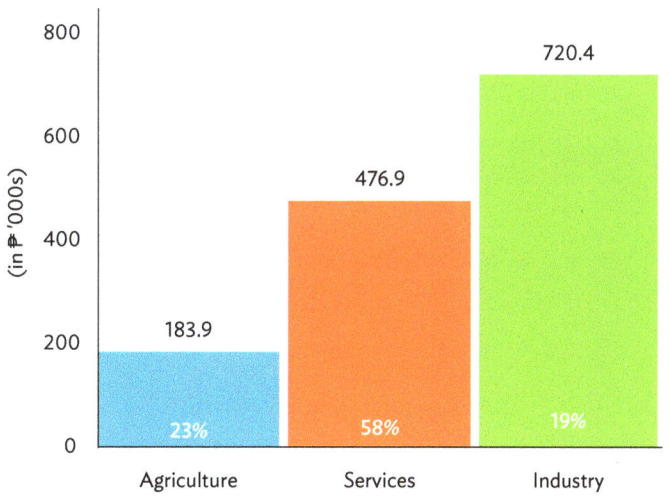

Sources: National Accounts and Labor and Employment, Philippine Statistics Authority for 2019 figures; ADB estimates.

Figure 1.14: Decomposition of Aggregate Labor Productivity Change, 2000–2010

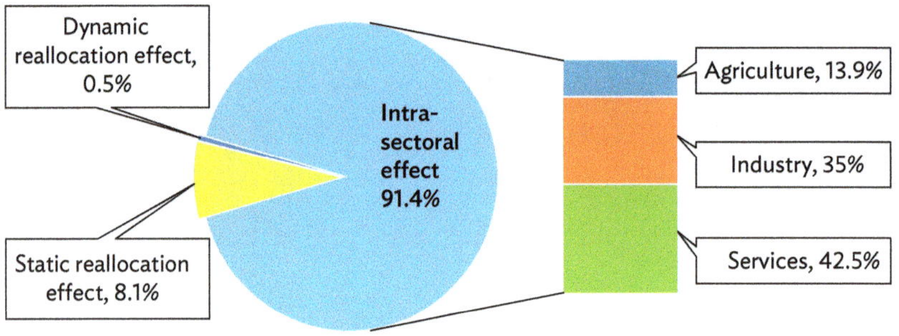

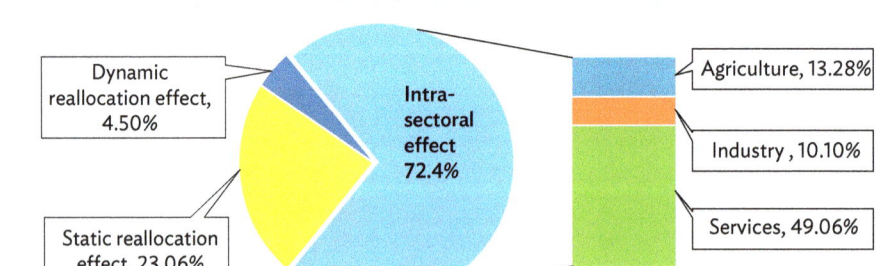

Note: Gross domestic product/gross value added at constant 2018 prices.
Sources: National Accounts and Labor and Employment, Philippine Statistics Authority for 2019 figures; ADB estimates.

Figure 1.15: Decomposition of Aggregate Labor Productivity Change, 2010–2019

Note: Gross domestic product/gross value added at constant 2018 prices.
Source: National Accounts and Labor and Employment, Philippine Statistics Authority for 2019 figures; ADB estimates.

At the lower end of the labor productivity scale are the largest labor absorbers, including agriculture and construction. Industries with below average labor productivity levels are also the larger industries, including agriculture; construction; and the traditional services industries of wholesale and retail trade, transport and storage, and food and accommodation services. The absorption of labor displaced from agriculture in the relatively high-value manufacturing and tradable business services industries would have a larger contribution to aggregate labor productivity than if agriculture labor shifted to other below average productivity industries such as construction and traditional service industries.

The reallocation effect of aggregate labor productivity growth has increased in importance in the more recent decade, with the high-value tradable business services taking up the largest contribution. This is followed by the less productive industries of construction, wholesale and retail trade, and nonmarket services. The manufacturing sector has the highest contribution of the within-sector effect, but very minimal role in the reallocation effect. This is partly due to the increasing technological intensity of the manufacturing sector with rapid and accelerated growth rates recorded for medium-high and high-technology industries that also require higher-skilled labor.

Conclusions and Policy Implications

Structural transformation in the last decade has been associated with signs of improved quality of employment. Although the manufacturing share of value added has remained largely unchanged, there was a shift in value-added structure from lower technology industries to medium-high and high-technology manufacturing industries. For the services sector, the reallocation in value-added share was toward the tradable services of financial intermediation, information and communication, and real estate and business activities. At the same time, economic growth in the more recent decade was associated with lower employment elasticity, but more aligned with improvements in decent work, as indicated by declining low-paid wage employment, vulnerable employment, and underemployment.

Despite high growth rates, the gains from growth have not been equitably shared and point to the potential for TVET to improve employment growth for youth and women. The employment intensity of output growth for youth and women was found to be significantly lower than adults and men despite the Philippines having reversed the gender gap in education and the younger labor force being more educated than older cohorts. There is need for more effective strategies of employment promotion that reduce the underutilization of the youth and female labor force, including strengthening TVET programs that facilitate the transition from school to work, intensifying the Youth Entrepreneurship Program of the Department of Trade and Industry, and increasing flexible work arrangements for mothers and other women with domestic responsibilities.

Labor productivity remains highly uneven across regions. The National Capital Region (NCR) is the frontier economy, with labor productivity at close to three times the national mean average and almost five times the national median average (Box 1.2). The rest of the regions follow far behind, with the ARMM having the lowest labor productivity at only 24% of the nation-wide aggregate level. The level of labor productivity across regions is negatively correlated with the share of agriculture to total regional employment and positively correlated with the share of manufacturing and tradable business services. This highlights the need for a more effective implementation of policies and programs under the Philippine Development Plan 2017–2022 for agricultural modernization, establishment of regional manufacturing hubs, and spatial dispersion of IT-BPO industries.

A regional education policy that is closely aligned with regional industrial policy may be the key to narrowing the inequality that undermines the process of growth acceleration. A strong education policy and targeted education programs should buttress an effective industrial policy in the regions as the low level of human capital in economically disadvantaged regions poses a critical barrier to agricultural modernization and accelerated structural transformation. The establishment of institutions of specialized higher education and research, including TVET that provide contextualized and experiential education in regional economies is crucial to: (i) capacitate agriculture manpower to utilize the appropriate technologies under a more modern and environmentally sustainable agriculture system and acquire entrepreneurial skills to meet the challenges of both the domestic and international competitive agri-food market systems; and (ii) fulfill regional labor market skill requirements under a more modern and dynamic process of regional industrialization and tertiarization that is necessary to facilitate a speedier productivity-enhancing structural transformation.

Box 1.2: Variations in Regional Labor Productivity

There are significant regional differentials in labor productivity. The National Capital Region is the frontier economy in labor productivity that was close to three times the national mean average and almost five times higher than the national median average. Variation in labor productivity across regions was driven by the differentials in the role of agriculture and the tradable industries of manufacturing and tradable business services to regional economies. Labor productivity is negatively correlated with the share of agricultural employment to total regional employment and positively correlated with manufacturing and the tradable business services of financial intermediation and real estate and business activities.

Low-income regions have regional aggregate labor productivity below the nationwide labor productivity level, and they have among the highest shares of agricultural employment, which makes for a strong potential for accelerated regional productivity growth from a reallocation of labor agriculture to the higher-productivity non-agriculture sectors. In the absence of a strong manufacturing industry, labor displaced from the primary industries of agriculture and mining were absorbed largely in construction, transport, and public administration industries, which have labor productivity levels below the regional aggregate labor productivity.[a] The experience of agricultural middle-income regional economies indicates that the presence of a manufacturing base is necessary to break out from a low-income, slow gross regional domestic product growth trajectory to a higher-income, faster-growth trajectory.

The role of wholesale and retail trade was also more prominent in the middle-income agricultural regions accounting for 10%–18% of regional aggregate labor productivity growth primarily through the within-sector effect. The labor productivity of wholesale and retail trade in the middle-income regions was more than three times that of low-income regions for the same industry. This indicates that more developed supply chains and better linkages to markets would be key to the more efficient distribution and sale of agricultural and agro-industrial products and increasing their market and competitive advantage. Accelerated value added growth in wholesale and retail trade may be partly due to regulatory reforms including the enactment of the Ease of Doing Business and Efficient Government Service Delivery Act of 2018, aimed at improving efficiency by the imposition of a shorter transaction period for business processes, automation of business licensing and certification systems, and the prescription of heavier penalties against administrative and criminal liabilities. This was supplemented by the wider enforcement of the Go *Negosyo* Act of 2014 which mandated the establishment of *Negosyo* (Business) Centers in all cities and municipalities that offer the full services of business registration facilitation; entrepreneurship education; product development; access to financial service providers; establishment of linkages with suppliers; and the promotion of products and services in the regional; national, and international markets.

Higher regional aggregate productivity growth is associated with a strong base in the tradable industries of manufacturing and tradable business services, which are experiencing accelerating growth. Cavite, Laguna, Batangas, Rizal, and Quezon (CALABARZON), the most industrial-based economy, had the lowest aggregate labor productivity growth among the high-income regions, hampered by the low productivity of its higher-value industries (at 3.1% in 2012–2018 for manufacturing, which is half that of the nation-wide level, and at –1.4% for the tradable business services). By comparison, regional aggregate labor productivity growth was highest in Davao Region (Region 11), by an above average growth in value added and labor productivity in manufacturing and tradable business services.

A low level of human capital can be a significant barrier to the development of a strong manufacturing base and robust services sector that would be critical to putting low-income regions on a higher growth path. Only a quarter of total employed in the low-income and middle-income regions had at least some post-secondary education compared to almost two-fifths of the major industrial regions of CALABARZON and Cordillera Autonomous Region, and close to half in the National Capital Region that has the highest labor productivity in services. Regional educational policy should be closely aligned with regional industrial policy to better match the knowledge and skills supplied in and demanded by the regional labor market and speed up the dynamics of productivity-enhancing regional structural transformation.

[a] The only exception is the public administration industry in Autonomous Region in Muslim Mindanao, which has labor productivity that was more than twice as high as the regional aggregate labor productivity.
Source: Authors.

Appendix 1.1: Gross Domestic Product per Capita Growth Decomposition

GDP per capita (Y/N) can be expressed algebraically as comprising four components:

$$\frac{Y}{N} = \frac{Y}{E} \times \frac{E}{L} \times \frac{L}{A} \times \frac{A}{N} \qquad [1]$$

where Y is GDP in real terms, N is total population, E is total employment, L is the labor force, and A is the working-age population. In equation [1], GDP per capita (Y/N) is the composite product of output per worker (Y/E), or aggregate labor productivity; employment rate (E/L), or the proportion of the labor force who are employed; labor force participation rate (L/A), or the share of the working-age population 15 years and over who are participating in the labor force; and the share of the working-age group to the total population (A/N). The latter is an indicator of the maximum productive population that can support the economically dependent of below 15 years old.

Following the Shapley decomposition approach (Gutierrez et al. 2007), GDP per capita growth can be decomposed into four components by taking the natural logarithm and obtaining the time derivative of equation [1]:

$$\frac{d}{dt}(Y-N) = \frac{d}{dt}(Y-E) + \frac{d}{dt}(E-L) + \frac{d}{dt}(L-A) + \frac{d}{dt}(A-N)$$

$$\dot{Y} - \dot{N} = (\dot{Y} - \dot{E}) + (\dot{E} - \dot{L}) + (\dot{L} - \dot{A}) + (\dot{A} - \dot{N}) \qquad [2]$$

where the overdot above a variable denotes a growth rate.

Thus, the growth rate in per capita GDP can be expressed as the sum of four growth components: (i) labor productivity, (ii) employment rate, (iii) labor force participation rate, and (iv) ratio of working-age population.

Appendix 1.2: Decomposition of Aggregate Labor Productivity Growth

Labor productivity at year t can be expressed as follows:

$$\rho_t = \frac{Y_t}{E_t} = \sum_{i=1}^{n} \frac{Y_{it}}{E_{it}} \frac{E_{it}}{E_t} = \sum_{i=1}^{n} \rho_{it} \theta_{it} \qquad [1]$$

where ρ is aggregate labor productivity, Y is the aggregate real output, E is the level of total employment, and ρ_i, Y_i and E_i are the corresponding labor productivity, and levels of output and employment for industry $i=1,...,n$, and θ_i is the share of employment in industry i to total employment. This section presents the decomposition of the aggregate labor productivity growth for 1-digit level industry classification for the periods 2000–2010 and 2010–2019, and 2-digit level industry classification for 2012–2019.

The change in aggregate labor productivity between the end period ($t = 1$) and the base period ($t = 0$) can be decomposed into three effects as follows[13]:

$$\Delta \rho = \rho_1 - \rho_0 = \sum_{i=1}^{n} \rho_{i1} - \rho_{i0} = \underbrace{\sum_{i=1}^{n} \Delta \rho_i \theta_{i0}}_{\text{intra-sector effect}} + \underbrace{\sum_{i=1}^{n} \rho_{i0} \Delta \theta_i}_{\text{static reallocation effect}} + \underbrace{\sum_{i=1}^{n} \Delta \rho_i \Delta \theta_i}_{\text{dynamic reallocation effect}} \qquad [2]$$

- Intra-sector effect denotes the effect of changes in labor productivity within a sector or industry on aggregate labor productivity.
- Static reallocation effect denotes the effect of inter-sector reallocation of labor, which is positive (negative) if the movement is from a less (more) productive sector to a more (less) productive sector. Labor inflow into (outflow from) sectors with above average labor productivity has a positive (negative) effect on the change in aggregate labor productivity.
- Dynamic reallocation effect denotes the effect of inter-sector reallocation of labor from sectors with decreasing labor productivity to sectors with increasing labor productivity. This is indicated in the third term of equation (2) by interacting the change in sectoral share to total employment and the sectoral change in labor productivity. A movement of labor away from (toward) sectors with increasing labor productivity results in a negative (positive) dynamic reallocation effect.

---

[13] G. de Vries, M. Timmer, and K. de Vries. 2015. Structural Transformation in Africa: Static Gains, Dynamic Losses. *The Journal of Development Studies* 51(6): 674–88.

2. Labor Market Diagnostics

Although recent economic growth may not have led to massive job creation, it is the structure and quality of employment that has changed most in the Philippines, with informality, underemployment, vulnerable and precarious employment, and wide disparities across regions and socioeconomic groups remaining a concern. In the coming years, to meet its more-inclusive development objectives, the Philippines will need to expand the scale of decent work creation, and engage more of its population in the labor force, with a particular focus on women, youth, vulnerable groups, and poorer regions. In that regard, skills and education have a major role to play.

This chapter provides a labor market diagnostic of the Philippines economy, and an overview of the changing occupational structure and demand for skills. It also examines recent labor market trends at the national level, focuses on the changing occupational structure and demand for skills, and provides an overview of these two dimensions at the regional level.

The Labor Market at a Glance

The Philippine population is relatively young, with nearly one-third below working age (Figure A2.1).[14] The population surpassed 100 million in 2015 and is estimated to have reached 105.8 million in 2018. With a labor force participation rate (LFPR) of 62.2%, the Philippine labor force stood at 44.1 million, including 41.8 million employed and 2.3 million (5.3%) unemployed.[15]

As outlined in Chapter 1, rapid economic growth over the last 2 decades has not been accompanied by sufficient employment creation. The Philippines has sustained a high GDP growth rate over the past decade, and, particularly from 2012, one that is well above the East Asia and the Pacific average (Figure 2.1). Despite this rapid economic growth, the employment-to-population rate (EPR) has remained generally constant, and has even decreased in recent years, indicating that employment growth has fallen short of the growth of the working-age population. The substantial drop in unemployment from 2014 onward was primarily due to a decline in labor force participation (Figure 2.2). The largest decline in LFPR took place in 2016, with the implementation of the K to 12 program, as cohorts that would have normally entered the labor market remained in school for an additional 2 years. Between 2013 and 2018, youth (aged 15–24) had a 4.3 percentage-point (p.p.) decline in LFPR (Table 2.1). This translated into significant declines in unemployment rates for young men and women (by 3.6 and 4.9 p.p., respectively) and "neither in employment nor in education or training" (NEET) rates

---

[14] It is worth noting that overseas Filipino workers (OFWs), who constitute just over 2% of the population based on the labor force survey (LFS), are not considered part of the working-age population for statistical purposes. OFWs play an important contribution to the Philippines economy via remittances. The TVET system in the Philippines plays a key role in preparing and skilling OFWs for employability overseas.

[15] The primary source of data in this chapter is the LFS. Due to data availability, the January round of the LFS is used as the annual estimate for each year. Therefore, data presented may slightly differ from other sources using the average of the four quarters for annual figures. Note that aggregate figures for 2014 exclude Region VIII, which was not included in the January round of the LFS that year.

Figure 2.1: Gross Domestic Product Growth and Employment-to-Population Ration in the Philippines and East Asia and the Pacific, 2000–2018

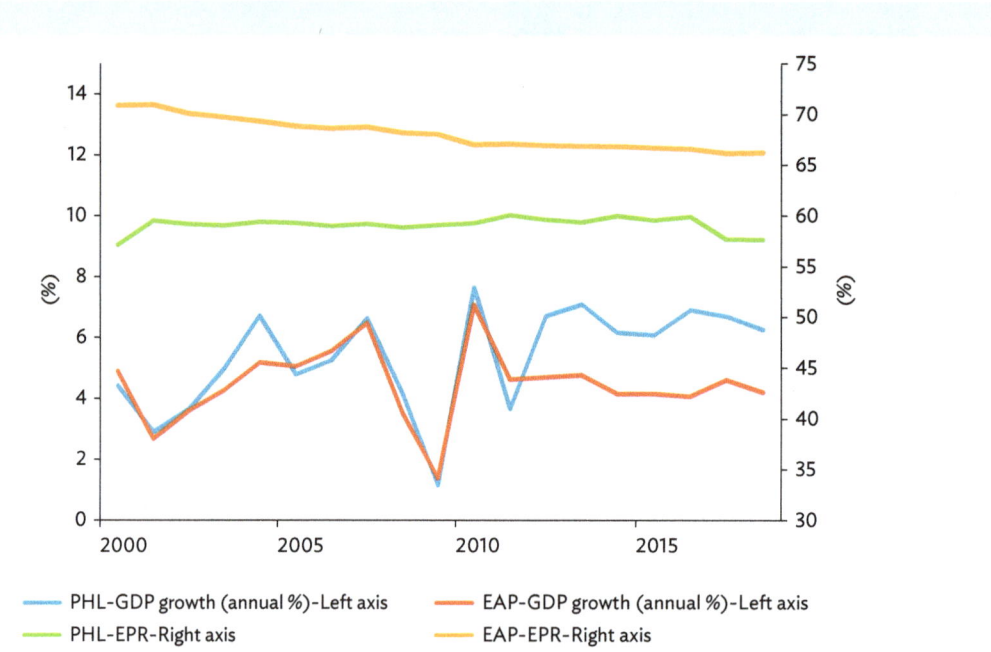

EAP = East Asia and the Pacific, EPR = employment-to-population rate, GDP = gross domestic product, PHL = Philippines.
Sources: World Bank. World Development Indicators. http://databank.worldbank.org/data/home.aspx (accessed 3 December 2020); and labor force survey.

(by 6.1 and 6.7 p.p.). Nevertheless, young people still represented over 40% of the unemployed in 2018, a disproportionate share given that they represented only 18.5% of the labor force.

The smaller numbers of young labor market entrants following the implementation of K to 12 coincided with significant job reduction in agriculture in 2016 and 2017, which further contributed to the decline in the overall EPR and LFPR (Table 2.1). A further decline in both the EPR and LFPR occurred in 2019 (Figure 2.2) due to Hurricane Usman, which led to a drop of nearly 20% in agriculture employment, reflecting the Philippine labor market's vulnerability to external shocks and natural disasters, the impacts of which are often considerable at the regional level. The decline in agriculture employment is reflected in the large drop in adult female EPR and LFPR between 2013 and 2018, as women represent a relatively large share of low-skill employment, including in agriculture. Despite having achieved gender parity in education and significantly narrowed the gender gap in health outcomes, the Philippines still has a persistent gender gap in terms of employment opportunities and labor force participation across age groups and educational achievement categories, largely due to entrenched gender roles.[16]

Although employment growth in the Philippines has been modest over the past decade, particularly in relation to the increase in the working-age population, the structure of employment has changed significantly. This

---

[16] Specifically, in addition to child-bearing and child-rearing, household and family duties are assigned primarily to women, while men are in charge of providing financially for the family. See Epetia (2019) for an elaborate discussion.

Labor Market Diagnostics 23

Figure 2.2: Key Labor Market Indicators, 2008–2019

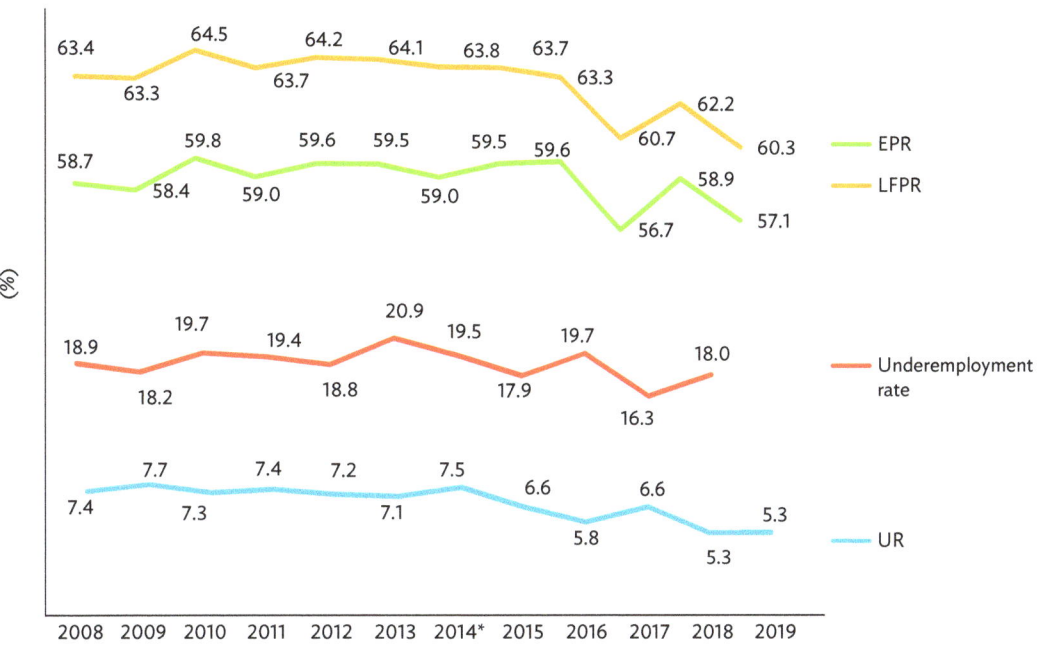

EPR = employment-to-population rate, LFPR = labor force participation rate, UR = unemployment rate.
Note: 2014 excludes Region 8.
Source: ADB estimates based on labor force survey.

Table 2.1: Change in Key Labor Market Indicators by Demographic Group, 2008–2018

| | | YOUTH (15–24 years old) | | | | ADULTS (25 years old and above) | | | |
| | | | Change (p.p.) | | | | Change (p.p.) | | |
		2018	2008–13	2013–18	2008–18	2018	2008–13	2013–18	2008–18
LFPR	Male	50.4	0.2	(4.8)	(4.6)	87.4	(1.4)	(0.2)	(1.6)
	Female	30.1	(0.3)	(4.1)	(4.4)	54	3	(3.5)	(0.4)
	Total	40.5	0	(4.3)	(4.3)	70.6	0.9	(1.8)	(0.9)
EPR	Male	44.2	0.5	(2.2)	(1.7)	83.9	(1.1)	0.7	(0.4)
	Female	26.2	(0.4)	(1.9)	(2.2)	52.3	2.9	(3)	0
	Total	35.4	0.1	(1.9)	(1.8)	68	1	(1.1)	(0.1)
UR	Male	12.3	(0.7)	(3.6)	(4.3)	4	(0.2)	(1.1)	(1.3)
	Female	12.9	0.3	(4.9)	(4.5)	3.1	(0.1)	(0.6)	(0.7)
	Total	12.5	(0.3)	(4.1)	(4.4)	3.7	(0.2)	(0.9)	(1.1)
NEET	Male	13.5	1.1	(6.1)	(5)				
	Female	25.5	0.8	(6.7)	(5.9)				
	Total	19.4	0.9	(6.5)	(5.5)				

EPR = employment-to-population rate, LFPR = labor force participation rate, NEET = neither in employment nor in education or training, p.p. = percentage points, UR = unemployment rate.
Note: ( ) = negative.
Source: ADB estimates based on labor force survey.

Figure 2.3: Employment Share by Broad Sector, 1998–2019

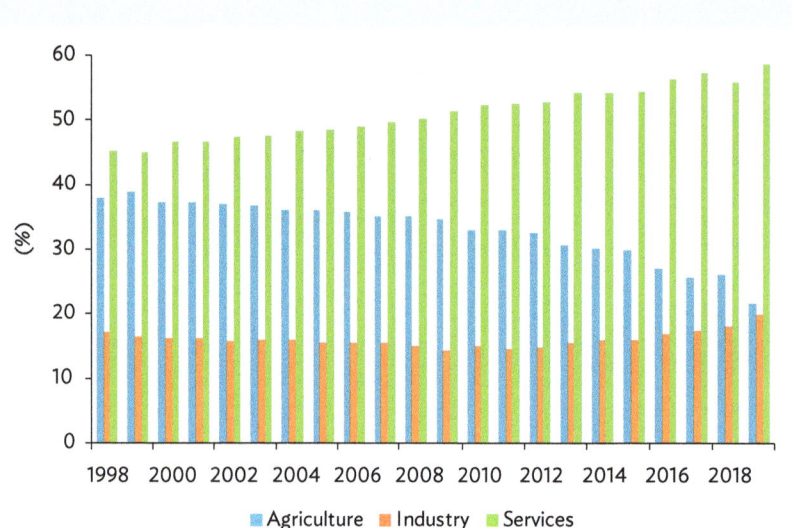

Source: ADB estimates based on labor force survey.

contributed to a decline in income inequality and the incidence and depth of poverty.[17] Agriculture's share in employment has continued to decline, reaching 26% in 2018 (Figure 2.3). The share of workers employed in services continued to grow, and in 2018, the sector accounted for nearly 56% of employment.

The highest employment growth rates between 2008 and 2018 were in service industries, specifically in administration and business support services, which includes the BPO industry, as well as in the professional, scientific, and technical activities (Figure 2.4). Accommodation and food services (tourism), real estate activities, and information and communication also had very high employment growth rates during this period. In absolute numbers, much of the increase in services employment was in the wholesale and retail industry, which accounted for nearly 20% of total employment in 2018 (Figure 2.5). This industry, which has a large share of own-account work and low-productivity jobs has continued to absorb the growing labor force in urban areas. Other service industries that accounted for large net increases in employment are administration and business support services, transportation and storage, public administration, tourism, and other services.

The industry sector's share in employment, which had remained more or less constant or even declined slightly between 2000 and 2010, has been growing since 2011. In 2018, the share reached 18.1%. The largest increase in industry employment, however, took place in construction, which surpassed manufacturing as the largest industry subsector in terms of employment in 2018, driven by the "Build, Build, Build" program of the Duterte administration.[18] The sector added almost as many jobs as the wholesale and retail trade industries between 2008 and 2018, with nearly 1.9 million (Figure 2.4).

---

[17] Based on World Bank estimates, the Gini coefficient for the Philippines declined from 47.7 in 2000 to 44.4; the poverty headcount ratio at the national poverty line fell from a high of 26.6% of the population in 2006 to 21.6% in 2015; and the poverty gap, measuring the depth of poverty, declined from 5.8% in 2006 to 5.1% in 2012 (World Bank, Poverty and Equity Database).

[18] The "Build, Build, Build" program, launched in 2017, consists of some 20,000 infrastructure projects around the country, including roads and highways, airports, seaports, terminals, schools, and hospitals, among others. Its substantial budget of approximately ₱8 trillion ($164.7 billion) over the 2017–2022 period constitutes a remarkable increase of the infrastructure budget from 3% of GDP in 2011–2016 to over 6% by 2021. Its objective is to enhance connectivity and infrastructure for a more widespread and balanced growth across the Philippines. The "Build, Build, Build" program has encountered some setbacks due to the COVID-19 pandemic, but is expected to play a central role in the recovery. See Malindog-Uy (2020) for a brief discussion.

Figure 2.4: Average Annual Employment Growth Rate and Net Employment Growth by Sector, 2008–2018

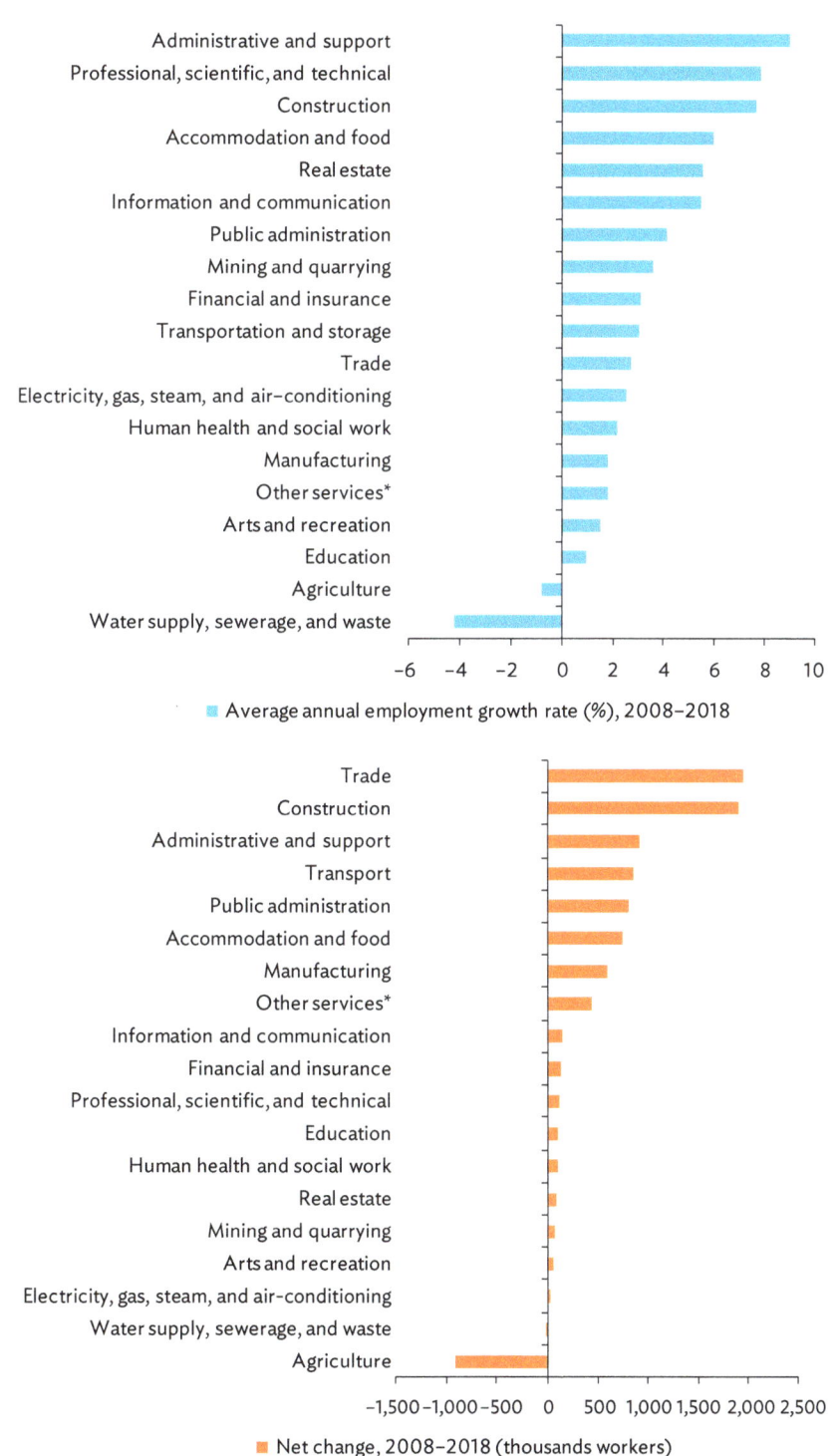

Source: ADB estimates based on labor force survey.

Figure 2.5: Employment by Industry, 2018 (1-digit PSIC)

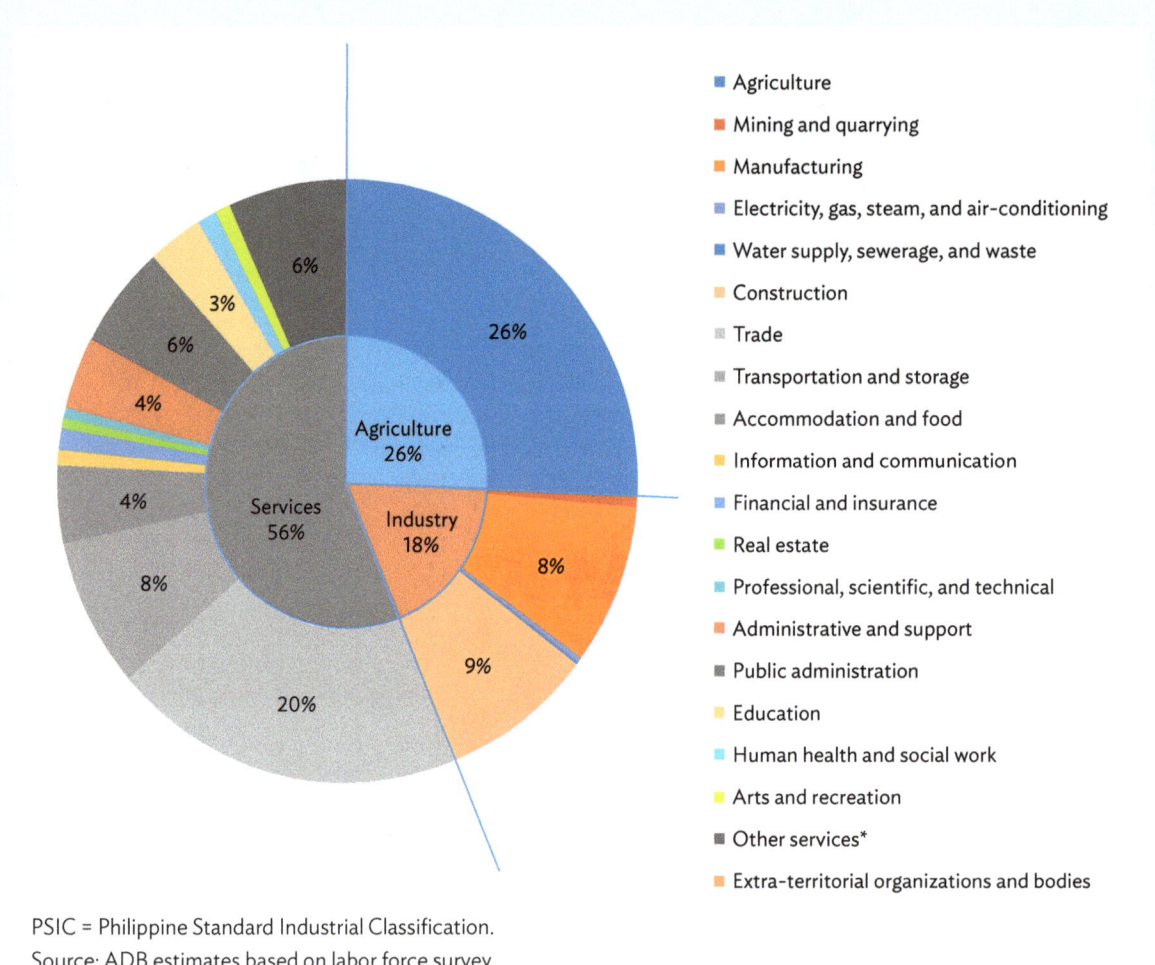

PSIC = Philippine Standard Industrial Classification.
Source: ADB estimates based on labor force survey.

Changing Occupation Distribution and Skills Demand

The changing structure of employment is reflected in the occupational distribution and skills demand composition. The share of agricultural and elementary occupations in total employment has steadily declined over the past 2 decades, while that of service and sales workers had steadily increased (Figure 2.6). The large drop in share of elementary occupations between 2016 and 2017 consisted to a large extent of female adult workers, primarily in agriculture, but also in manufacturing, wholesale and retail trade, and other services. During these years, many female adult workers dropped out of the labor force, driving the decline in EPR and LFPR among adults, in particular (Figure 2.2; Table 2.1).

Figure 2.6: Employment Share by Major Occupational Group and Skill Category, 2001–2019

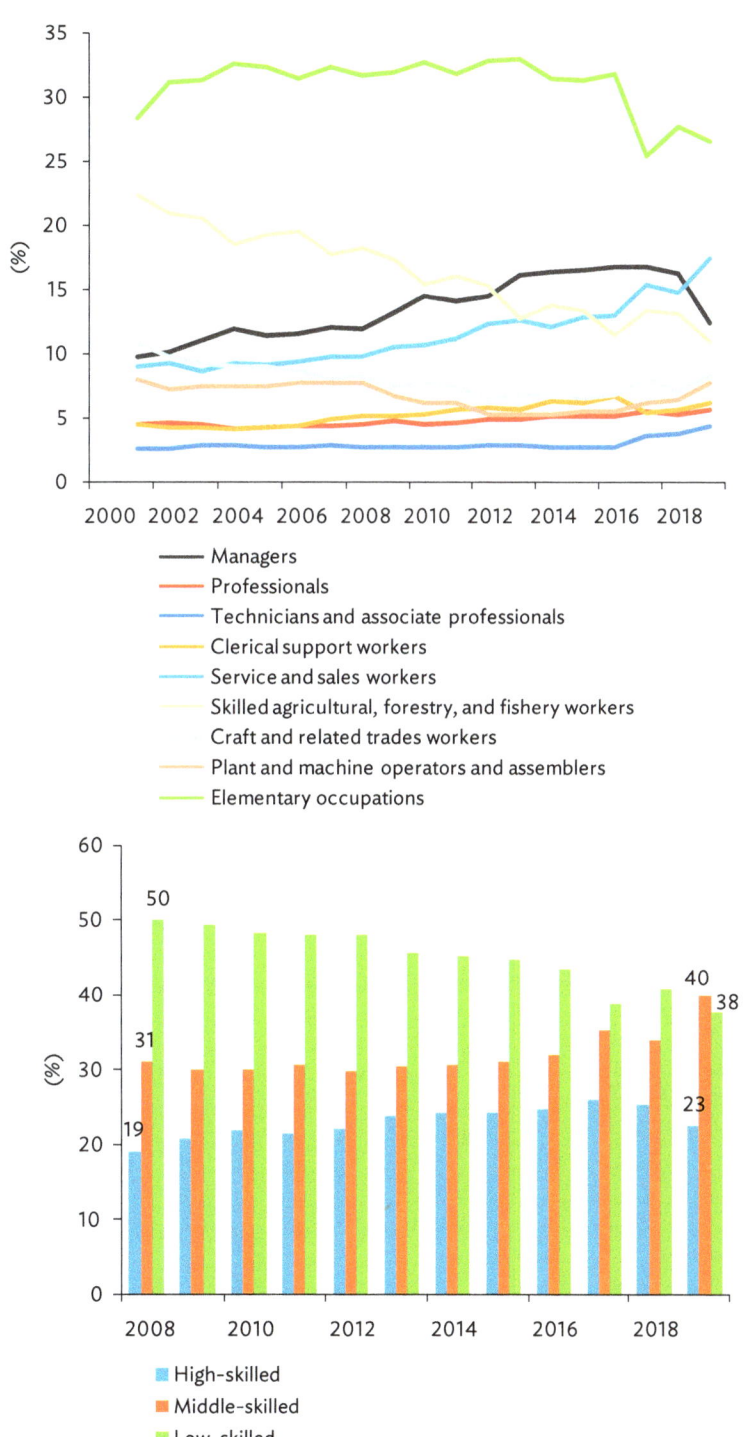

Source: ADB estimates based on labor force survey.

In particular, the employment shares of high-skilled occupations, i.e., managers, professionals and technicians, and associate professionals, have increased over time, as have the shares of clerical support workers, a middle-skilled occupational group. A rise in the share of the latter groups is associated with high employment growth rates in administrative and support service activities; professional, scientific, and technical services; information and communications technology (ICT); and public administration (Figure 2.4). There has been a good amount of reshuffling of jobs within the middle-skill occupational groups over the past decades. Craft and related trades workers had negative employment growth between 2001 and 2008, while plant and machine operators and assemblers had positive growth (Figure 2.6), reflecting a restructuring from labor-intensive to capital-intensive production, within and across manufacturing industries. The plant and machine operators and assemblers category was hit hardest during the Great Recession, with a –4.9% average annual employment growth rate between 2008 and 2011 (Figure 2.7). Both the craft and related trades workers, and plant and machine operators and assemblers categories, have increased since, due to rapid growth in manufacturing and construction.

At the aggregate level, the skills demand and supply structures are converging in the Philippines, but mismatch remains a concern. In previous decades, the increasing educational attainment of the Philippines was not met with sufficient creation of middle- and high-skilled employment opportunities. This resulted in vertical skills mismatch

Figure 2.7: Average Annual Employment Growth Rates by Major Occupational Group, 2001–2018

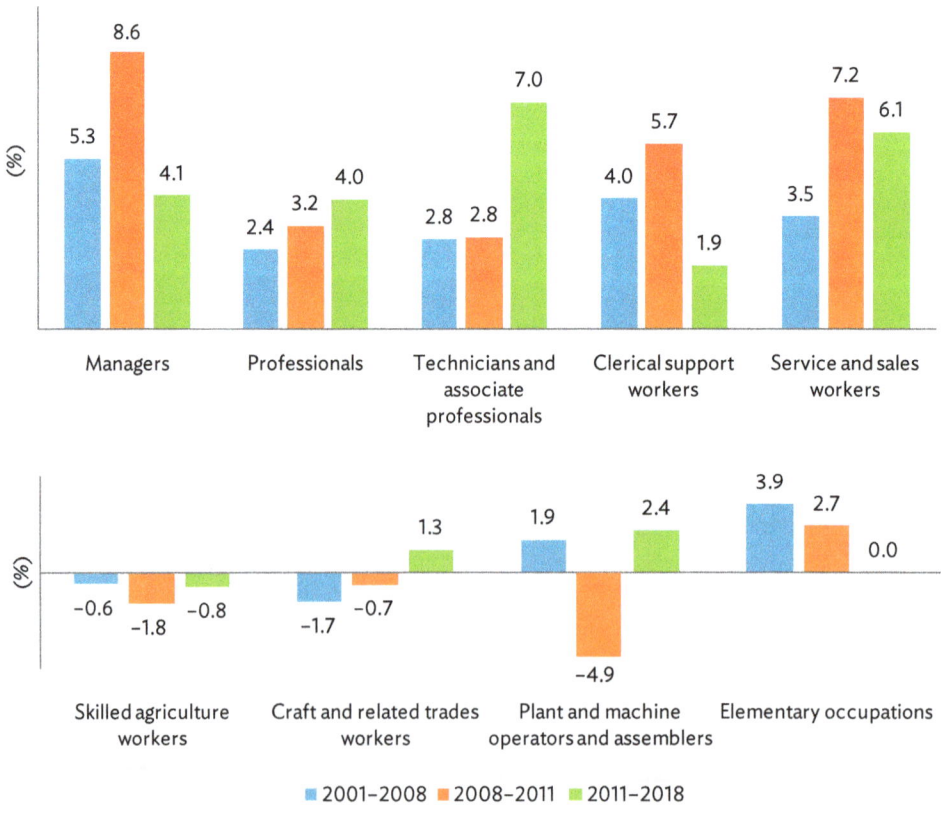

Source: ADB estimates based on labor force survey.

whereby high-skilled workers were employed in middle- or low-skill occupations (e.g., engineering students employed on the assembly lines of aerospace manufacturers)[19] and middle-skilled workers employed in low-skilled occupations.

A recent study estimated that around one-third of college graduates in the Philippines were "overeducated" or overqualified for the positions they hold.[20] The study also found that those with lower socioeconomic status were more likely to be overeducated than their higher socioeconomic status counterparts due to limited access to opportunities through social networks, and greater willingness to accept lower-skilled, lower-pay jobs, (particularly in the absence of unemployment insurance and due to limited access to credit markets). In more recent years, with rapid employment growth in high-skilled service industries, manufacturing, and construction, there is no longer an oversupply of high-skilled workers at the aggregate level, and the oversupply of middle-skilled workers had narrowed from 15 p.p. in 2012 to 11 p.p. in 2017 (Figure 2.8). This does not mean that skills mismatch is no longer a concern in the Philippines, but rather that the skills demand associated with the country's economic structure and the skills supply reflecting the educational attainment of the workforce, are slowly becoming better aligned.

Despite some progress in terms of employment quality in the Philippines, underemployment, informality, and vulnerable and precarious employment remain a concern. The employment shift away from agriculture toward industry and services has been accompanied by an increase in the share of wage and salaried employment, and a decrease in the share of own-account workers and unpaid family workers. The share of the latter two status-in-employment categories, often referred to as the vulnerable employment rate (VER), has declined from nearly 45% of employed persons in 2008 to approximately one-third of workers in 2019 (Figure 2.9). Although the growing share of wage and salaried workers is considered a positive development, it is important to note that, in many industries, this increase has also been accompanied by a rise in precarious

Figure 2.8: Skills Demand and Supply, 2012–2017

Source: ADB estimates based on labor force survey.

---

[19] P. Bamber, S. Frederick, and G. Gereffi. 2016. *The Philippines in the Aerospace Global Value Chain: Opportunities for Upgrading.* Durham, NC: Duke University Centre on Globalization, Governance and Competitiveness.

[20] M. C. Epetia. 2018. *College Graduates in Non-College Jobs: Measuring Overeducation in the Philippine Labor Market.* PhD dissertation. Diliman, Quezon City: University of the Philippines School of Economics.

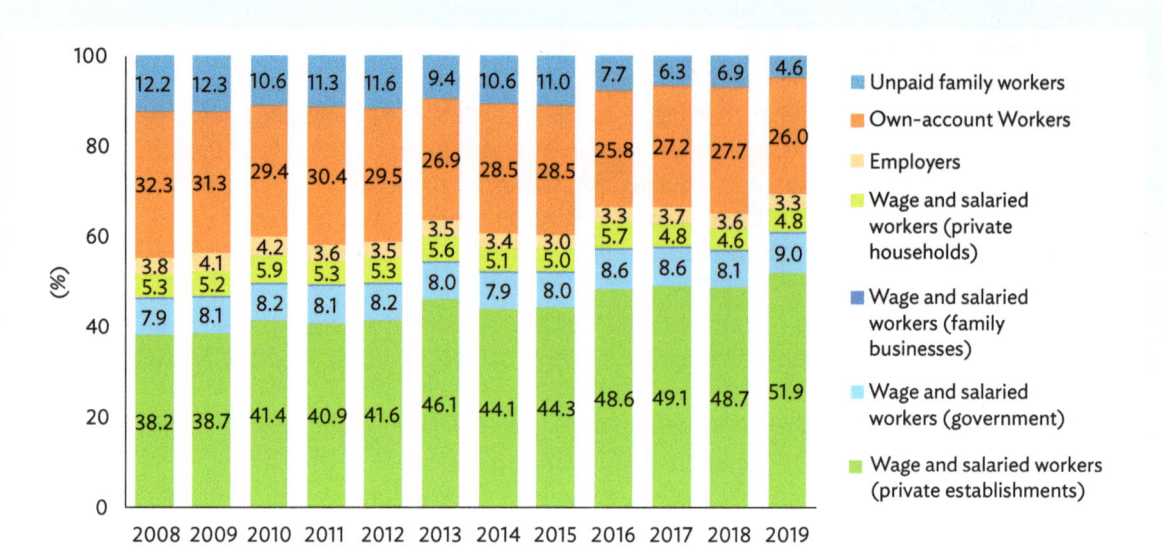

Figure 2.9: Status in Employment Distribution, 2008–2019

Source: ADB estimates based on labor force survey.

employment, defined as fixed-term, short-term, seasonal, or casual work, including employment through contracting or subcontracting agencies.

Non-regular or nonstandard forms of employment increasingly characterize working arrangements in the context of Industry 4.0 and the future of work (see Chapter 3). Workers in precarious employment often do not have the benefits associated with wage and salaried work, such as stability and security in terms of job tenure, access to social protection, and other labor rights.[21] At the aggregate level, it is estimated that 27% of wage and salaried workers (employees) were in precarious employment in 2018, with a particularly elevated share in certain high-growth industries such as automotive manufacturing (nearly 70%) and electrical and electronics (approximately 57%). Using the sum of workers in vulnerable and precarious employment as a proxy,[22] it is estimated that nearly 52% of workers in the Philippines were in informal employment in 2018, down from 57% in 2010. Finally, underemployment, another indicator of employment quality, is a persistent challenge in the Philippines. Despite the decline in unemployment over the past decade, time-related underemployment, defined as the share of employed wanting additional work, remains elevated at 18% in 2018 (Figure 2.2).

Regional Diagnostics

Going beyond the aggregate figures reveals significant disparities across regions. Over the past decade, unemployment has decreased in all but two regions (Figure 2.10). In many regions, the decline was primarily due to a decrease in labor force participation, rather than employment growth. In fact, employment growth, although positive for all regions except for ARMM, fell below working-age population growth, resulting in a declining EPR in all but seven regions between 2008 and 2018.

---

[21] ILO. 2017. *Decent Work Country Diagnostics: Philippines 2017*. Geneva.
[22] This is consistent with the approach of ILO (2017).

Figure 2.10: Change in Regional Labor Market Indicators, 2008–2018

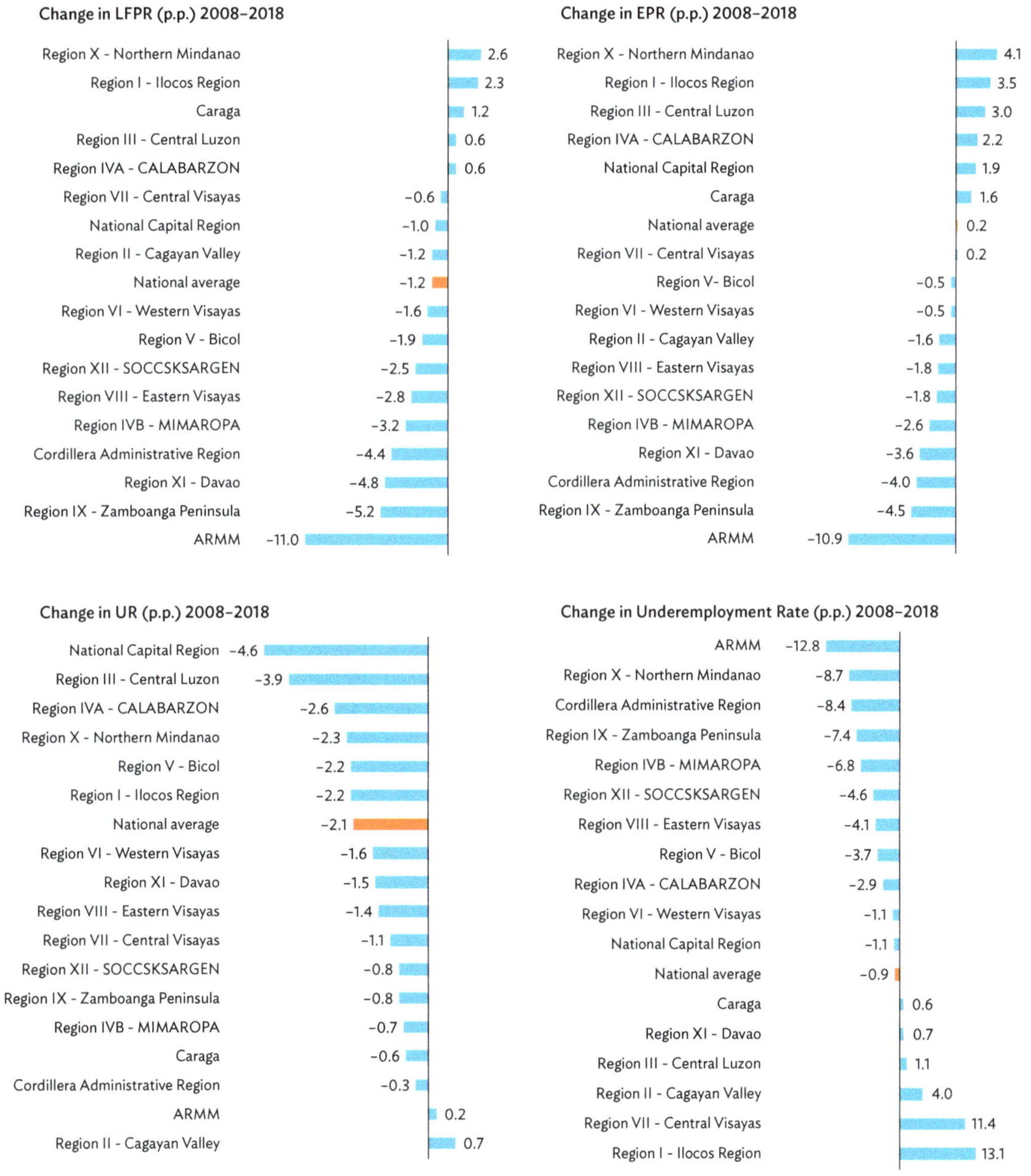

Change in LFPR (p.p.) 2008–2018

Region X - Northern Mindanao	2.6
Region I - Ilocos Region	2.3
Caraga	1.2
Region III - Central Luzon	0.6
Region IVA - CALABARZON	0.6
Region VII - Central Visayas	-0.6
National Capital Region	-1.0
Region II - Cagayan Valley	-1.2
National average	-1.2
Region VI - Western Visayas	-1.6
Region V - Bicol	-1.9
Region XII - SOCCSKSARGEN	-2.5
Region VIII - Eastern Visayas	-2.8
Region IVB - MIMAROPA	-3.2
Cordillera Administrative Region	-4.4
Region XI - Davao	-4.8
Region IX - Zamboanga Peninsula	-5.2
ARMM	-11.0

Change in EPR (p.p.) 2008–2018

Region X - Northern Mindanao	4.1
Region I - Ilocos Region	3.5
Region III - Central Luzon	3.0
Region IVA - CALABARZON	2.2
National Capital Region	1.9
Caraga	1.6
National average	0.2
Region VII - Central Visayas	0.2
Region V - Bicol	-0.5
Region VI - Western Visayas	-0.5
Region II - Cagayan Valley	-1.6
Region VIII - Eastern Visayas	-1.8
Region XII - SOCCSKSARGEN	-1.8
Region IVB - MIMAROPA	-2.6
Region XI - Davao	-3.6
Cordillera Administrative Region	-4.0
Region IX - Zamboanga Peninsula	-4.5
ARMM	-10.9

Change in UR (p.p.) 2008–2018

National Capital Region	-4.6
Region III - Central Luzon	-3.9
Region IVA - CALABARZON	-2.6
Region X - Northern Mindanao	-2.3
Region V - Bicol	-2.2
Region I - Ilocos Region	-2.2
National average	-2.1
Region VI - Western Visayas	-1.6
Region XI - Davao	-1.5
Region VIII - Eastern Visayas	-1.4
Region VII - Central Visayas	-1.1
Region XII - SOCCSKSARGEN	-0.8
Region IX - Zamboanga Peninsula	-0.8
Region IVB - MIMAROPA	-0.7
Caraga	-0.6
Cordillera Administrative Region	-0.3
ARMM	0.2
Region II - Cagayan Valley	0.7

Change in Underemployment Rate (p.p.) 2008–2018

ARMM	-12.8
Region X - Northern Mindanao	-8.7
Cordillera Administrative Region	-8.4
Region IX - Zamboanga Peninsula	-7.4
Region IVB - MIMAROPA	-6.8
Region XII - SOCCSKSARGEN	-4.6
Region VIII - Eastern Visayas	-4.1
Region V - Bicol	-3.7
Region IVA - CALABARZON	-2.9
Region VI - Western Visayas	-1.1
National Capital Region	-1.1
National average	-0.9
Caraga	0.6
Region XI - Davao	0.7
Region III - Central Luzon	1.1
Region II - Cagayan Valley	4.0
Region VII - Central Visayas	11.4
Region I - Ilocos Region	13.1

ARMM = Autonomous Region in Muslim Mindanao; CALABARZON = Cavite, Laguna, Batangas, Rizal, and Quezon; EPR = employment-to-population rate; LFPR = labor force participation rate; MIMAROPA = Occidental Mindoro, Oriental Mindoro, Marinduque, Romblon, and Palawan; p.p. = percentage points; SOCCSKSARGEN = South Cotabato, Cotabato, Sultan Kudarat, Sarangani and General Santos; UR = unemployment rate.

Source: ADB estimates based on labor force survey.

Limited employment growth in most regions over the past decade conceals significant changes in the composition of employment that took place, reflecting the ongoing structural transformation process (see Chapter 1). In particular, all regions, except Zamboanga Peninsula, had a decline in agriculture share in employment over this period, with a corresponding increase in the shares of industry and services (Figure 2.13). For 5 out of the 17 regions, the declining agriculture share reflected positive net employment growth in agriculture that was slower than in industry and services. For the other regions, the agriculture sector shed jobs over the past decade, pulling down the regions' net employment growth. Because a large share of own-account workers and unpaid family workers are employed in agriculture, the decline in the sector's employment share correlates to a large extent with the decline in vulnerable employment (Figure A2.2).

The large urban agglomerations of the National Capital Region (NCR), along with neighboring CALABARZON and Central Luzon, had relatively high employment growth, and the largest declines in unemployment. The three regions, which account together for over 37% of the Philippine population (Table 2.2), had the fastest average annual employment growth rates between 2008 and 2018, with 3.4% for CALABARZON, 2.7% for Central Luzon, and 2.2% for the NCR (Figure 2.11), among the highest increases

Table 2.2: Regional Diagnostics and Labor Market Indicators, 2018

	Regional share of population (%)	Urbanization rate (%)	Poverty incidence rate in families - 2015	LFPR (%)	EPR (%)	UR (%)	VER (%)	Under-employment rate (%)
Region I - Ilocos Region	5	10.1	9.6	63.3	59.1	6.7	33	27.9
Region II - Cagayan Valley	3.4	11.4	11.7	65.3	62.6	4.2	27.8	24.8
Region III - Central Luzon	10.9	54.1	8.9	60.7	57.5	5.4	27.4	11.5
Region V - Bicol	6	17.1	27.5	62	59.5	4	42.8	33.8
Region VI - Western Visayas	7.5	29.4	16.6	62	58.9	4.9	31.9	22.9
Region VII - Central Visayas	7.3	36.8	23.6	63.1	59.5	5.8	33.7	24.4
Region VIII - Eastern Visayas	4.5	6	30.7	61.6	59.4	3.7	48.2	19.4
Region IX - Zamboanga Peninsula	3.7	25.9	26	59.3	57.4	3.4	52.7	16.1
Region X - Northern Mindanao	4.6	43.9	30.3	72	69.8	3	45.5	21
Region XI - Davao	4.9	58.1	16.6	62.2	59.3	4.7	35.9	17.8
Region XII - SOCCSKSARGEN	4.6	44.1	30.5	62.4	60	3.8	47.4	17.9
National Capital Region	12.3	100	2.7	60.6	55.9	7.8	16.8	7.2
Cordillera Administrative Region	1.8	33.2	14.9	62.2	59.9	3.6	44.1	14.8
Autonomous Region in Muslim Mindanao	3.7	10.4	48.2	46.1	44.9	2.6	78.3	8.1

Table 2.2: *continued*

	Regional share of population (%)	Urbanization rate (%)	Poverty incidence rate in families - 2015	LFPR (%)	EPR (%)	UR (%)	VER (%)	Under-employment rate (%)
Caraga	2.7	35.1	30.8	67.1	64.4	4	50	24.7
Region IVA - CALABARZON	14	63.6	6.7	62.9	58.7	6.7	25.8	13.1
Region IVB - MIMAROPA	3.1	20.7	17.4	65.9	63.3	4	38.9	22.4
AGGREGATE (National Average)	**100**	**44.6**	**16.5**	**62.2**	**58.9**	**5.3**	**34.7**	**18**

CALABARZON = Cavite, Laguna, Batangas, Rizal, and Quezon; EPR = employment-to-population rate; LFPR = labor force participation rate; MIMAROPA = Occidental Mindoro, Oriental Mindoro, Marinduque, Romblon, and Palawan; UR = unemployment rate; VER = vulnerable employment rate.

Sources: ADB estimates based on labor force survey January 2018; TESDA. 2018a. *National Technical Education and Skills Development Plan (NTESDP) 2018–2022*. Taguig.

Figure 2.11: Average Annual Employment Growth, 2008–2018

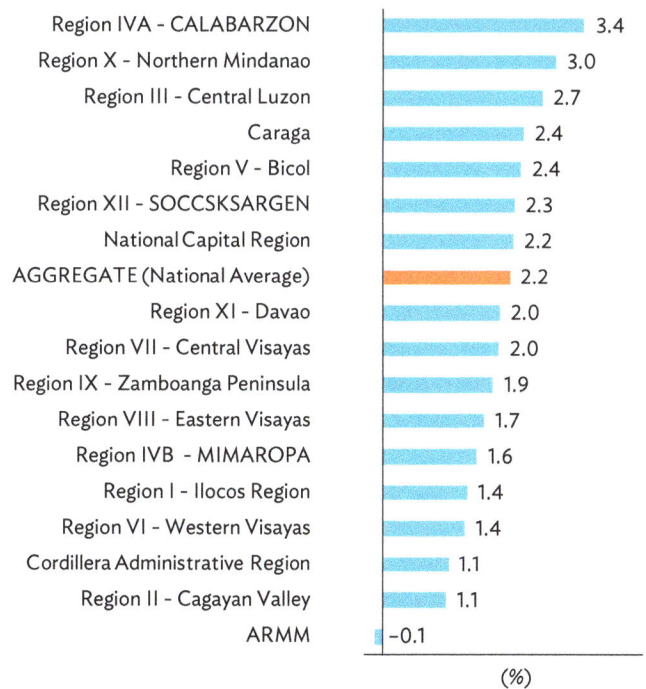

ARMM = Autonomous Region in Muslim Mindanao; CALABARZON = Cavite, Laguna, Batangas, Rizal, and Quezon; MIMAROPA = Occidental Mindoro, Oriental Mindoro, Marinduque, Romblon, and Palawan; SOCCSKSARGEN = South Cotabato, Cotabato, Sultan Kudarat, Sarangani and General Santos.

Source: ADB estimates based on labor force survey.

in EPR, and the largest drops in unemployment (Figure 2.10). However, their unemployment rates remained high, with 7.8% for the NCR, 6.7% for CALABARZON, and 5.4% for Central Luzon, and these regions still had among the lowest LFPRs and EPRs in 2018 (Table 2.2). In the Philippines, as in many developing countries, there is a negative association between poverty incidence and unemployment, and, conversely, a positive one between poverty and employment and participation rates (Figure 2.12). The three regions also had the lowest agricultural employment shares (below 15%), the highest services sector employment shares (over 60%), and among the highest shares of industry employment (over 20%) (Figure 2.14). CALABARZON, the region with the highest population growth rate over the past decade (averaging 2.7% annually between 2008 and 2018), also had the highest employment growth rate in services over this period (Figure 2.15).

Other regions with above average employment growth over the past decade are those where growth in industry and services was not offset by a large decline in agricultural employment. These were Northern Mindanao (3.0%), Caraga (2.4%), Bicol (2.4%), and SOCCSKSARGEN (2.3%) (Figure 2.11). Northern Mindanao, SOCCSKSARGEN, and Bicol had the highest average annual employment growth rate in the industry sector between 2008 and 2018, with 7.0%, 6.4%, and 6.1%, respectively (Figure 2.14). Northern Mindanao and Caraga were among the few regions that had an increase in both the LFPR and EPR between 2008 and 2018 (Figure 2.10). Northern Mindanao, in particular, also had an important decline in unemployment during this period. In 2018, these four regions had relatively low unemployment rates (3.8%–4.0%), but still high vulnerable employment rates (42.8%–50%) and underemployment rates (Table 2.2). Bicol had the highest rate of time-related underemployment among all regions, with over one-third (33.8%) of employed persons in 2018.

Figure 2.12: Poverty Incidence and Regional Labor Market Indicators, 2018

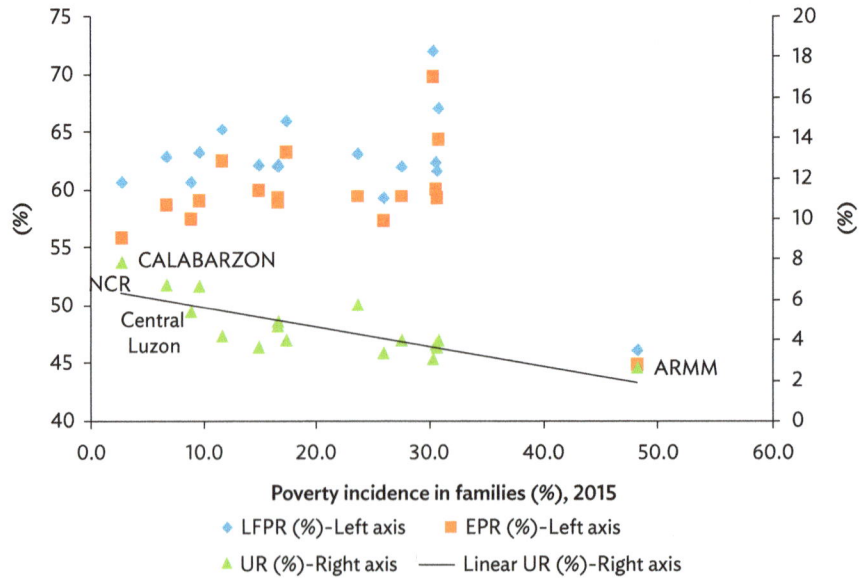

ARMM = Autonomous Region in Muslim Mindanao; CALABARZON = Cavite, Laguna, Batangas, Rizal, and Quezon; EPR = employment-to-population rate; LFPR = labor force participation rate; NCR = National Capital Region; TESDA = Technical Education and Skills Development Authority; UR = unemployment rate.

Sources: ADB estimates based on labor force survey; TESDA National Technical Education and Skills Development Plan 2018–2022.

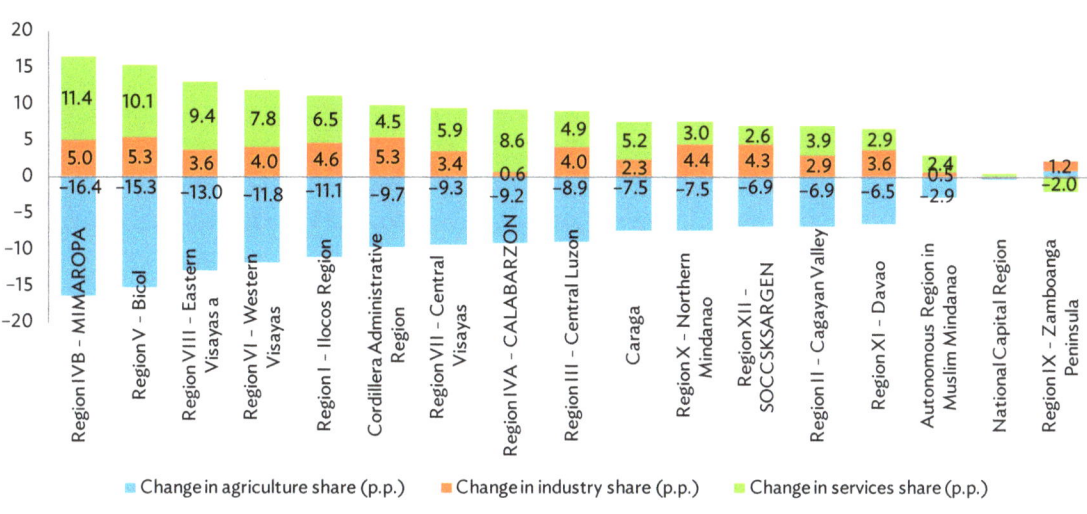

Figure 2.13: Employment Shift from Agriculture to Industry and Services at the Regional Level, 2008–2018

CALABARZON = Cavite, Laguna, Batangas, Rizal, and Quezon; MIMAROPA = Occidental Mindoro, Oriental Mindoro, Marinduque, Romblon, and Palawan; p.p. = percentage points; SOCCSKSARGEN = South Cotabato, Cotabato, Sultan Kudarat, Sarangani and General Santos.
Source: ADB estimates based on labor force survey.

A shift away from agriculture employment resulted in a declining vulnerable employment rates in many regions. Although underemployment and vulnerable employment remain elevated in Bicol, the region had a major decline in the vulnerable employment rate (–16.0 p.p.) over the past decade, driven by an important decline in agriculture employment and rapid employment growth in both industry and services (Figure 2.14, Figure A2.2). On the other hand, SOCCSKSARGEN, where the employment shift from agriculture to industry and services was smaller, had nearly no change in its VER over the same period.

In some regions, demographic factors have had a greater impact on EPRs than employment creation. In Davao and SOCCSKSARGEN, relatively high employment growth fell short of even faster population growth and urbanization, resulting in declines in EPRs (Figure 2.10, Figure A2.3). In contrast, the region of Ilocos had the slowest population growth rate and a decline in urbanization between 2008 and 2018, resulting in an important increase in LFPR and EPR. The Ilocos region's employment growth, averaging 1.4% annually between 2008 and 2018 fell below the national average, but was nevertheless higher than its annual population growth of 0.7% (Figure 2.11, Figure A2.3). The region saw a 2.2 p.p. decline in unemployment rate, but a 13.1 p.p. increase in the underemployment rate over this period. It also had a decline in agriculture employment (–1.9% annually) and corresponding shift in employment share from agriculture to industry and services (Figure 2.13; Figure 2.15).

In other regions, rapid employment growth in industry and services was partly offset by large-scale job losses in agriculture. Agricultural employment declined significantly over the past decade in MIMAROPA (–2.0% annually), and the Visayas regions, with –1.8% annually for Western Visayas, and –1.4% for both Eastern and Central Visayas (Figure 2.15). MIMAROPA had the largest shift in employment share from agriculture to industry and services, and the greatest decline in VER (Figure 2.13, Figure A2.2). The Visayas regions, which collectively account for nearly 20% of the country's population (Table 2.2), also had important employment

Figure 2.14: Regional Employment Shares by Broad Sector, 2018

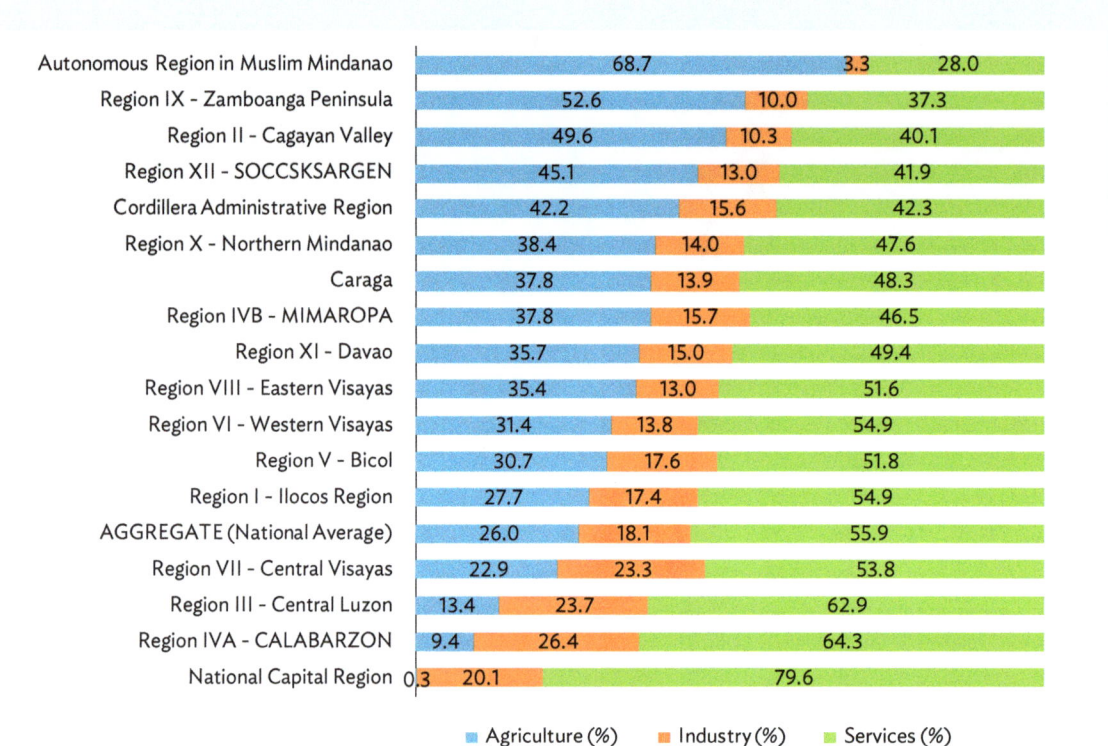

CALABARZON = Cavite, Laguna, Batangas, Rizal, and Quezon; MIMAROPA = Occidental Mindoro, Oriental Mindoro, Marinduque, Romblon, and Palawan; SOCCSKSARGEN = South Cotabato, Cotabato, Sultan Kudarat, Sarangani and General Santos.
Source: ADB estimates based on labor force survey.

shifts away from agriculture to industry and services. In 2018, the latter regions had a large share of employment in services (50%–55%), with the Central Visayas region having a relatively large share of industry employment (23.3%) as well (Figure 2.14). Although Central Visayas still had a relatively high unemployment rate, with 5.8% in 2018, it is one of the regions where the average annual employment growth (2.0%) surpassed working-age population growth, leading to a small increase in the EPR between 2008 and 2018 (Figure 2.10).

The slowest employment growth was in ARMM, Cagayan Valley, and the Cordillera Administrative Region (CAR), and in relation to working-age population growth, in the Zamboanga Peninsula. In CAR and Cagayan Valley, employment growth averaged 1.1% annually over 2008–2018, while ARMM was the only region with negative employment growth over the past decade (Figure 2.11). These three regions had a small decline in agricultural employment and an employment shift from agriculture toward industry and services, even if these shifts were smaller in magnitude than for other regions (Figure 2.13, Figure 2.15). The three regions had a decline in LFPR and EPR, and their unemployment rate declined slightly (−0.3 p.p. for CAR) or increased (by 0.2 p.p. and 0.7 p.p. for Cagayan Valley and ARMM, respectively) (Figure 2.10). The Zamboanga Peninsula, despite a higher employment growth rate than the other three regions (1.9% annually), had an important decline in EPR (4.5 p.p.) between 2008 and 2018 (Figure 2.10). In the latter region, the only one that had a

Figure 2.15: Average Annual Growth Rate by Broad Sector and Region, 2008–2018

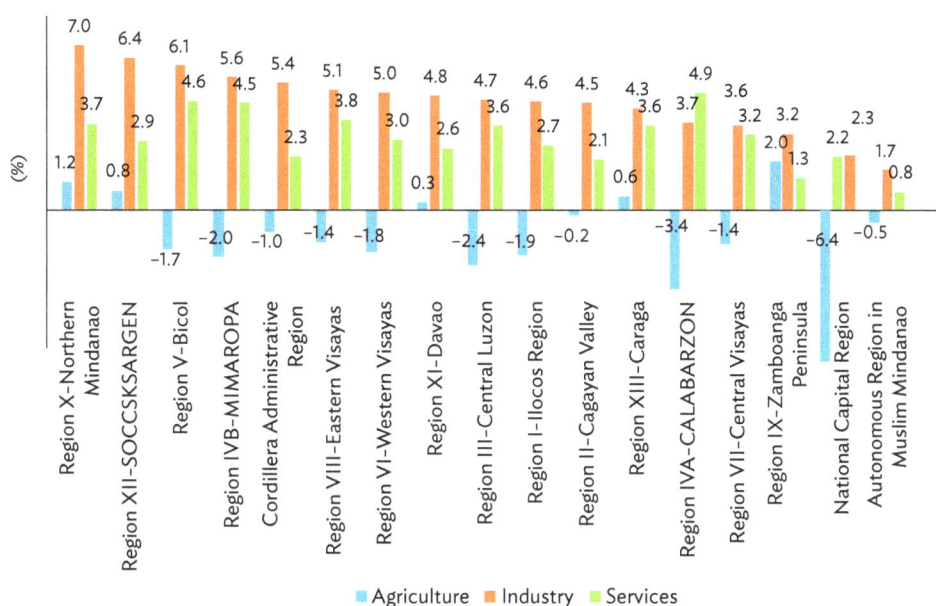

CALABARZON = Cavite, Laguna, Batangas, Rizal, and Quezon; MIMAROPA = Occidental Mindoro, Oriental Mindoro, Marinduque, Romblon, and Palawan; NCR = National Capital Region; SOCCSKSARGEN = South Cotabato, Cotabato, Sultan Kudarat, Sarangani and General Santos.

Note: The large negative growth rates for agricultural employment for the metropolitan regions of NCR, CALABARZON, and Central Luzon do not represent large absolute numbers, as these are calculated from a smaller base than for other regions.

Source: ADB estimates based on labor force survey.

small increase in the agriculture share of employment over the past decade, a decline in VER was driven by the decline in services share in employment (Figure 2.13, Figure A2.2). However, the Zamboanga Peninsula still had the second-highest VER (after ARMM) with 52.7% of workers in 2018 (Table 2.2).

ARMM continues to lag far behind other regions in terms of most labor market outcomes. The region experienced the most significant drop in LFPR (–11.0 p.p.) and EPR (–0.9 p.p.) between 2008 and 2018, further increasing the gap between it and other regions with respect to these labor market indicators. Out of ARMM's working-age population, less than half were economically active in 2018, and less than 45% were employed (Table 2.2). This is largely due to low female LFPRs, as only 28% of female adults and only 12% of young females (aged 15–24) were economically active in 2018. The region's female NEET rate was as high as 40%, in comparison to the national average of 26% (Table A2.1). More than two-thirds of ARMM workers were employed in agriculture, and less than 4% in industry (Figure 2.14). The region's VER was more than double the national average (in 2018), and poverty incidence was three times as high as the national average in 2015 (Table 2.2). It is the only region where poverty incidence in families increased between 2006 and 2015 (Figure A2.4).

Conclusions

The high economic growth in the Philippines in preceding the COVID-19 pandemic has led to some decent work creation, but not on a sufficient scale to keep up with the growing population and its aspirations. Despite rapid economic growth, the EPR has remained generally constant, and has even decreased in recent years, indicating limited employment growth, which has fallen short of growth in working-age population. Furthermore, underemployment, informality, and vulnerable and precarious employment remain a concern despite some progress in terms of employment quality.

Limited net employment growth over the past decades conceals a significant shift in the structure of employment in the Philippines. There has been a major shift in employment from agriculture toward services, including both high-productivity and low-productivity services subsectors. Industry employment has also increased, particularly in the construction sector, but also manufacturing.

The changing structure of employment has been reflected in the occupational distribution and skills demand composition. In particular, the employment shares of high-skilled occupations have increased over time: those of low-skilled occupations have been decreasing, and there has also been considerable reshuffling of middle-skill jobs, reflecting rapid employment growth in services, construction, and restructuring from labor-intensive to capital-intensive production within and across manufacturing industries. Current trends suggest a continued demand for middle-skilled and skilled TVET graduates to support growth sectors of the Philippine economy.

Growth has not been inclusive, however, with large disparities in access to quality employment opportunities across socioeconomic and demographic groups and regions, due to geographical clustering of industries; differential access to skills acquisition; skills mismatch; and other labor market entry barriers (e.g., limited geographical mobility, limited access to information and resources, including social networks, finance to start their own businesses, and institutional factors for instance related to gender roles). In particular, youth unemployment and NEET rates remain elevated, female labor participation remains low, and poverty incidence remains high in regions beyond the urban agglomerations and industrial centers.

In this context, and due to Industry 4.0's potential to exacerbate existing inequalities, TVET has a major role to play, particularly through the delivery of high-quality programs in line with the demands and requirements of growth sectors, and the targeting of disadvantaged groups, particularly youth, women, and the poor population residing in largely agricultural regions.

Appendix 2.1: National Labor Market Information

Figure A2.1: A Snapshot of the Philippines Labor Market, 2018

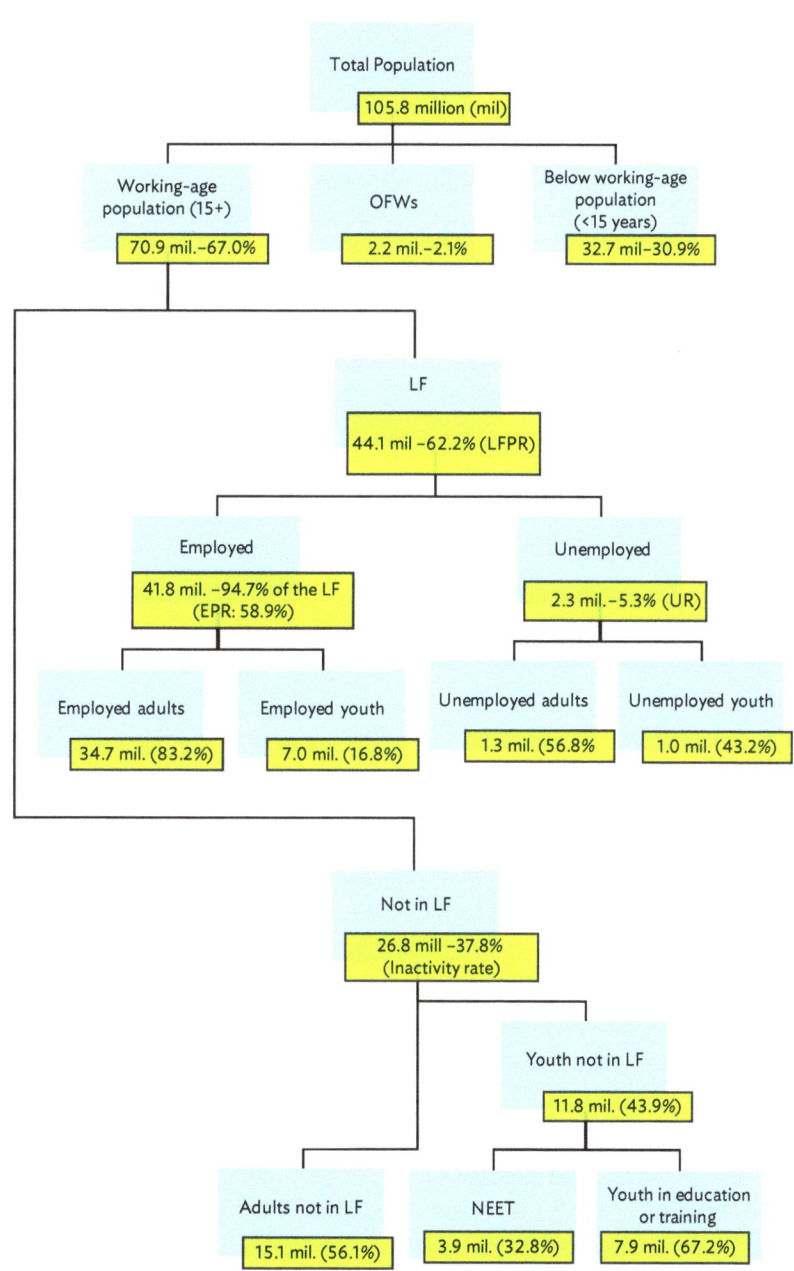

EPR = employment-to-population rate, LF = labor force, LFPR = labor force participation rate, NEET = neither in employment nor in education or training, OFW = overseas Filipino worker, UR = unemployment rate.
Source: ADB estimates based on labor force survey.

Figure A2.2: Change in Agriculture Share in Employment and Decline in Vulnerable Employment Rate, 2008–2018

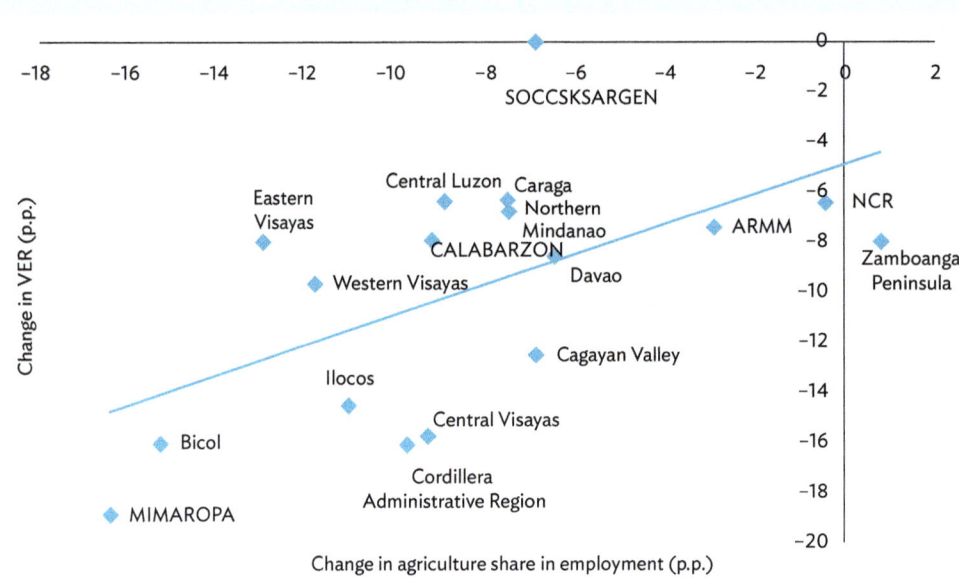

ARMM = Autonomous Region in Muslim Mindanao; CALABARZON = Cavite, Laguna, Batangas, Rizal, and Quezon; MIMAROPA = Occidental Mindoro, Oriental Mindoro, Marinduque, Romblon, and Palawan; NCR = National Capital Region; p.p. = percentage points; SOCCSKSARGEN = South Cotabato, Cotabato, Sultan Kudarat, Sarangani and General Santos; VER = vulnerable employment rate.
Source: ADB estimates based on labor force survey.

Figure A2.3: Population Growth Rates and Change in Urbanization Rates at the Regional Level, 2008–2018

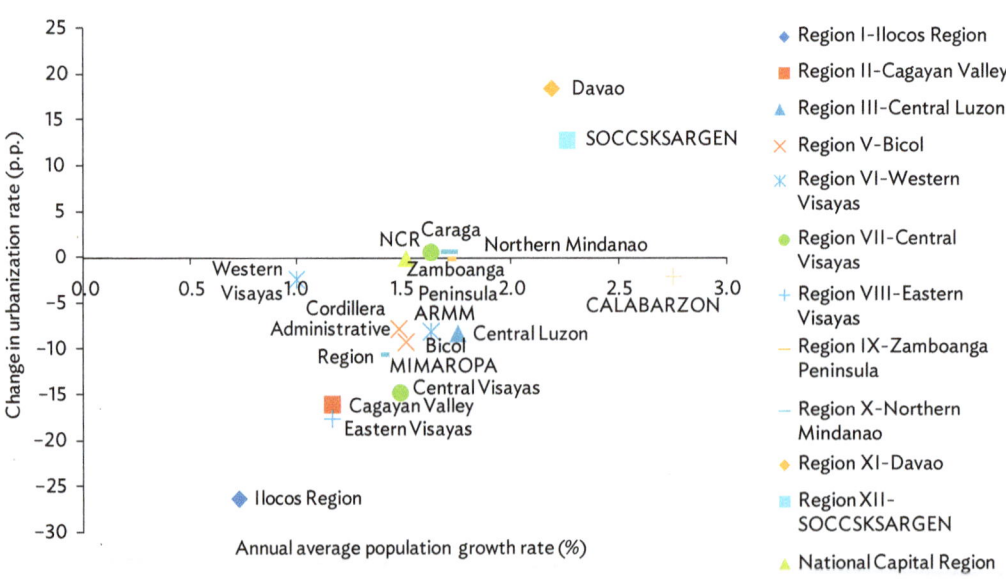

ARMM = Autonomous Region in Muslim Mindanao; CALABARZON = Cavite, Laguna, Batangas, Rizal, and Quezon; MIMAROPA = Occidental Mindoro, Oriental Mindoro, Marinduque, Romblon, and Palawan; NCR = National Capital Region; p.p. = percentage points; SOCCSKSARGEN = South Cotabato, Cotabato, Sultan Kudarat, Sarangani and General Santos.
Source: ADB estimates based on labor force survey.

Figure A2.4: Poverty Incidence, Change in Poverty Incidence, and Public Share of Technical and Vocational Education and Training Enrollment by Region

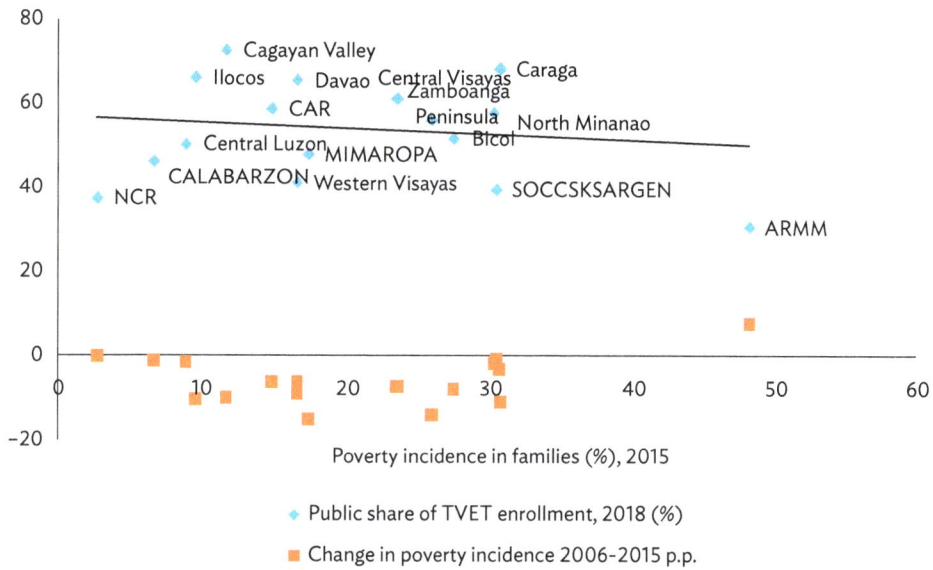

ARMM = Autonomous Region in Muslim Mindanao; CALABARZON = Cavite, Laguna, Batangas, Rizal, and Quezon; MIMAROPA = Occidental Mindoro, Oriental Mindoro, Marinduque, Romblon, and Palawan; NCR = National Capital Region; p.p. = percentage points; SOCCSKSARGEN = South Cotabato, Cotabato, Sultan Kudarat, Sarangani and General Santos; TESDA = Technical Education Skills and Development Authority; TVET = technical and vocational education and training.
Source: ADB estimates based on labor force survey and TESDA.

Appendix 2.2: Regional Labor Market Information

Table A2.1: Regional Labor Market Indicators by Demographic Groups, 2018

	Youth			Adults		
	Male	Female	Total	Male	Female	Total
Employment-to-population Rate						
Region I - Ilocos Region	47	25.9	36.9	81.5	52.6	67
Region II - Cagayan Valley	51	21.7	37.1	88.2	54	71.9
Region III - Central Luzon	43	31.6	37.5	82.4	47.6	64.7
Region V - Bicol	50.4	26.1	38.7	85.5	52.7	69.2
Region VI - Western Visayas	41.5	26.4	34.2	84.2	52.2	68.2
Region VII - Central Visayas	41.7	27.5	34.8	82.8	55.4	68.9
Region VIII - Eastern Visayas	46.8	23.4	35.6	84.5	55.1	70
Region IX - Zamboanga Peninsula	43.3	21.7	32.8	89.4	45.7	67.9
Region X - Northern Mindanao	63.8	40	52.4	89	64.7	76.9
Region XI - Davao	46.9	23.2	35.3	85.6	50.2	68.4
Region XII - SOCCSKSARGEN	51.2	21.2	36.7	87.1	51.3	69.8
National Capital Region	33.9	25.6	29.8	79.1	50.9	64.2
Cordillera Administrative Region	40.4	19.2	30.1	85.1	58.3	72
Autonomous Region in Muslim Mindanao	33.9	10.5	22.3	88.9	27.4	57.4
Caraga	54.9	32.3	44.2	87.2	58.5	73.2
Region IVA - CALABARZON	40.6	28.2	34.5	81.4	54.8	67.6
Region IVB - MIMAROPA	44.5	24.5	34.8	89.2	61.2	75.6
AGGREGATE	**44.2**	**26.2**	**35.4**	**83.9**	**52.3**	**68**
Labor force participation rate						
Region I - Ilocos Region	55.6	32	44.3	86	54.4	70.1
Region II - Cagayan Valley	54.5	27.5	41.7	90.6	55.6	74
Region III - Central Luzon	49.7	36.2	43.2	85.8	49.1	67.1
Region V - Bicol	54.9	29.1	42.5	87.9	54	71
Region VI - Western Visayas	47	30.2	38.9	87.7	53.7	70.7
Region VII - Central Visayas	48.9	32	40.7	87	56.8	71.7
Region VIII - Eastern Visayas	51.6	26.7	39.7	86.5	55.9	71.4
Region IX - Zamboanga Peninsula	48.5	23.2	36.2	91.3	46.6	69.2
Region X - Northern Mindanao	67.1	42.6	55.3	91.1	66.3	78.8
Region XI - Davao	53.3	27.3	40.6	88.5	51.3	70.4
Region XII - SOCCSKSARGEN	55	24.2	40.2	89.4	52.8	71.7
National Capital Region	43.5	30.8	37.2	84.6	53.2	68.1
Cordillera Administrative Region	44.9	21.6	33.6	87.5	59.4	73.7

Table A2.1: *continued*

	Youth			Adults		
	Male	Female	Total	Male	Female	Total
Autonomous Region in Muslim Mindanao	35.7	11.6	23.8	90.5	27.9	58.5
Caraga	59.9	34.5	47.8	89.9	60.2	75.4
Region IVA - CALABARZON	48.8	32.3	40.7	86	57.2	71.1
Region IVB - MIMAROPA	50.3	27.7	39.3	91.3	62.7	77.4
AGGREGATE	**50.4**	**30.1**	**40.5**	**87.4**	**54**	**70.6**
Unemployment Rate						
Region I - Ilocos Region	15.5	19	16.7	5.2	3.2	4.4
Region II - Cagayan Valley	6.5	21.2	11.1	2.7	3	2.8
Region III - Central Luzon	13.3	12.8	13.1	3.9	3	3.6
Region V - Bicol	8.2	10.3	8.9	2.8	2.4	2.6
Region VI - Western Visayas	11.6	12.6	12	3.9	2.7	3.5
Region VII - Central Visayas	14.7	14.1	14.5	4.8	2.6	3.9
Region VIII - Eastern Visayas	9.1	12.5	10.2	2.4	1.5	2
Region IX - Zamboanga Peninsula	10.7	6.6	9.4	2	2	2
Region X - Northern Mindanao	4.8	6	5.3	2.4	2.5	2.4
Region XI - Davao	12	15.2	13.1	3.3	2.1	2.8
Region XII - SOCCSKSARGEN	6.9	12.5	8.5	2.6	2.8	2.7
National Capital Region	22	17.2	20	6.6	4.4	5.7
Cordillera Administrative Region	10.1	11.1	10.4	2.8	1.8	2.4
Autonomous Region in Muslim Mindanao	5.1	9.6	6.2	1.8	1.8	1.8
Caraga	8.3	6.4	7.6	3	2.9	3
Region IVA - CALABARZON	16.7	12.9	15.2	5.4	4.3	5
Region IVB - MIMAROPA	11.5	11.4	11.5	2.3	2.4	2.3
AGGREGATE	**12.3**	**12.9**	**12.5**	**4**	**3.1**	**3.7**
NEET Rate						
Region I - Ilocos Region	14.3	24.3	19.1			
Region II - Cagayan Valley	9	28	18.1			
Region III - Central Luzon	14.4	23.4	18.8			
Region V - Bicol	12.7	26.2	19.2			
Region VI - Western Visayas	12.2	24	17.9			
Region VII - Central Visayas	14.1	25	19.4			
Region VIII - Eastern Visayas	12.9	24.6	18.5			
Region IX - Zamboanga Peninsula	12.8	28.3	20.4			
Region X - Northern Mindanao	8.2	24.1	15.8			
Region XI - Davao	13.5	29.1	21.1			
Region XII - SOCCSKSARGEN	8.7	31.7	19.9			

continued on next page

Table A2.1: *continued*

	Youth			Adults		
	Male	Female	Total	Male	Female	Total
National Capital Region	15.5	23	19.2			
Cordillera Administrative Region	10.2	23	16.4			
Autonomous Region in Muslim Mindanao	17.9	40.2	29			
Caraga	10.7	22	16.1			
Region IVA – CALABARZON	17.1	23.1	20			
Region IVB – MIMAROPA	12.1	24.5	18.1			
AGGREGATE	**13.5**	**25.5**	**19.4**			

CALABARZON = Cavite, Laguna, Batangas, Rizal, and Quezon; LMI = labor market information; MIMAROPA = Occidental Mindoro, Oriental Mindoro, Marinduque, Romblon, and Palawan; NEET = neither in employment nor in education or training; SOCCSKSARGEN = South Cotabato, Cotabato, Sultan Kudarat, Sarangani and General Santos.

Source: ADB estimates based on labor force survey January 2018.

3. Industry 4.0 and the Changing Demand for Labor

The potential impact of Industry 4.0 on jobs is multifaceted and far from clear cut. Building upon and combining automation (more machines) and IT (more efficient and intelligent machines), rapidly evolving technologies could lead to job losses and displacement on an unprecedented scale. On the other hand, scale and productivity gains, technological spillover effects, complementarity of technology and employment, income effects, and other mechanisms could result in job creation.[23]

Regardless of whether Industry 4.0 results in net overall employment gains or losses, it will certainly have major distributional impacts through shifts in countries' economic structures, within-industry changes in firm composition and within-firm changes in business models and processes resulting in changes in occupational structures, and in the task content of occupations. Ultimately, there will be consequences in terms of skills demand and the return on skills. Examples of disruptive Industry 4.0 technologies presenting both challenges and opportunities in the Philippines context include cloud technology and robotic process automation. In the IT-BPO industry, for instance, cloud computing, allowing for Big Data analytics, can enable designing targeted programs, while robotic process automation technology, making use of artificial intelligence in the form of chatbots, can potentially substitute for humans in interacting with customers.[24]

In the Philippines, there is a high level of awareness of Industry 4.0-related challenges and opportunities, and of the centrality of skills in determining outcomes during the transition and beyond. This comes across explicitly and implicitly in the goals and objectives of TESDA's National Technical Education and Skills Development Plan 2018–2022,[25] and its strategic focus on both global competitiveness and workforce readiness, and social equity for workforce inclusion and poverty reduction (see Chapter 5). This chapter examines the changing demand for labor in the Philippine context, drawing out implications for skills development and TVET, in particular. It analyzes the impact that Industry 4.0 and related factors are having on the quantity, structure, nature, and quality of employment in the country, identifying major trends and differential effects across groups. It concludes with insights regarding the readiness of the national TVET system to confront the challenges and considerations for the way forward.

---

[23] See Acemoglu and Restrepo (2016), Autor (2015), Vivarelli (2007), ADB (2018b), and ADB (2020).
[24] ADB. 2021. *Reaping Benefits of Industry 4.0 through Skills Development in High-Growth Industries in Southeast Asia: Insights from Cambodia, Indonesia, the Philippines, and Viet Nam.* Manila.
[25] Technical Education and Skills Development Authority (TESDA) (2018a).

Technological Change and Employment

Recent trends suggest that Industry 4.0 is not yet having a major impact on employment levels in the Philippines.[26] In recent years, until the onset of the COVID-19 pandemic, employment growth has remained positive, although not very high, and real wages and job quality have risen on average. It may be that disruptive technologies have not yet been or have only begun to be implemented, or that scale, productivity, and income effects are outweighing the potential displacement of labor. Nevertheless, there are undeniable signs that the structure and nature of jobs is changing, and distributional effects are real and significant, with skills playing a key role in the equation. As technological innovation benefits capital owners, patent holders, high-skilled workers, and those with technology-compatible skills, it is lower-skilled workers, those whose tasks are more easily automated, and those who face structural barriers to education and skills acquisition who, more than ever, run the risk of being left behind.[27]

Intensified globalization and specifically the interplay of trade and technology are leading to the rise of industries and decline of others, shifting jobs across borders. With the fragmentation of production processes facilitated by technology, global value chains (GVCs) and their regional equivalents now account for a growing share of global production, trade, and employment. The Asia and the Pacific region's participation in GVCs has been growing, but remains still largely centered around labor-intensive production and assembly stages in low- to medium-technology manufacturing industries.[28] However, with rapid technological change, the availability of lower-cost labor is becoming less relevant as a comparative advantage, while innovation capacity and a skilled workforce increasingly determine competitiveness. In this context, improving countries' positions in GVCs and moving toward higher-value and more knowledge-intensive sectors and segments represents a more sustainable development path (footnote 28). Such a shift is already taking place within the Philippines' manufacturing sector, and to some extent in its higher-productivity service sectors.

Technological change has been accompanied by shifts within the manufacturing sector in the Philippines. Although the Philippines, like many countries in Asia, entered GVCs through apparel manufacturing, it is now a player in the electronics sector, its automotive industry has expanded, and it has entered the aerospace industry (footnote 28). Within some of these industries, there is a push by both industry and government to shift activities further up along the value chain, e.g., in the electronics industry, there are efforts to move from parts manufacturing toward assembly and production centers (footnote 27). Although the manufacturing share in value added in the Philippines declined between 2010 and 2017, and its share in employment remained more or less constant, significant shifts took place within the sector, generally away from lower-technology industries to other low-, medium-low, and medium-high technology industries.

For instance, important job losses in the wood and wood products manufacturing industry, in textiles and wearing apparel, and machinery and equipment were offset by net increases in employment in food and beverages, electrical and electronics, leather and footwear, automotive, and rubber and rubber products (Figure 3.1). In

---

[26] The analysis presented in this section uses labor market data obtained from the labor force surveys 2001–2018. Due to data availability, only the January LFS is used as the annual estimate over this period. As a result, data and indicators presented may differ slightly from other published annual estimates for the same year. Data on industry output and gross value added (GVA) are obtained from the input–output tables for 2010 and 2017, from ADB (2018a). For consistency of time periods across the analysis, industry-level trends presented in tables and figures are calculated over 2010–2017. See Box 3.1 for a brief overview of what is meant by Industry 4.0.

[27] S. El Achkar Hilal. 2018. Creative destruction? Technological Progress, Employment Growth, and Skills for the Future in Indonesia, the Philippines, Thailand and Vietnam. In *Skills and the Future of Work: Strategies for Inclusive Growth in Asia and the Pacific*, edited by Akiko Sakamoto and Johnny Sung, 182–255. Bangkok: International Labour Organization.

[28] K. Fernandez-Stark and P. Bamber. 2018. Skills Development for Economic and Social Upgrading: The Case of Asian Developing Countries in the Global Value Chains. In *Skills and the Future of Work: Strategies for Inclusive Growth in Asia and the Pacific*, edited by Akiko Sakamoto and Johnny Sung, 62–97. Bangkok: International Labour Organization.

Box 3.1: What is Industry 4.0?

Over the past 5 years, the "Future of Work" debate has become increasingly focused on the labor market implications of the Fourth Industrial Revolution (4IR, or Industry 4.0). While the first three industrial revolutions, involving mechanization, assembly lines, and automation, completely transformed production processes, the fourth wave currently underway is expected to have far greater impacts.

INDUSTRY 1.0	INDUSTRY 2.0	INDUSTRY 3.0	INDUSTRY 4.0
Mechanization of industry using water and steam-powered machines	Railroads and telegraph networks connecting people and ideas Mass production with assembly line powered by electricity	The advent of computers, the internet, robots and automation, and electronics	First conceptualized to describe data exchange technologies used in manufacturing, this term is now widely used to refer to technologies applied across sectors; technologies include cyber-physical systems, the Internet of Things (IoT), artificial intelligence, cloud computing, and cognitive computing
18th Century	19th Century	1990s	Today

Source: Adapted from ADB 2021. *Reaping Benefits of Industry 4.0 through Skills Development in High-Growth Industries in Southeast Asia: Insights from Cambodia, Indonesia, the Philippines, and Viet Nam.* Manila.

The impacts of Industry 4.0 are due to the use of highly advanced technologies characterized by the convergence of "the physical, biological and digital worlds, impacting all disciplines, economies and industries, and even challenging ideas about what it means to be human."

Source: K. Schwab. 2016. *The Fourth Industrial Revolution.* Geneva: World Economic Forum. SkillsFuture. n.d. https://www.skillsfuture.sg/.

---

other medium-low technology manufacturing industries with a smaller employment base, such as chemicals and petroleum products, employment growth was limited in absolute terms, but significant in terms of growth rate (Figure 3.2).

In the services sector, employment has expanded in most industries, with the most significant job growth in the high-productivity business and professional services, including the rapidly growing BPO industry. Employment growth has also been high in public administration and banking and finance, but also in retail and wholesale trade sector, hotels and restaurants, and land transportation, lower-productivity sectors employing lower-skilled workers (Figure 3.3, Figure 3.4).

The inter-industry shift from low- to medium- and high-technology manufacturing, and toward high-productivity services, has been accompanied by a change in skills demand. In the medium- and high-technology industries, a large segment of the value chain consists of the mid-level jobs typically involving processing and performing complex activities requiring specific technical competencies, often acquired through TVET (Figure 3.5).

Figure 3.1: Net Employment Growth in Manufacturing by Technology Intensity, 2010–2017

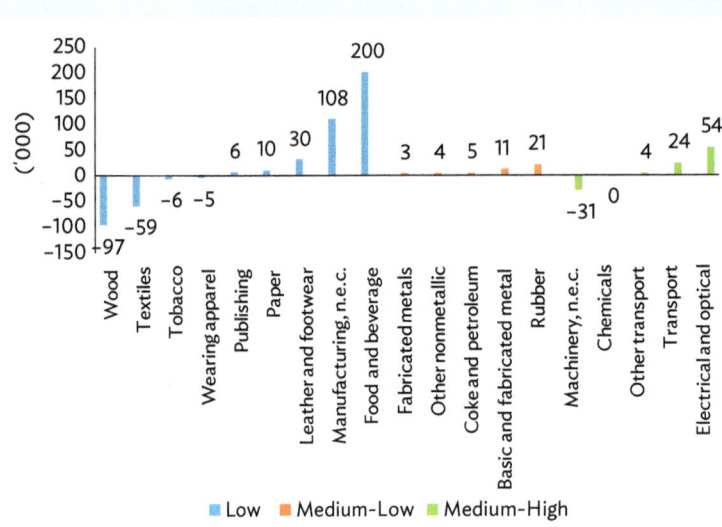

n.e.c. = not elsewhere classified.
Source: ADB estimates based on labor force survey.

Figure 3.2: Average Annual Employment Growth Rate in Manufacturing by Technology Intensity, 2010–2017

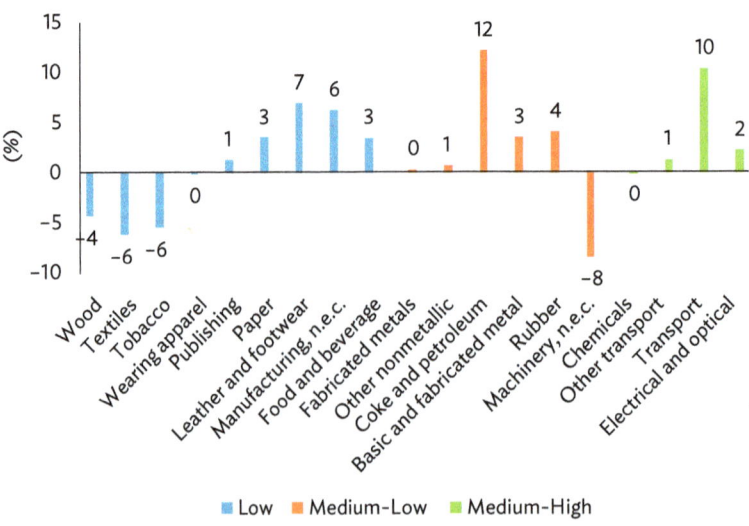

n.e.c. = not elsewhere classified.
Source: ADB estimates based on labor force survey.

Figure 3.3: Net Employment Growth by Labor Productivity Group, 2010–2017

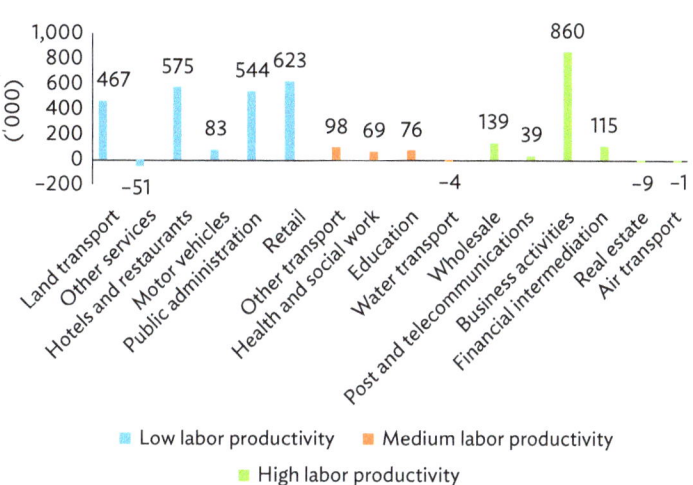

Sources: ADB estimates based on labor force survey; the ADB Multi-Regional Input–Output Database.

Figure 3.4: Average Annual Employment Growth Rate in Services by Labor Productivity Group, 2010–2017

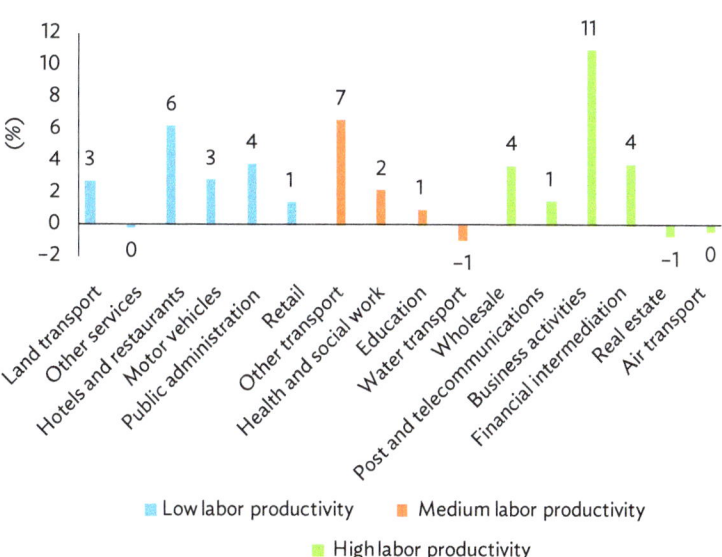

Source: ADB estimates based on labor force survey, and ADB Multi-Regional Input–Output Database.

Figure 3.5: Workforce Composition across Global Value Chains

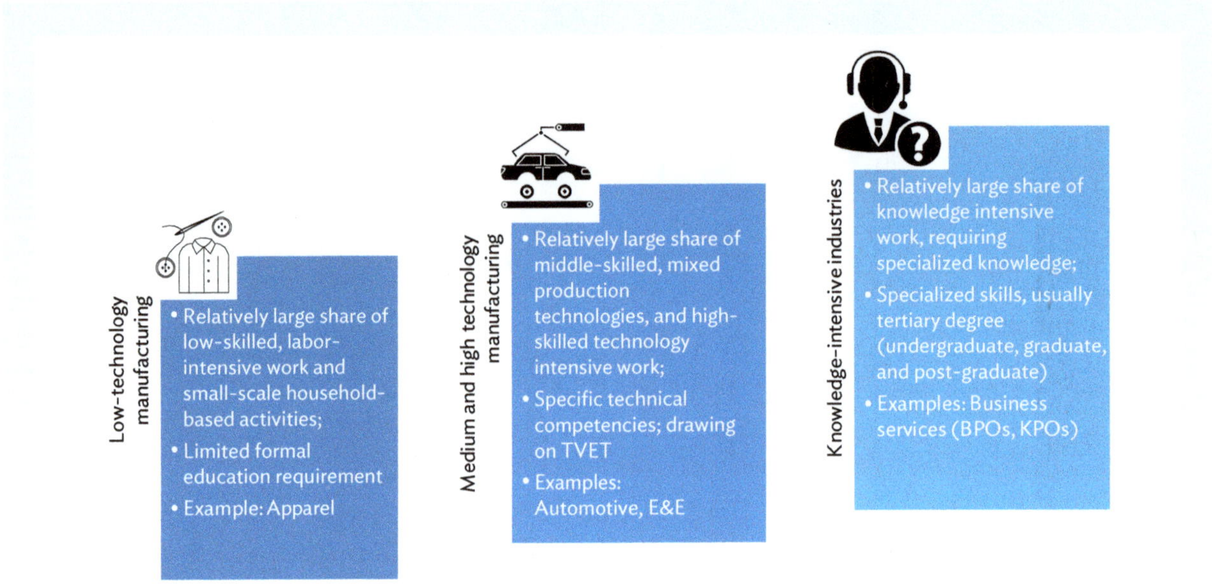

Low-technology manufacturing
- Relatively large share of low-skilled, labor-intensive work and small-scale household-based activities;
- Limited formal education requirement
- Example: Apparel

Medium and high technology manufacturing
- Relatively large share of middle-skilled, mixed production technologies, and high-skilled technology intensive work;
- Specific technical competencies; drawing on TVET
- Examples: Automotive, E&E

Knowledge-intensive industries
- Relatively large share of knowledge intensive work, requiring specialized knowledge;
- Specialized skills, usually tertiary degree (undergraduate, graduate, and post-graduate)
- Examples: Business services (BPOs, KPOs)

BPO = business process outsourcing, E&E = electrical and electronics,
KPO = knowledge process outsourcing, TVET = technical and vocational education and training.
Source: Authors' adaptation based on Fernandez-Stark and Bamber (2018).

In the high-productivity services sectors, workers often must conduct nonroutine cognitive tasks, requiring specialized knowledge and analytical capacity, usually acquired through tertiary education. In the Philippines, which has a relatively highly educated workforce, this shift in skills demand should lead to a narrowing of the skills mismatch whereby highly educated workers are employed in mid-level positions due to limited opportunities in high-skilled occupations,[29] as well as a shortage of qualified graduates from post-secondary education with the required technical competencies (TVET graduates).

Within industries, there has been a shift in firm composition, as reflected in the rise in wage and salaried work as a share of employment. Each industry is composed of heterogeneous firms in terms of size, formality, export orientation, target customers, or market segment. The adoption of technologies can involve high upfront costs that many smaller and informal enterprises may not be able to afford, leading them to exit the market. This can result in a shift of market share towards large, more productive formal enterprises, thus increasing the wage and salaried share in employment. On the other hand, productivity increases could lead to higher wages, thus raising the cost of formality and pushing firms at the margin toward informality.[30] In the latter case, the employment share of own-account and unpaid family work could increase. In the Philippines, all manufacturing industries, except for rubber and rubber products and basic metals, had an increase in the share of paid employees among their workforces between 2010 and 2017, reflecting within-industry changes toward larger and more formal enterprises.

---

[29] Epetia, Maria Christina F. 2018. "College Graduates in Non-College Jobs: Measuring Overeducation in the Philippine Labor Market." PhD dissertation. Diliman, Quezon City: University of the Philippines School of Economics.

[30] B. Aleman-Castilla. 2006. *The Effect of Trade Liberalization on Informality and Wages: Evidence from Mexico*. CEP Discussion Papers No. 763. London: London School of Economics and Political Science, Centre for Economic Performance.

An increase in nonstandard forms of employment in several high-growth industries is reflecting within-firm changes in business models and hiring practices. This is linked to another trend accompanying technological change, which is the expansion of fixed-term or temporary working arrangements, contract labor or casual work, and part-time work, collectively referred to as nonstandard forms of employment. At the global level, a rise in these forms of employment is resulting from a number of interconnected factors, including technological innovation, changing consumption and production patterns associated with GVCs and global production networks, and contractor–subcontractor relationships.[31] Consumption patterns, such as "fast fashion" for the apparel industry, have added to the pressure on firms, particularly those at the lower end of GVCs, to increase their organizational efficiency through flexible business models and production processes. This has led firms to increasingly resort to nonstandard forms of employment whereby they can hire workers temporarily based on demand. In services, a rise in part-time, temporary, or on-call jobs has been facilitated by digital technologies, which allow work to be done remotely. However, from the workers' perspective, these forms of employment are often precarious, associated with less regular incomes and limited access to social safety nets, while being more vulnerable to economic shocks. Workers in nonstandard forms of employment are generally not unionized, which contributes to low bargaining power, and relatively low wages and poor working conditions. Furthermore, from a skills development perspective, these workers lack the institutional support to build up their skills and remain competitive in a rapidly changing environment.

In some rapidly growing medium- to high-technology intensity manufacturing industries and in high-productivity service sectors in the Philippines, the increase in share of wage employment has been accompanied by a rise in precarious employment, which is defined as employees in nonstandard forms of employment (Figure 3.6). In low-technology intensity manufacturing industries, however, it was accompanied by a decline in precarious employment. Similarly, low-productivity service industries had more limited increases in wage employment shares, but also declines in precarious employment, while higher-productivity industries generally had increases in precarious employment (Figure 3.7). Due to an increase in precarious employment in many industries, average weekly working hours declined across the board in the Philippines (with the exceptions of coke and refined petroleum manufacturing, real estate activities, and public administration), and labor productivity measured in terms of value added per hour worked increased faster than labor productivity measured as value added per worker (Figure 3.8). Although shortened working hours may be a means of labor sharing in productivity gains,[32] in a context of high time-related underemployment and rising nonstandard forms of employment, it may be a less desirable outcome.

Within-industry and within-firm changes are reflected in a change in occupational structures, and in the task content of occupations. Even within industries, firms differ in terms of business models and skills utilization. For instance, one financial firm can offer relatively standard products to a large number of customers in the personal finance sector, while another targets a smaller number of high-net-worth customers with personalized services and business planning.[33] In the former model, many tasks are routine, while the latter involve nonroutine, situation-specific tasks, and a higher level of knowledge and skill. These different business models are differently impacted by technology; in the former case, a larger share of workers may be substituted by technology. However, technology may also be driving a shift toward models closer to the

---

[31] Global production networks are often characterized by permanent employees at the top who engage in core tasks, have specialized knowledge and expertise, and are encouraged to further build their skills through exposure and work across different departments; and temporary employees in the bottom tiers who "are primarily used to maximize organizational efficiency – to contribute to cost reduction," regardless of their level of vocational skills. See Yamazaki (2018) and ILO (2015).

[32] I. Nübler. 2016. New Technologies: A Jobless Future or Golden Age of Job Creation? *ILO Working Paper 13*. Geneva: International Labour Office.

[33] J. Sung. 2018. Business Model, Skills Intensity and Job Quality for Inclusive Society. In *Skills and the Future of Work: Strategies for Inclusive Growth in Asia and the Pacific*, edited by Akiko Sakamoto and Johnny Sung, 24–40. Bangkok: International Labour Organization.

Figure 3.6: Change in Wage and Salaried Work and Precarious Employment in Manufacturing by Technology Intensity, 2010–2017

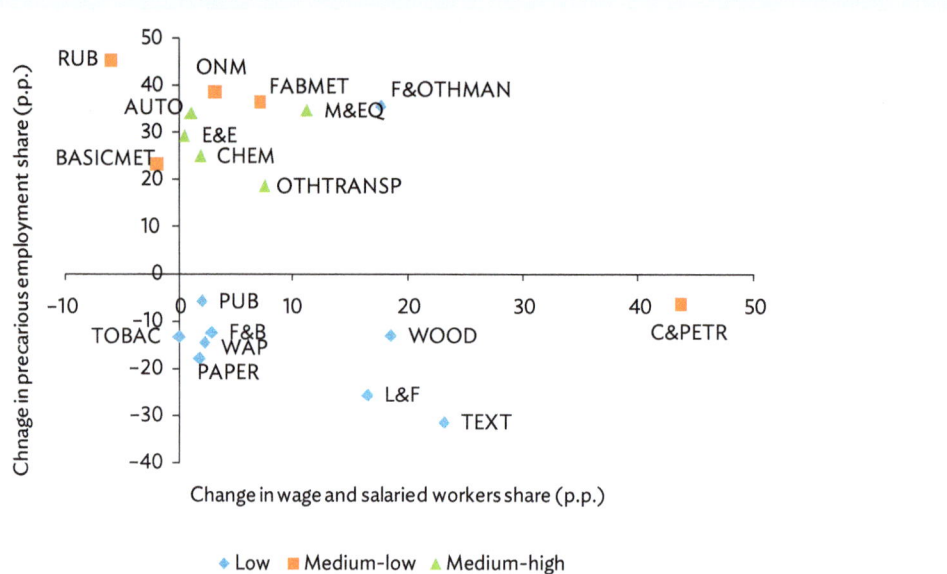

AUTO = Automotive, BASICMET = Basic metals, C&PETR = Coke and petroleum, CHEM = Chemicals, E&E = Electrical and electronics, F&B = Food and beverage, F&OTHMAN = Furniture and other manufacturing, n.e.c., FABMET = Fabricated metals, L&F = Leather and footwear, M&EQ = Machinery and equipment, n.e.c., ONM = Other nonmetallic, OTHTRANSP = Other transport, PAPER = Paper, p.p. = percentage points, PUB = Publishing, RUB = Rubber and plastic, TEXT = Textiles, TOBAC = Tobacco, WAP = Wearing apparel, WOOD = Wood.
Source: ADB estimates based on labor force survey.

latter; by substituting for routine tasks, it can free up resources to be assigned to nonroutine interpersonal or nonroutine analytical tasks for which technology is complementary. Such shifts in skills demand are reflected in both a change in occupational structures and in the task content of occupations. Unfortunately, due to data constraints, most analyses, including the one presented in this chapter, are limited to changes in occupational structures, rather than changes in the task content of occupations. It is important then to re-emphasize that observed changes in occupational demand, further described in the following paragraphs in the context of the Philippines, are not—at least not yet—primarily attributable to the effect of technology on the task content of occupations, but are driven by a number of factors at different levels of impact as described earlier. These include, at the macro level, structural shift in the composition of output resulting in inter-industry employment shifts; at the sector level, a change in the structure of industries resulting in within-industry changes in workforce composition; and finally within-firm changes in occupations. The driving forces behind these changes are therefore not limited to technological progress in the context of Industry 4.0, but include other related megatrends[34] such as intensified globalization and shifts in economic power, demographic and social change, urbanization, climate change, and resource scarcity, all of which are having major impacts on labor markets all over the world.

---

[34] See for example: PwC (2017).

Figure 3.7: Change in Wage and Salaried Share and Precarious Employment Share in Services, 2010-2017

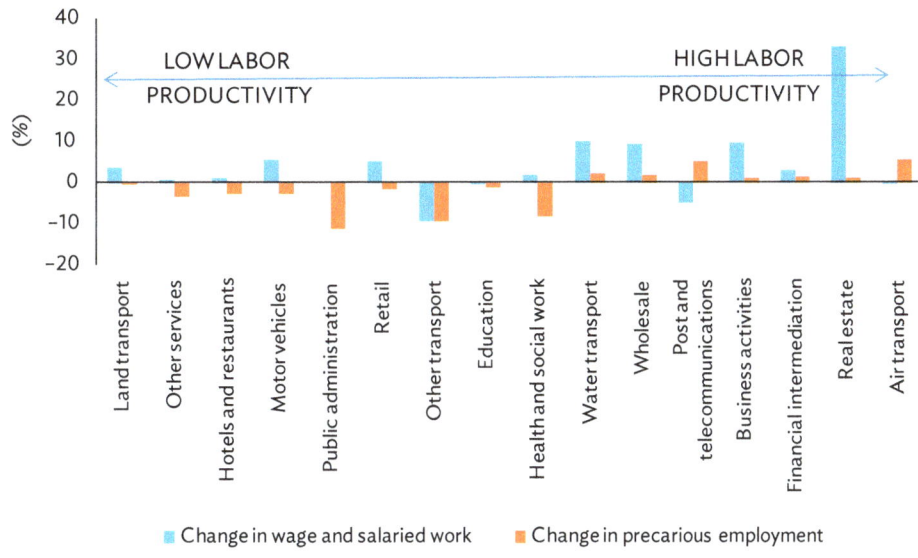

Source: ADB estimates based on labor force survey.

Figure 3.8: Change in Working Hours and Labor Productivity Growth by Industry, 2010–2017

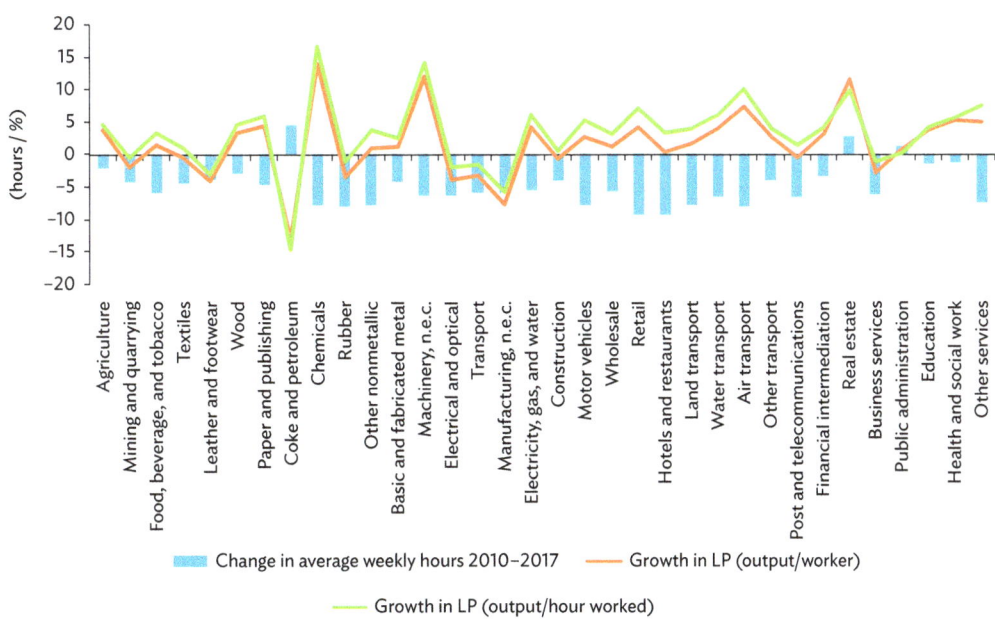

LP = labor productivity, n.e.c. = not elsewhere classified.
Source: ADB estimates based on labor force survey and ADB Multi-Regional Input–Output Database.

In the Philippines, there has been an increase in skill intensity of employment driven by an increase in demand for middle-skilled and high-skilled occupations, and a decline in the share of low-skilled workers (elementary and agriculture workers) between 2010 and 2017 (Figure 3.9, Figure 3.10). A decline in low-skilled employment in agriculture and, to a lesser extent, in retail trade and other personal and community services was partly offset by low-skilled employment growth in construction and tourism. As a share of employment, low-skilled work increased in the latter two industries, as well as in utilities, air transport, and mining and quarrying. The share of middle-skill occupations has not declined, but there has been a shift in the composition of these occupations at the aggregate level toward sales and service occupations, driven by high growth in service sector employment. Sales and services employment growth was highest in retail trade, tourism, and other personal and community services, as well as in the business services industries; as a share of employment, it also grew in the post and ICT industries and in real estate. Clerical support workers increased mainly in the business services industries and to a lesser extent in finance, but decreased as a share of employment in most other industries. Plant and machine operators and crafts and related trades workers have also had a small increase in their share of employment since 2012 at the aggregate level (Figure 3.11) driven by employment in manufacturing and construction. In a number of manufacturing industries, such as textiles, electrical and electronics, and automotive, a declining share of crafts and related trades occupations has been offset by an increase in plant and machine operators (Figure 3.12). This trend has been observed in some industries across several countries in the region, reflecting the restructuring of manufacturing industries away from small-scale and labor-intensive work toward relatively more capital-intensive production processes in medium and larger firms.[35] However,

Figure 3.9: Employment Distribution by Skill Level and Skills Intensity at the Aggregate Level, 2010–2018

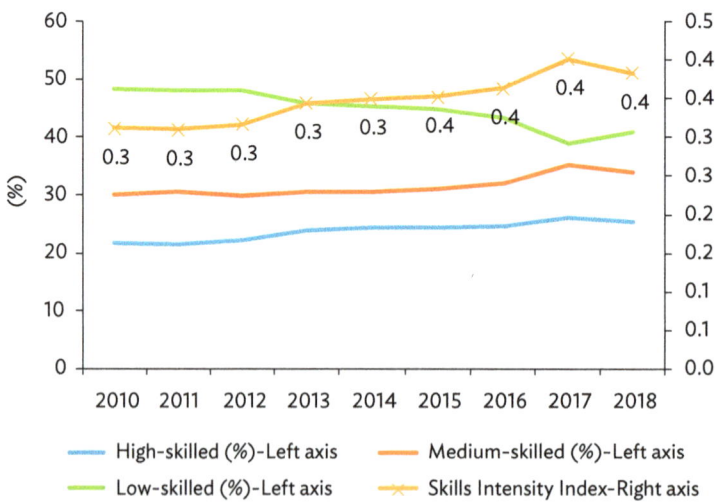

Skills intensity index = [high-skilled % / (high-skilled % + low-skilled %)]
Source: ADB estimates from labor force survey.

---

[35] S. El Achkar Hilal. 2018. Creative destruction? Technological Progress, Employment Growth, and Skills for the Future in Indonesia, the Philippines, Thailand and Vietnam. In *Skills and the Future of Work: Strategies for Inclusive Growth in Asia and the Pacific*, edited by Akiko Sakamoto and Johnny Sung, 182–255. Bangkok: International Labour Organization.

Figure 3.10: Demand Share by Task Content of Occupations, 2010–2018

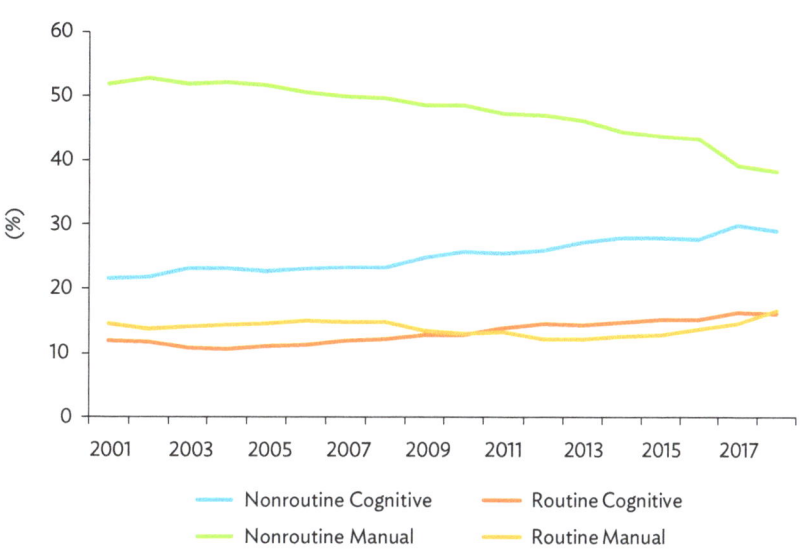

Note: Excludes skilled agriculture workers and armed forces occupational groups.
Source: ADB estimates from labor force survey, based on Generalao (2019) and Acemoglu and Autor (2011).

Figure 3.11: Employment Distribution by Broad Occupational Group, 2010–2018

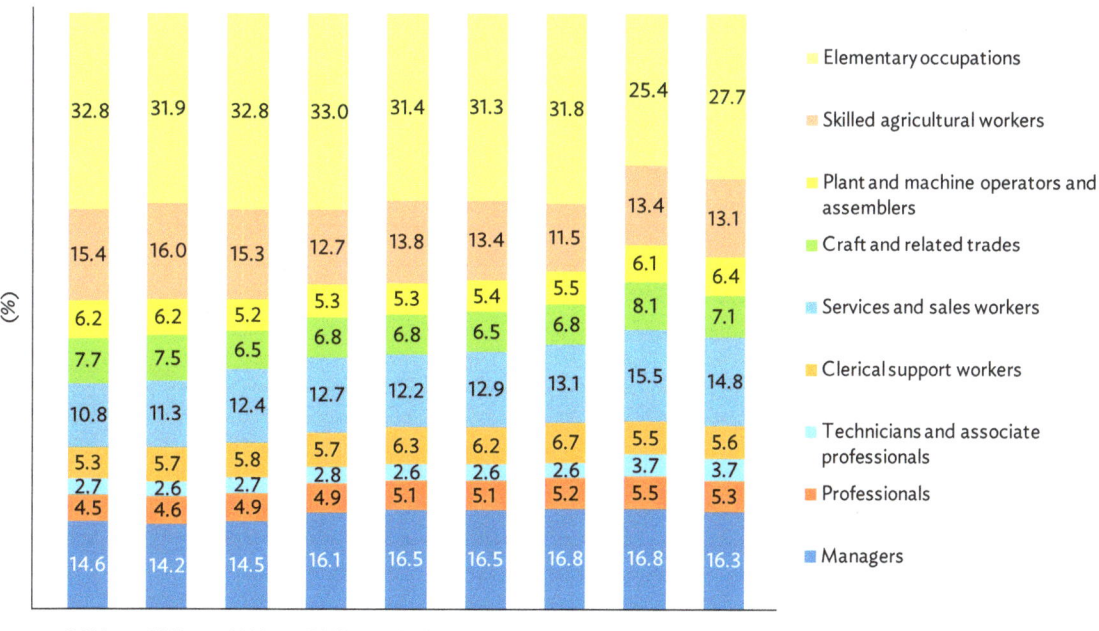

Source: ADB estimates from labor force survey.

Figure 3.12: Change in Occupational Demand by Skill Category, Selected Manufacturing Industries, 2010–2017

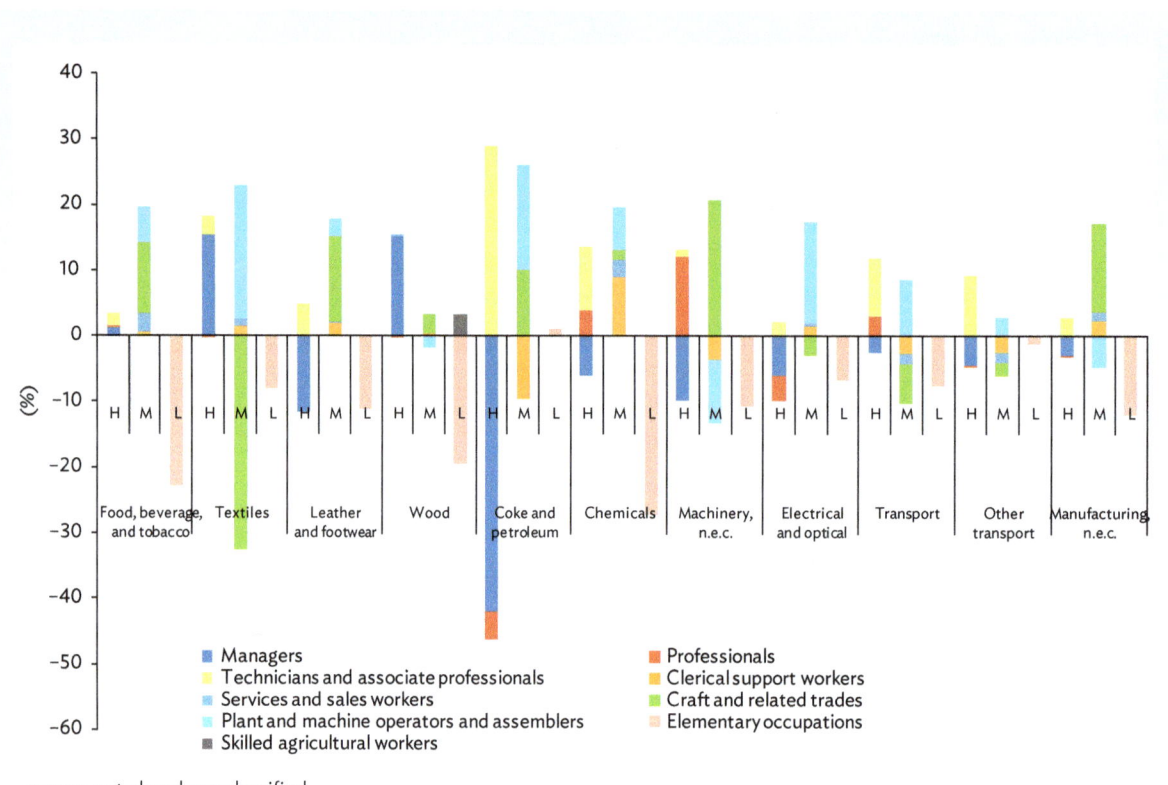

n.e.c = not elsewhere classified.
Source: ADB estimates from labor force survey.

the opposite is true for machinery and equipment, and for furniture and other manufacturing. In other low-skill intensity manufacturing industries (e.g., food and beverages, or leather and footwear), the share of crafts and related trades workers increased, as that of elementary occupations fell.

The shifting skills demand reflects a notable increase in occupations that primarily involve nonroutine cognitive (including analytical, interpersonal) tasks, and a decline in relative demand for occupations that primarily involve nonroutine manual tasks (Figure 3.10). The former generally correspond to the high-skilled occupational groups, and the latter to elementary occupations as well as crafts and related trades workers. The demand shares of occupations that are routine cognitive, consisting mainly of clerical occupations, have slightly increased over time, partly due to growth in the business services industries. That of occupations involving primarily routine manual, mainly plant and machine operators, which had decreased during the global financial crisis, has been increasing since 2012. The recent increase in routine cognitive and routine manual occupations stands in contrast to the routine-biased technological change hypothesis (Box 3.2). Thus, trends so far suggest that impact of Industry 4.0 on employment has not reached a tipping point in the Philippines yet, possibly because the adoption of advanced technologies remains limited in many sectors (Box 3.3).

Interestingly, the increase in skill intensity of employment has been accompanied by a decrease in the skill premium over the 2010–2018 period in the Philippines (Figure 3.13). Note that the premium calculated here using data on basic pay likely underestimates the real premium, which would be obtained if other compensation

Box 3.2: Routine-Biased Technological Change and the Task Content of Occupations

Skill-biased technological change (SBTC)—in brief, the idea that technology complements and benefits high-skilled workers at the expense of the less-skilled—has emerged partly to explain an observed increase in the skills premium or difference between returns to high skills relative to low skills. But SBTC failed to explain the "job polarization" trend observed initially in the United States,[a] and subsequently in many advanced but even in some developing economies.[b]

With job polarization, the share of employment increases at both ends of the skills spectrum, with a corresponding "hollowing out" of mid-level occupations. This trend has been observed both at the overall economy level, and within industries. An alternative to SBTC, more consistent with the observed trends, is *routine-biased technological change* (RBTC) through which different occupations face different risks of being substituted by technology based on their task content. In particular, occupations involving mainly routine tasks with clear and precise procedures, which are often repetitive, are more likely to be replaced through automation, or outsourced/offshored to workers in other countries.[c] Note that SBTC and RBTC are not mutually exclusive, and may be taking place in parallel.

Based on the concept of RBTC, most of the recent literature on the impact of technology, trade, and globalization on labor demand has used a task-based framework.[d] In these studies, tasks are divided into a classification scheme (usually between two to six categories), the categories of which are then used to develop the task profile of occupations. In the Philippine context, Generalao (2019a) mapped 3,281 tasks of 427 occupations from the Philippines Standard Occupational Classification onto five task groups, based on the literature: nonroutine analytical, nonroutine interpersonal, nonroutine manual, routine manual, and routine cognitive.[e] The classification schemes from Generalao (2019) and Acemoglu and Autor (2011) are used in the analysis presented in this chapter.

[a] D. Acemoglu. 1999. Changes in Unemployment and Wage Inequality: An Alternative Theory and Some Evidence. *The American Economic Review* 89(5): 1259–78.
[b] P. K. Goldberg and N. Pavcnik. 2007. Distributional Effects of Globalization in Developing Countries. *Journal of Economic Literature* 45(1): 39–82.
[c] M. Goos, A. Manning, and A. Salomons. 2014. Explaining Job Polarization: Routine-Biased Technological Change and Offshoring. *American Economic Review* 104(8): 2509–26.
[d] See Autor, Levy, and Murnane (2003); Acemoglu and Autor (2011); Autor and Dorn (2013); and Goos, Manning, and Salomons (2014).
[e] I. N. Generalao. 2019a. Skill Transferability and Mismatch Among Post-Training Graduates: An Application of the Task-Based Approach. Master's Thesis. Diliman, Quezon City: University of the Philippines School of Economics.
Source: Authors.

and benefits were included. Specifically, although real wages have increased across all occupational groups based on task content (Figure 3.14), that of unskilled workers, many of whom are engaged in nonroutine manual task-intensive occupations, increased faster than that of skilled workers employed in nonroutine cognitive (analytical and interpersonal) task-intensive occupations (Figure 3.13). This seems puzzling due to the decline in demand for the former group, and increased demand for the latter. However, the greater rise in real wages for nonroutine manual workers can be explained by the shedding of low-productivity, low-pay jobs in agriculture, driving the average wage of their occupational group upward. Nonroutine manual skills have the lowest returns in the Philippines, and also the largest gender gap in pay at 33% in 2018, unchanged since 2010 (Figure 3.15). The gender pay gap has increased slightly in nonroutine analytical occupations, and in routine manual occupations, but has decreased in routine cognitive ones, and has been reversed in nonroutine interpersonal occupations (Figure 3.15). The latter reversal is due to a decline in real wages of managers—which include many own-account workers—that was more pronounced for males (−2.5% annually between 2010 and 2018) than for females (−0.6%).

Box 3.3: Adoption of Industry 4.0 Technologies in the IT-BPO and Electronics Manufacturing Industries

In a survey undertaken for an ADB study, 59% of employers in the IT-BPO industry and 49% of employers in the electronics manufacturing industries reported having already adopted Industry 4.0 technologies in their operations, and the share is expected to increase significantly by 2025 in both industries (figure).[a]

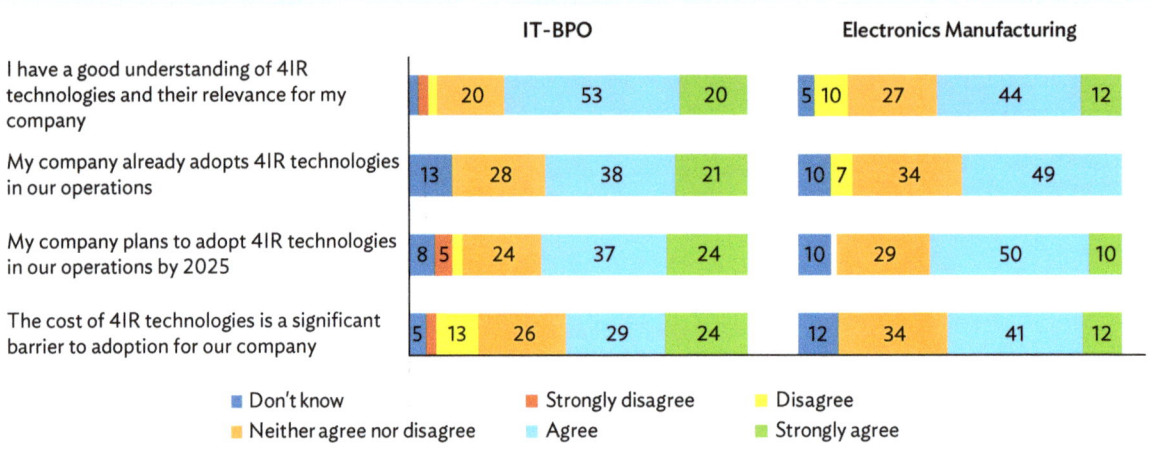

Sentiments toward Industry 4.0 in the IT-BPO Industry in the Philippines

4IR = Industry 4.0, IT-BPO = information technology–business process outsourcing.
Source: ADB. 2021. *Reaping Benefits of Industry 4.0 through Skills Development in High-Growth Industries in Southeast Asia: Insights from Cambodia, Indonesia, the Philippines, and Viet Nam.* Manila: ADB.

However, over half of surveyed employers consider the high cost of Industry 4.0 technologies as a significant barrier to adoption for their company. Indeed, in many industries, the economic feasibility of adoption can be expected to lag technical feasibility.

[a] The study was commissioned by ADB and undertaken by the consultancy firm AlphaBeta, which examined trends on technology and skills linked to Industry 4.0 in two key growth sectors, in each of four Southeast Asian countries: Cambodia, Indonesia, the Philippines, and Viet Nam. The objective of the study was to assess the countries' readiness for the transition to Industry 4.0, by identifying challenges and opportunities in the two sectors. In the Philippines, the two selected sectors were the IT-BPO and the electronics manufacturing industries. The Philippines' IT-BPO industry accounts for 10%–15% of the global market. It represented 2.7% of the country's employment in 2016 and 6% of its gross domestic product in 2015. The electronics manufacturing industry represented 2% of employment and 10.5% of the country's exports in 2018.

Sources: Authors; ADB. 2021. *Reaping Benefits of Industry 4.0 through Skills Development in High-Growth Industries in Southeast Asia: Insights from Cambodia, Indonesia, the Philippines, and Viet Nam.* Manila.

Industries at high risk of labor substitution from Industry 4.0 technologies, whether in manufacturing or services, include some key growth sectors of the Philippine economy. Under a task-based framework (Box 3.2), plant and machine operators, which involve mainly routine manual tasks, face the highest risk of job losses due to substitution, followed by occupations involving primarily routine cognitive tasks. Therefore, industries where these occupations are more prominent, such as electrical and electronics, face a greater risk than leather and footwear, for instance, where craft and related trade occupations, involving mainly nonroutine manual tasks, represent a larger share of employment (Figure 3.16). See Box 3.4 for more in-depth findings for the IT-BPO sector and electronics manufacturing industry. Other manufacturing industries in the Philippines facing high risk of labor substitution are paper and paper products and rubber and rubber products (Figure 3.17). Similarly, in the services sector, the finance, insurance, and auxiliary services industries with a relatively larger share of primarily routine

Figure 3.13: Basic Daily Pay by Task-Based Occupational Group, 2010 and 2018

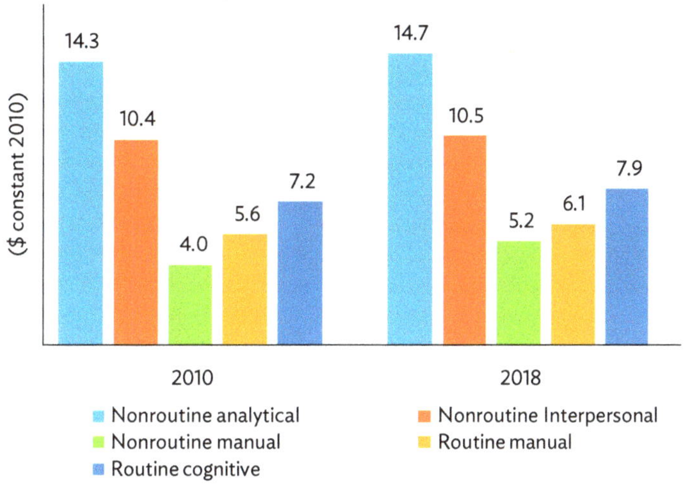

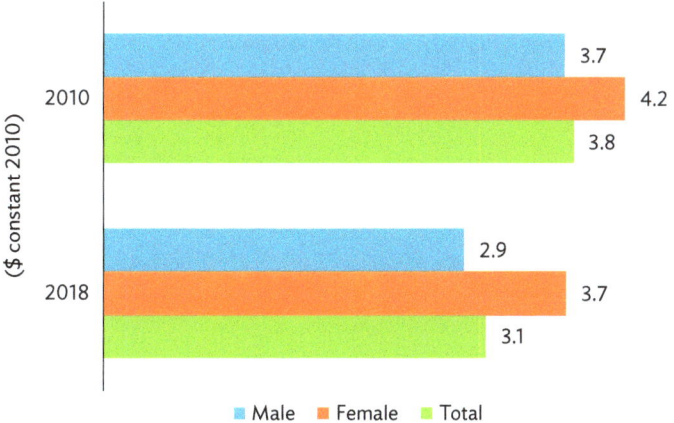

Source: ADB estimates from labor force survey.

Figure 3.14: Skill Premium by Sex, 2010 and 2018

Source: ADB estimates from labor force survey.

cognitive jobs face a greater risk than education, for instance, where jobs primarily involve tasks that are nonroutine interpersonal (Figure 3.16). Even among low-productivity service sectors, industries with relatively high routine manual (e.g., land transportation) and routine cognitive (e.g., retail trade) task content face higher risks from automation than industries with relatively higher shares of nonroutine manual jobs (e.g., sale and repair of motor vehicles) or nonroutine interpersonal jobs (e.g., tourism). In most of these industries, the share of jobs at risk of substitution has actually increased over the 2010–2017 period (Figure 3.17).

Figure 3.15: Gender Pay Gaps and Change in Real Wages (Basic Pay), 2010 and 2018

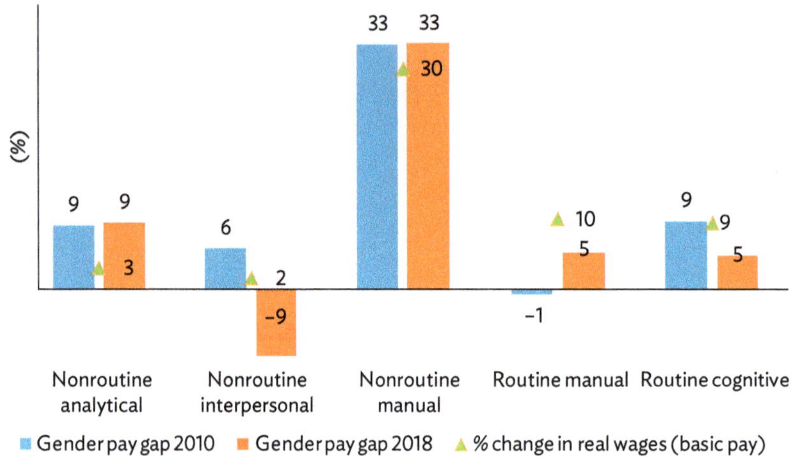

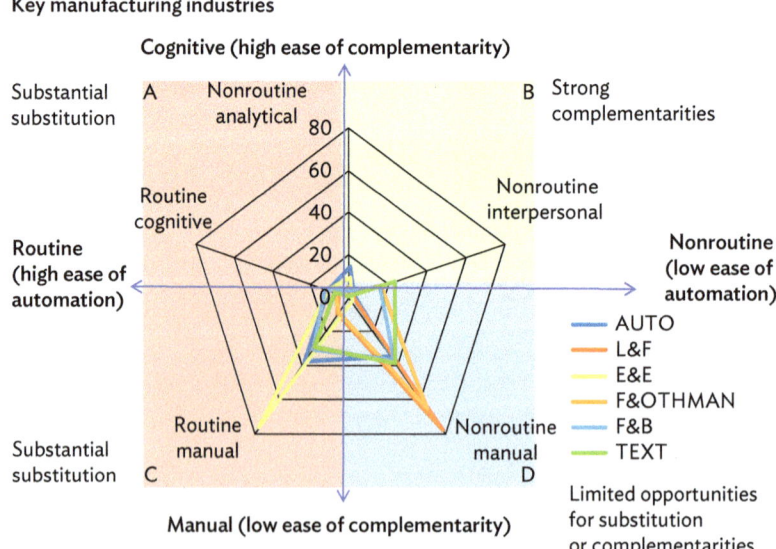

Source: ADB estimates from labor force survey.

Figure 3.16: Labor Substitution Risk in Key Industries

Figure 3.16: *continued*

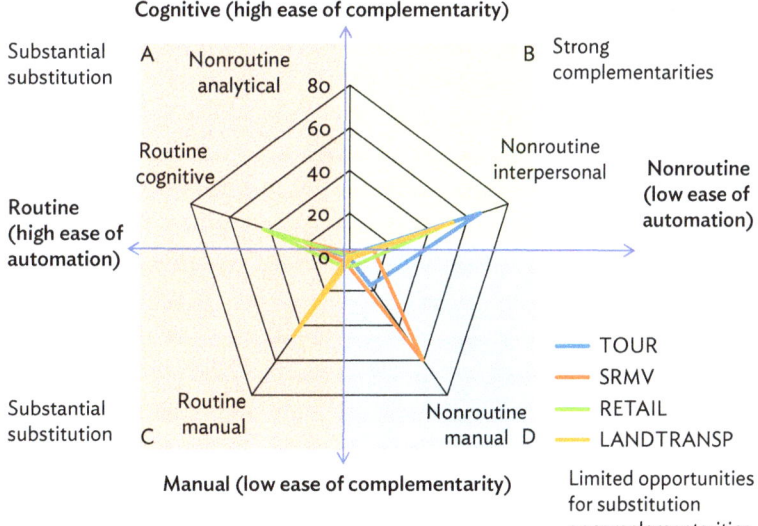

AUTO = Automotive, BUSERV = Business services, E&E = Electrical and electronics, EDUC = Education, F&B = Food and beverage, F&OTHMAN = Furniture and other manufacturing, n.e.c., FINA = Financial services, HSW = Health and social work, L&F = Leather and footwear, LANDTRANSP = Land transport, P&ICT = Postal and telecommunication, RETAIL = Retail trade, SRMV = Motor vehicles, TEXT = Textiles, TOUR = Accommodation.
Source: ADB estimates from labor force survey.

Box 3.4: Impact of Industry 4.0 on Jobs and Skills in the IT-BPO and Electronics Manufacturing Industries

Based on an ADB study on the IT-BPO and electronics manufacturing industries in the Philippines, Industry 4.0 would bring about both job displacement (due to automation) and job gains (due to improved productivity and new labor demand) in the two high-growth industries. In both cases, the net effect is projected to be positive.

Modeled Impact of Industry 4.0 on Number of Jobs in the Electronics Industry—Displacement and Income Effects of Industry 4.0 on Jobs, 2018–2030

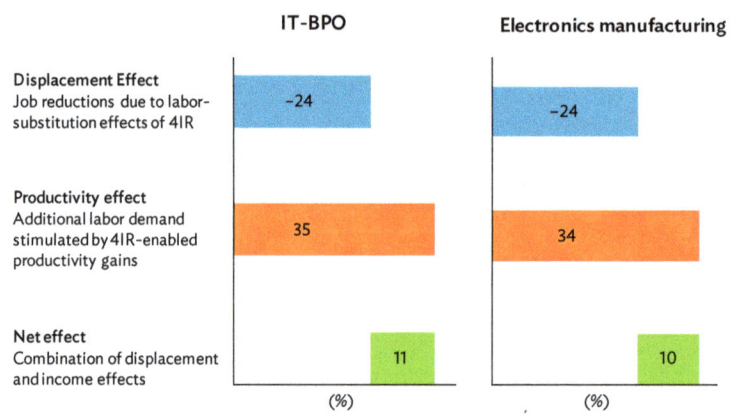

The study also confirmed the relative decline in the importance of routine physical tasks, and increase in importance of analytical and nonroutine tasks, as technology takes over responding to simple queries and basic processes, while more complex issues requiring problem-solving abilities will remain the responsibility of humans. A relatively larger task shift is expected in the electronics manufacturing industry, where workers are expected to spend an additional 16% of their work week on interpersonal and nonroutine tasks and 16% less time on routine physical and routine interpersonal tasks.

Change in Work Hours Spent on Different Tasks in the IT-BPO and Electronics Manufacturing Industries (%)

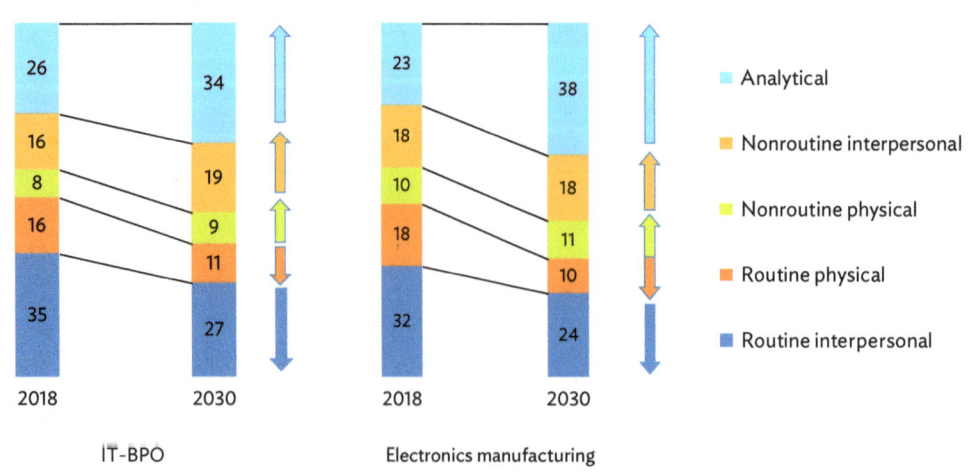

4IR = Industry 4.0, IT-BPO = information technology-business process outsourcing.
Note: Change in jobs based on accelerated adoption scenario of Industry 4.0 technologies.
Source: ADB. 2021. *Reaping Benefits of Industry 4.0 through Skills Development in High-Growth Industries in Southeast Asia: Insights from Cambodia, Indonesia, the Philippines, and Viet Nam.* Manila.

Figure 3.17: Industries Facing Highest Risk of Job Losses due to Automation

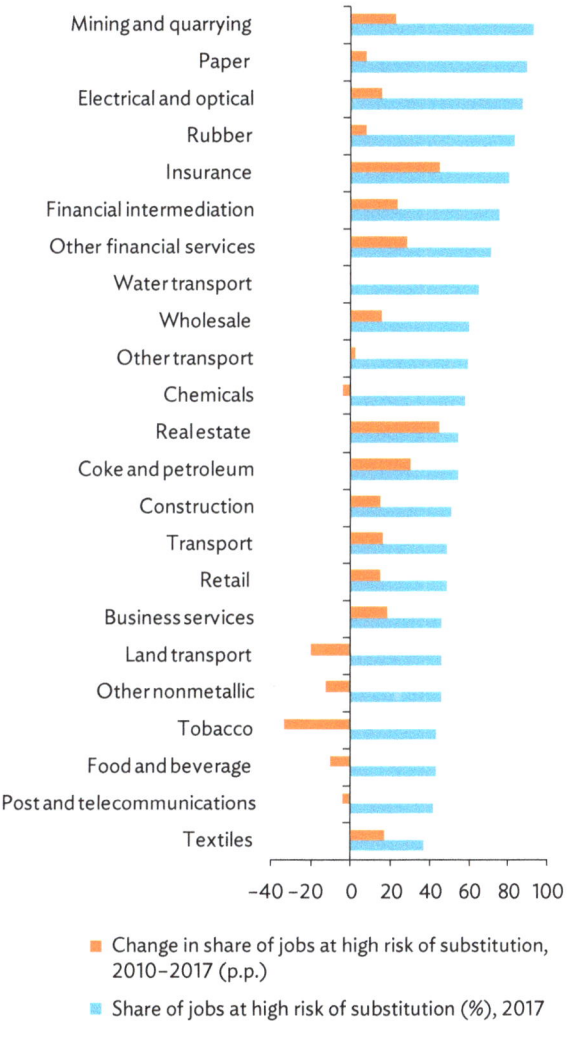

p.p. = percentage points.
Source: ADB estimates from labor force survey.

Female workers represent a disproportionate share of jobs at risk of automation in the Philippines as they account for large shares of routine jobs across many sectors. Within industries facing the highest risk of job losses due to automation (with the exceptions of mining and quarrying and retail trade), the female share of employment in routine occupations, whether in manufacturing or services, is greater than their share in industry employment (Figure 3.18). Most notably, although female workers represent only one-third of business services employment, they account for nearly 60% of jobs at risk of substitution in the industry. Other service industries where female workers represent a larger share of jobs at risk are finance (59%), insurance and pensions (72%), real estate (69%), and retail trade (59%). In manufacturing, women represent the majority of jobs at risk in textiles (73%), tobacco (69%), and in electrical and electronics (67%).

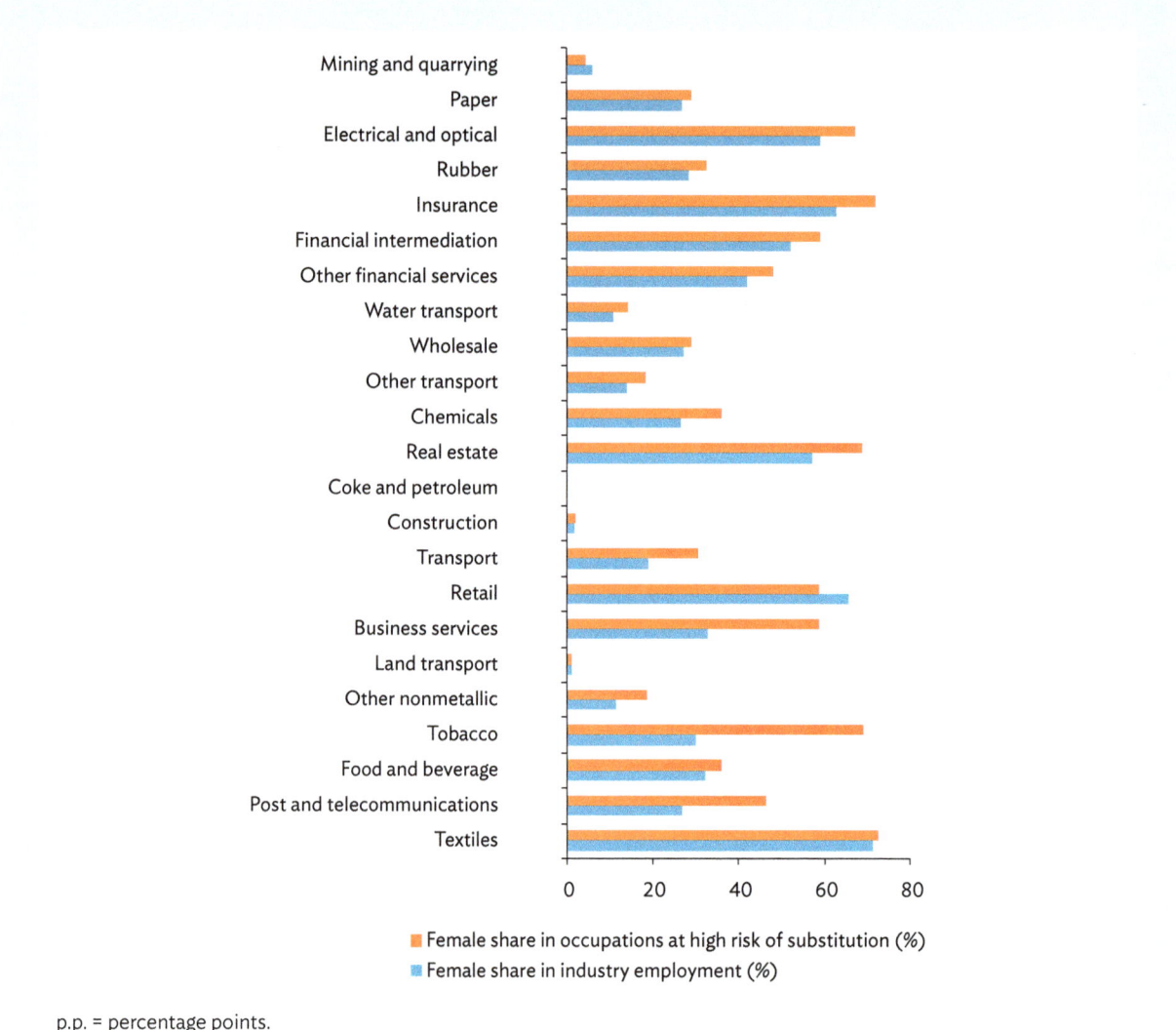

Figure 3.18: Female Share of Employment in Industries at High Risk of Automation

p.p. = percentage points.
Source: ADB estimates from labor force survey.

Distributional Impacts and the Centrality of Skills

The inter- and intra-industry shifts in employment structure, changes in occupational demand, and changes in the task content of occupations ultimately change skills demand. The skills that workers possess will therefore be central to the distributional impacts of Industry 4.0. First, a change in demand for different skills will influence returns to these skills (e.g., increasing the "skills premium" of wage differential between high-skilled and low-skilled workers). Second, skills play a critical role in determining not only the likelihood of being displaced by technology, but also the ease or difficulty of reallocation (transitioning to another job), including adjustment costs (e.g., costs associated with job search and acquiring new skills).

Workers positioned to benefit are those whose skills cannot be easily substituted by technology, those whose skills can complement and be complemented by technology, and those whose skill sets enable them to adapt to new task requirements and to move across jobs and occupations. Skills that cannot be easily substituted by technology include social and communication skills, and skills required for routine and nonroutine interpersonal tasks. Skills complementary to technology are specialized, technical, and technological skills (digital/ICT and science, technology, engineering, and math [STEM]), as well as "21st-century skills" like complex problem-solving, creativity, critical thinking, judgment, and decision-making, i.e., skills required for nonroutine cognitive analytical tasks. The latter skills are often called transversal, and include adaptability, flexibility, and the skills that enable individuals to move across jobs and occupations. Another important skill set,

Table 3.1: Changing Importance of Different Skills in the IT-BPO and Electronics Manufacturing Industries, 2018 and 2030

	Survey respondents who consider skill will be much more important over the next 5 years (%)			Importance of skill ranking by employers			
	Training Institutions	IT-BPO employers	Electronics Employee	IT-BPO 2018	IT-BPO 2030	Electronics Manufacturing 2018	Electronics Manufacturing 2030
Technical	52	53	54	9	9	9	3
Digital/IT	47	53	54	10	10	10	10 (Advanced digital skills)
Complex problem-solving	45	38	34	7	7	7	7
Computer literacy	45	53	54	6	5	6	4 (Basic digital skills)
Written and verbal communication	45	25	5	1	3	1	5
Evaluation, judgment, and decision-making	44	38	20	5	1	3	2
Critical thinking and active learning	42	41	24	8	6	8	8
Management	39	28	15	2	8	2	6
Social	32	22	5	4	4	5	9
Numeracy	31	22	12	3	2	4	1

■ Skills of increasing relative importance in the industry, 2018–2030
■ Skills of decreasing relative importance in the industry, 2018–2030
■ Skills with no change in relative importance in the industry, 2018–2030

BPO = business process outsourcing, IT = information technology.
Source: ADB. 2021. *Reaping Benefits of Industry 4.0 through Skills Development in High-Growth Industries in Southeast Asia: Insights from Cambodia, Indonesia, the Philippines, and Viet Nam.* Manila.

due to the continuous need to learn and relearn within a technology-driven economy, is that of "foundational skills," which initially included reading, writing, and numeracy, but have been expanded to include social and emotional skills and digital literacy.[36] Note that although these skills and skill sets are important in all sectors in the context of Industry 4.0, their relative importance can differ significantly across industries (see Table 3.1 for differences and similarities in the skills importance ranking by employers in the IT-BPO and electronics manufacturing industries).

Conclusion

Although Industry 4.0 has not yet led to major job displacement in the Philippines, industries at high risk from greater adoption of advanced technologies, whether in manufacturing or services, include key growth sectors of the economy. Within these sectors, technology is already transforming the nature of jobs, with an increase in precarious or nonstandard forms of employment.

In an Industry 4.0 environment, where change is the only constant, efficiency considerations favor enterprise-based training (EBT) and private TVET provision. With rapid technological change, some tasks may become redundant and some skills irrelevant. In this context, EBT has an edge, as this modality delivers TVET that is more in line with rapidly evolving workplace and workshop needs. For institutional TVET provision, this highlights the importance of continuous and rigorous industry involvement to mitigate the risk of technological change exacerbating existing skills mismatches between TVET output and market demand.

But equity and inclusion warrant continued public provision. The centrality of skills in determining the impacts of technological change across groups and individuals, and existing inequalities in terms of skills distribution and access to skills acquisition, upgrading, or reskilling across groups (by gender, geography, etc.) points to a key role for skills policy and delivery—alongside labor regulation, social protection, and income redistribution—in achieving inclusive societies.

In this context, workers must be able to move across industries and occupations, along career paths that may be nonlinear. In that regard, all levels of the education and skills supply system need to work in tandem to ensure that flexible pathways exist between different levels of formal education, and for the recognition and development of skills acquired outside formal education (lifelong learning). With respect to TVET, vocational streams and clusters should be used to impart transferable skills and prepare students not only for an entry-level job, but for careers during which they may transition between jobs with similar skill requirements. This suggests a shift away from narrowly defined competencies. Furthermore, although foundational and transversal skills need to be instilled early on in the education process, emphasis on these skills must continue through to post-secondary and tertiary education. In particular, even "generic" skills like problem-solving can be highly context-specific and need to be further developed alongside specialized training in TVET or higher education.[37]

The COVID-19 pandemic has increased the urgency of Industry 4.0 preparedness by precipitating automation and the shift toward digital and technological solutions in many fields, all the while putting a strain on government resources. TESDA must strive to meet its objectives with respect to Industry 4.0, during and beyond the recovery period, while also answering to emerging priorities like reskilling workers displaced by the pandemic.

---

[36] ADB. 2018b. *Asian Development Outlook 2018: How Technology Affects Jobs.* Manila: ADB.
[37] J. Buchanan, L. Wheelahan, and S. Yu. 2018. Increasing Young People's Adaptability and Mobility: From Competency Approach and Twenty-First Century Skills To Capabilities and Vocational Streams. In *Skills and the Future of Work: Strategies for inclusive growth in Asia and the Pacific*, edited by Akiko Sakamoto and Johnny Sung, 125–59. Bangkok: International Labour Organization.

4. Impact of COVID-19 on the Labor Market

The COVID-19 pandemic has had significant economic and labor market impacts worldwide, including in the Philippines. The measures imposed to contain the spread of the virus have effectively shut down major sectors of the economy and had an immediate and sweeping impact on employment. How deep and lasting these labor market effects are remains to be seen, but these will undoubtedly shape the future direction of TVET and work-based learning in the country. As the economy grapples with unprecedented levels of unemployment and job loss, the role of innovative and flexible learning programs such as TESDA's online programs become critical in retooling and upskilling displaced workers. Many trends already underway, like the use of digital tools, have also been accelerated by the pandemic. This provides a unique opportunity for an intensified shift toward learning solutions that use distance and online learning, but also amplify access barriers faced by disadvantaged learners and those in remote areas, with significant implications on social equity and workforce inclusion.

This chapter delves into how COVID-19 has impacted the world of work in the Philippines and, consequently, how TVET can help mitigate the effects. It opens with an estimate of the employment impact of the COVID-19 pandemic using the employment elasticity of growth approach at the sector level. The three rounds of the Philippines' quarterly labor force survey (LFS) are used, conducted in 2020 and available at the time of drafting this report, to analyze how profound and widespread the impacts of this crisis have been. This also allows comparison and validation of the projections presented in this chapter. We find that our projections underestimate the actual labor market impact due to the nature and scale of the COVID-19 crisis. It is also in this chapter that poverty impacts of the pandemic are explored.

Estimating the Effects of the COVID-19 Pandemic on Employment

Employment impacts of COVID-19 are far worse than anything the country has experienced in recent history, with up to 2.1 million projected to lose their jobs in 2020. Measures put in place to contain the spread of COVID-19—lockdowns, travel restrictions, social distancing policies, and workplace and school closures—have impeded economic activity and had an immediate and sweeping impact on employment. Using ADB's latest growth forecast for the Philippines[38] and sector employment elasticities of growth, it is estimated that annual employment growth will decelerate to –2.4% in 2020 (Figure 4.1).[39] This represents a –4.4% deviation from the baseline forecast for 2020 and translates to 2.1 million workers who may lose their jobs as a result of the COVID-19 pandemic.

---

[38] Note that we also used the International Monetary Fund's June 2020 World Economic Outlook and the Department of Budget and Management's revised forecast released in August 2020 to estimate the employment effects of COVID-19. However, in this chapter, we only present the estimates derived using ADB's Asian Development Outlook (ADO) growth forecast for simplicity and clarity of analysis. ADB's ADO forecast is also the most recent at the time of writing.

[39] Refer to Appendix 4.1 for a detailed discussion of the methodology for the estimating employment impacts of the COVID-19 pandemic.

Figure 4.1: **Real Gross Domestic Product Growth Rate and Employment Growth Rate, 2008–2021**

GDP = gross domestic product.
Source: ADB estimates.

COVID-19 has disrupted economic activity, pushing the Philippines into its first recession in 29 years. The extended lockdown measures, particularly in Luzon, which accounts for 70% of the country's GDP, propelled the Philippines into an economic recession by the second quarter of 2020—the first in 29 years. Before the COVID-19 pandemic, the government projected GDP growth to increase to 6.5% in 2020 and 7% in 2021 (Figure 4.1).[40] The most recent GDP growth forecast of ADB's Asian Development Outlook released in September, forecasts a 7.3% GDP contraction in 2020, a steeper decline than the earlier 3.2% forecast in July, signaling the severity of the COVID-19 shock to the economy and worsening economic prospects.

Not all of those who lose their jobs will become unemployed; many will drop out of the labor force and others are expected to move to lower-productivity sectors. Of the 2.1 million workers who may lose their jobs in 2020, relative to the pre-COVID baseline scenario, about 1.5 million (about 68%) could become unemployed, raising the unemployment rate from 5.1% in 2019 to 8.5% in 2020. An additional 389,000 workers (about 18%) may drop out of the labor force altogether. Finally, about 288,000 workers are expected to shift to lower-productivity sectors, predominantly agriculture. Such labor reallocation is typical following economic shocks in the context of developing economies, where in the absence of social protections, displaced workers cannot afford

---

[40] NEDA. 2019b. Joint Statement on the 176th DBCC Meeting: Review of the Macroeconomic Assumptions and Fiscal Program for the 2020 President's Budget. 18 July. https://www.neda.gov.ph/joint-statement-on-the-176th-dbcc-meeting-review-of-the-macroeconomic-assumptions-and-fiscal-program-for-the-2020-presidents-budget/ (accessed 11 December 2020).

to remain unemployed and therefore shift to lower-productivity employment often in agriculture or in informal employment in low-productivity services.

The industrial sector displays both the largest economic and employment impacts. Gross value added (GVA) growth in industry decreased by −22.9% (year-on-year) compared to that of the services sector at −15.8% (year-on-year) (Figure 4.2). Within the industry sector, the economic shutdown disproportionately affected construction and manufacturing (Figure 4.4). The strict quarantine measures suspended economic

Figure 4.2: Real Gross Value Added Growth Rate by Industry Group, Year-on-Year

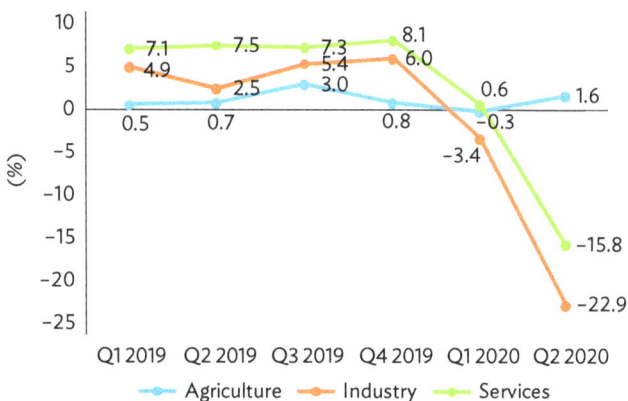

Note: Gross value added at constant 2018 prices.
Source: National Accounts, Philippine Statistics Authority; ADB estimates.

Figure 4.3: Estimated Change in Employment by Broad Industry Group

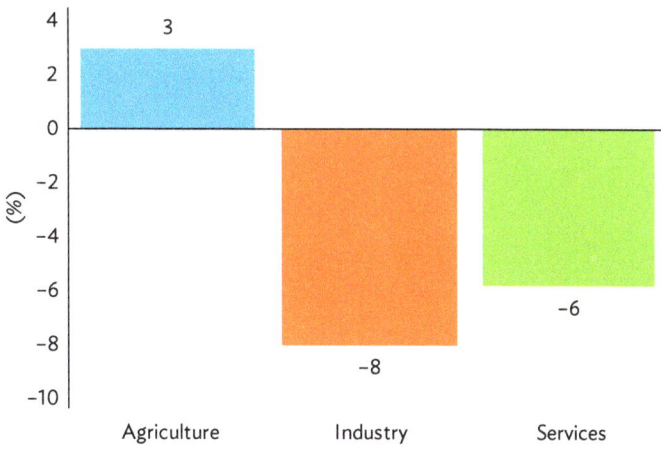

Source: ADB estimates.

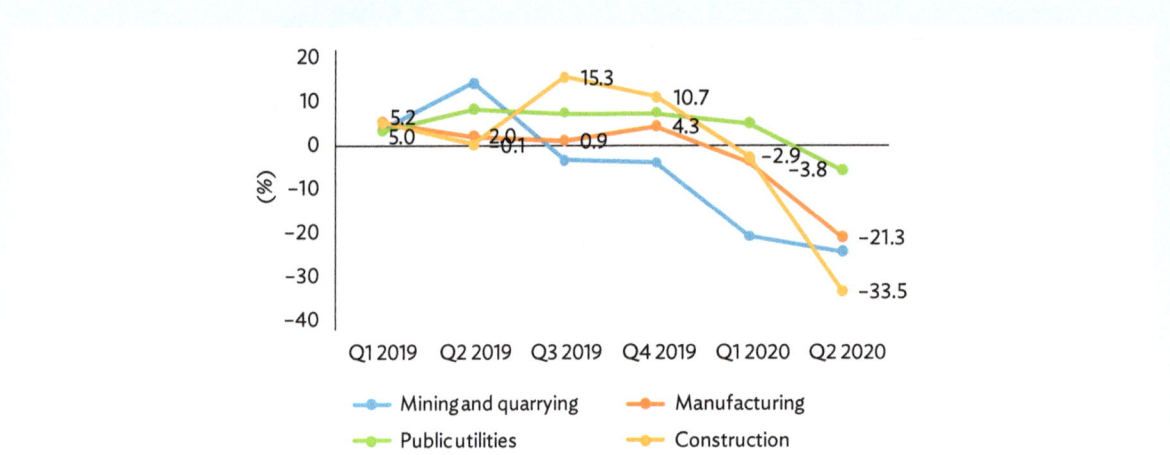

Figure 4.4: Real Gross Value Added Growth Rate by Industry Sectors, Year-on-Year

Note: Gross value added at constant 2018 prices.
Source: National Accounts, Philippine Statistics Authority; ADB estimates.

activities, including infrastructure development projects, and triggered the sharp construction drop. The closure of all establishments except those providing essentials such as food and medicine had negatively impacted manufacturing. Using sector employment elasticities, it was estimated that the industry sector would exhibit an 8% decline in employment as a result of COVID-19, equivalent to 670,000 jobs—around 500,000 accounted for by construction and another 100,000 in manufacturing (Figure 4.5).

The agriculture sector, relatively resilient to the COVID-19 impact, is expected to exhibit a net increase in employment, in part reflecting worker relocation. The agriculture sector, bolstered by a strong rice production growth and a sustained domestic demand for food, has been more resilient, and is posting a positive growth (Figure 4.2). While the employment elasticity estimates suggest this corresponds to an increase in employment, the estimated increase of 3% also includes job relocation to lower-productivity sectors, of which agriculture is anticipated to be a major recipient (Figure 4.3).

Areas of the services sector reliant on tourism were among the hardest hit by the COVID-19 outbreak. Visitor arrivals in January–July 2020 dropped by about 3.5 million and tourism receipts dropped by about P208 billion compared to the same period in 2019. Real GVA of tourism-related industries such as accommodation and food services plunged from a 7.8% growth rate in the last quarter of 2019 to –16.4% in the first quarter of 2020 and to –68% in the second quarter of 2020 (Figure 4.6). Precipitous declines in year-on-year growth were also recorded in transport and storage and arts and recreation industries at –63.2% and –59.2%, respectively (Figure 4.6). Examining the estimated job loss in the services sector, we find the steepest decline in wholesale and retail trade, north of 500,000 (Figure 4.7). There is also significant job loss in accommodation and food services, estimated at around 265,000. We also estimate a decline of about 100,000 jobs in transportation and storage, public administration and defense, and other services (Figure 4.7).

Overall, non-tradable sectors exhibit the steepest decline in employment. The projected estimates indicate a decline in employment across tradable sectors, such as manufacturing and transportation and storage, due to declining global demand. However, there were higher net job losses in non-tradable industries

Figure 4.5: Estimated Job Losses in the Industry Sectors

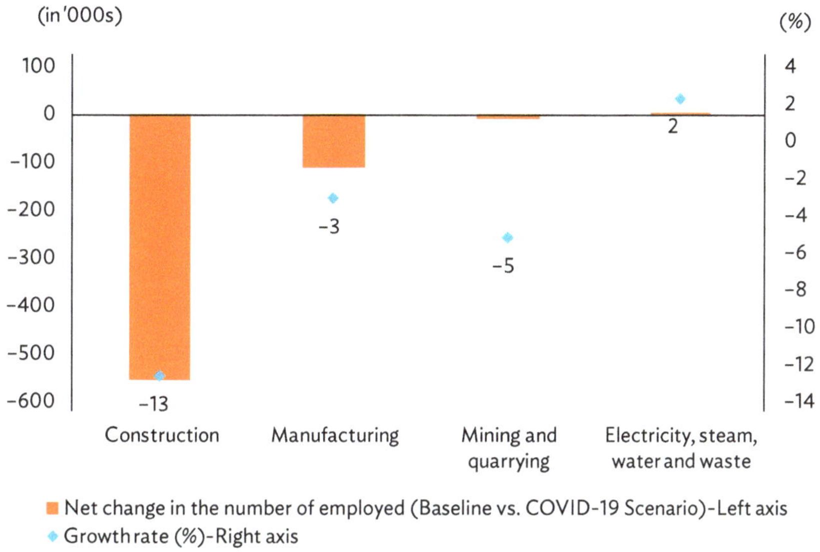

■ Net change in the number of employed (Baseline vs. COVID-19 Scenario)-Left axis
◆ Growth rate (%)-Right axis

Source: ADB estimates.

Figure 4.6: Real Gross Value Added Growth Rate for Most Affected Services Sectors, Year-on-Year

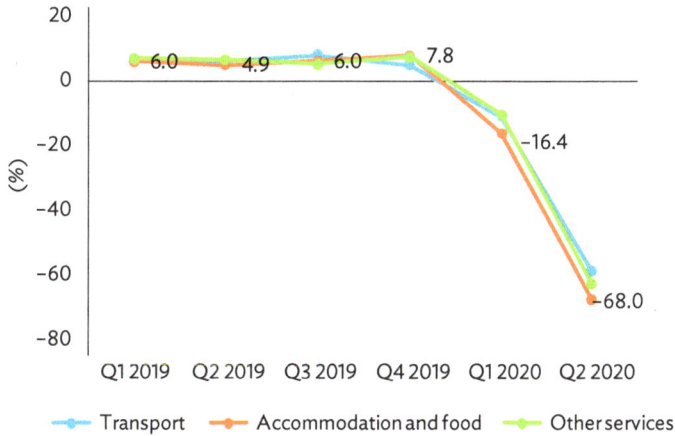

Note: Gross value added at constant 2018 prices.
Source: National Accounts, Philippine Statistics Authority; ADB estimates.

Figure 4.7: Estimated Job Losses in the Services Sectors

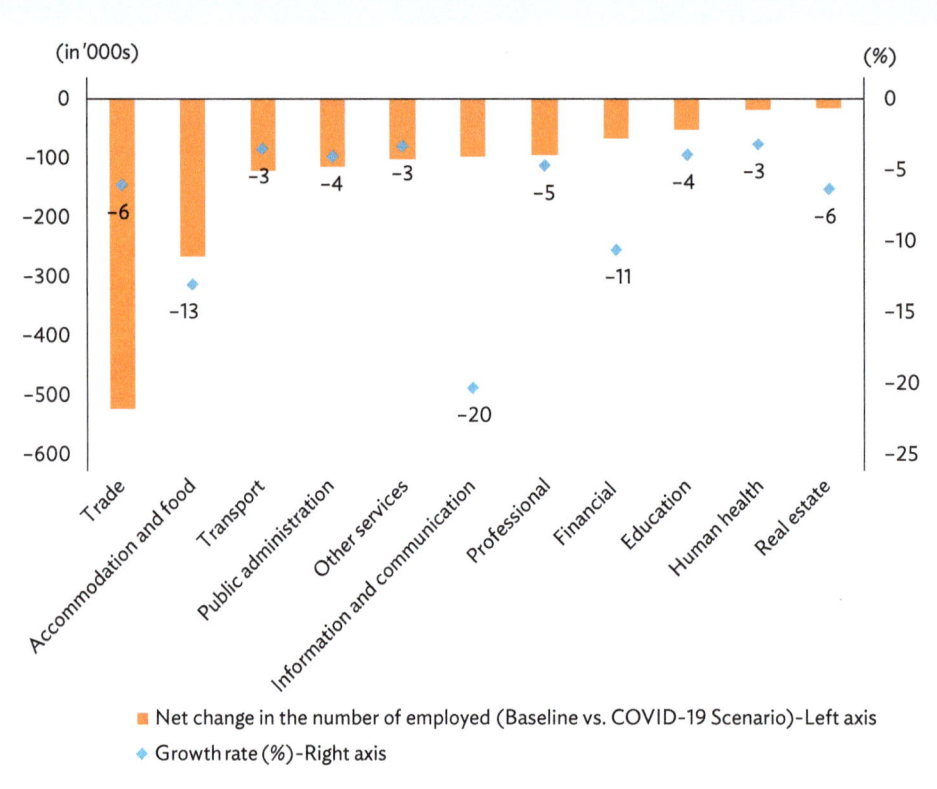

Source: ADB estimates.

(construction, retail trade, accommodation and food services, and public administration) due to the lockdown measures imposed during this crisis.

Recent Labor Force Survey Findings

Unemployment surged following lockdown measures to contain the COVID-19 outbreak. The country's unemployment rate, which has hovered at around 5%–8% over the past 15 years, soared to 17.7% in April 2020 following stringent lockdown measures (Figure 4.8). This corresponded to 7.3 million unemployed in April, mostly following job losses in services—mainly wholesale and retail trade, transport, accommodation and food services, arts and entertainment—and industry, primarily manufacturing.

Lower-income and lower-skilled workers have been disproportionately affected during this period of the country's most widespread and stringent lockdowns. The increase in the number of unemployed in terms of percentage growth was highest among those with no education, only elementary, and those with junior high school education (Table 4.1). Moreover, 64% of the unemployed in April 2020 are those with no education, only elementary, and junior high school education. Workers with higher education are more likely to be in more secure, less vulnerable jobs, where their working time may have been reduced, but their jobs are preserved. Moreover, as shown by a recent study of von Gaudecker et al. (2020) in the Netherlands,

Figure 4.8: Unemployment, April 2005–July 2020

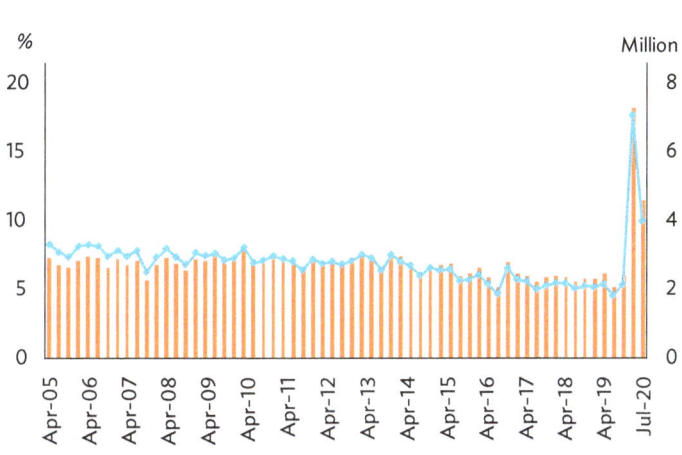

Source: CEIC Data Company. https://www.ceicdata.com/en (accessed 14 September 2020).

Table 4.1: Unemployed Persons by Highest Grade Completed, April 2020 versus April 2019

	April 2020	April 2019	Growth (%)
UNEMPLOYED PERSONS	7,254	2,267	220
HIGHEST GRADE COMPLETED (% of total)			
No grade completed	0.7	0.5	336
Elementary	19.3	14.1	336
Junior high school	43.6	37.2	275
Senior high school	3.6	5.1	123
Post-secondary	5.1	8.5	94
College	27.8	34.5	157

Source: Philippine Statistics Authority, labor force survey.

workers with higher education are more likely to be employed in jobs where remote work is possible and thus experienced lower likelihood of job loss and substantial reductions in hours worked.

Around 7.5 million jobs were restored with the easing of restrictions. Data for July 2020 show evidence of improvements in the labor market, whereby about 2.7 million jobs were recovered, and another 4.9 million workers rejoined the labor force (Figure 4.9). There is even a recovery in sectors that experienced sharp declines in April, such as the wholesale and retail trade, construction, manufacturing, agriculture, and transport and storage.

Projected impacts fall short of the actual job loss shown by the 2020 preliminary numbers. Comparing the projected job losses derived earlier to the actual numbers from the most recent LFS tells us only one thing—despite the bleak estimates presented in the preceding section, the actual employment numbers paint an even graver picture. Using preliminary 2020 employment numbers—the average of the January, April, and July LFS rounds—around 3.2 million workers would lose their jobs in 2020 (Table 4.2). Around 77% of workers who may lose their jobs would become unemployed, raising the unemployment rate in 2020 to about 10.8% from 5.1% in 2019. Around 749,000 workers would drop out of the labor force, and about 59,000 would shift to other sectors, mainly agriculture.

Figure 4.9: Working-Age Population by Labor Market Status

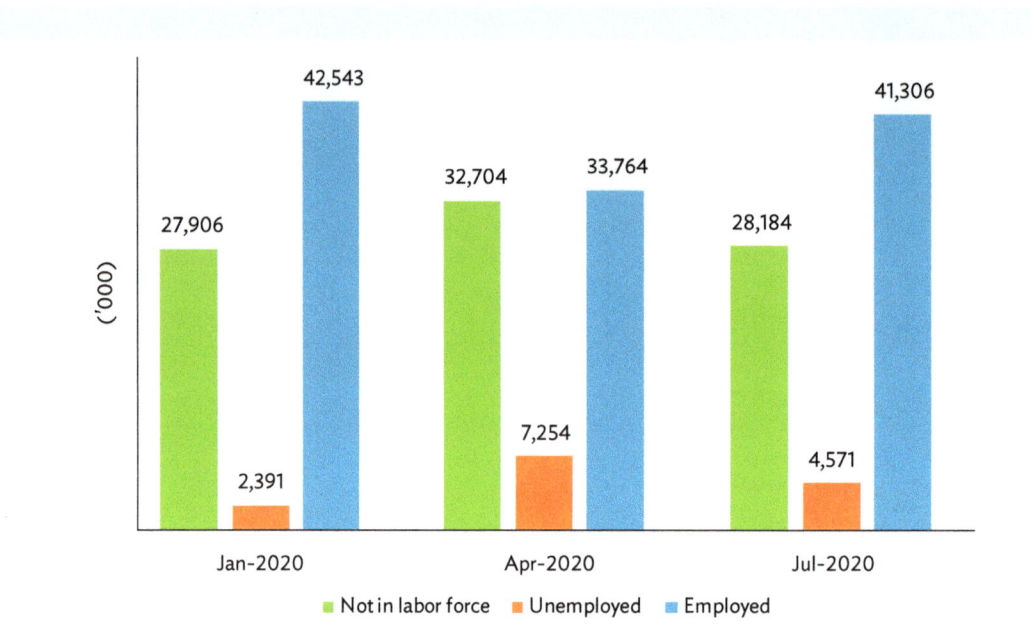

Source: CEIC Data Company. https://www.ceicdata.com/en (accessed 14 September 2020).

Table 4.2: Job Losses and Labor Reallocation, 2020

Item	Projections/Estimates ('000)	(%)	Actual (Q1–Q3) ('000)	(%)
Workers who would lose their job in 2020	2,136		3,282	
And become unemployed	1,459	68	2,475	76
Drop out of the labor force	389	18	749	23
Shift to low productivity sectors	288	13	58	2

Source: ADB estimates.

Most affected sectors in 2020 in terms of job loss are similar to projected estimates, although job losses were often underestimated. Projected estimates fall short in terms of magnitude, particularly in construction, wholesale and retail trade, transportation and storage, accommodation and food services, other services, manufacturing, and public administration (Table A4.1). These sectors account for 87% of the job loss in 2020, with 2.9 million jobs lost. Projections indicate that we have underestimated the job losses in accommodation and food services, manufacturing, other services, and transportation and storage by as much as 1 million (Figure 4.10). The underestimate reflects the nature of the measures imposed to contain the COVID-19 crisis in the country, which has effectively shut down all non-essential businesses beginning mid-March. The Philippines imposed one of the most stringent containment policies in the region, considering it also had the highest number of COVID-19 cases in Southeast Asia (Figure 4.11).[41] Although restrictions have eased up a bit,

---

[41] The stringency index comes from Oxford University's COVID-19 Government Response Tracker, which measures the stringency of government measures imposed as a response to the COVID-19 outbreak—including school and workplace closures, travel and transport bans, stay-at-home requirements, and restrictions on large gatherings and public events. As of 30 September 2020, the Philippines has 311,694 COVID-19 cases in total.

Figure 4.10: Job Losses due to COVID-19 in Selected Sectors, 2020 Preliminary versus Projections

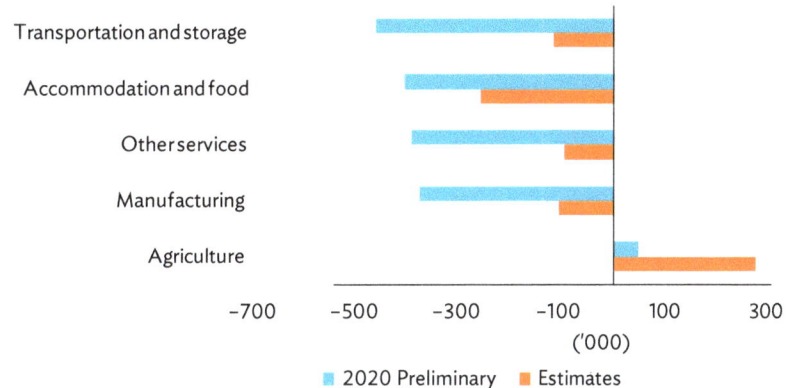

Note: 2020 data based on the average of the January, April, and July labor force survey rounds.
Source: ADB estimates.

Figure 4.11: COVID-19 Stringency and Mobility in the Philippines

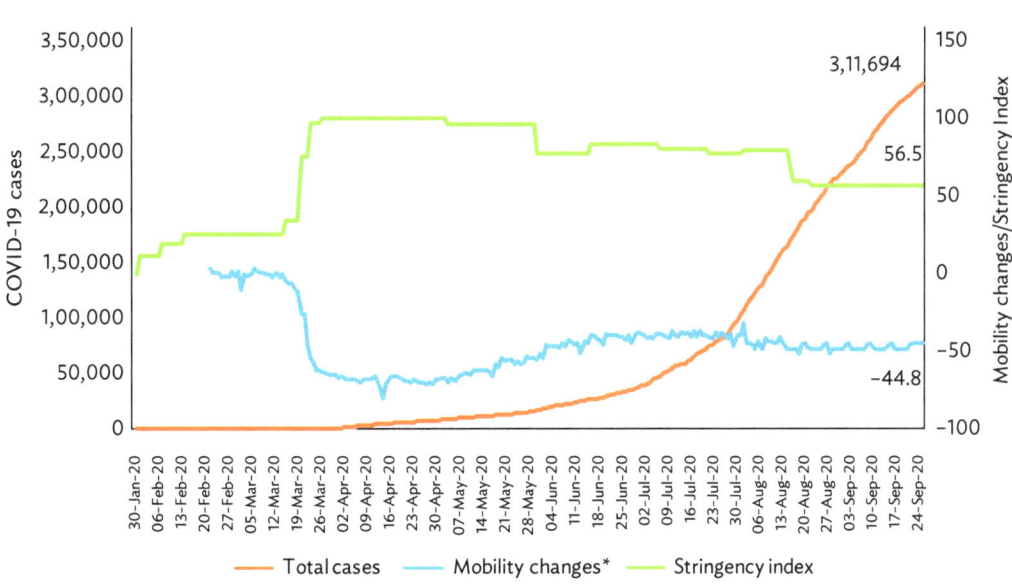

Source: ADB COVID-19 Monitoring Dashboard. https://app.klipfolio.com/published/f0c6657be7cff11c4e82ec35888bb0e9/covid19-monitoring-dashboard (accessed 5 October 2020).

Figure 4.12: Change in Employment by Working Time, Selected Sectors

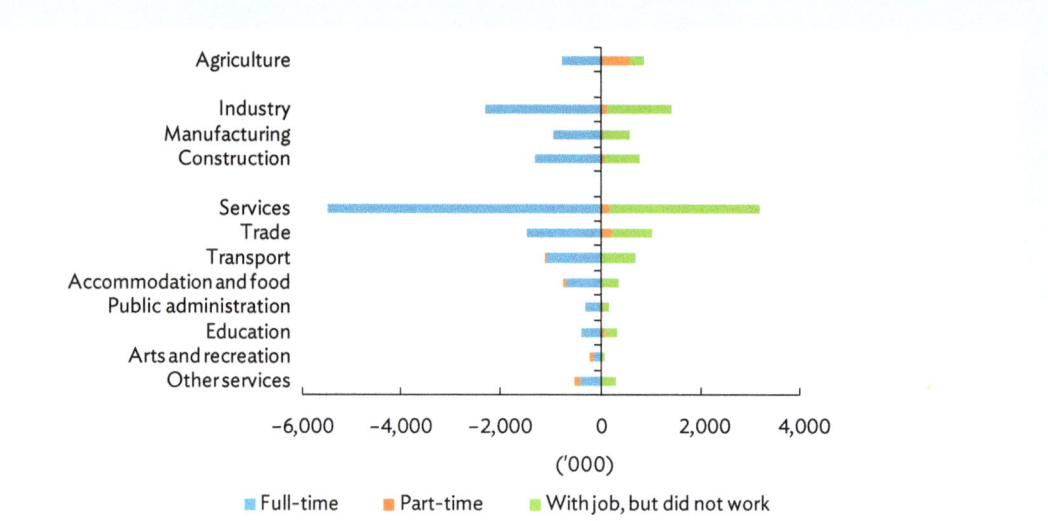

Note: Data based on the average of the January, April, and July labor force survey rounds.
Source: Philippine Statistics Authority.

movement outside the home remains dramatically diminished, down by 45% relative to the baseline before the COVID-19 pandemic.[42]

Moreover, although some displaced workers shifted to agriculture, the stringent lockdown measures severely constrained mobility and thus prevented large-scale labor reallocation to agriculture. Restrictions on movement also prevented farmers from accessing markets and resulted in food waste, especially in the early days of the lockdown in April.[43] Thus, we see that we have also overestimated the extent of labor reallocation to agriculture in our projections (Figure 4.10).

The pandemic also had a significant impact on hours worked—a sharp rise in part-time work and those employed but who did not work. While many workers lost their jobs, others shifted to part-time work, and a larger number reported having a job but not having worked, particularly in the most affected sectors (Figure 4.12). The decline in full-time employment is especially severe in the arts, entertainment, and recreation (–59%); accommodation and food services (–47%); real estate activities (–45%); transportation and storage (–43%); and information and communication (–41%). There is an increase number of workers that worked part-time (defined as less than 40 hours a week) notably in agriculture, wholesale and retail trade, education, construction and public administration and defense, and administrative and support services.

---

[42] Refers to the percentage change in visitor numbers to specific locations—such as shopping centers, grocery stores, parks, transit stations, workplaces—relative to the baseline before the pandemic. Mobility outside the home data comes from Google's COVID-19 Community Mobility Reports.
[43] R. Rivas. 2020. Farmers Trash Spoiled Vegetables While Poor Go Hungry. *Rappler*. 6 April. https://www.rappler.com/newsbreak/in-depth/farmers-trash-spoiled-vegetables-urban-poor-hungry-coronavirus-lockdown.

The most marked change in 2020 is the sharp rise in workers in all sectors who reported they had a job but did not work during the reference period. In 2019, there were only 349,000 workers in this situation. In 2020, this number jumped to 4.9 million, a worrying change since some of these workers likely earned no income during the period of inactivity, especially workers paid per day, per hour, per piece of output, or on a commission basis.

Impact of COVID-19 on Working Poverty

This section estimates the impact on the working poor as a result of COVID-19, through reduced number of jobs and working hours.[44] The estimates suggest that the number of working poor increased to around 5.6 million in 2020, up by 6% compared to 2018, reflective of an additional 403,000 workers to be pushed into poverty because of COVID-19 (Figure 4.13). The bulk of the working poor, around 57%, are employed in agriculture (Figure 4.13). Further, we see that the number of working poor is also high in sectors most affected by the pandemic: wholesale and retail trade, construction, other services, and manufacturing. By the number of hours worked, we see that most working poor were employed in part-time work.

Limiting the analysis to working poverty may significantly underestimate the poverty impacts of COVID-19 by excluding the large number of workers who became unemployed. This becomes apparent when we look at the change in the number of working poor in 2020 relative to 2018, where we see a reduction in the number of working poor in sectors that experienced sharp declines in the number of employed, such as in construction, other services, accommodation and food services, and transportation and storage (Figure 4.14a). Therefore, adjusting our estimates to account for the workers who shift from employed to the unemployed status, we estimate the number of workers potentially to be pushed into

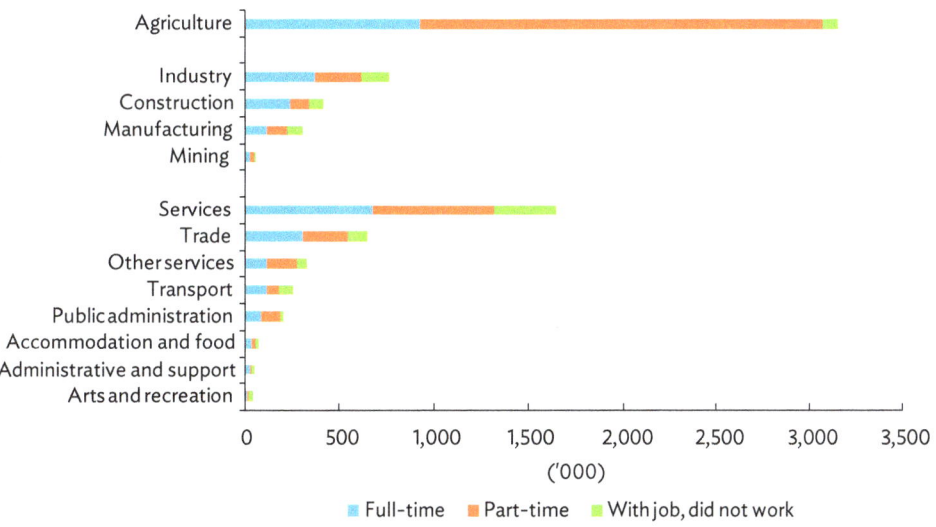

Figure 4.13: Number of Working Poor in Select Sectors, 2020

Source: ADB estimates.

---

[44] Appendix 4.2 provides a detailed discussion of the methodology used in estimating the poverty effects of COVID-19.

Figure 4.14: Change in the Number of Poor, 2020 versus 2018, Various Approaches

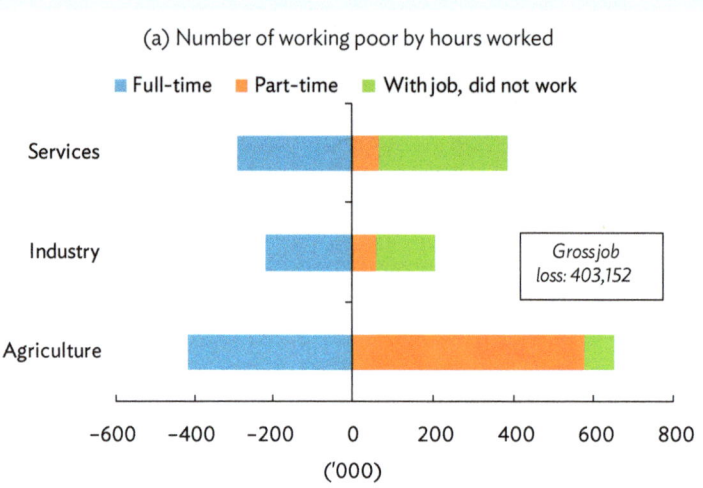

(a) Number of working poor by hours worked

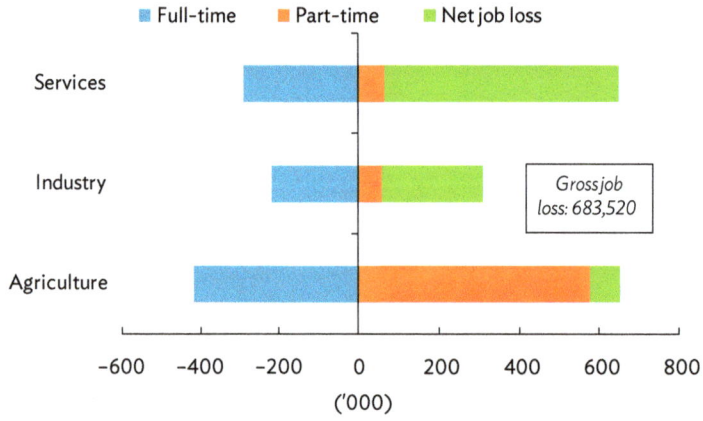

(b) Added those who newly lost their jobs to "with a job, did not work" to get the net job loss

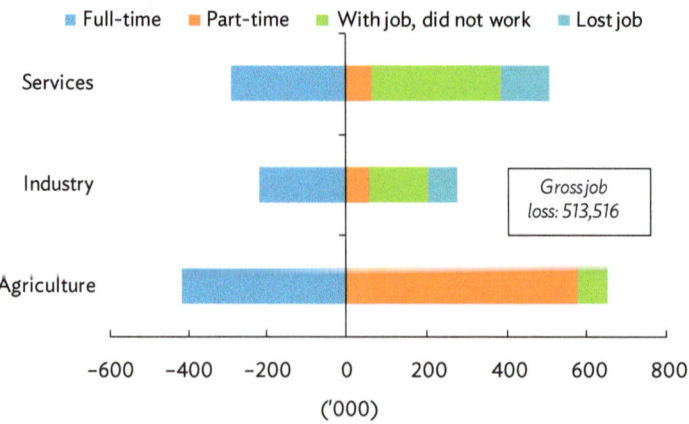

(c) Used the share of workers with income >20% of the poverty threshold to get the number of additional poor due to unemployment

Figure 4.14: *continued*

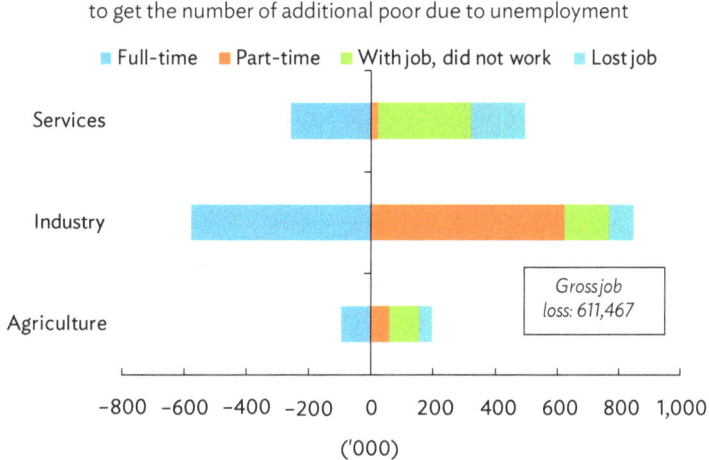

Note: Appendix 4.2 provides a discussion of the approaches used to estimate the poverty effects of COVID-19.
Source: ADB estimates.

poverty to be around 514,000–684,000 (Figure 4.14b to Figure 4.14d) in 2020. These estimates refer neither to the working poor per se nor to overall poverty. The adjusted estimates presented here capture the increase in the number of working poor due to reduced work hours, the increase in the number of working poor due to sectoral reallocation of labor, and the additional poverty effect as workers shift from employment to unemployment.

Conclusions

Using sectoral employment elasticities to project the impact of COVID-19 on the Philippines labor market in 2020 and the first three rounds of labor force surveys available for the year to estimate the actual impacts, we find that these impacts of the pandemic have been substantial and unprecedented. The number of unemployed increased, the number of employed decreased, labor force participation dropped, and, among those who remained employed, there was a massive inflow into part-time work and an increase in the ranks of those with a job but who did not work.

We find that job loss disproportionately affected those in low-productivity sectors, primarily low-skilled workers, and that lockdown measures significantly prevented large-scale labor reallocation toward low-productivity sectors like agriculture and trade. Most affected sectors included construction, transportation, tourism, and trade that employ large numbers of low-skilled workers. The limited labor reallocation resulted in greater unemployment hikes than would have occurred if more displaced workers shifted to other sectors, as in previous economic shocks.

The adverse impacts of the COVID-19 pandemic threaten to wipe out the gains in poverty reduction achieved over the past decade and push a significant number of displaced workers into poverty. The pandemic amplifies the existing inequality faced by the working poor and those in low-paid jobs who cannot afford to stay at home and thus must choose between risking their health or losing their income.

Much is expected from TVET during this time. The COVID-19 shock has not only resulted in massive job displacements, disproportionately affecting lower-skilled workers, but has also affected learning. The surge in the number of registered users of TESDA's Online Program amid the pandemic underscores the value of using digital platforms to make TVET more accessible and relevant. However, transitioning to more IT-based teaching and learning approaches can exclude learners who lack the equipment and technology to gain meaningful access. Thus, TESDA's adoption of flexible learning—which utilizes online, blended (online and face-to-face), and distance learning (for those without internet connection and computers)—ensures everyone has access to learning.[45] However, TESDA may not have sufficient equipment to roll out blended learning programs in the country's provinces. Thus, the procurement of ICT equipment such as laptops, computers, and ICT structures form part of TESDA's P13.5 billion proposed 2021 budget.[46]

The COVID-19 pandemic has demonstrated that TESDA can respond swiftly and relevantly to the country's massive economic and social demands. However, there is a need for a greater, more targeted effort toward reskilling workers who have lost their jobs, especially in the hardest-hit sectors. Moreover, besides ensuring that TVET provision is resilient to school disruptions and responsive to the digital economy's challenges, the curricula should reflect the increasing importance of technical and ICT skills—skills that allow Filipinos to thrive in the post-COVID-19 workplace.

---

[45] TESDA defines distance learning as the use of print learning materials and non-digital electronic resources. The following is the exact definition from TESDA Circular No. 062 series 2020: "Distance Learning: takes place outside the training institution for both the knowledge contents and skills components with print learning materials and non-digital electronic resources. This is preferred for TVET programs that require no, or limited use of large and/or complicated learning equipment and suitable for TVIs, trainers and learners with limited capacity to adopt Blended Learning and Online Learning delivery modes."

[46] CNN Philippines. 2020. *TESDA Lacks Equipment for Blended Learning*. 9 September. https://cnnphilippines.com/news/2020/9/9/TESDA-lacks-equipment-blended-learning.html.

Appendix 4.1: Elasticities-Based Approach for Projecting the Impact of COVID-19 on Employment

Employment elasticity of growth is a labor market indicator that provides a useful insight into how employment varies with economic growth, i.e., how much employment growth is associated with 1 percentage point of economic growth.[47] We use this measure to generate the projected impact of COVID-19 on employment in the Philippines.

Thus, the analysis involves estimating the following log-linear equation for the time period 2007–2019:

$$\ln(Employment_i) = \alpha + \beta_i \ln(GVA_i) + \varepsilon_i$$

where $Employment_i$ refers to the number of employed in sector i, GVA_i is the gross value added of sector i, and β_i is the sectoral employment elasticity of sector i. We adjusted the employment elasticity of the public administration sector to reflect the observed job security aspect of public sector jobs (Kopelman and Rosen, 2014). We added an exogenous assumption that permanent jobs in this sector are unaffected by the COVID-19 shock—no job loss and no job growth for 2020–2021. Thus, only nonpermanent status workers in this sector experienced job loss due to the pandemic.

To calculate the projected job losses due to COVID-19 by sector, we first extrapolate sectoral GVA projections for 2020–2021. We use the pre-COVID real GDP projections of the Department of Budget and Management for the baseline scenario and ADB's Asian Development Outlook real GDP forecast for the COVID-19 scenario. Using the GVA projections and the derived employment elasticities (β_i), we obtain the sectoral employment projections for 2020–2021.

Labor market indicators—labor force, working-age, employed, and unemployed—for 2020 and 2021 were estimated by extrapolating the labor force participation rates using projected employment numbers and working-age population (which we assumed does not change due to the pandemic). Other employment indicators were derived from the employment and labor force estimates using standard definitions.

All data used in this chapter—the labor market, real GDP, and GVA series—come from the Philippine Statistics Authority (PSA).

---

[47] S. Kapsos. 2005. *The Employment Intensity of Growth: Trends and Macroeconomic Determinants*. ILO Employment Strategy Papers 2005/12. Geneva: International Labour Office.

Appendix 4.2: Methodology of Estimating the Poverty Impact of COVID-19

To estimate the poverty impacts of COVID-19, we use microdata from the 2018 merged Family Income and Expenditure Survey (FIES) with the LFS and the 2020 LFS. The 2018 merged FIES–LFS data set matches employment data from the LFS with the FIES household income data, which allows us to identify employed persons living in a household whose income falls below the poverty threshold. We note that the methodology utilized here is constrained by the availability of only 1 year of the merged FIES–LFS data.

- Step 1. Calculate the number (and rate) of working poor by sector in 2018. Working poor are employed persons living in a household whose annual per capita income is below ₱25,813.
- Step 2. Find the working poverty rates by the number of hours worked in 2018 (part-time, full-time, or with a job, but did not work).
- Step 3. Estimate the change in working poverty in 2020 due to (i) sector reallocation effect, i.e., the change in working poverty due to sector shifts in employment; and (ii) within-sector effect, i.e., the change in working poverty due to changes in the number of hours worked.

The analysis, however, only captures the poverty effects concerning the employed. Given the massive unemployment brought about by the COVID-19 pandemic, we broaden our scope to include these workers. To account for the poverty effect of workers going from employed to unemployed status, we try out various alternative approaches. First, we add the number of unemployed to workers with a job but did not work during the reference period. Second, we hypothesize that workers who become unemployed do not automatically fall into poverty if they were not at the margin of poverty initially.

- Step 4. Add the number of unemployed to the workers with a job but who did not work during the reference period. Apply the 2018 working poverty rate of "with a job, did not work" to estimate the 2020 number of working poor for this group.
- Step 5. Calculate the share of workers with incomes higher than 10%, 20%, or 30% of the poverty threshold in 2018 by sector. Use this rate to estimate the number of workers that could be pushed into poverty due to unemployment in 2020.

Thus, the poverty effect we are capturing in the analysis goes beyond working poverty but does not pertain to overall poverty as well. The estimates presented here can be defined as the: (i) increase in the number of working poor because of reduced work hours; (ii) increase in the number of working poor due to sectoral reallocation of labor; and (iii) additional poverty effect due to workers shifting from employment to unemployment.

Appendix 4.3: Employment Impact of COVID-19 and Estimated Job Losses by Sector, 2020

Industry	2020 Employment Projections ('000)			Actual employment ('000)		
	Baseline	COVID-19 Scenario	Net change in the number of employed (Baseline vs. COVID-19 Scenario)	2019	2020p	Net change in the number of employed (2019 vs. 2020p)
Agriculture, forestry and fishing	9,568	9,852	284	9,698	9,746	48
Mining and quarrying	189	179	−10	184	194	9
Manufacturing	3,667	3,556	−111	3,618	3,236	−382
Electricity, steam, water and waste mgt.	154	158	4	156	143	−13
Construction	4,393	3,840	−553	4,153	3,605	−548
Wholesale and retail trade	8,704	8,180	−524	8,453	7,979	−474
Transportation and storage	3,487	3,366	−121	3,432	2,965	−467
Accommodation and food service activities	2,038	1,773	−265	1,918	1,506	−411
Information and communication	471	376	−95	425	315	−110
Financial and insurance activities	612	548	−65	582	540	−41
Real estate and ownership of dwellings	239	224	−15	232	197	−35
Professional and business services	2,003	1,909	−93	1,961	1,817	−144
Public administration and defense	2,839	2,725	−114	2,785	2,613	−172
Education	1,305	1,254	−51	1,283	1,221	−62
Human health and social work activities	553	535	−17	543	524	−19
Other services	3,055	2,955	−100	3,006	2,608	−399
	43,277	41,429	−1,848	42,428	39,209	−3,220
	Gross job loss		**−2,136**			**−3,277**

p = preliminary.
Note: 2020 data based on the average of the January, April, and July labor force survey rounds.
Source: ADB estimates.

Technology-based learning. Keeping up with the needs of Industry 4.0 through in-demand skills provision.

PART II
TECHNICAL AND VOCATIONAL EDUCATION AND TRAINING AND THE EDUCATION SYSTEM IN THE PHILIPPINES

Part II of the technical and vocational education and training (TVET) sector study provides an overview of TVET provision in the Philippines, including in the context of the education system. Chapter 5 addresses the structure of the Technical Education and Skills Development Authority (TESDA), key features in the national development agenda, and system preparedness for Industry 4.0. Chapter 6 addresses education system reform over the past 3 decades, highlighting TVET imperatives. Finally, Chapter 7 addresses TVET trends over the last decade in the Philippines, including a regional breakdown.

5. Technical and Vocational Education and Training Provision in the Context of Industry 4.0

TESDA is the TVET authority in the Philippines. TESDA's programs and policies ensure quality and clarify priorities for TVET through research studies, standards development, and certification and information dissemination. For the last 25 years, TESDA has evolved to play a multifaceted role providing varied technical education and skills development (TESD) programs and activities, including for the marginalized sector of Philippine society and responding to needs such as those arising from COVID-19 (Boxes 5.1 and 5.2). These functions have represented both strengths and challenges for TESDA given resources constraints, demands of emerging technologies associated with Industry 4.0, and implications for the future of skills development in the Philippines.

This chapter provides an overview of the structure of TESDA, key features of TVET in the Philippines, TVET in the national development agenda, TVET system preparedness for Industry 4.0, and key issues for TESDA's relevance and effectiveness.

Structure of the Technical Education and Skills Development Authority

TESDA's policy direction is grounded in the legal mandate of Republic Act (RA) 7796.[48] The vision and mission, outlined in Figure 5.1, express the aspirations and purpose of TESDA, and provides a reference point for plans and programs of the organization. TESDA's current reform and development agenda is described in the National Technical Education and Skills Development Plan (NTESDP) 2018–2022 (Appendix 5).[49]

The policymaking structure of TESDA is composed of the TESDA Board and various local TESD committees. The TESDA Board is the highest policymaking body, while the local TESD committees oversee the regions and provinces. Both regional and provincial TESD committees provide the necessary inputs through resolutions for policy development for adoption by the TESDA Board. The final decision and policy promulgation are made by the TESDA Board. Composition of the board and local TESD committees are from the government, industry, labor, and academia. Advisory councils for TESDA technology institutions (TTIs) serve as additional policymaking bodies, composed of government, industry, and academe.[50] The purpose of these advisory councils is to provide policy advice and guidance and to build networks of the TESDA-administered schools and regional training centers.

The corporate structure of TESDA is composed of the TESDA Board and Secretariat. While the board is the policymaking body, the secretariat takes charge of organizational management. COROPOTTI—which stands for the Central Office, Regional Office, Provincial Office and TTIs—serves as the Secretariat of TESDA (Figure 5.2). The organizational arrangements of the field offices are linked to the major final outputs of

---

[48] Republic Act (RA) No. 7796. 1994a. An act creating the Technical Education and Skills Development Authority, providing for its powers, structure and for other purposes. Philippines.
[49] TESDA. 2018a. *National Technical Education and Skills Development Plan (NTESDP) 2018–2022*. Taguig.
[50] TESDA Circular No. 49. 2019. Implementing Guidelines on the New TVET Governance Ecosystem: Creation of the TESDA Technology Institution (TTI) Advisory Council. Taguig: TESDA.

Figure 5.1: **Organizational Anchors of Technical Education and Skills Development Authority**

LEGAL MANDATE

RA 7796 or TESDA Act of 1994 - sets out the policy and goals of the government with respect to technical education, provides for a technical education plan, and establishes the Technical Education and Skills Development Authority (TESDA) to implement the policy and plan.

VISION

TESDA as the transformational leader in the technical education and skills development of the Filipino workforce.

MISSION

TESDA sets direction, promulgates relevant standards, and implements programs geared toward a quality-assured and inclusive technical education and skills development and certification system.

REFORM AND DEVELOPMENT AGENDA

National Technical Education and Skills Development Plan (NTESDP) 2018-2022. The NTESDAP was developed by TESDA in consultation with key stakeholders across the technical and vocational education and training (TVET) sector, and sets the policy direction of TVET programs and action plans from 2018 to 2022 in line with the twin goals of achieving global competitiveness and ensuring social equity.

Source: Authors' depiction based on various sources.

Figure 5.2: **Structure of Technical Education and Skills Development Authority Secretariat**

TESDA Secretariat (COROPOTTI)

Central office	Contains the offices of the director general and deputy director generals along with the executive offices tasked to handle the key organizational processes, which are planning, qualifications and standards; support for the National Institute for Technical Education and Skills Development; partnerships and linkages; certification; Regional Operations Management Office; administrative service; and financial and management services
Regional offices Provincial offices	The field offices (regional and provincial) perform the line functions under the auspices of the central office, which provides guidance and direction in the delivery of services to the clientele.
TESDA Technology Institutions (TTIs)	The TTIs provide direct training services. TESDA has a total of 124 TTIs, with 5 special training centers, 16 regional training centers, 46 provincial training centers, and 57 TESDA-administered schools.

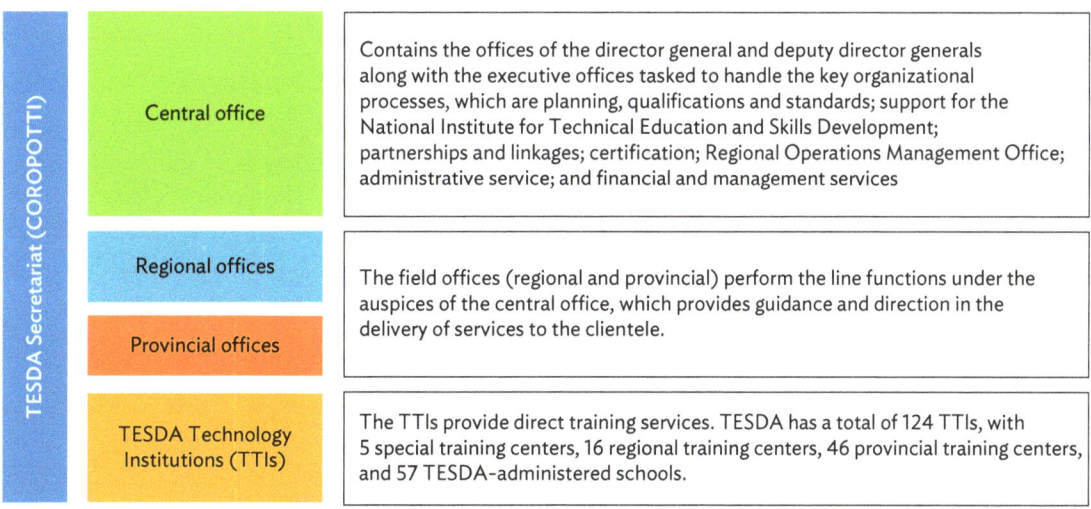

COROPOTTI = Central Office, Regional Office, Provincial Office and TESDA Technology Institutions;
TESDA = Technical Education and Skills Development Authority.

Source: Authors' depiction based on various sources.

TESDA, i.e., policy services, TESD services, and regulatory services. Each major final output has corresponding processes or programs, like the Unified TVET Program Registration and Accreditation System (UTPRAS) and the competency assessment and certification (CAC) for regulatory services; scholarships for TESD services; and planning, monitoring, and management IT and other processes for the major final output on policy services. On the other hand, the TTIs have teaching and training staff for their operations and technical division.

TESDA has established programs and systems to ensure quality of all TVET efforts. This is achieved through: (i) development of standards or training regulations and assessment tools, (ii) registration and accreditation of TVET programs through the UTPRAS, and (iii) conduct of the CAC system. These programs, systems, and procedures have already been well established in TESDA with several manuals that document the process flow and guidelines and templates to ensure consistency. The training regulations and assessment tools are developed in the central office, while the UTPRAS and CAC are conducted by the field offices.

For quality assurance in training service delivery, capacity building of TVET trainers and administrators are provided by TESDA. The majority of TVET providers (90%) are from the private sector, with 10% from the TTIs and other government units.[51] To ensure quality and support the TVET sector, the National Institute for TESD (NITESD) and National TVET Trainers Academy under the Planning and Policy office are in charge of the development and continuous improvement of the TVET learning system. The NITESD covers technology research, learning development, and curriculum and training aids development, while trainers' training and development is with the National TVET Trainers Academy. The Quality Management System was established in TESDA as a means of quality assurance and monitoring toward the goals and objectives outlined in the NTESDP.

TESDA's Partnership and Linkages Office at the Central Office is responsible for establishing and managing partnerships with key stakeholders. At the same time, the field offices build alliances and maintain stakeholder relations at the local level to leverage resources and achieve set objectives. To strengthen linkages with industry, TESDA came under supervision by the Department of Trade and Industry (DTI) in 2018. Under this arrangement, the chairperson of the TESDA board is now the secretary of the DTI, whereas previously it was the secretary of the Department of Labor and Employment (DOLE). This has helped establish memoranda of agreement with multisector groups to provide scholarships and mutual assistance related to TVET.[52]

Role of Industry and Private Sector

TESDA exercises a regulatory role over private technical-vocational institutions (TVIs) on the principle of reasonable supervision. This is done through the UTPRAS, which covers programs offered by both public and private institutions. TESDA ensures that TVET programs are compliant to promulgated standards and that appropriate opportunities are available from both public and private providers. Focus is also given to building the capability and capacity of TVET providers including the local government units (LGUs). Career guidance and scholarships are also made available to enhance access and equity to quality TVET opportunities.

---

[51] United Nations Educational, Scientific, and Cultural Organization - International Centre for Technical and Vocational Education and Training (UNESCO-UNEVOC) 2019. TVET Country Profile: Philippines. Bonn: UNESCO-UNEVOC.

[52] Executive Order No. 67. 2018. Rationalizing the Office of the President through the Consolidation of its Core Mandates and Strengthening the Democratic and Institutional Framework of the Executive Department. Philippines.

Box 5.1: Technical Education and Skills Development Authority
Responses to the COVID-19 Pandemic

The Technical Education and Skills Development Authority (TESDA) has responded proactively to the pandemic, releasing a strategy to help the country respond to the ongoing crisis and adjust to the "new normal." Immediately after the country was placed under lockdown, TESDA released "OPLAN TESDA ABOT LAHAT–TVET towards the New Normal" geared toward adjusting to the new normal.[a] TESDA's online programs (TOPs) form part of its strategic plan.

TESDA also proactively engaged with the private sector to boost participation in its flexible training programs and create more job opportunities for its graduates. Starting 10 Aug 2020, all Globe and TM mobile phone subscribers get free data access to TOP—a positive development that can reduce access barriers to online learning.[b] TESDA also recently signed an agreement with mobile application developer Bizooku Philippines to create a service booking platform for more job opportunities for TESDA graduates.[c] The platform allows customers to book services of verified TESDA graduates.

At the start of the pandemic, TESDA called on employees of regional and provincial offices and trainees of TESDA training institutes to help augment the supply of personal protective equipment for front-liners in the country. As of 10 September, TESDA had already produced 420,433 face masks; 40,807 face shields; 12,621 sanitizers; and 10,060 protective suits.[d] Earlier in April, TESDA also released a video on how to sew face masks when wearing them became mandatory.[e] Relevant and timely courses regarding coronavirus disease (COVID-19), including a course on prevention in the workplace, were also added to those offered in TESDA's online program.

An additional P1 billion was recently approved for TESDA's work scholarship programs and its specialized training programs. These funds give the agency a greater capacity to accommodate displaced workers and overseas Filipino workers, especially after the realignment of around P2.1 billion of its 2020 budget under the Bayanihan 1 Act, which mostly came from TESDA's scholarship fund.

[a] According to (IATF-TWG for AFP, 2020), the new normal is, "characterized by the need to observe social distance and strict personal hygiene and other sanitation protocols. There may still be sporadic lockdowns, though over a smaller geographic unit. At the same time, the COVID-19 threat looms large in the minds of individuals – consumers and business alike."

[b] TESDA. 2020a. Globe/TM Customers Get Free Data Access to TESDA Online Courses. 21 August. https://www.tesda.gov.ph/News/Details/18965.

[c] D. Nazario. 2020. TESDA Partners with Mobile App Developer to Assist Graduates. *Manila Bulletin*. 29 September. https://mb.com.ph/2020/09/29/tesda-partners-with-mobile-app-developer-to-assist-graduates/.

[d] M. C. Arayata. 2020. Filipinos Can Expect More from TESDA amid Pandemic: Lapeña. *Philippine News Agency*. 15 September. https://www.pna.gov.ph/articles/1115538.

[e] TESDA. 2020b. TESDA Encourages Public to Make Washable Face Masks. 10 April. https://pia.gov.ph/news/articles/1038559.

Source: Authors.

Key Features of TVET in the Philippines

As one of the three national education agencies, TESDA plays a key role in establishing and maintaining the country's national qualifications framework, which was institutionalized through the Philippine Qualifications Framework (PQF) Act of 2017 (Republic Act No. 10968).[53] The PQF is a unified system that sets the standards for qualification outcomes from the completion of high school, to certificates of initial entry to the workplace, to doctoral degrees. It is a quality-assured national system based on standards of knowledge, skills, and values acquired in different ways and methods by learners and workers of the country.

---

[53] The Philippine Qualifications Framework (PQF) is discussed in greater detail in Chapter 7.

Technical and Vocational Education and Training Quality Assurance

As part of the agency's mandate to ensure quality TVET, TESDA sets program standards, regulates TVIs, and provides recognition of competencies and qualifications. TESDA is guided by its Quality Management System Manual that covers the systems and process under the Quality Assured Philippine TVET System.

- **Training regulations.** TESDA develops competency standards for workers in the form of units of competency containing descriptors for acceptable work performance. These are packaged into qualifications corresponding to critical jobs and occupations. The qualifications correspond to specific levels in the Philippine TVET Qualifications Framework. Each qualification level has corresponding assessment tools that serve as instruments in evaluating the level of knowledge and skills competence for a particular occupation. There are usually four qualification levels (National Certificate, or NC Levels I-IV of increasing levels of competency and ability). The competency standards and qualifications, packaged with training standards and assessment arrangements, comprise the national training regulations. Promulgated by the TESDA Board, training regulations serve as the basis for the development of the curricula, instructional materials, registration, and delivery of training programs. Private sector representatives and industry experts are involved in developing training regulations to ensure relevance and alignment with labor market needs. Training regulations are periodically revisited and upgraded based on the changing requirements of the industry.
- **Unified TVET Program Registration and Accreditation System.** The Unified TVET Program Registration and Accreditation System (UPTRAS) is the quality assurance mechanism for technical-vocational programs. The system covers a two-stage process of quality assurance: (i) mandatory registration of TVET programs; and (ii) voluntary accreditation of programs or institutions that leads to the issuance of a certificate of accredited status attesting to the quality or standard of a public or private TVET schools to any of its programs or courses. Registration in the UTPRAS signifies compliance with the minimum requirements prescribed by training regulations. A TVET institution must comply with the requirements of registration prior to its offering of a program. Upon completion of all the requirements, a *Certificate of Program Registration* is issued to the TVI. All registered programs are reflected in TESDA's *Compendium of Registered Programs*, which is usually uploaded to the websites of TESDA regional offices. Compliance audits are conducted to ensure that TVIs are continuously complying with TESDA's program requirements. On the other hand, accreditation is a form of quality assurance, which is over and above the requirements for program registration in UTPRAS. It is voluntary and deals with establishing institutional quality management systems.
- **Philippine TVET Competency Assessment and Certification System.** Assessment and certification of the competencies of the middle-level skilled workers are conducted through the Philippine TVET Competency Assessment and Certification (CAC) System. The assessment seeks to determine whether the graduate or worker can perform to the standards expected in the workplace based on the defined competency standards. It is conducted by TESDA-accredited assessors through any of the following methods: demonstration/observation with oral questioning, written test, interview, third-party report, portfolio, and submission of work projects. Individuals may apply for assessment and certification in private TESDA-accredited assessment centers, TESDA regional and provincial offices, and assessment centers in TESDA technology institutions. A National Certificate (NC) is issued when a candidate has demonstrated competence in all units of competency that comprised a qualification. On the other hand, a certificate of competency (COC) is issued to individuals who have satisfactorily demonstrated competence on a particular or cluster of units of competency.

Box 5.2: Relevance of the Technical Education and Skills Development Authority Online Programs to COVID-19

TESDA's Online Programs (TOP) plays a critical role as the country grapples with record-high unemployment and migrant workers' mass return during the coronavirus disease (COVID-19) pandemic. A significant number of workers would require retooling and upskilling, especially those whose livelihoods have been affected by the COVID-19 pandemic. TOP is an open educational resource launched in 2012 to make technical and vocational education and training (TVET) more accessible through information and communication technology (ICT). Enrollment in TOP surged during the COVID-19 pandemic. As of August 2020, TOP had around 794,211 registered users (figure). During this period, registered users accounted for more than one-third (about 36%) of the total number of TOP users (2.2 million) since its launch in 2012. TOP currently has 71 available online courses under 16 categories. Most-enrolled TOP courses include tourism (21%), entrepreneurship (16%), 21st-century skills (14%), and ICT (10%).[a]

TESDA Online Programs, 2012–2020

- Number of registered users in TESDA's Online Programs (TOP)-Left axis
- Cumulative number of course offerings-Right axis

Note: Number of registered users as of 3 August 2020.

Sources: M. Dumaua-Cabautan et al. 2018. *E-Education in the Philippines: The Case of Technical Education and Skills Development Authority Online Program.* Discussion Paper Series No. 2018-08. Quezon City: Philippine Institute for Development Studies; TESDA. 2019b. *2018 TESDA Annual Report.* Taguig: TESDA; TESDA. 2020c. *TESDA Commemorates 26th Founding Anniversary with the Theme "TESDA@26: Bringing Hope in Times of Crisis."* 25 August. https://www.tesda.gov.ph/News/Details/18969; TESDA. 2020d. *2019 TESDA Annual Report.* Taguig: TESDA.

TESDA adopted flexible learning in the delivery of TVET to address the disruptions due to school closures. Since not all learning can be done remotely, TESDA also adopted flexible learning arrangements that involve using a combination of conventional and ICT-based teaching/learning approaches to achieve more involvement among TVET institutions, trainers, and learners. The various flexible learning platforms consider the institutions', trainers', and learners' differing capacities and access to computers and the internet. Thus, TVET institutions may adopt online training programs, blended learning (online and face-to-face), and distance learning for those without internet connection and computers (via learning materials and non-digital electronic resources).

[a] NEDA. 2020. "Innovative and Flexible Training Needed to Retool and Upskill Labor Force –NEDA." 16 June. http://www.neda.gov.ph/innovativeand-flexible-training-needed-to-retool-and-upskill-labor-force-neda/ (accessed 11 December 2020).
Source: Authors.

Training Provision

Aside from its mandated functions in direction setting, standard setting, and regulation of TVIs, TESDA also provides direct training programs through the following modalities:

- **School-based programs.** Direct delivery or provision of TVET programs by TESDA-administered schools (including post-secondary offerings of varying duration not exceeding 3 years)
- **Center-based programs.** Training undertaken in the TESDA regional and provincial training centers in selected trade areas in the different regions and provinces in the country
- **Community-based programs.** Primarily addressed to the poor and marginalized groups, those who cannot access, or are not accessible by formal training provisions; done in partnership with LGUs, nongovernment organizations, people's organizations, and other organizations; programs are primarily designed to enable its clientele build skills for livelihood enterprises
- **Enterprise-based programs.** Training programs being implemented within companies or firms (e.g., apprenticeship, learnership, dual training program arrangements)

Further, TESDA is promoting e-learning as a means of upskilling and reskilling. TESDA Online Program, a free open education resource, was rolled out to make technical education more accessible to professionals, laborers, unemployed, out-of-school youths, students, and OFWs who want their skills upgraded.

As of the end of 2018, TESDA manages 122 TTIs. These consist of 16 regional training centers; 45 provincial training centers; 5 specialized training centers; and 56 TESDA-administered schools (14 agricultural schools, 5 fishery schools, and 37 trade schools) (TESDA, 2018b). Aside from training provision, TTIs are also intended to cultivate innovation by testing new training schemes and serving as laboratories for new technology.

TESDA also provides scholarships and financial assistance to TVET enrollees to address access and equity. Several student financial assistance programs are available in TVET. These scholarships are described and assessed in chapter 12 of this report.

TVET in the National Development Agenda

In the context of contributing to the further development of smart, innovative Filipinos, the 25-year vision emphasizes the significant role of government in setting the agenda for education and skills development. In 2016, the Philippine government adopted a long-term vision entitled *Ambisyon Natin 2040* as a guide for development planning. As stipulated in Executive Order No. 5 (series of 2016),[54] the Philippine Development Plan (PDP) 2017–2022 and the succeeding PDPs until 2040 shall be anchored in the long-term vision and reflect the aspirations of the Filipino people for themselves and for the country: "By 2040, the Philippines is a prosperous middle-class society where no one is poor. People live long and healthy lives and are smart and innovative. The country is a high-trust society where families thrive in vibrant, culturally diverse, and resilient communities."[55]

---

[54] Executive Order No. 5. 2016. Approving and Adopting the Twenty-Five-Year Long Term Vision Entitled Ambisyon Natin 2040 as Guide for Development Planning. Philippines.
[55] See page 3 of NEDA (2016).

Philippine Development Plan 2017–2022: Strategic Framework for Accelerating Human Capital Development

For the 2017–2022 development plan period, key strategies and targets were set to ensure access to lifelong learning opportunities to enable Filipinos attain both personal and national goals. The goals stated in the long-term vision, the Administration's *0-10 Point Socioeconomic Agenda,* and *2030 Agenda for Sustainable Development* are translated into coherent strategies and policies in the PDP 2017–2022, with an overall goal of laying down a solid foundation for a more inclusive growth, a high-trust and resilient society, and a globally competitive knowledge economy. The thrust is to equip Filipinos with 21st-century skills that will help them engage in meaningful and rewarding careers in today's changing world of work. The TVET subsector will particularly focus on facilitating and improving access to quality and relevant TVET opportunities. Community-based training will be enhanced with particular focus on providing training for special groups (such as informal workers, indigenous peoples, farmers, fisherfolk, OFWs, persons with disabilities, and drug dependents). Global competitiveness will also be ensured by scaling up technical education, aligning Philippine TVET qualifications to international standards, recognizing higher TVET qualifications, expanding public–private partnerships, and strengthening stakeholder collaboration.

In the PDP human capital development framework, TVET is also emphasized not only as a crucial sector in education and skills development, but also for increasing income-earning abilities. Retooling, upskilling, and strengthening enterprise-based TVET programs (internships, apprenticeships, and dual training system programs) are particularly highlighted to enhance employability.

National Technical Education and Skills Development Plan 2018–2022

In line with the priorities set in the PDP, TESDA issued the *National Technical Education and Skills Development Plan 2018-2022*[56] as the blueprint for the TVET subsector, including responsive policies and implementing programs in support of the broader goals and objectives of the national government. Guided by the *Ambisyon Natin 2040,* PDP 2017–2022 and the United Nations' Sustainable Development Goals 4 (quality education) and 8 (decent work and economic growth), the NTESDP 2018–2022 envisions a "Vibrant Quality TVET for Decent Work and Sustainable Inclusive Growth." The NTESDP's five major objectives are to:

(i) Create a conducive and enabling environment for the development and quality service delivery of the TVET sector.
(ii) Prepare the Philippine workforce for the challenges posed by the Fourth Industrial Revolution.
(iii) Assure industries with high economic and employment growth potentials and provide them the required quantity of quality workforce.
(iv) Directly and more vigorously address workforce needs of the basic sectors and the disadvantaged.
(v) Instill values and integrity in the conduct and delivery of TVET in the whole sector.

The NTESDP identifies eight priority sectors as the industries expected to generate higher economic value. These are also seen as providing much larger employment markets and are projected to require an estimated 6 million quality workers in 6 years. These sectors include:

(i) Tourism (Hotel and Restaurants)
(ii) Construction

---

[56] TESDA. 2018b. Strategic Direction. In *National Technical Education and Skills Development Plan 2018–2022*. Taguig: Technical Education and Skills Development Authority.

(iii) ICT and IT-BPM

(iv) Transport, communication, and storage

(v) Agriculture, fisheries, and forestry (including agro-processing)

(vi) Manufacturing (including food manufacturing and electronics)

(vii) Health, wellness, and other social services

The NTESDP recognizes that the Fourth Industrial Revolution "will accelerate the convergence of industrial technology and information technology and will pervade all facets of human activities," while emphasizing social equity and flexibility in developing their competencies toward gainful employment and livelihood.[57] In addition, the NTESDP also takes into account new sector demands and responsibility brought by legislative and policy reforms such as the inclusion of a technical–vocational–livelihood track in senior high school, the *Universal Access to Quality Tertiary Education Act* (Republic Act No. 10931), and the *Philippine Green Jobs Act of 2016* (Republic Act No. 10771), among others. To achieve the sector's two-pronged strategic thrust of (i) global competitiveness and workforce readiness, and (ii) social equity for workforce inclusion and poverty reduction, the NTESDP strategies are hinged on the following strategic responses:

- **Agility.** Fast reaction time, immediate responsiveness, innovative ways of doing things in the advent of the Fourth Industrial Revolution.
- **Scalability.** Intensify and scale up TVET programs; programs to address the huge demand for a skilled and conscientious workforce.
- **Flexibility and sustainability.** More practical, culturally sensitive approaches to the needs of the disadvantaged sector.

The NTESDP strategies are linked to TVET subsector goals and the broader national goal articulated in the PDP 2017–2022. These strategies will be supported by organizational initiatives, which aim to create a conducive and enabling environment for development and quality service delivery, and ensure integrity to instill sector credibility. The NTESDP also emphasizes improving the adaptability of the TVET sector to emerging trends and developments. As such, it highlights the importance of anticipating stakeholders' needs through skills forecasting and other research and development approaches; close engagement with clients to keep pace with their demands for the world of work and to be responsive with the needs of society in general; and the development of comprehensive, inclusive, and equitable service delivery to all Filipinos. Strong collaboration among government units, industries, academe, and relevant organizations will be crucial in undertaking these initiatives.

TVET System Preparedness for Industry 4.0

Industry 4.0 and its associated challenges have been on the policy agenda in the Philippines, including with respect to TVET. As described, this awareness of the challenges and opportunities involved is reflected in various government initiatives, including through the selection of key industries to be priorities for Industry 4.0 technology adoption. Some industry association such as the IT and Business Process Association of the Philippines have already developed a technology road map in consultation with the government.[58] In the NTESDP 2018–2022, Industry 4.0 preparedness is explicitly stated as a main objective, along with strategies to achieve it (Box 5.3). The challenge will be implementation. As industry involvement is crucial, TESDA must

---

[57] See page 81 of TESDA (2018b).
[58] Initial consultations are done by ADB (2020).

seek new and innovative means of incentivizing private sector participation to reverse the downward trend in enterprise-based training (EBT). Furthermore, efforts to engage with industry must not be done at the policy level only, but also at the level of TVIs and other providers across the country. Because of the regional clustering of industries, there is a need to enhance EBT in a way that will not exacerbate disparities across groups and regions. This will necessitate a great amount of political will, coordination, and resources.

Despite widespread awareness of Industry 4.0 in the Philippines, an apparent implementation gap underscores the need to enhance and support TVI preparedness. Awareness of Industry 4.0 in the Philippines is not limited to the policy level. For instance, a recent ADB study found strong alignment between the perceptions of training institutions and employers regarding skills requirements for the future in the BPO and electronics manufacturing industries.[59] While 80% of surveyed TVIs believed they had a good understanding of skills needs in relation to Industry 4.0, 88% agreed or strongly agreed that they needed additional technical and financial support specifically for Industry 4.0 skills provision (Figure 5.3). There may be a gap between awareness on one hand, and implementation on the other. For instance, less than half of training institutions reported reviewing their curricula and course offerings on an annual basis (or more frequently) or providing trainees with information on labor market conditions.

Figure 5.3: Technical and Vocational Education and Training Institutions and their Perception of Readiness for Industry 4.0

4IR = Industry 4.0, N/A = not applicable.
Source: ADB. 2021. *Reaping Benefits of Industry 4.0 through Skills Development in High-Growth Industries in Southeast Asia: Insights from Cambodia, Indonesia, the Philippines, and Viet Nam*. Manila.

---

[59] ADB. 2021. *Reaping Benefits of Industry 4.0 through Skills Development in High-Growth Industries in Southeast Asia: Insights from Cambodia, Indonesia, the Philippines, and Viet Nam.* Manila: ADB.

Box 5.3: Strategies to Prepare for Industry 4.0 in the National Technical Education and Skills Development Plan 2018–2022

Objective 2 of the National Technical Education and Skills Development Plan (NTESDP) 2018–2022 is to prepare the Philippine workforce for the challenges posed by the Fourth Industrial Revolution or Industry 4.0.

Strategies	Programs/projects	Indicators
2.1 Push for the active participation of industries in assessment and certification processes	Intensify involvement of industries in competency assessment and training delivery	• Number (No.) of assessed and certified by industry sector • Certification rate by industry sector, gender • No. of accredited assessment centers which are industry-based • No. of partners for on-site assessment • No. persons trained under EBT
2.2 Gear the synergy of education agencies with the industries toward synchronizing with international standards of/for decent work	PQF/AQRF alignment Participation in skills competitions	• No. of registered programs by PQF level • No. of international skills competition participated • No. of areas with competitor in international skills venue • No. of medals/awards given
2.3 Rationalize TVET delivery system to meet demands and requirements of technologies, industries, and world of work by enlarging the scope and impact of EBT as a dominant delivery mode	TESD regulatory services Partnership/linking Research studies TVET delivery	• No. of EBT programs • No. trained in EBT • No. of trainers/assessors who are industry practitioners • No. of industry consultations held • Employer surveys conducted • No. of specialized/special training centers • No. of TVET graduates in at least NC III level • No. of NC III, IV, and V (Diploma) level qualifications promulgated • % of registered programs under NC III–V
2.4 Institute separate and faster mechanisms to address rapidly changing jobs	Skills needs anticipation	• No. of sectors with skills projections • Area-based tracking/monitoring of skills needs (with Philippine pesos) • No. of diploma programs with STEM • No. of industry practitioners trained as TVET trainers
2.5 Address skills requirements not yet attended or covered by the TVET sector	Skills needs anticipation	• No. of new training regulations approved and promulgated • Infusion of 21st-century skills in secondary, TVET curricula • % of scholarship funding allotment in emerging technology qualifications, with and without training regulations

AQRF = ASEAN Qualifications Reference Framework, EBT = employment-based training, NC = national certificate, PQF = Philippines Qualifications Framework, STEM = science, technology, engineering, and math, TESD = technical education and skills development, TVET = technical and vocational education and training.

Source: TESDA. 2018b. Strategic Direction. In *National Technical Education and Skills Development Plan 2018–2022*. Taguig: Technical Education and Skills Development Authority.

Key Issues for the Technical Education and Skills Development Authority's Relevance and Effectiveness

This subsection adopts a methodological approach drawing on principles of Positive Organization Development, which is based on the notion of planned, purposive and methodical processes to identify what is already present in an organization and building on this.[60] Furthermore, the organizational assessment presented here uses as a key reference, a study by the European Centre for Development Policy Management on core capabilities of organizations, i.e., capabilities to commit and engage, to carry out functions or tasks, to relate and attract resources and support, to adapt and self-renew, and finally, to balance coherence and diversity.[61] Specifically, the latter study, which outlines drivers of organizational and systems behavior, is used to shape our approach for assessing the organizational capacities and organizational development of TESDA.

Our assessment is based on primary and secondary data collection, including key informant interviews, focus group discussions, and a review of secondary literature. Regional consultations and field visits were initially conducted by the study team in selected areas of the Philippines in 2018. The study findings were updated in 2020, by incorporating new data obtained from the Project Development Division of TESDA's Planning Office, as well as comments and information gathered from the workshop on "TVET in the Age of Fourth Industrial Revolution: Future of Skills Development in the Philippines."

The following paragraphs summarize key issues and challenges identified in our assessment, while corresponding recommendations are integrated with our findings from other parts of the TVET sector study, and presented in Part IV.

Unsettled Issue of Devolution of Direct Training Function

Despite TESDA's accomplishments in implementing training programs, there is an ongoing debate on the devolution of its direct training function. TESDA provides a range of training programs in various fields including language training, entrepreneurship, human relations training, and skills training for internally displaced people. It recently also launched the TESDA Online Program offering free TVET courses through the internet. Despite this, there has been an ongoing debate on the issue of TESDA's direct training function through the administration of TTIs. On the one hand, there is a clear provision in the TESDA law, as well as recommendations from previous organizational studies, to devolve TTIs. As far back as 2000, an ADB study emphasized the need for TESDA to divest its responsibility for direct administration of training operations and assume a supporting role in systems monitoring and information dissemination (ADB, 2000). The report suggested freeing up staff resources for higher priority activities, including policy and standards development, training materials support, and overall monitoring.

The main argument for devolution is that TESDA should focus its resources and efforts on its unique role as an authority of the TVET sector, regulating the training providers. This school of thought describes TESDA's role in TVET as *"Judge, Jury, and Executor,"* since it sets the standards, conducts direct training service delivery, assesses and certifies as well as regulates compliance and dispenses sanctions to its own TTIs and other TVIs. Further, duplication in the content of programs offered by TESD centers with their more modern TVI counterparts further undermine TESDA's training function. There are private technical education institutions located in the same area of the TTIs, offering the same programs but with more

---

[60] See Cooperrider et al. (2005) and Cooperrider and Goodwin (2012) for more information.
[61] European Centre for Development Policy Management. 2008. Capacity, Change and Performance Insights and Implications for Development Cooperation. *Policy Management Brief. No. 21.* Maastricht: European Centre for Development Policy Management.

modern and world-class equipment and infrastructure that are responsive to emerging industries and with strong industry partnership.[62]

However, devolution is neither straightforward nor does it have universal support. A significant obstacle to the devolution of TESDA's training function is the reluctance of LGUs to take over the function. Devolution would require LGUs to take responsibility of administering the TTIs. This requires substantial capitalization for new technologies, with potential additional burden on staff and budget. There are also arguments that this would compromise the sustainability of TTIs as LGU priorities change, and have major implications in terms of inclusion.

Limited Resources and Staff

Limited budget for capital outlay is a major obstacle for developing up to date and modern facilities. Capital outlay accounts for around 8% of the 2020 annual budget and is allotted for land outlay, buildings and other structures, machinery and equipment, and transportation equipment. Limited capital outlay means that there are limited funds available for needed construction or even rehabilitation of facilities, like buildings or training workshops. Access to capital outlay to update tools and equipment, especially in the TTIs and field offices also remains a challenge. This presents a major difficulty considering that TESD requires appropriate and updated equipment and facilities for training on emerging technologies. Moreover, the TTIs have difficulty in accessing funds for capital outlay because of the provision of the law for TESDA to devolve its training function to the LGUs. As such, it is imperative that action should be taken to resolve on the provision of training service delivery by TESDA.

The number of regular staff is minimal in most of the TTIs, particularly the TESD centers. There are some concerns that the limited number of trainers/facilitators in TTIs is insufficient to adequately cover the number of qualifications and programs offered by their centers, including bundled programs and diploma programs. Furthermore, the need for additional personnel is even more important, given the expected influx of students, especially with free access to TVET education. This disproportionately low number of staff in the TTIs is also the result of the provision in the TESDA law to devolve the training function of TESDA, starting with the TESD centers and eventually also the TESDA administered schools.

Shortage of Technology Competency Assessors

There is a prevailing issue on the declining number of qualified assessors due to transfer of assessors to the Department of Education following the K to 12 reform, and the need to upgrade qualifications. With the opening of the technical-vocational and livelihood (TVL) track in senior high school, many assessors left TESDA to join the faculty of the Department of Education for higher salaries and regularization of employment. Another reason for the decline of the number of assessors is the requirement of industry immersion/experience and conflict of schedule. The Industry Work Experience Required or IWER is a quality standard requirement of TESDA to ensure that assessors are updated with industry practice. However, there is apparent difficulty in gaining IWER because the assessors also act as trainers in the TTIs and have limited time to immerse themselves in an actual industry setting for updates and continuous improvement.

The availability of assessors for higher levels of technology, particularly in the ICT subsector is limited. The rapid change of technology requires assessors who are updated with competencies relevant to the industry. In 2018 alone, at least four training regulations on ICT, mainly on visual graphic design and animation, were superseded.[63] A number of industry vendors, such as Microsoft, conduct their own assessments for qualifications that have

---

[62] In Region VII for example, the regional TESD center offers tourism courses like housekeeping qualifications, which are also offered by the School of Knowledge for Industrial Labor, Leadership, and Service and Banilad Center for Professional Development.
[63] TESDA. 2018c. *2017 TESDA Annual Report*. Taguig: TESDA.

no assessors from TESDA. These industry vendors have the competencies to better assess the competencies of interested individuals for assessment, and TESDA can issue the needed National Certificate (NC).

Lengthy Processes for Developing Standards and Assessment Tools

A slow process of developing or updating standards and assessment tools means that with new and emerging technology, standards quickly become obsolete. Processes for updating standards can take up to 8 months. Regional stakeholder consultations revealed that some sectors (e.g., construction) have already developed their own competency standards. Other findings from field visits showed that some programs with internationally comparable standards (e.g., advanced shoemaking) could not be registered because of lack of training regulations and assessors. Some initiatives, especially among the local chamber of commerce and industry in some regions are underway to develop standards that are relevant and meaningful to specific industries in their localities. Such initiatives involving industry leadership in standards development and assessment represent good practice and help ensure standards and competencies are in sync with what is needed in the workplace.

Resource and capacity constraints delay the registration of new programs and compliance audits as well as the conduct of assessment and certification. The field offices face a considerable administrative burden ranging from program registration to overseeing the assessment procedures, while enforcing policies and attending to clients' concerns. Recently, a new ruling was promulgated on reducing the process time of program registration and certification to simplify requirements and procedures so as to provide efficient service delivery to the public.[64] A major challenge of the field offices is to meet requirements and maintain quality assurance given this new ruling.

Lack of Industry Engagement

There are potential opportunities for TESDA to further promote Recognized Industry Bodies (RIBs) in more industry sectors and strengthen partnership with industry to achieve goals of TVET, including anticipation of skills priorities. Mature industry organizations can be key partners in the delivery of TVET programs or services and participate in the design and implementation of TESD. It is also in the mandate of TESDA to establish institutional arrangements with industry boards and such other bodies or associations to provide an avenue for their direct participation in TESD.[65] As such, there are already six RIBs from the ICT-BPO, electrical and electronics, metals and engineering, tourism, and printing sectors which TESDA shall engage in pursuing the development and implementation of activities related to TVET.

Limited Organizational Capacity

Many of the challenges identified in this chapter relate to some degree with limited organizational capacity. For instance, building up the RIBs as a key partner in TVET governance would require an internal review of the organizational arrangements of TESDA to facilitate the changes in implementing the proposed enhanced functions of the RIBs. Such changes require capacity building and organizational change management.

Limited resources and capacity hinder staff learning and development activities. Learning and development activities are conducted in the TESDA Development Institute at the central office and managed by the Human Resources office. Capacity-building needs of the staff are identified in a competency-based training needs analysis conducted in coordination with the local human resources staff in the field offices and TTIs. The results of the training needs analysis are prioritized and translated into programs for the year that are then included in the Workforce Training Development and Investment Plan. Since the TESDA Development Institute is located

---

[64] TESDA Circular No. 18. 2019. Revised Process Cycle Time for Program Registration and Assessment and Certification. Taguig City: TESDA.
[65] RA 7796. 1994b. Rules and Regulations Implementing the TESDA Act of 1994. Philippines.

at the central office in Metro Manila, there are often difficulties in sending staff from the field offices and TTIs because of heavy workload and minimal personnel to cover their assigned tasks while away for training. The field offices and TTIs are also constrained to conduct their own training activities in their locality given limited training budgets. Nonetheless, there are efforts to build capacity of the staff through the implementation of a quality management system, which emphasizes continuous improvement of processes and tasks in the workplace.

Conclusions

While TESDA has made strides over the years, questions around its appropriate role, endemic resource constraints, and organizational capacity weigh on its ability to respond to Industry 4.0. For the last 25 years, TESDA has evolved to play a multifaceted role providing varied TESD programs and activities, including for the marginalized sector of Philippine society. However, a range of challenges exist: there is the unsettled issue of devolution of its direct training function; resource constraints, which impact capital outlay reducing its ability to provide up-to-date and modern facilities as well as trained staff; shortages of technology competency assessors and lengthy processes for developing standards and assessment tools, which undermine its ability to provide up to date services; and insufficient industry engagement, which hinders the ability to respond to changing private sector demand for skills.

A key challenge for TESDA is how to redefine its role and enhance its relevance as the authority of TVET in the context of a fast-changing environment and the realities of its own organizational resources. Moreover, with the new demands of emerging technology in the age of Industry 4.0, the organization needs to move beyond the confines of bureaucratic space and set the tone of a learning organization that models the 21st-century skills of creativity, critical thinking, communication, and collaboration. Recommendations to address challenges, shaped around reinforcing strengths and processes that are positive to organizational effectiveness, are presented in Part IV of this TVET Sector Study. These are based on the assessment and foregoing discussion on TVET governance and TESDA's organizational management.

Appendix 5: Technical Education and Skills Development Authority Initiatives

Current Technical Education and Skills Development Authority (TESDA) initiatives include:[66]

(i) TESDA's scholarship programs to continue to give priority allocation to the key sectors identified in the National Technical Education and Skills Development Plan (NTESDP) 2018–2022: (a) agriculture, fisheries, and forestry; (b) construction (general infrastructure); (c) tourism, hotels, and restaurants; (d) manufacturing; (e) IT-BPO (BPM); (f) health, wellness, and other services (including language and culture); (g) TVET; and (h) transportation, communication, and storage (logistics).

(ii) Fully implement the *Tulong Trabaho* Program, which intends to fund programs critical to industry needs in terms of new and emerging skills and skills relevant to the Fourth Industrial Revolution (4IR) or Industry 4.0.

(iii) Further operationalize the NTESDP Action Programming, which involves industry and other stakeholders coming up with actionable programs for the priority sectors identified in the plan.

(iv) Ensure the conduct of the Workplace Skills and Satisfaction Survey, which aims to determine the skills requirements of priority sectors/industries identified in the NTESDP.

(v) Pursue the institutionalization of the Philippines' Technical and Vocational Education and Training (TVET) 4.0 Framework, which aims to produce 4IR-ready learners via TVET programs, projects, and strategies such as the inclusion of essential skills/21st-century skills in training regulations, among others.

(vi) Strengthen and improve the National TVET Trainers Academy to improve trainers' training and expand the pool of qualified and 4IR-ready TVET trainers.

(vii) Establish innovation centers throughout the country to provide state-of-the-art learning systems and authentic learning environment to constituents.

(viii) Expand the implementation of the dual training system by streamlining various processes.

(ix) Continue to prioritize agriculture-related TVET programs in line with the government's food security and food sufficiency thrusts. These would include the continuous implementation of the Rice Competitiveness Enhancement Program and Programs in Accelerating Farm School Establishment, as well as the development and updating of training regulations in the area of agri-fisheries, agribusiness, and agro-industrial subsectors.

(x) Strengthen implementation of skills training and livelihood interventions under Executive Order 70 as the head of the Poverty Reduction, Livelihood and Employment Cluster.

(xi) Strengthen accessibility of TVET programs by establishing provincial training centers in all provinces nationwide.

(xii) Allocate scholarships equitably between TESDA technical institutions (TTIs) and other technical–vocational institutions (TVIs).

(xiii) Intensify the recruitment and selection process of the agency nationwide in order to expedite the filling up of vacancies, specifically in view of the approved additional 996 *plantilla* positions from the Department of Budget and Management.

(xiv) Capacitate TTIs to be assessment centers.

(xv) Monitor closely and ensure proper fund utilization of TESDA scholarship programs.

---

[66] Data provided by Project Development Division, TESDA's Planning Office, 4 March 2020.

6. Education System Reforms and the Implications for Technical and Vocational Education and Training

As the TVET subsector keeps up with Industry 4.0 and addresses the accompanying challenges, it must be vigilant in keeping abreast with other emerging issues and developments that will also alter the skills and employment landscape. For instance, the COVID-19 pandemic brought disruptions that will necessitate wider-scale adoption of flexible and/or technology-based learning in the country, including TVET.[67] The subsector will have to increase its efforts in shifting to flexible or blended training arrangements and expand its Mobile Training Laboratory Program to better serve far-flung areas. The country is also expecting a higher demand for adult learning skills retooling and upskilling to cater to displaced workers and Filipinos lacking digital skills. TESDA, through its *TESDA Online Program* and a wide range of training programs, holds high potential in addressing such needs.

Given these challenges, it becomes more important to ensure that latest legislative reforms and investments are prioritized well. For instance, on top of the free TVET program in public, TVIs under the Universal Access to Quality Tertiary Education Act, the Tulong Trabaho Act (Republic Act No. 11230) was signed into law 22 February 2019. The latter act establishes the Tulong Trabaho Fund, which will cover training fees and additional financial aid such as transportation allowances of qualified beneficiaries enrolling in selected training programs. There is a need to ensure that new initiatives and funds will not duplicate existing programs and subsidies to students. In this context, this legislative measure may serve as a good opportunity to address key challenges in the sector. The Tulong Trabaho Fund may be tapped to further promote enterprise-based modalities in TVET, and upscale retooling/upskilling efforts in the workforce through "training vouchers," as recommended by the National Economic and Development Authority (NEDA) (footnote 74).

From a planning perspective, TESDA has demonstrated its ability to assess and respond to the needs and challenges of the TVET subsector of the Philippines' broader education sector. This is evident in its conscientious effort to prepare a subsector medium-term plan, the latest of which is the NTESDP 2018–2022. TESDA is the only one of the three education agencies that has continuously prepared and officially adopted fully articulated subsector plans that are aligned with the national development planning process. The current NTESDP already provides a rich and nuanced perspective on the priorities and reforms that the TVET subsector would need to pursue in the intermediate term. It would be strategic, however, from a broader sector perspective for it to equally pay attention to areas of reform and adjustment that overlap with the other two subsectors. While experience since the education sector has been "trifocalized" has shown the particular difficulty and complexity of trans-subsector coordination, there are current opportunities that should be maximized by TESDA. These would benefit not only TVET but also bring about better outcomes for the governance of the sector as a whole.

This chapter provides an overview of TVET in the context of reform milestones, followed by reform imperatives in the broader education sector.

---

[67] IATF-TWG for AFP. 2020. *We Recover as One*. https://www.neda.gov.ph/wp-content/uploads/2020/05/We-Recover-As-One.pdf.

TVET in the Context of Reform Milestones

The historical reform context of TVET as it relates to the broader education sector is important in determining strategic and meaningful reform actions for the present. In this regard, it is relevant to look at the major education reform initiatives beginning from the Congressional Commission on Education (EDCOM) of 1991, which initiated the trifocalization of the education sector. In this section, six reform milestones spanning 3 decades will be discussed (Figure 6.1) that have had and continue to impact TVET's functioning within the whole of the education sector in terms of planning, policy formulation, regulation, and implementation coordination.

Congressional Commission on Education of 1991

In 1990, the Philippine Senate and House of Representatives enacted *Joint Resolution No. 2* creating EDCOM. Beginning its work in 1991, this specially constituted government reform body had a comprehensive scope, covering the entire education sector (i.e., basic education, TVET, and higher education; both the formal and non-formal modalities), that included the goals and structure of Philippine education; access and equity; quality and relevance; teacher education, training, and welfare; special topics and concerns (such as special education, education for indigenous cultural communities, and educational technology and innovations); sector targets and functional linkages; financing; and governance and management.

EDCOM paved the way for the creation of TESDA, a single agency primarily responsible for both technical education and skills development. This organizational reform was also seen as a means to strengthen existing linkages between technical and vocational institutions, both public and private, and industry by engaging the latter in policy making, planning, and standard setting. Furthermore, this would facilitate close coordination and linkages of education and manpower planning with employment by rationalizing and putting all programs that are directly and closely related to employment under one coherent administration. One of the key legislative measures proposed by EDCOM was the Republic Act No. 7796, or *The TESDA Act of 1994*.[68]

Figure 6.1: Time Frame of Selected Reform Milestones

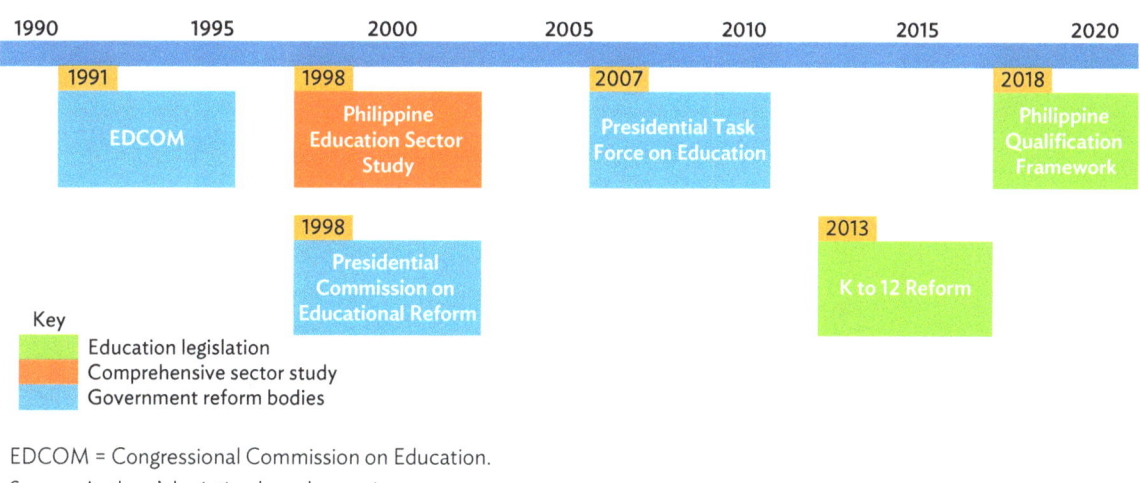

EDCOM = Congressional Commission on Education.
Source: Authors' depiction based on various sources.

---

[68] Republic Act (RA) No. 7796. 1994a. An act creating the Technical Education and Skills Development Authority, providing for its powers, structure and for other purposes. Philippines.

A *National Council for Education* (NCE) was proposed by EDCOM as a means of maintaining cohesion of the sector under a trifocalized regime. A key and lasting institutional reform by EDCOM is the trifocalization of the education sector. This entailed restructuring the existing Department of Education Culture and Sports (DECS)[69] to focus solely on basic education and transferring all its functions related to TVET and higher education to the proposed TESDA and the Commission on Higher Education (CHED), respectively. The NCE was to ensure that an integrative, coordinative, and comprehensive sector framework is maintained, while each of the three agencies are operating autonomously. The NCE was envisioned to maintain systems integration and program unity at the highest level of the education system, balancing the autonomy and independence of the three education agencies: DECS, TESDA, and CHED.

The EDCOM saw the NCE performing an essential role in the implementation of its recommendations. Pursuant to this, it proposed the passage by Congress of an omnibus enabling law or resolution, which shall have three main provisions, one of which is quoted as follows.

'That an institution, in this case the National Council for Education, be immediately set up to formulate plans, programs, guidelines and projects to implement the legislative measures based on EDCOM recommendations, as well as the executive actions meant to carry out such recommendations.'

(EDCOM, 1993, p. 112)

While the government was successful in trifocalizing the sector following EDCOM's recommendations, it was unable to realize the establishment of NCE. This was a key reform, and the NCE was deemed critical in pursuing the totality of its reform vision. As can be seen in the almost 3 decades post-EDCOM, the failure to permanently put in place the NCE (or any coordinating body that effectively performed the intended function) resulted in program fragmentation and coordination issues, scenarios that EDCOM highlighted as risks in the absence of a mechanism that will pull all three subsectors together.

The 1998 Philippine Education Sector Study

ADB and the World Bank undertook a review of the education sector, resulting in the *Philippine Education Sector Study* (PESS).[70] This was seen as an opportunity to influence the policy and reform priorities of a new set of education agency heads for the next 6 years of the administration, while ensuring the continuity of reforms initiated by EDCOM. The study focused on four areas: (i) financing of education and training and the efficiency of resource use, (ii) equity in basic education (for whom and of what quality), (iii) skills for competitiveness—the adequacy of middle- and higher-level skills development for the future competitiveness of the economy, and (iv) management of the education sector. Compared to previous reviews and analyses of the sector, PESS was the first to be able to look at each subsector and generate initial operational insights under the new governance setup (Box 6.1).

---

[69] DECS is now known as the Department of Education or DepEd.
[70] Asian Development Bank (ADB) and World Bank. 1999. *Philippine Education for the 21st Century. The 1998 Philippines Education Sector Study.* Manila: ADB.

Box 6.1: Policy Recommendations on Three Technical and Vocational Education and Training Areas As Outlined in the Philippine Education Sector Study

- **Improving and expanding private provision.** The study noted that private training provision is more cost-effective and responsive to labor demand than those publicly provided. It suggested that the constraints on the lack of access to commercial credit by private providers and unfair competition stemming from heavy subsidies to public providers be addressed by giving private providers easier access to commercial credit markets, expanding the Private Education Student Financial Assistance scholarship program to support disadvantaged students and increase the revenues of private providers, and introduction of fees in state universities and colleges (SUCs) providers for cost recovery and to reduce unfair public–private competition.
- **Focusing on policy development and quality assurance.** The Technical Education and Skills Development Authority (TESDA) faced the challenge of being understaffed and under resourced for what it has set to do in policy and programs, mainly because of its heavy responsibility on the management of training provision. The study recommended the following to TESDA: devolution of responsibility on training provision to nongovernment organizations and local government units, or to private providers through public subsidies, leasing of facilities, and providing vouchers to trainees instead of direct financing of training institutions; focusing on its role and tasks in the development of institutional accreditation standards and occupational standards; and assuming the authority to accredit the technical education programs of SUCs.
- **Improving equity of access and outcomes.** The Philippine Education Sector Study noted that while students of public training institutions, including SUCs, can avail it for free, these are programs of lower quality compared to those offered by private institutions for a fee. The limited access of poor students entering private institutions to financial assistance was also noted, as well as the lack of equivalency standards for post-basic technical and vocational education and training (TVET). Introducing cost recovery in public training institutions was one of the measures that could help promote equity. On equivalency, it suggested the following policy options: reconstituting the Commission on Equivalency to provide students with options to move from post-basic education and training programs to higher levels of education; and initiating equivalency development in technical education programs of SUCs.

Source: Authors.

The PESS noted that the trifocalization of the sector had made it difficult to formulate sector-wide policies and to make decisions on the allocation of sector resources. This had been part of the logic behind the coordinating mechanism involving the three education agencies (i.e., the NCE). As an alternative to the creation of an NCE was a "process whereby the leaders of DECS, CHED, TESDA work more collaboratively with one another," which it recognizes "will require some effort and considerable goodwill on the part of the three leaders."[71] It further noted that that the agencies should voluntarily and informally participate in this process. It meant that the desired inter-agency coordination under an NCE did not work out because of the lack of a strong legal or policy instrument (given the inaction on the original EDCOM proposal for a law creating the NCE); enforcing the desired coordination instead became dependent on whether the agency heads or the President saw it as a priority and ensured that this kind of coordination was enforced. This issue of sector management and inter-agency coordination would arise time and again throughout different reform processes.

Presidential Commission on Educational Reform

In 1998, the *Presidential Commission on Educational Reform* (PCER) was part of a 10-point action plan under the new administration. The PCER was a multisector body composed of representatives from both the public and private sector, and included the heads of the Department of Education (DepEd),[72] TESDA, and CHED. Its mandate was to do a broad review of the education system, including, among others, the recommendations of

---
[71] See p. 67 of ADB and World Bank (1999)
[72] Previously known as DECS.

the EDCOM and PESS, and to come up with reform proposals that were considered urgent and feasible within the President's term.[73]

Nine proposals constituted the PCER's *Agenda for Reform*; however, these excluded anything specific to TVET, despite recommendations in different committee reports. Among the PCER proposals, it is noticeable that there was nothing specific to the TVET subsector. It has been interpreted that the silence of PCER on TVET implies affirmation of the thrust to mainly depend on private providers to respond to the market for TVET services, which was in essence what the PESS also recommended.[74] Despite this, some TVET-related recommendations were included within the PCER committee reports (six committees focused on different areas and comprised of PCER members and other experts). Specific recommendations are highlighted in Box 6.2.

The issue of coordination among DECS, TESDA, and CHED continued to be an area of concern, to the extent that it became the first of the PCER's nine specific reform proposals. While the trifocalization of the system had facilitated the pursuit of reforms in each of the subsectors, EDCOM had correctly anticipated the

---

Box 6.2: Related Recommendations by Committees under the Presidential Commission on Educational Reform on Technical and Vocational Education and Training

- **The Presidential Commission on Educational Reform (PCER) Financing Committee report included recommendations to improve post-secondary technical and vocational education and training (TVET) through equity-enhancing measures.** These included the adoption of socialized fees by charging students based on family income, consistent with the government's promotion of equity. It also recommended the provision of subsidy for skills training, with priority accorded to government-sponsored programs.
- **The PCER Financing Committee report also recommended measures for improving certification systems and enhancing training for trainers.** These included: (i) establishing a career path for upward occupational mobility for technicians, which includes a system for certification to attest to skills acquired along the career path; (ii) encouraging professional and craft organizations to certify job proficiency; and (iii) setting and enforcing minimum academic qualifications and industry experience for TVET trainers, as well as the implementation of continuing education programs.
- **The PCER Financing Committee report also recommended institutionalization of ladderized TVET courses based on a model considering the dual training system.** The creation of linkages between schools and industries for skills training was also emphasized, as well as the strengthening of TVET programs provided by different institutions (technical-vocational institutions and community colleges). The latter is intended to promote improvement in science and math content and occupational offerings that are more attuned and relevant to the needs and resources of the community.
- **The PCER Quality Assurance Committee report recommended the adoption of a competency-based framework.** Specifically, it endorsed the competency-based framework that had already been developed by TESDA at that time in articulating the curriculum from basic to post-secondary education levels and in its assessment and evaluation.

Source: Authors.

---

[73] Presidential Commission on Educational Reform (PCER). 2000. *Philippine Agenda for Educational Reform: The PCER Report.* Manila.
[74] World Bank. 2004. Philippines - Education Policy Reforms in Action: A Review of Progress Since PESS and PCER. *World Bank Other Operational Studies 14367.* Washington, DC.

"possibility of overlapping, duplicative, disjointed and inconsistent plans and policies, priorities and concerns," and saw the necessity of a "broader perspective transcending subsector concerns in determining program priorities and education budgetary allocations."[75] The PCER revived the recommendation, as the first of its nine specific reform proposals, of having a formally constituted mechanism for coordination by means of the establishment of a *National Coordinating Council for Education* (NCCE).

While the proposal to establish the NCCE was immediately acted upon after the submission of PCER's reform proposals to the President, it failed to become operative. The Executive Order (No. 273)[76] creating the NCCE was issued in August of 2000. However, despite the official issuance, the NCCE remained inoperative. This was mainly attributed to the first rotating chair's view that formally convening the coordinating body and constituting the prescribed high-powered secretariat were not priorities (footnote 74). The funding from the General Appropriations Act for its operations in succeeding years likewise did not materialize due to the NCCE's non-operation. As such, trans-subsector coordination remained informal, with issues being resolved in an ad hoc basis and with no deliberate sector-wide decisions being made.

Presidential Task Force for Education

In 2007, the new administration abolished the NCCE and established a Presidential Task Force for Education (PTFE). President Gloria Macapagal-Arroyo issued Executive Order No. 632 that abolished the NCCE, which was not functioning as mandated. The Arroyo administration, however, recognized that "the need to synchronize and harmonize the government's educational policies, programs and initiatives becomes all the more urgent given the country's ranking in world competitiveness," and mandated, given the dissolution of the NCCE, "a Presidential Assistant to exercise [the NCCE's] functions" (footnote 76). The following month after the NCCE was abolished, another Executive Order (No. 652)[77] was issued, this time creating a Presidential Task Force to Assess, Plan and Monitor the Entire Educational System.

The functions of the PTFE were similar to that of the NCCE, but were translated to be more recommendatory in nature. For instance, while the NCCE's function was "to serve as the regular forum for trans-subsectoral consultations" (footnote 76), the PTFE was tasked "to design a mechanism in the holding of regular *fora* for trans-subsectoral consultations" (Executive Order No. 632, 2007). The PTFE articulated the concept of a "Philippine Main Education Highway," which represents a continuum from pre-school to basic education, to TVET, or higher education. At each level, particular goals and metrics are defined. It was seen as the PTFE's "strategic platform" from which its envisioned goal of "producing quality and world-class graduates" in a knowledge-based economy will be realized. This framework emphasized the tighter linkage between tertiary education and industry, and the availability of mechanisms and interventions for lifelong learning.

The PTFE convened the first-ever biennial congress in 2008, bringing together a wide range of stakeholders from both the public and private sectors in each of the education subsectors, including business groups and industry associations. The Congress focused on themes that had significance across basic education, TVET, and higher education, and included the harmonization of the TVET and higher education subsystems, and the management, regulatory, and coordination issues among the three education agencies. A major discussion point of the biennial congress was on the interface between TESDA and CHED in the implementation of the *Ladderized Education Program* (LEP) (Executive Order No. 358, 2004). The LEP

---

[75] See p. 16–17 of PCER (2000).
[76] Office of the President. 2000. *Executive Order No. 273. Institutionalizing the System of National Coordination, Assessment, Planning and Monitoring of the Entire Educational System.* https://www.officialgazette.gov.ph/2000/08/07/executive-order-no-273-s-2000/.
[77] Office of the President. 2007. *Executive Order No. 652. Creating the Presidential Task Force to Assess, Plan and Monitor the Entire Educational System.* https://www.officialgazette.gov.ph/2007/08/21/executive-order-no-652-s-2007.

> **Box 6.3: Selected Recommendations in the First Biennial Congress under the Presidential Task Force for Education**
>
> In the thematic discussion on the harmonization of technical and vocational education and training (TVET) and higher education, some of the other key recommendations included the following:
>
> - The Technical Education and Skills Development Authority (TESDA) and the Commission on Higher Education to agree on competency-based assessment and credit units, including a policy to standardize credit transfer from technical-vocational or tech-voc education to higher education degree courses.
> - Explore other pathways of interfacing tech-voc education and higher education.
> - Develop more model curricula to expand the coverage of ladderized education programs;
> - Have tech-voc education leading to TESDA National Certificate levels I and II in secondary education in general and not just in selected tech-voc high schools; and
> - Include the Department of Education in the policy and program harmonization process. Another issue that needed to be addressed in relation to the Ladderized Education Program was the observation that while vocational qualifications incorporated into the degree programs were based on TESDA promulgated competency standards, these were not well articulated or defined in many of the higher education degree programs.
>
> Source: Authors.

allowed learners to progress between TVET and higher education and vice-versa. A PTFE proposal to the President prior to the biennial congress for removing a perceived bureaucratic bottleneck affecting the smooth implementation of the LEP was approved by the President and Executive Order No. 694 (2008) effecting this change was issued just days before the biennial congress. Other recommendations around the harmonization of TVET and higher education are provided in Box 6.3.

An Inter-agency Coordination for Education (ICE) Framework was also proposed to strengthen coordination among the three education agencies. The PTFE's post-congress report's proposed ICE Framework emphasized the optimal utilization of mechanisms, bodies, and working groups already available to education agencies, and empowering a "coordinating body" to facilitate tighter inter-agency coordination and linkage with other external stakeholders such as the legislature, and other government entities. In principle, the ICE Framework articulated what was desired in terms of promoting a seamless functioning of the three education agencies into one coherent system. However, this has always been the vision since the trifocalized system was conceptualized. Unfortunately, that "coordinating body" identified in the ICE Framework was never fully realized before the PTFE ceased its operations by the end of the Arroyo administration in 2010.

The K to 12 Reform

In 2010, the new administration under President Benigno Aquino III prioritized several education reforms. The reforms comprised 10 action points that included the expansion before the end of his administration in 2016 of basic education from a 10-year cycle to a globally comparable 12 years, and the "reintroduction" of technical–vocational education "as an alternative stream in senior high school...to better link schooling to local industry needs and employment."[78] President Aquino's appointed Secretary of Education Armin Luistro made this shift to a K to 12 system the primary objective of his tenure.

---

[78] B. Aquino III. 2010. 10 Ways to Fix Philippine Basic Education. *Philippine Daily Inquirer.* February. https://www.scribd.com/document/26541154/POLICY-NOTE-10-Ways-to-Fix-Philippine-Basic-Education (accessed 11 December 2020).

The K to 12 basic education program is one of the most significant reforms in the history of Philippine education.[79] The proposal of DepEd was to adopt a "K-6-4-2" model: 1 year of kindergarten, 6 years of elementary education, 4 years of junior high school, and 2 years of senior high school, known as the K to 12 basic education program. At the time, the K to 12 reform was proposed, the Philippines was the only remaining country in Asia and one of only three countries (the other two being Djibouti and Angola) in the world with a 10-year pre-university program. By early 2013, the *Enhanced Basic Education Act of 2013* (Republic Act No. 10533), popularly known as the K to 12 Law, was passed.[80] This law officially adopted the DepEd-proposed model and mandated its implementation, along with other major reforms in the curriculum, such as allowing for more flexibility so the curriculum can be suitably contextualized based on the school's specific educational and social context.

Among the objectives of the K to 12 reform was to contribute to the expansion of job opportunities by reducing jobs–skills mismatch and providing better preparation for higher learning. A notable development that stemmed from the new K to 12 program was the introduction of senior high school. Four tracks were introduced in senior high school: academic, technical–vocational and livelihood (TVL), sports, and arts and design. When students complete this terminal stage of basic education, they are supposed to be prepared for four possible exits: employment, entrepreneurship, middle-level skills development, and higher education (footnote XX). The senior high school TVL track provides students an opportunity to acquire a National Certificate from TESDA for courses that follow the agency's training regulations.

The introduction of the TVL program was a pivotal development where closer coordination and collaboration between DepEd and TESDA has been critical. The program required the two education agencies to work together in the integration of TVET skills, competencies, and qualifications (including in Technology and Livelihood Education in junior high school) as translated into the corresponding Curriculum Guides; ensuring that senior high school TVL graduates are eligible for TESDA assessments (i.e., COC, NC I, or NC II); developing learning resources that are aligned with TESDA's training regulations; and developing in-service training and certification programs for Technology and Livelihood Education and TVL teachers.

In 2017, the DepEd also introduced the Joint-Delivery Voucher Program for Senior High School TVL Specializations.[81] Consistent with what has been highlighted in the K to 12 Law and recommendations of previous education reform bodies, the Joint-Delivery Voucher Program for Senior High School TVL Specializations operates within the framework of recognizing the complementary roles of public and private educational institutions, and maximizes the use of public–private partnerships in the fulfillment of the state's mandate to make quality education accessible to all. It is a form of tuition fee assistance for Grade 12 TVL students enrolled in DepEd schools with inadequate learning resources (i.e., specialized teachers or trainers, equipment, workshops, and tools) to offer TVL specializations.

A significant change in the Philippine education landscape that was brought about by the shift to K to 12 was that of DepEd suddenly becoming a major provider of TVET. From a whole sector perspective, the increasing enrollment in the TVET system coupled with the introduction of the senior high school TVL track program, has boosted the growth of the TVET subsector and its potential to improve workforce competitiveness and poverty reduction efforts.

---

[79] Department of Education. DepEd Order No. 21. 2019. *Policy Guidelines on the K to 12 Basic Education Program*. Pasig.
[80] Congress of the Philippines. 2013. *Republic Act (RA) No. 10533. An act enhancing the Philippine basic education system by strengthening its curriculum and increasing the number of years for basic education, appropriating funds therefor and for other purposes.*
[81] Department of Education. 2017. *DepEd Order No. 68. Guidelines on the Implementation of the Joint Delivery Voucher Program for Senior High School Technical-Vocational-Livelihood Specializations (JDVP-TVL) for School Year (SY) 2017–2018.* Pasig

The Philippine Qualifications Framework

A key milestone in sectoral reform is the institutionalization of the Philippine Qualifications Framework (PQF). The proposal to adopt a national qualifications framework had long been discussed as a reform area in the sector, including by the PTFE and the *Medium-Term Philippine Development Plan 2004–2010*.[82] In 2012, together with the developments in the K to 12 reform, the operationalization of the PQF was achieved through the issuance of Executive Order No. 83 (Institutionalization of the Philippine Qualifications Framework).[83]

To serve as the government focal point in the management of the PQF, a National Coordinating Committee was created, chaired by the secretary of education (DepEd). This also included the heads of TESDA, CHED, DOLE, and the Professional Regulation Commission, as members. The PQF has a three-fold objective: (i) adoption of national standards and levels for education outcomes; (ii) support for the development and maintenance of pathways and equivalencies that enable access to qualifications and facilitate the movement between the different education and training subsectors, and between these subsectors and the labor market; and (iii) alignment of the PQF with the international qualifications framework to facilitate the mobility of workers within and outside the country through enhanced recognition of the value and comparability of Philippine qualifications. Unlike the longstanding proposal to create an NCE/NCCE, the PQF National Coordinating Committee was actually institutionalized by law. This compels the different education agencies (and other agency members) to operationalize the PQF National Coordinating Committee.

The PQF was set to have eight qualifications levels with descriptors that will define each in terms of knowledge, skills and values, application, and degree of independence. CHED, DepEd, and TESDA were tasked to formulate the level descriptors drawing from the learning standards in basic education, competency standards of training regulations in TVET, and the policies and standards in higher education. The education agencies were also mandated to carry out the national piloting of programs to ascertain relevance and applicability in the different education levels. Consistent with the desire to guarantee the alignment of education outcomes to labor requirements, the participation of various industry sector representatives was underscored in further defining and articulating the PQF. At the time when Executive Order No. 83 was newly issued, the critical task for TESDA was the review and revision of the training regulations to align with the new qualifications level descriptors (for DepEd, it was the alignment of the K to 12 curriculum being developed with the new descriptors; and for CHED, the transformation of the policies, standards, and guidelines of degree programs into an outcomes-based format).[84]

Another milestone that further bolstered the pursuit of the PQF was the passage of Republic Act No. 10647 (An Act Strengthening the Ladderized Interface Between Technical-Vocational Education and Training and Higher Education), otherwise known as the *Ladderized Education Act of 2014*.[85] In this legislation, CHED, DepEd, and TESDA were tasked to work closely in the implementation of a unified PQF with the "end view of creating a seamless and borderless education system." The three education agencies were mandated to formulate harmonized guidelines and equivalency competency courses to enhance the delivery of high-quality TVET and higher education courses; synchronize standards and upgrade curriculum design; and develop a strategic implementation scheme, which includes extensive consultations and information dissemination.

---

[82] National Economic and Development Authority (NEDA). 2004. *Medium-term Philippine Development Plan 2004–2010*. Pasig City.
[83] Office of the President. 2012. *Executive Order No. 83. Institutionalization of the Philippine Qualifications Framework*. https://www.officialgazette.gov.ph/2012/10/01/executive-order-no-83-s-2012/.
[84] TESDA. 2012a. The Philippine Qualifications Framework. *TESDA Policy Brief, Issue 2*. Taguig.
[85] Congress of the Philippines. 2014. *Republic Act (RA) No. 10647. An act strengthening the ladderized interface between technical-vocational education and training and higher education*. https://www.officialgazette.gov.ph/2014/11/21/republic-act-no-10647/.

Education System Reforms and the Implications for Technical and Vocational Education and Training   111

As the pursuit of the PQF was gradually becoming more organized and coherent, a law that provided a stronger legal basis for the institutionalization of the PQF was passed. In 2018, Republic Act No. 10968 (An Act Institutionalizing the Philippine Qualifications Framework (PQF), Establishing the PQF-National Coordinating Council and Appropriating Funds Therefor) or the *PQF Act* was enacted.[86] Under this act, the PQF National Coordinating Committee was transformed into a National Coordinating Council (NCC) and expanded its membership to include one representative each from the economic sector and the industry sector. In the law's implementing rules and regulations, seven distinct Working Groups, each to be chaired by a designated member of the PQF NCC, were established focusing on the following areas: Qualifications Register, Quality Assurance, Pathways and Equivalencies, Information and Guidelines, International Alignment, Government–Industry–Education Sector, and Lifelong Learning (footnote 86). The PQF Act also introduced the identification of priority sectors to ensure its more focused implementation. CHED, DepEd, and TESDA, in consultation with industry and other relevant stakeholders, DOLE, Professional Regulation Commission, DTI, NEDA, Department of Science and Technology, and other relevant agencies, were tasked to identify priority sectors and programs considering the realities of the labor market.

A recent accomplishment in line with the intent of the PQF Act to align Philippine qualification standards with international qualification frameworks was the acceptance by the Association of Southeast Asian Nations (ASEAN) Qualifications Reference Framework (AQRF) Committee of the Referencing Report of the Philippines in June 2019. This acceptance confirmed that the Philippine report has met the AQRF referencing criteria and has been endorsed to the ASEAN ministers of economy, education, and labor. The AQRF serves as a common reference framework to allow comparisons of qualifications across ASEAN member states. It is underpinned by a set of agreed quality assurance principles and standards articulated in 11 referencing criteria.

Figure 6.2:   The Philippine Qualifications Framework

Level	Basic education	TVET	Higher education
Level 8			Doctorate and post-doctorate
Level 7			Post-baccalaureate
Level 6			Baccalaureate
Level 5		Diploma	
Level 4		NC IV	
Level 3		NC III	
Level 2		NC II	
Level 1		NC I	
	Grade 12		

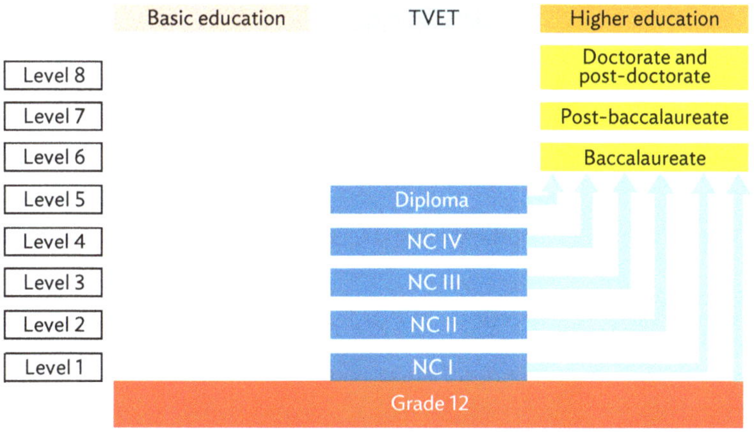

NC = National Certificate, TVET = technical and vocational education and training.
Source: Government of the Philippines. Undated. Philippine Qualifications Framework. https://pqf.gov.ph.

---

[86] Congress of the Philippines. 2017a. *Republic Act (RA) No. 10968. An act institutionalizing the Philippine Qualifications Framework (PQF), establishing the PQF-National Coordinating Council (NCC) and appropriating funds therefor.*

Reform Imperatives for TVET in the Broader Education Sector

In light of the reform milestones outlined in the previous section, the following actions are suggested:

Revisit TVET and TVET-related program frameworks, institutional arrangements, and implementation in light of the K to 12 reform and PQF. The shift to K to 12 and the strengthened implementation of PQF have far-reaching implications to the governance of the TVET subsector within the trifocalized education system. One concern that should be addressed given the relatively fast rollout of the K to 12 program, together with changes being brought about by the PQF, is determining the full extent of its implications to TVET and TVET-related program frameworks, design, and institutional arrangements. This is also an opportunity to look more closely at the training-related programs and projects of other government agencies outside the education sector (such the Department of Agriculture, for example) and determine how the government, through TESDA, can better rationalize the implementation and regulation of these activities given the changing education and training context in the country.

Fast-track the formulation of an action plan to operationalize the PQF. Substantial gains have been achieved since 2012, culminating with the passage of the PQF Act in 2018 and the designation of a permanent governance mechanism mandated by law (i.e., the PQF-NCC). The urgent task for the PQF-NCC is the formulation of an action plan that would operationalize what to many may still seem to be an abstract framework of qualifications and recognitions. The critical work on the development of a Philippine Credit Transfer System to establish pathways between TVET and higher education should be sustained and finalized. A strategic action plan should include effective communications and advocacy that would promote meaningful understanding of the PQF among the various education and training institutions across the subsectors, the extended group of education stakeholders in the public and private sectors, and the general public.

Strengthen and support TESDA's role in quality assurance in the senior high school TVL education program. As the senior high school TVL track has already been implemented for some years now, it would now be opportune to further clarify TESDA's role in the quality assurance of public and private senior high schools offering TVL courses. While it is noted that TVL graduates subject themselves to the necessary TESDA assessments to acquire their NCs, and the TVL teachers obtain the necessary credentials (such as the Trainers Methodology Certificate and requisite NCs), it will be beneficial to assess how these schools could be gradually integrated into the Unified TVET Program Registration and Accreditation System (UTPRAS). As previous reform bodies have consistently highlighted the importance of strengthening TESDA's regulatory and quality assurance functions in the sector, as well as the developments in the PQF, it is important to pursue this policy dialogue now, especially given the huge impact that the TVL track program has on the TVET subsector. A more active role for TESDA in the TVL program, rather than being seen as merely a regulatory compliance concern, should be framed and pursued as a means for the continuous enhancement of the program offerings by providing the metrics for improvement, better planning, evaluation, and generating objective bases for resource allocation.

Strengthen institutional mechanisms between TESDA and DepEd for coordination and policy setting. The recent effort to establish a *DepEd-TESDA Joint Working Group on the TVL Track in the K to 12 Program* is a welcome development.[87] It may be advantageous to set up a similar mechanism at the regional and even provincial/city level as a means for field offices to address operational issues and promote collaborative efforts. The localization of such a working group could be an effective measure to ensure that the distinct roles of DepEd and TESDA, and how they complement in the TVL program, are effectively communicated to the different stakeholders at the

---

[87] Department of Education. 2019. DepEd, *TESDA Formalize Agreements on TVL Education*. July 12. https://www.deped.gov.ph/2019/07/12/deped-tesda-formalize-agreements-on-tvl-education/.

various levels of governance.[88] It is also necessary to guarantee that standards are consistently communicated, understood, and observed by those directly involved in the management of the program, especially at the level of the schools division offices of DepEd and provincial offices of TESDA, and the implementing schools themselves. More than addressing coordination and overlapping issues between DepEd and TESDA, collaboration in program implementation, and policy review and formulation should be encouraged.

Strengthen industry engagement in the implementation of the senior high school TVL education program. Another area where synergy between DepEd and TESDA can contribute to better outcomes in the senior high school TVL track program is in industry engagement, particularly at the regional and provincial/city/schools division levels. The representation of industry in policy making and standard setting had been a hallmark of TESDA's operations. Rather than DepEd having to develop its own mechanism, it could explore a partnership arrangement with TESDA where the regional and provincial TESD committees can be maximized as a means to align senior high school TVL offerings with sectors that have high growth and high value addition, as well as high prospects of employment.

Revive efforts to create a mechanism for broader trans-subsector coordination comprised of CHED, DepEd, and TESDA. Effective sector governance takes on renewed significance now in light of the K to 12 system and the three agencies being pulled closer together as a result of the adoption of the PQF. The present conditions warrant the revival of the proposal to put in place a coordinating body. Certainly, successful attempts for trans-subsector collaboration were evident in the development and transition into the K to 12 program. However, sustaining a state of collaboration and coordination cannot merely be dependent on executive priority or whether there is interest on the part of the agency heads to do so. Rather than pursue this through executive action (i.e., via a presidential issuance or executive order), perspective gained from the years of experience after Congressional Commission on Education (EDCOM) would suggest that this is a reform best secured by legislation. This will provide a stronger legal backbone to exact compliance and lessen the impact of political fluctuations that have hampered its full implementation through the years. Successful reforms are precisely those that can take root in the system and withstand political changes and pressures. The establishment of this coordinating body will also enable agencies to act strategically across subsectors and address cross-cutting concerns. In particular, it will allow for the much-desired interface in setting policy and priorities, planning, budgeting, and program implementation and review. The existence of this coordinating body will also facilitate collaborative and complementary sector approaches, for example, in targeting the poor and disadvantaged and adopting holistic and integrated approaches to interventions.

Develop and implement a sector-wide communications strategy to promote better appreciation of TVET and its distinct niche in the sector and in national development. Removing the low regard for TVET relative to college education through advocacy has always been part of recommendations to improve the subsector and has been duly pursued by TESDA. Better outcomes could be achieved in this regard by shifting into a broader, sector-wide communications strategy that actively engages the other two subsectors of basic education and higher education. As a key entry point, TESDA should seek opportunities for increased collaboration with CHED and DepEd in promoting understanding of the senior high school curriculum exits (i.e., employment, entrepreneurship, middle-level skills development, higher education) among various stakeholders, and how a learner can navigate through equivalency pathways for seamless education transfer and/or progression between education levels in accordance with the PQF qualification levels. A recent law, Republic Act No. 11206 (Secondary School Career Guidance and Counseling Act),[89] that came into effect in 2019 should provide added impetus in pursuing this as it mandates CHED and TESDA, among other agencies, to work with DepEd in the development and implementation of a career guidance and counseling program in secondary education.

---

[88] Asian Development Bank–Senior High School Support Program (ADB-SHSSP). 2019. *Field Visit Findings: Senior High School Support Program Review Mission Aide Memoire*. Manila: ADB.

[89] Congress of the Philippines. 2018. *Republic Act (RA) No. 11206. An act establishing a career guidance and counseling program for all secondary schools and appropriating funds therefor*. https://www.officialgazette.gov.ph/downloads/2019/02feb/20190214-RA-11206-RRD.pdf.

7. Technical and Vocational Education and Training Trends Over the Last Decade

TVET in the Philippines has significantly changed in recent years due to major education reforms, labor market developments, and changes related to Industry 4.0, among other factors. This chapter draws on data from TESDA surveys, statistics, and publications, and from the labor force survey, to provide an overview of trends in TVET over the last decade (prior to COVID-19) both at the national and regional levels. It concludes with remarks on the contribution of TVET in making the country's economic growth more inclusive, in line with TESDA's twin objectives of a competitive workforce and social equity for workforce inclusion.

Descriptive Trends on TVET at the National Level

The number of TVET enrollees has been increasing, while the gap between graduates and those that are assessed and certified has narrowed. In 2018, nearly 2.5 million Filipinos were enrolled in TVET courses. The numbers of TVET enrollees and graduates have steadily grown since 2010 (Figure 7.1). The share of assessed graduates more than

Figure 7.1: Technical and Vocational Education and Training Enrollment, Program Completion, Assessment, and Certification, 2008–2018

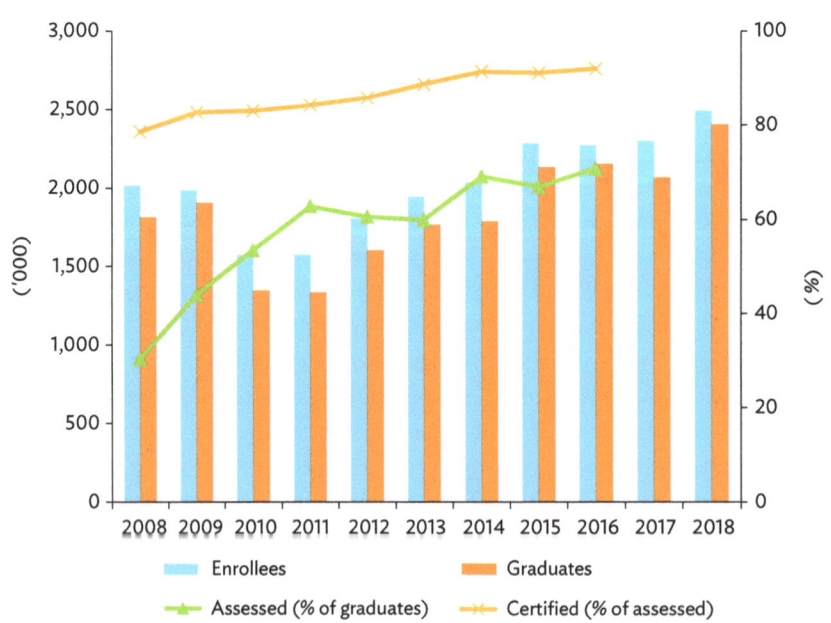

Source: Technical Education and Skills Development Authority. 2018a. *National Technical Education and Skills Development Plan 2018–2022*. Taguig.

doubled from 2008 to 2011 (going from 30% to 63%) and has continued to increase to 71% in 2016. Certification rates have also continued to rise, from 79% in 2008, to 92% in 2016, reflecting important improvements in terms of meeting industry standards.

Enterprise-based TVET provision has continued to represent a minor share of TVET enrollment, declining from 5%–6% in 2009–2012, to 3%–4% since 2013 (Figure 7.2). This is due to an important decline in the number of participating companies from 801 in 2011 to 348 in 2016, which TESDA attributes to difficulties relating to legal matters (e.g., tax emptions, duration of training) and to economic difficulties in certain industries (footnote 50). The declining trend in enterprise-based training (EBT) should be a concern for TESDA due to the increasing relevance of this modality, which tends to deliver training more aligned with industry demand. The share of community-based TVET provision has increased and the share of institution-based TVET decreased from 2012 to 2017. Community-based training in the Philippines is often delivered through partnerships with TVIs and can be more responsive to local needs. However, concerns about it being of poorer quality and largely supply driven, due to limited resources/facilities and linkages with industry, warrant continuous monitoring efforts from TESDA, particularly as these issues may be exacerbated in the context of Industry 4.0.

Figure 7.2: Technical and Vocational Education and Training Enrollment by Delivery Mode, 2009–2018

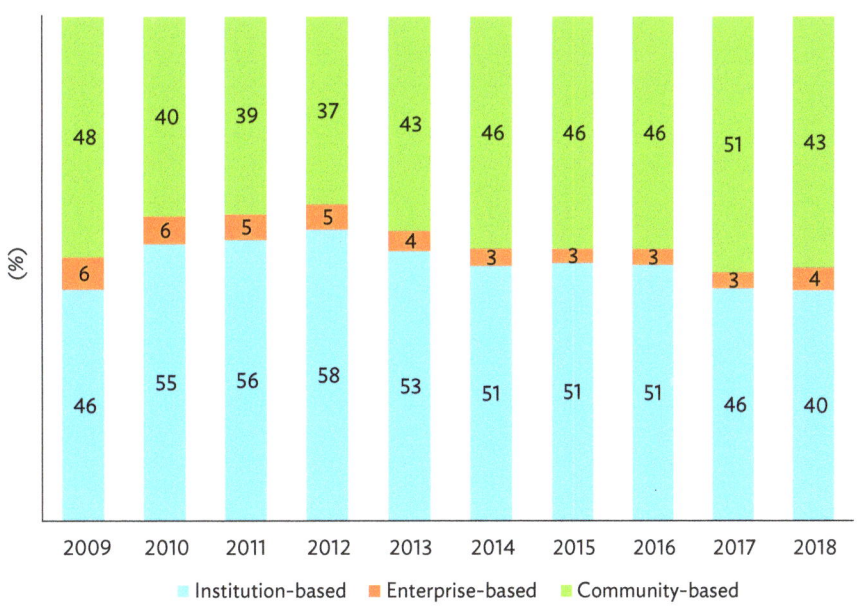

Source: Technical Education and Skills Development Authority. 2018a. *National Technical Education and Skills Development Plan 2018–2022*. Taguig.

Publicly provided TVET in the Philippines accounts for more than half of enrollment, and targets the poor and vulnerable population, consistent with TESDA's objectives of social equity and inclusion. As of 2017, there were 3,966 TVET providers nationwide (3,625 private and 341 public).[90] TVET providers are institutions with TESDA-registered programs or courses, including TVIs, higher education institutions, TESDA technical institutions (TTIs), and others. Despite representing less than 10% of TVET providers, public institutions, including TESDA's 124 TTIs, accounted for 52% of the country's TVET enrollment in 2018. The distribution of those enrolled in post-secondary and TVET differs significantly between public and private schools, and this difference has increased in recent years. While the poorest income deciles' share in post-secondary courses enrollment has increased in 2013–2017 for public institutions, the largest shares of enrollment in private institutions have shifted from middle-income toward the highest income deciles (Figure 7.3). Note that this shift is exacerbated by the inclusion of senior high school with TVL track in the data for 2016 and 2017, following the implementation of the K to 12 program. In 2017, the three poorest income deciles represented 38% of enrollment in public post-secondary courses and senior high school, and 14% of enrollment in private ones. Conversely, the three richest deciles represented 15% of enrollment in public institutions, and 58% of enrollment in private institutions. The availability of scholarships and scholarship funds appears to have an important impact on enrollment figures (footnote 50). TESDA scholarships include the Special Training for Employment Program (STEP) targeting poorer and informal sector families (Chapter 11).

Figure 7.3: Enrollment in Post-Secondary Courses (2013–2017) and Senior High School (2016 and 2017)

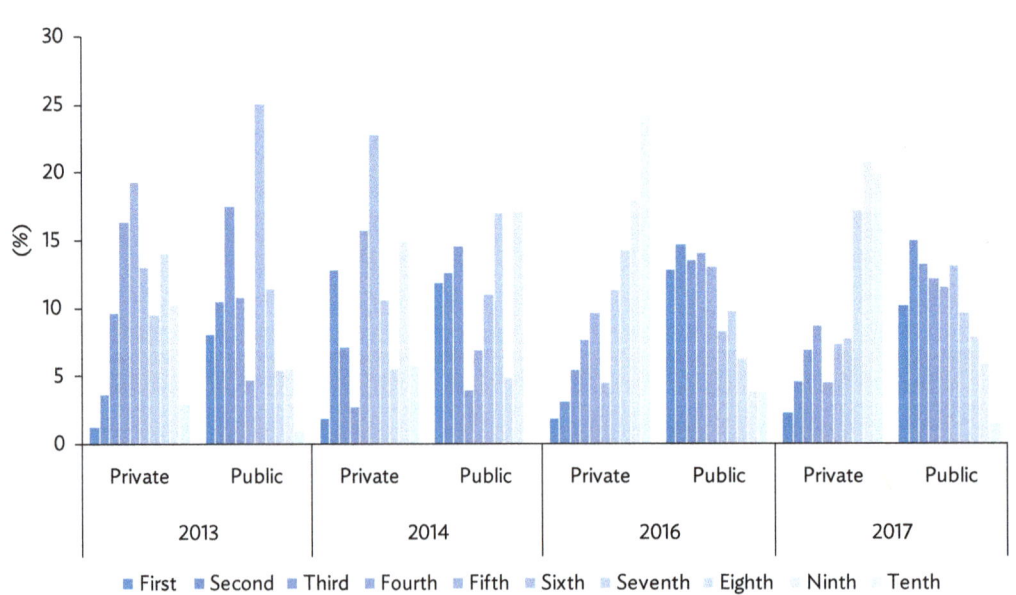

Source: ADB estimates using Annual Poverty Indicators Survey.

---

[90] Note that the number of TVET providers had grown to 4,670 in 2015, but declined subsequently following a national technical audit in 2016, which led to some TVI closures. The number of public TVIs also declined partly due to some being absorbed into rapidly expanding state universities and colleges. See TESDA (2018a).

Figure 7.4: Employment-to-Population Rate and Labor Force Participation Rate of Technical and Vocational Education and Training Graduates, 2012–2018

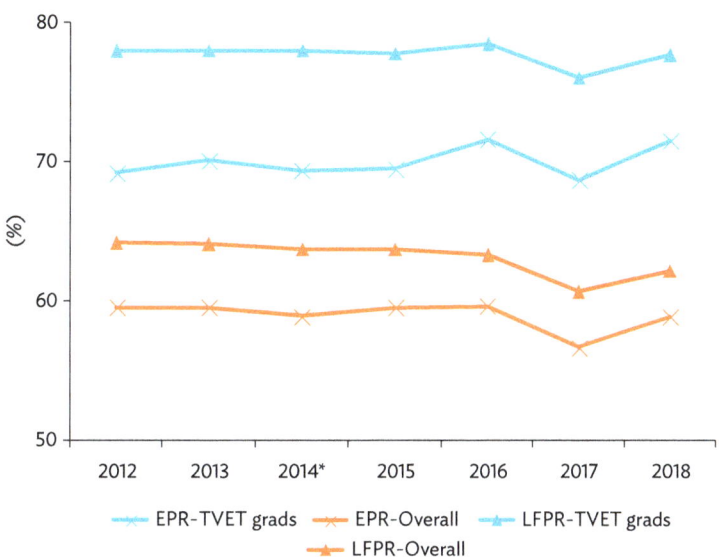

EPR = employment-to-population rate, LFPR = labor force participation rate, TVET = technical and vocational education and training.

Figure 7.5: Unemployment Rate of Technical and Vocational Education and Training Graduates and Share of Working-Age Population, 2012–2018

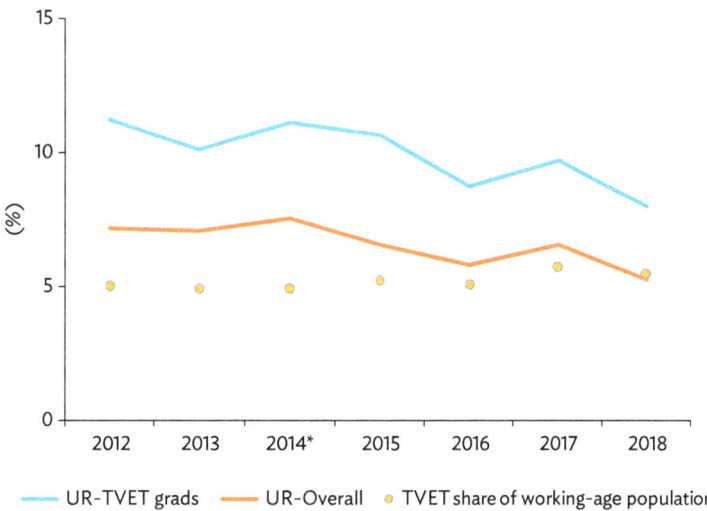

TVET = technical and vocational education and training, UR = unemployment rate.
Note: 2014 excludes Region 8.
Source: ADB estimates based on labor force survey.

Over 5% of the Philippines' working-age population has completed some form of TVET, and TVET graduates are far more likely than average to participate in the labor market. Between 2012 and 2018, the share of the Philippines' working-age population that had completed some form of TVET, henceforth referred to as TVET graduates, increased slightly from 5.0% to 5.4% (Figure 7.5). Labor market indicators for TVET graduates have generally followed the same trend as the national average for 2012–2018 (Figure 7.4, Figure 7.5).

TVET graduates have significantly higher labor force participation and employment rates than the national average, but also higher unemployment rates (Figure 7.4, Figure 7.5). This largely reflects the fact that many of those engaging in TVET do so with the objective of improving their employability and finding employment, and are therefore more likely to be economically active. Thus, the higher unemployment rate of TVET graduates does not necessarily signal poor labor market performance, as those who take up TVET are more likely than average to be unemployed in the first place (i.e., not in employment and seeking work). For instance, an estimated 74% of TVET graduates in 2012 were unemployed before training.[91] TVET programs are often part of active labor market policies (ALMPs) targeting the unemployed, including with opportunities for reskilling. This function of TVET is particularly important in the context of rapidly changing labor demand.

The gender gap in TVET has been closed in the Philippines, with a larger share of females than males among enrollees in recent years. Analyzing data from the labor force survey (LFS) and from TESDA databases provides complementary insights on TVET trends in the Philippines. The former source covers all TVET graduates among the working-age population, regardless of when their course or program was completed or the highest grade completed, while the second source provides statistics on TVET enrollees and graduates by year. For instance, in the 2018 LFS, men still accounted for 59% of all TVET graduates among the Philippines' working-age population. However, in recent years, the gender gap in TVET enrollment has narrowed and even reversed—in 2017 and 2018, respectively, 53% and 54% of TVET graduates were female as per TESDA records.

TVET remains highly gender-segregated; female students dominate enrollment in courses geared for the growing services subsectors, while male students dominate those geared toward construction and manufacturing. While some courses that have always been among the top TVET programs in the Philippines (such as automotive and mechanics, electronics and electricians, and welding) have remained among the most popular in recent years, particularly for male TVET graduates, other courses that are traditionally the most popular among women TVET graduates (e.g., those related to garments, secretarial work, and the beauty/cosmetics industry) seem to have fallen behind courses geared toward sales and services occupations in retail and wholesale trade and tourism (hotels and restaurants), and personal services (Figure 7.6, Figure 7.7).[92] Specifically, the top TVET courses in terms of enrollment at the national level in 2018 (among courses with training regulations only) included the following, all of which were NC II courses, and all of which were particularly popular among female TVET enrollees: bread and pastry production, food and beverage services, cookery, housekeeping, wellness massage, and domestic work (Figure 7.7). Other top courses in terms of enrollment in 2018, where male students dominate enrollment, were linked to construction, specifically Shielded Metal Arc Welding (NC I and II) and electrical Installation and Maintenance NC II; and to automotive manufacturing and repair of motor vehicles, specifically Automotive Servicing NC I.

---

[91] C. Orbeta, Jr. and E. Esguerra. 2016. The National System of Technical Vocational Education and Training in the Philippines: Review and Reform Ideas. *Philippine Institute for Development Studies (PIDS) Discussion Paper Series*, No. 2016-07. Quezon City.

[92] In the overall working-age population as represented in the 2016 LFS, men accounted for 90%–100% of graduates of TVET courses linked to the automotive, construction, and marine transportation industries, while women accounted for similar shares of graduates of courses linked to garments, midwifery, secretarial work, and beauty care (Table A7.1).

Figure 7.6: Top Programs and Courses among Male and Female Technical and Vocational Education and Training Graduates in the Overall Population, 2016

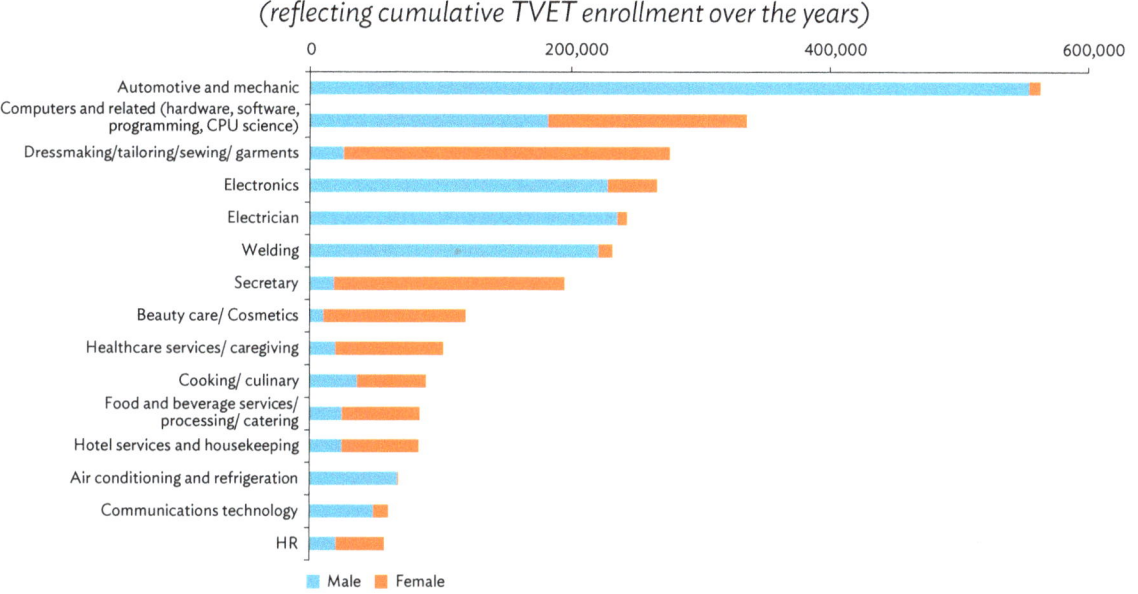

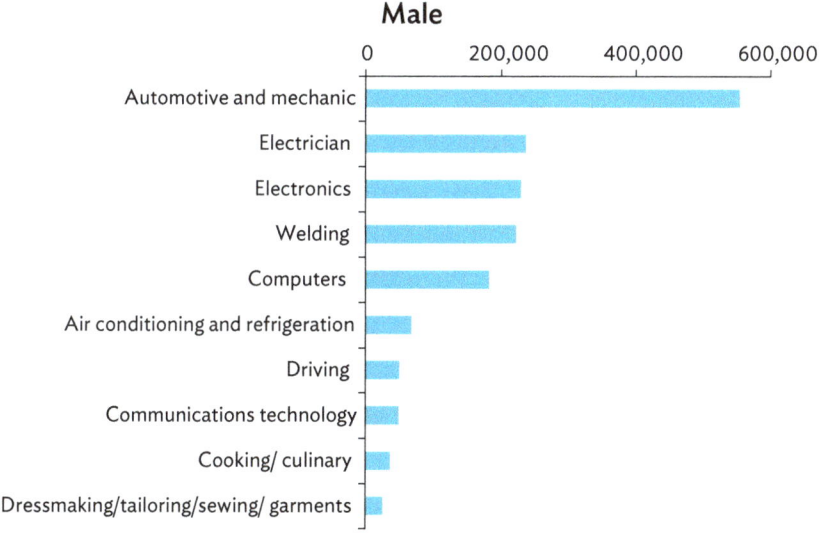

continued on next page

Figure 7.6:   continued

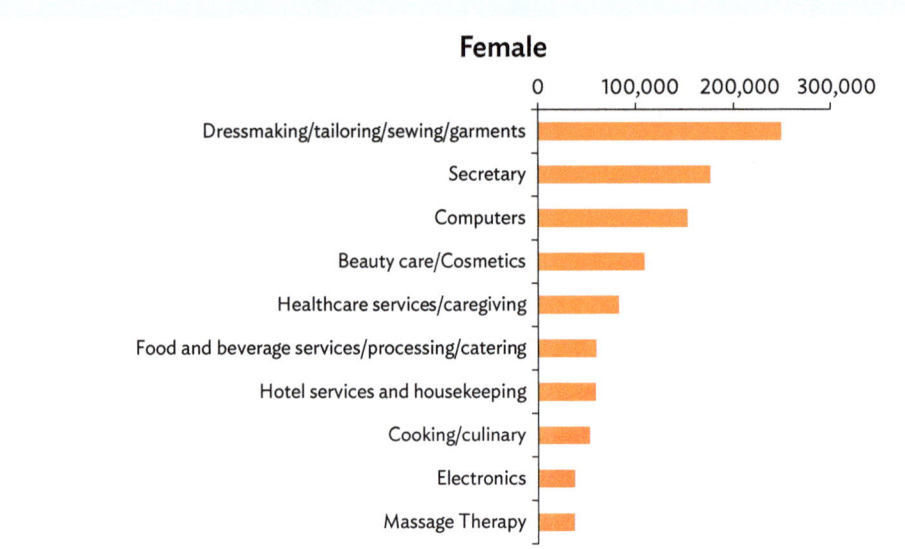

CPU = central processing unit, HR = human resources, TVET = technical and vocational education and training.
Source: ADB estimates based on labor force survey, January 2016.

Figure 7.7:   Top Courses in Terms of Total Male and Female Technical and Vocational Education and Training Enrollment, 2018

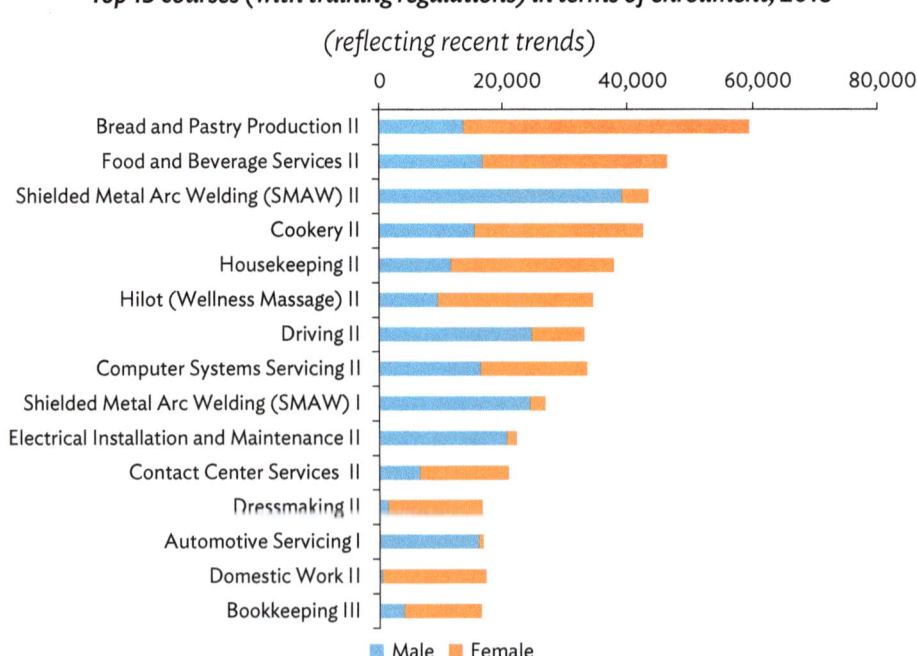

Figure 7.7: continued

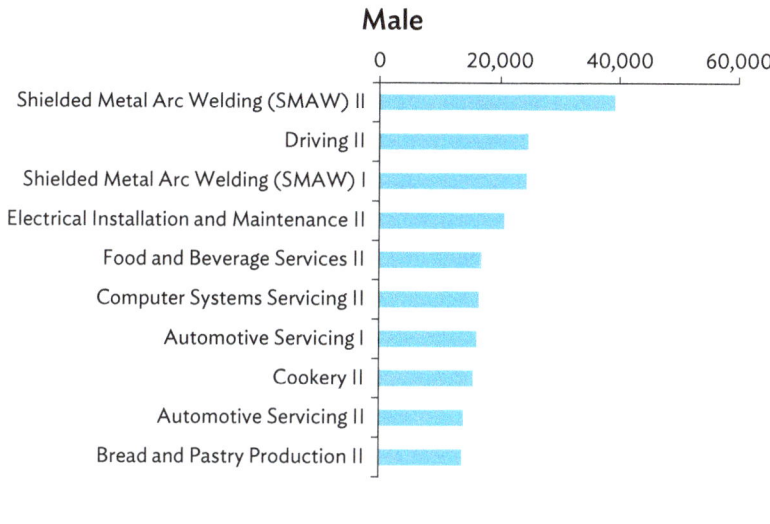

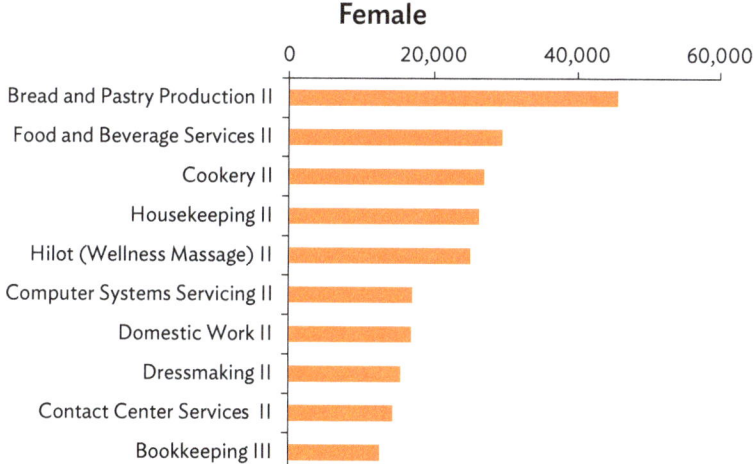

TVET = technical and vocational education and training.
Source: Technical Education and Skills Development Authority. 2018a. *National Technical Education and Skills Development Plan (NTESDP) 2018–2022.* Taguig.

The most popular courses in recent years reflect growth sectors of the Philippines' economy, including those conducive to employment in call centers and business process outsourcing: Computer Systems Servicing NC II, popular with both sexes, and Contact Center Services II, popular for female enrollees, in particular. These courses have more or less been constant on TESDA's list of top 10 most-availed courses between 2014 and 2018. Other courses that have been on the top 10 list over this period include Computer Hardware Servicing NC II and Programming NC II, Front Office Services NC II, which are courses conducive to employment in the IT-BPO industries, and Bartending NC II, which is conducive to employment in tourism. Although the hotels and restaurants industry, health care and social work, and "other services" industries accounted for less than 15% of employment among the Philippines' TVET graduates in 2018 (Figure 7.7), these industries represented about 40% of TVET enrollment, specifically tourism (24%), social and community development (10%), and human health/health care (6%) (Figure 7.8). This reflects perceptions and expectations on the continued expansion of employment opportunities in these growth sectors of the Philippines economy, but also the transferability of skills across certain sectors. For instance, the expected post-training occupations of bread and pastry production and food and beverage services courses belong to the service and sales workers occupational group (Table 7.1); graduates may find employment in tourism, but also in the wholesale and retail trade industry.

The distribution of TVET graduates across industries parallels that of the overall workforce, but TVET graduates are more likely than average to be employed in manufacturing, and less likely to be employed in agriculture. Among the employed TVET graduates, some 23% were employed in wholesale and retail trade and repair of motor vehicles in 2018, and 14% in manufacturing (Figure 7.8). TVET graduates are therefore far more likely than average to work in manufacturing, which employed 8.5% of the Philippine workforce in 2018. On the other hand, they are also far less likely to be employed in agriculture (only 12.4% of employed TVET graduates, compared to 26% of the country's employed). Other industries

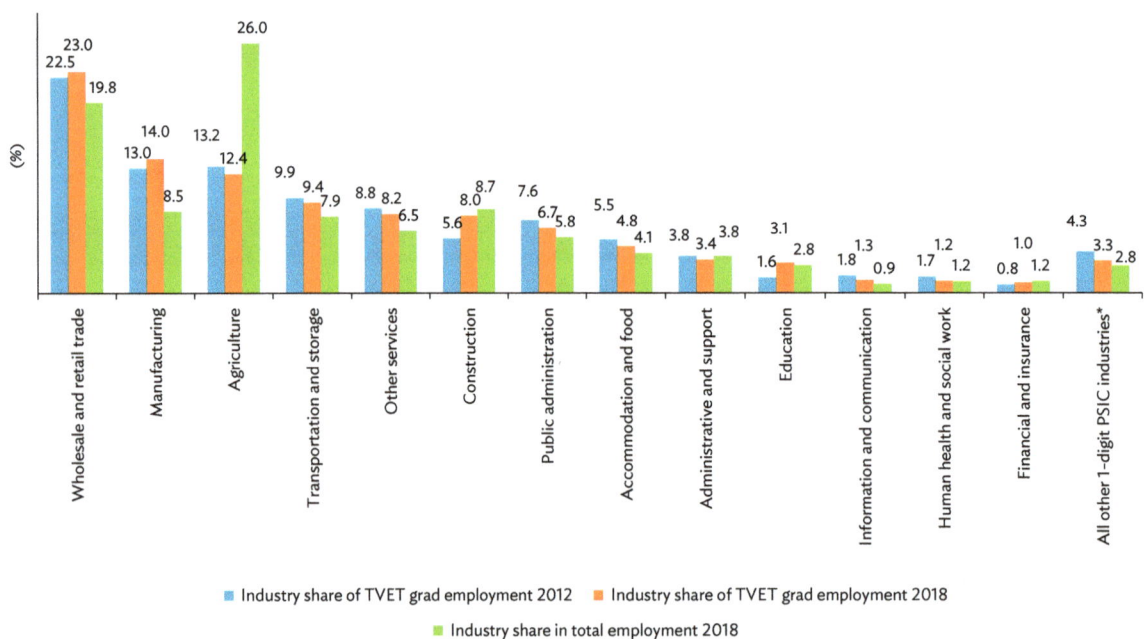

Figure 7.8: Industry Shares of Technical and Vocational Education and Training Graduate Employment and Overall Employment, 2012 and 2018

PSIC = Philippine Standard Industrial Classification, TVET = technical and vocational education and training.
Note: All other 1-digit PSIC industries include arts, entertainment and recreation; professional, scientific and technical services; real estate activities; mining and quarrying; electricity, gas, steam, and air-conditioning supply; water supply, sewerage, waste management, and remediation; extraterritorial organizations and bodies; and activities of private households as employers and undifferentiated production activities of private households.
Source: ADB estimates based on labor force survey.

Table 7.1: Top 10 Qualifications with Expected Occupations and Corresponding Occupational Groups, 2013–2016

Qualification	Expected Occupations	PSOC Group
Food and Beverage Services II	Waiter; Food and Beverage Service Attendant	Service and sales workers
Housekeeping NC II	Junior Cleaner; Assistant Cleaner; Assistant Public Area Cleaner; Cleaner; Public Area Cleaner; Attendant; Room/Cabin Attendant/Room Maid; Laundry Attendant; Housekeeping Attendant; Butler	Elementary Occupations
Computer Hardware Servicing NC II	Computer Assembler; Computer Service Technician; Network Technician; Computer Maintenance Technician	Technicians and associate professionals
Shielded Metal Arc Welding (SMAW) II	Plate Welder (Flux-core arc welding)	Craft and related trades workers
Bread and Pastry MC II	Commis - Pastry; Baker	Service and sales workers
Electrical Installation and Maintenance NC II	Building-Wiring Electrician; Residential/Commercial-Wiring Electrician; Maintenance Electrician	Craft and related trades workers
Bartending NC II	Barista	Service and sales workers
Automotive Servicing NC II	Automotive Engine Rebuilder; Machinist	Craft and related trades workers
Consumer Electronics Servicing NC II	Consumer Electronics Products Assembly Supervisor; Domestic Appliance Senior Technician; Cellular Phone Senior Technician; Audio-Video Senior Technician	Technicians and associate professionals
Cookery NC II	Cook or Commis; Assistant Cook	Service and sales workers

NC = National certificate, PSOC = Philippines Standard Occupational Classification.
Source: ADB compilation based on Technical Education and Skills Development Authority documents.

with large shares of TVET grad employment are transportation and storage, construction, and other service activities.

TVET graduates represent an important share of the workforce in specialized construction activities, utilities, and in several manufacturing industries. Between 2016 and 2018, TVET graduates represented on average more than 10% of the workforce of a number of manufacturing industries, such as fabricated metal products, machinery and equipment, basic metals, motor vehicles, and other transport equipment and wearing apparel (Figure 7.8). Specialized construction activities and utilities (electricity, gas, steam, and air-conditioning) also had high shares of TVET graduates among the workforce. In all these industries, the TVET share of the workforce increased in more recent years (2016–2018), compared to the 2012–2015 average. The expanding construction sector saw the largest increase in its share of overall TVET employment (from 5.6% to 8.0% between 2012 and 2018), followed by education (from 1.6% to 3.1%) and manufacturing (from 13% to 14%) (Figure 7.9).

Figure 7.9: Technical and Vocational Education and Training Graduates' Share in Employment by Detailed Industry, 2012–2015 and 2016–2018

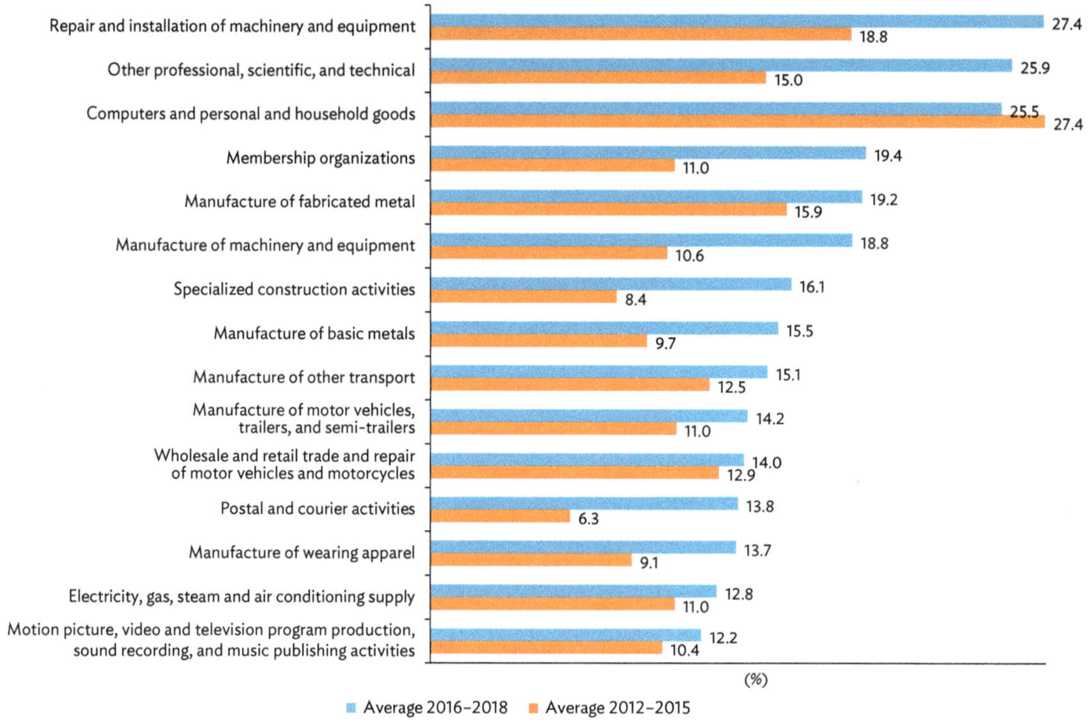

Industry	Average 2016–2018 (%)	Average 2012–2015 (%)
Repair and installation of machinery and equipment	27.4	18.8
Other professional, scientific, and technical	25.9	15.0
Computers and personal and household goods	25.5	27.4
Membership organizations	19.4	11.0
Manufacture of fabricated metal	19.2	15.9
Manufacture of machinery and equipment	18.8	10.6
Specialized construction activities	16.1	8.4
Manufacture of basic metals	15.5	9.7
Manufacture of other transport	15.1	12.5
Manufacture of motor vehicles, trailers, and semi-trailers	14.2	11.0
Wholesale and retail trade and repair of motor vehicles and motorcycles	14.0	12.9
Postal and courier activities	13.8	6.3
Manufacture of wearing apparel	13.7	9.1
Electricity, gas, steam and air conditioning supply	12.8	11.0
Motion picture, video and television program production, sound recording, and music publishing activities	12.2	10.4

Source: ADB estimates based on labor force survey.

Service industries that employ graduates of electronics- and computer-related programs, were among those with the highest shares (over 25%) of TVET graduates among their workforce (Figure 7.9). These include repair and installation of machinery and equipment; other professional, scientific, and technical activities; and repair of computers and personal household goods. The electrical and electronics sector accounted for an important share (8%) of TVET enrollment in 2018, with approximately one-third of its enrollees being female (Figure 7.10).

Regional TVET Diagnostics

Regional TVET representation is generally proportional to regional population size, with CALABARZON, Central Luzon, and the NCR regions jointly accounting for nearly 40% of TVET enrollment in 2018 (Figure A7.1). The lowest regional shares of TVET enrollment are in ARMM and CAR, which in 2018 accounted, respectively, for 0.8% and 2.3% of the country's TVET enrollment. ARMM has a particularly low share in TVET enrollment relative to its share in the overall population (Figure A7.1), and the lowest ratio of TVET graduates to working-age population (Figure 7.11). The region has had a decline in TVET enrollment in recent years, as has Central Visayas. The fastest growth in TVET enrollment took place in SOCCSKSARGEN, followed by Eastern and Western Visayas,

Figure 7.10: Technical and Vocational Education and Training Enrollment by Sector, 2018

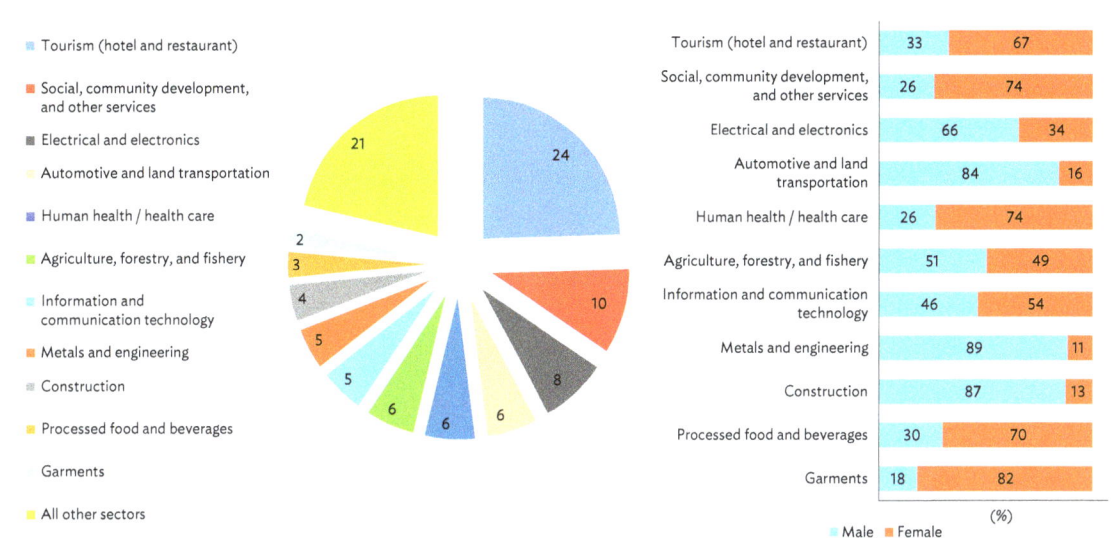

TVET = technical and vocational education and training.
Source: Technical Education and Skills Development Authority, TVET Statistics, https://www.tesda.gov.ph/About/TESDA/53 (accessed 1 December 2020).

Ilocos, and Davao. The growth rate of TVET enrollment has been far lower in the NCR, albeit from a larger base, but also in the CAR, MIMAROPA.

The more urban industrialized regions that have a more diverse private sector have relatively higher shares of TVET enrollment in private institutions and in enterprise-based training. CALABARZON, Central Luzon, and SOCCSKSARGEN have lower than average public share in TVET enrollment, limited community-based TVET, and the highest shares of enterprise-based TVET. The NCR has the second-lowest public share in TVET enrollment, and accounts for less than 5% of enrollment in TESDA's TTIs (Table 7.2). It has among the highest share of institution-based TVET enrollment, due to the presence of a large number of private sector providers, and lowest shares of community-based TVET (Table 7.2). Set against these industrialized regions, however, there does not appear to be any correlation between poverty incidence and the public share of enrollment, or, if any, it seems to be a slightly negative correlation.[93] The poorest region, ARMM, also has the lowest public share of TVET enrollment, with just over 30% in 2018, and the lowest share of TTI enrollment (Table 7.2). It has virtually no enrollment in enterprise-based TVET; enrollment is split in half between institution-based and community-based providers. ARMM also has the lowest certification rate as a percentage of those assessed among the regions.

Females represented more than half of TVET enrollment in all but three regions in 2018 (Table 7.2). Even in ARMM, where female labor force participation and employment are far lower, females accounted for 54% of TVET enrollment. TVET is therefore a potentially useful tool to improve female labor market outcomes and contribute to poverty reduction in this disadvantaged region.

[93] Refer to Figure A2.4 in Chapter 2.

Table 7.2: Regional Technical and Vocational Education and Training Statistics

	Share of TVET enrollment (2018)	Share in TTI enrollment, 2018	Number of TESDA TTIs, 2018	Public share of TVET enrollment, 2018 (%)	Female share of TVET enrollment, 2018 (%)	TVET enrollment by delivery mode			Certification rate (% of assessed), 2016
						Institution-based (%)	Enterprise-based (%)	Community-based (%)	
Region I – Ilocos Region	7.3	12.1	7	66	52	60.9	2.7	36.4	91
Region II – Cagayan Valley	3.5	5.1	6	73	53	44.5	2.3	53.1	93
Region III – Central Luzon	9.7	4.2	10	50	55	54.6	4.5	40.9	91
Region V – Bicol	3.6	6.6	12	52	56	49.6	0.2	50.3	82
Region VI – Western Visayas	7.2	8.1	10	41	50	32.7	1.8	65.5	88
Region VII – Central Visayas	7.4	4.2	12	61	58	54.3	3.2	42.5	94
Region VIII – Eastern Visayas	3.8	6.4	9	68	56	46.3	1.6	52.1	96
Region IX – Zamboanga Peninsula	4	7.3	5	56	46	44.8	2.5	52.7	86
Region X – Northern Mindanao	4.9	9.9	10	58	57	44.8	2.1	53.2	91
Region XI – Davao	5.4	4.6	6	65	55	29.8	0.7	69.6	95
Region XII – SOCCSKSARGEN	6.2	2	3	40	46	51.2	4.6	44.2	90

Table 7.2: continued

	Share of TVET enrollment (2018)	Share in TTI enrollment, 2018	Number of TESDA TTIs, 2018	Public share of TVET enrollment, 2018 (%)	Female share of TVET enrollment, 2018 (%)	TVET enrollment by delivery mode			Certification rate (% of assessed), 2016
						Institution-based (%)	Enterprise-based (%)	Community-based (%)	
National Capital Region	14.2	4.8	5	38	64	60.8	2.3	36.9	97
Cordillera Administrative Region	2.3	3.2	6	59	52	56.9	1.9	41.2	90
Autonomous Region in Muslim Mindanao	0.8	1.1	3	31	54	50.4	0	49.6	84
Caraga	3.4	5.4	5	68	50	52.6	1.5	45.9	87
Region IVA - CALABARZON	13	7.1	10	46	46	49.9	7.8	42.4	88
Region IVB - MIMAROPA	3.1	7.6	5	48	55	57.3	0.3	42.3	90
Aggregate or national average	100	100	124	52	54	50.7	3.2	46.1	92

CALABARZON = Cavite, Laguna, Batangas, Rizal, and Quezon; MIMAROPA = Occidental Mindoro, Oriental Mindoro, Marinduque, Romblon, and Palawan; SOCCSKSARGEN = South Cotabato, Cotabato, Sultan Kudarat, Sarangani and General Santos; TESDA = Technical Education and Skills Development Authority; TTI = TESDA technical institution; TVET = technical and vocational education and training.

Sources: TESDA, TVET Statistics, https://www.tesda.gov.ph/About/TESDA/53 (accessed 1 December 2020); TESDA. 2018a. *National Technical Education and Skills Development Plan (NTESDP) 2018–2022.* Taguig.

Figure 7.11: Technical and Vocational Education and Training Share of Working-Age Population and Annual Growth Rate of Enrollment by Region

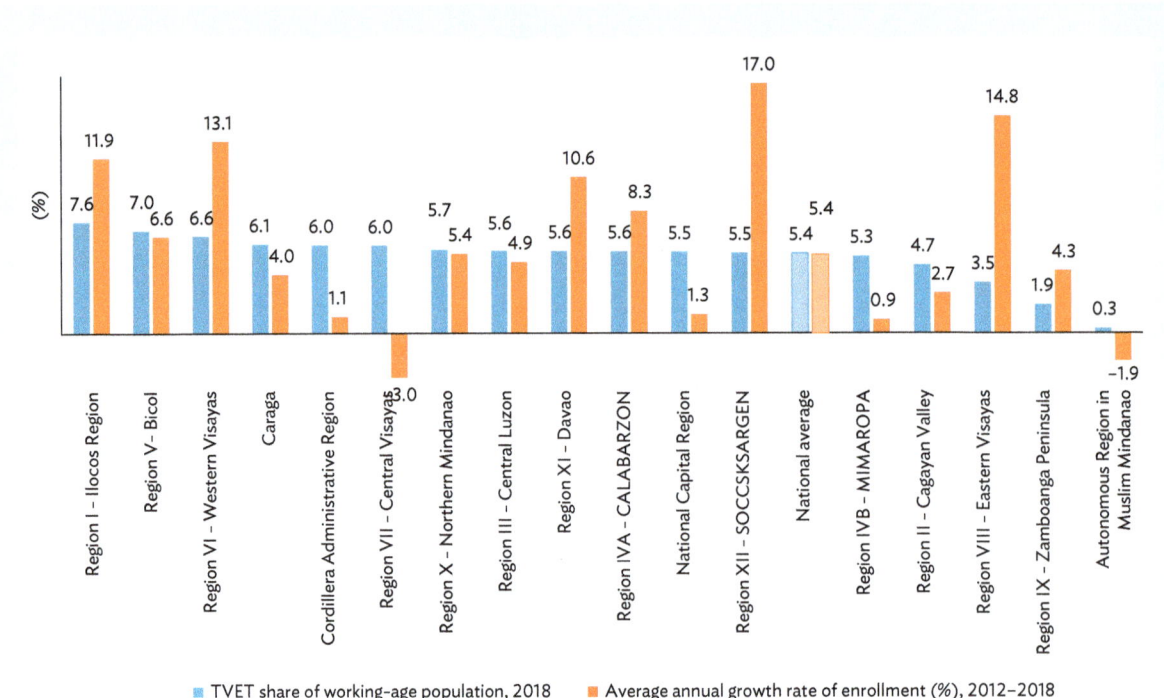

CALABARZON = Cavite, Laguna, Batangas, Rizal, and Quezon; MIMAROPA = Occidental Mindoro, Oriental Mindoro, Marinduque, Romblon, and Palawan; SOCCSKSARGEN = South Cotabato, Cotabato, Sultan Kudarat, Sarangani and General Santos; TESDA = Technical Education and Skills Development Authority; TVET = technical and vocational education and training.
Source: ADB estimates based on labor force survey and TESDA.

Conclusions

TVET enrollment has been on the rise, and the gap between graduates and those that are assessed and certified has narrowed. The most-availed programs in recent years reflect growth sectors of the Philippine economy. These include courses conducive to employment in call centers and business process outsourcing, hotels and restaurants industry, health care and social work, among others.

A concerning trend in the context of Industry 4.0 is the decline in enterprise-based training (EBT) at the national level, and its complete absence in certain regions. EBT already accounted for a limited share of TVET and has further declined to 3%–4% of enrollment since 2013. At the same time, the advantages of this modality are likely to be enhanced with Industry 4.0. With respect to its objective of a developing competitive workforce, TESDA must therefore intensify its efforts to expand EBT, including through a review of the Dual Training System Act of 1994 (DTS Law) and the Apprenticeship Bill, both of which are already on its legislative agenda as per the NTESDP 2018–2022. It must also continue to push for sustained industry involvement in training provision and in other areas of TVET, including assessment and certification, and continuous identification of the changing needs and requirements in the Industry 4.0 context (with respect to skills, but also equipment, processes, etc.).

On the social inclusion front, TESDA must actively encourage enrollment of youth, females, and disadvantaged groups in courses and programs conducive to decent work in manufacturing and services, through scholarships and other incentives, and partnerships with industry and other stakeholders. The gender gap in TVET enrollment has narrowed and has even been reversed, but enrollment remains highly segregated, with female students clustering in courses geared toward sales and services occupations, involving mainly nonroutine manual tasks, and less pay, in lower-productivity services sectors like retail trade and tourism. TVET offers a promising means of labor market inclusion for women; female enrollment in TVET is high even in regions with low female labor force participation.

Publicly provided TVET in the Philippines accounts for more than half of TVET enrollment, and targets the poor and vulnerable population, consistent with TESDA's objectives of social equity and workforce inclusion. However, while public TVET targets disadvantaged segments of the population, enrollment shares in public institutions are not necessarily higher in the poorer regions. Public TVET provision in poor regions and remote areas must be focused on local needs, including agriculture and other sectors of rural economies.

Attracting youth to the agriculture sector will remain difficult as long as agriculture wages and productivity remain low. Despite the ongoing structural transformation underway in the Philippines, the agriculture sector remains important for the livelihoods of many, particularly in poorer regions outside the urban and industrial centers. TESDA must promote enrollment in agriculture programs and courses that can prepare workers for employment along agricultural supply chains. This also is a challenge recognized in the NTESDP 2018–2022. Thus, TESDA must join efforts with other initiatives aimed at boosting agricultural growth, and develop partnerships with investors in agribusiness and agro-processing ventures.

Appendix 7: Labor Market Characteristics of Technical Education Skills Development Authority Graduates

Table A7.1: Male and Female Share of Graduates, Employment-to-Population Rate, Unemployment Rate, and Labor Force Participation Rate by Course/Program

Rank (By number of TVET graduates)	Course/program	Male share	Female share	EPR	UR	LFPR
1	Automotive and mechanic	98	2	84	6	90
2	Computers and related (hardware, software, programming, computer science)	54	46	66	14	76
3	Dressmaking/tailoring/sewing/garments	9	91	60	5	63
4	Electronics	86	14	75	10	84
5	Electrician	97	3	82	8	89
6	Welding	95	5	78	9	86
7	Secretary	10	90	62	5	66
8	Beauty care/Cosmetics	9	91	69	3	71
9	Health care services/caregiving	20	80	54	13	63
10	Cooking/culinary	41	59	60	12	68
11	Food and beverage services/processing/catering	29	71	59	16	70
12	Hotel services and housekeeping	30	70	51	24	67
13	Air-conditioning and refrigeration	99	1	81	7	87
14	Communications technology	81	19	78	1	79
15	HR	36	64	63	17	76
16	Driving	91	9	87	3	90
17	Massage therapy	18	82	77	8	83
18	ICT	38	62	63	16	75
19	Nursing	19	81	59	4	61
20	Baking and pastry	29	71	64	13	74
21	Manufacturing technology/industrial technology/machine shop/machinist/instrumentation	81	19	83	7	90
22	Bar tending and baristas	75	25	65	24	85
23	Seaman/seafarer	98	2	85	6	91
24	Hairdressing	28	72	61	12	69
25	Plumbing	100	0	58	14	68
26	Hotels and restaurants management	32	68	63	15	74
27	Midwifery	0	100	60	0	60
28	Architecture/civil engineering/interior design/graphic design/drafting	73	27	79	6	84
29	Pipe fitting	100	0	68	13	78
30	Reflexology	13	87	79	0	79

Table A7.1 continued

Rank (By number of TVET graduates)	Course/program	Male share	Female share	EPR	UR	LFPR
31	Carpentry	100	0	82	0	82
32	Drafting	74	26	65	0	65
33	General construction/maintenance	100	0	75	17	91
34	Bookkeeping	15	85	80	0	80
35	Other marine transport	100	0	71	25	95
36	Heavy equipment/machinery operators	94	6	96	4	100
37	Farming/animal production	94	6	59	23	77
38	Physical/occupational therapy	22	78	84	8	91
39	N/A	68	32	50	18	61
40	Pharmacy	37	63	64	0	64
41	Agriculture/agribusiness/forestry	42	58	76	0	76
42	Business management/office management/institutional management	29	71	59	20	75
43	Education/teaching	20	80	64	11	72
44	Airlines/travel/ other tourism	46	54	71	10	79
45	Aquaculture/ fishing	52	48	84	0	84
46	Call centers	22	78	56	28	79
47	Agricultural technology	73	27	78	0	78
48	Front office services	21	79	60	0	60
49	Languages	18	82	94	6	100
50	Aircraft	100	0	95	0	95
51	Masonry	100	0	100	0	100
52	Furniture making/woodwork	100	0	100	0	100
53	Entrepreneurship	31	69	50	0	50
54	Religion	100	0	100	0	100
55	Marine engineering	100	0	85	0	85
56	Security	55	45	61	0	61
57	Arts	16	84	34	0	34
58	Aeronautics	72	28	67	22	86
59	ICT	23	77	100	0	100
60	Scaffolding	100	0	57	43	100
61	Electrical engineering	79	21	100	0	100
62	Police and criminology	100	0	61	25	81
63	Medical laboratory/medical technician/x-ray	44	56	44	0	44
64	Other manufacturing	22	78	45	0	45
65	Dentistry	83	17	61	0	61
66	Mechanical engineering	100	0	100	0	100
67	Other engineering	100	0	78	0	78

continued on next page

Table A7.1 continued

Rank (By number of TVET graduates)	Course/program	Male share	Female share	EPR	UR	LFPR
68	Liberal arts/international studies/governance	25	75	100	0	100
69	Safety	100	0	100	0	100
70	Clerical (general)	0	100	50	0	50
71	Painting	100	0	100	0	100
72	Sales and service	31	69	100	0	100
73	Lineman	100	0	53	0	53
74	Banking and finance	0	100	67	0	67
75	Alternative learning system	0	100	0		0
76	Paramedic	0	100	100	0	100
77	Optical technician	100	0	0		0
78	Marketing	0	100	100	0	100

EPR = employment-to-population rate, HR = human resources, ICT = information technology, LFPR = labor force participation rate, LFS = labor force survey, TVET = technical and vocational education and training, UR = unemployment rate.
Source: ADB estimates based on labor force survey January 2016.

Figure A7.1: Regional Share in Technical and Vocational Education and Training Enrollment and Population Share, 2018

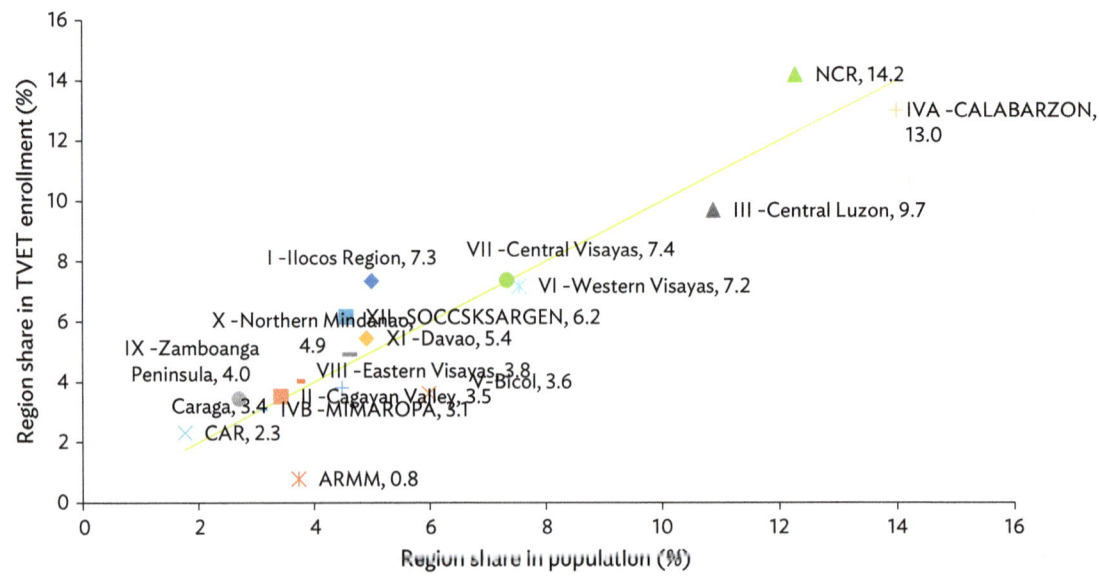

ARMM = Autonomous Region in Muslim Mindanao; CALABARZON = Cavite, Laguna, Batangas, Rizal, and Quezon; CAR = Cordillera Administrative Region; MIMAROPA = Occidental Mindoro, Oriental Mindoro, Marinduque, Romblon, and Palawan; NCR = National Capital Region; SOCCSKSARGEN = South Cotabato, Cotabato, Sultan Kudarat, Sarangani and General Santos; TESDA = Technical Education and Skills Development Authority; TVET = technical and vocational education and training.
Source: ADB estimates based on labor force survey and TESDA.

Switched on. Expanding TVET in key growth areas to ensure a globally competitive workforce.

PART III

EMPIRICAL FINDINGS FOR TECHNICAL AND VOCATIONAL EDUCATION AND TRAINING PERFORMANCE

Part III presents empirical findings on several areas used to gauge TVET performance, from employment outcomes to the impact of scholarships. Each chapter is drawn from background studies commissioned as part of this TVET sector study, also to be released as individual working papers. Chapter 8 provides an overview of employment outcomes for TVET graduates. Chapter 9 provides an overview of the returns for TVET graduates, estimating the private rates of return to TVET at the upper secondary, post-secondary, and tertiary levels. Chapter 10 investigates the effectiveness of TVET programs in terms of matching the expected and actual post-training occupations of graduates. Finally, Chapter 11 estimates the impacts of three major scholarships offered by TESDA.

8. Employment Outcomes for Technical and Vocational Education and Training Graduates

Effective skills development programs, such as TVET, can upskill and reskill the workforce and improve their overall employability and employment outcomes in the face of Industry 4.0. One of the primary goals of TVET, as per the TESDA NTESDP 2018–2022, is to equip its trainees with useful and relevant skills to make them workforce-ready and globally competitive (footnote 50). Thus, it is imperative to measure the impact, or the lack thereof, of completing a TVET program on employment outcomes.

Youth are particularly at risk due to persistently high unemployment over the past decade and now incur a higher risk of displacement as a result of COVID-19. In this study, we focus our attention on individuals aged 15 to 24 for two reasons. First, youth have been persistently experiencing poorer employment outcomes compared to adults in the past decade (Figure 8.1). In particular, the youth unemployment rate has consistently been almost four times that for adults. Second, a recent report of the ADB and the International Labour Organization (ILO) identifies youth as facing the most risk of displacement due to COVID-19.[94] The same report estimates that the pandemic caused 700,000 to 1,000,000 youth job losses in the Philippines as reflected by the twofold to threefold increase of youth unemployment rate from 6.8% in 2019 to 15.1%–19.5% in 2020, depending on the duration of the government's containment measures.

This chapter presents estimated employment outcomes of TVET graduates, focusing on youth. It provides an overview of literature assessing employment outcomes globally from skills development programs, and presents the methodology, findings, and conclusions to the assessment outcomes.

Employment Outcomes from Technical and Vocational Education and Training in Recent Literature

There are myriad studies assessing the employment effects of active labor market programs such as TVET, on the youth in different country development contexts. The empirical evidence across countries and regions vary. Using meta-analysis methods, Kluve et al. (2016) identify and review evidence of 113 counterfactual impact evaluations, which utilize different interventions, methods across countries. They find that only one-third of these youth employment programs have shown a significant positive impact on labor market outcomes, either in terms of employment rates or earnings. Using a similar methodology, but on 97 studies from 1995 to 2007, Card, Kluve, and Weber (2010) assess the effects of active labor market policies (ALMPs) on employment and determine that programs that target the youth are less effective in bringing positive effects. This affirms an earlier review by Kluve and Schmidt (2002) on studies on European ALMPs from 1983 to 1999. Most of these studies are in the context of high-income countries. Interestingly, however, Kluve et al. (2016) and Betcherman et al. (2007) determine that youth interventions in low- to middle-income countries are more effective in improving employment outcomes than in high-income countries.

---

[94] ADB and ILO. 2020. *Tackling the COVID-19 Youth Employment Crisis in Asia and the Pacific.* Bangkok: ILO and Manila: ADB.

Figure 8.1: Youth and Adult Unemployment Rate, 2006–2016

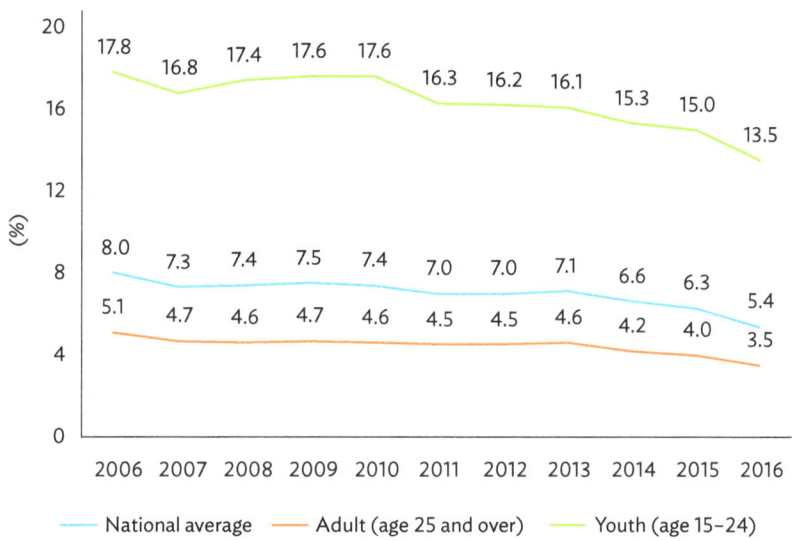

Source: Philippine Statistics Authority, labor force surveys.

Estimated employment impacts are mixed, with a range of contrasting findings across available studies. For instance, in the context of low- to middle-income countries, McKenzie (2017) provides recent evidence on the effects of ALMPs and reveals that many of these are much less effective than policy makers perceive, with evaluations estimating no significant impact on employment and earnings. By contrast, Tripney and Hombrados (2013) focus their assessment from studies in Latin American countries and show that TVET interventions have small, positive, and significant mean effects on overall paid and formal employment, and monthly earnings. Attanasio, Kugler, and Meghir (2011) study the impact of a unique randomized training program in Colombia and identify that it significantly raises the earnings and employment outcomes for women. Hicks et al. (2011) describe how the ongoing Technical and Vocational Vouchers Program in Kenya had positive supply-side impacts among institutions and short-run impacts, not only on labor market outcomes, but also on expectations and behaviors of participants. Bidani et al. (2009) use different methodologies to assess the employment effects of public retraining programs in two cities in the People's Republic of China, Wuhan and Shenyang, and find strong evidence to suggest that the programs improved employment of workers in Wuhan, but not in Shenyang.

Although TESDA collects and publishes regular statistics (e.g., graduate tracer surveys) and studies (e.g., employment satisfaction survey reports) on TVET graduates, the literature estimating the employment impact of TVET in the Philippines has been scant.[95] These statistics have not yet been analyzed rigorously to establish correlation and causality of TVET on employment outcomes such as earnings, employment, employability, and mismatch. Nevertheless, the numbers suggest that, despite important employment gains, TVET graduates experience high unemployment and underemployment rates. Using the individual graduate tracer surveys covering graduates from 2010–2017, TVET graduates' overall unemployment rates were found

---

[95] A literature review and discussion of the impact of TVET on wages is presented in Chapter 9.

to decline from 60%–70% before training to 28%–35% post-training. Despite these gains in employment post-training, unemployment rates remain high, and 37%–43% of employed graduates are considered underemployed or still want additional hours of work. Using a unique data set, the World Bank STEP Survey, Vandenberg and Laranjo (forthcoming) employ probabilistic regression techniques to estimate the effects of TVET on employment and find that TVET graduates are more likely to be employed.

Employment outcomes are determined by both demand-side and supply-side factors, and the interaction of the two. Specifically, there needs to be demand for the output of TVET (i.e., employment opportunities must exist), the output of TVET needs to be adequate to meet this demand in terms of quantity (no excess supply of graduates in certain fields) and quality (meeting industry standards and employer expectation, i.e., employability). Thus, employment outcomes are not equivalent to employability (Box 8.1), which is one of the factors determining these outcomes.

Box 8.1: Employability of Technical and Vocational Education and Training Graduates—Case of the Philippines

Employability is an important indicator of whether the current quantity and quality of technical and vocational education and training (TVET) graduates match the industry needs and standards and employers' expectations. Using the Philippines Enterprise Survey of World Bank in 2015, Acosta et al. (2017) present evidence of inadequate workforce skills, particularly in terms of socio-emotional skills, usually known as "noncognitive skills," "soft skills," or "behavioral skills." About one-third of employers cites difficulty in filling vacancies, primarily attributing to the skill shortage of applicants.

Bayan Academy (forthcoming), in partnership with the Technical Education and Skills Development Authority (TESDA) and with support from J.P. Morgan, also presents some anecdotal evidence on the readiness of graduates from key players in the eight priority industries identified in the National Technical Education and Skills Development Plan (NTESDP) 2018–2022. They conducted forums, focus group discussions, and technical working group sessions to identify gaps in the supply and demand (i.e., lack of which type of skills, reasons for not hiring, etc.) of trainees for each industry. Most industries identified a lack of sector- and firm-specific skills, particularly nontechnical core skills, which affirms the findings of Acosta et al. (2017). These skill shortages are prevalent in the information technology-business process management (IT-BPM), construction, health and wellness, and transportation and logistics industries. Technical skills seem to be lacking among graduates in the agriculture, construction, manufacturing, and transportation and logistics industries.

Using the recently available Employers' Satisfaction Surveys[a] of TESDA,[b] we find a slight decline in the employer's degree of satisfaction on the work performance of employees who underwent TVET in two out of the three aspects, theoretical and practical knowledge in performing tasks and work attitudes. The set of indicators under work attitudes pertain to socio-emotional skills such as teamwork, confidence, and self-motivation. The mean rating of TVET graduates recorded a small uptick in terms of trainability on the relevant job skills. Overall, the proportion of establishments satisfied with TVET graduates' performance decreased from 94% in 2011 to 90% in 2014.

The Employer and Training Institute Surveys conducted by the Asian Development Bank (ADB)[c] also provide valuable insights on the quality of TVET graduates employed in the IT-business process outsourcing (IT-BPO) and electronics industries. The survey results of employers in the IT-BPO industry reveal that employers are somehow satisfied with the graduates in terms of "general" and "job-specific" skills, with about 51%–55% of firms with a positive response (strongly agree and agree). However, industry interviews highlighting some challenges employers face in finding qualified graduates, consistent with Acosta et al. (2017), which identifies lack of skills or competency as the top reason for the unfilled vacancies in the industry. There seems to be better satisfaction on the overall skill level of graduates among employers in the electronics industry. The employers survey for the industry shows that 58% of employers agree that graduates possess the right level of "general" and "job-specific" skills and are ready for entry-level occupations.

Box 8.1: *continued*

The perspective of training institutions on the quality of their graduates are reflected in the results of the training institute survey. Training institutions point to the lack of recognition of certifications by employers and the lack of preparedness of their graduates as the top employment barriers. Comparing the results from the two surveys reveals the wide discrepancy in terms of the expectations of training institutions and employers on the skill level of graduates: 90% of training institutions are optimistic of their graduates' labor market preparedness, while only 52% and 58% of employers from the IT-BPO and electronics industries respectively agree. ADB (2020) further concludes that the implementation and the content of these skills training often do not match industry requirements.

[a] The Workplace Satisfaction Survey 2019 of TESDA, which covers the construction and IT-BPM industries, is not yet available at the time of the study.

[b] TESDA. 2012b. Employer Satisfaction Survey. Taguig; TESDA. 2014. 2014 Employers' Satisfaction Survey. Taguig.

[c] ADB. 2021. *Reaping Benefits of Industry 4.0 through Skills Development in High-Growth Industries in Southeast Asia: Insights from Cambodia, Indonesia, the Philippines, and Viet Nam.* Manila.

Source: Authors.

Methodological Approach

This chapter uses treatment effect methods and probabilistic regression techniques for the assessment of employment outcomes of TVET.[96] We are interested in three sets of outcomes of our sample: labor force participation, employment, and underemployment status. We evaluate these outcomes using labor force survey data. Further, to determine the correlates of these employment outcomes in terms of program characteristics, we use TESDA's graduate tracer surveys, specifically, the Employability of Technical Vocational Education and Training Graduates (SETG) data, to account for the program-specific characteristics (e.g., training modality, registration status, and sector of the TVET program) and individual-specific, TVET-related behavior and status (e.g., taking, passing, or failing the competency exam and scholarship status).

Treatment Effects Estimators

Since treatment status in this case is obtained from observational data, it is therefore not randomized. This suggests that our outcome and treatment variables are not necessarily independent. Thus, we use treatment effects estimators to utilize the covariates to ensure that treatment and outcome are independent after conditioning on those covariates.[97] We measure the average treatment effect on the treated or the average causal effect of a variable in the sample of interest (e.g., TVET graduates), commonly binary (e.g., TVET completion), on outcome variables of interest, which are employment outcomes in our context. However, the problem with using observational data is that all the potential outcomes of the same individual cannot be observed, which gives rise to the missing-data problem and thus no estimates for individual-level effects.[98] Given the binary nature of our outcome variable, we employ the inverse-probability weighted regression adjustment (IPWRA).[99]

---

[96] The background and technical details of the empirical methodology are presented in Appendix 8.1.
[97] For a detailed description of treatment effects estimators used and its assumptions, see Appendix 8.1.
[98] Potential-outcome models provide a solution to these by specifying the potential outcomes that each individual would obtain under each treatment level, the treatment assignment process, and the dependence on the treatment assignment process. See Appendix 8.1 for an elaborate discussion.
[99] Other treatment effect estimators are regression adjustment estimators, inverse-probability-weighted estimators, doubly robust estimators, and matching estimators.

The IPWRA is a doubly robust estimator that combines the outcome modeling strategy of regression adjustment and the treatment modeling strategy of inverse probability weights.[100] If the treatment models are well specified, then the outcome will be conditionally independent of the treatment and the covariates are balanced (i.e., the distributions of covariates do not vary over treatment levels). Before inferring from the results of the treatment effect estimation, we employ an overidentification test for covariate balance.[101] The null hypothesis of the test is that the treatment model balanced the covariates. Thus, the rejection of the null hypothesis implies that the covariates are still unbalanced and the estimates are unreliable. Further, to account for possible endogeneity, i.e., the treatment assignment is correlated with the potential outcomes, we use endogenous treatment effects estimators to calculate treatment effects.[102] Specifically, using a probit model for both the treatment assignment and potential outcomes, we estimate the two models using the endogenous treatment-effects estimators. Finally, to verify the presence of endogeneity in our sample and, therefore, decide on the more appropriate estimator, we perform a post-estimation test, i.e., a Wald test. The null hypothesis of the test is that the correlations are jointly zero. Thus, rejection of the null hypothesis would suggest endogeneity and justify the use of the endogenous treatment effect estimator over the IPWRA and other treatment effect estimators.

Probabilistic Regression Techniques

To measure the impact of program characteristics on employment outcomes, we employ a logit regression, which uses maximum likelihood estimation on dichotomous dependent variables.[103] The marginal effects derived from the post-estimation reflect the correlation between TVET program characteristics and employment outcomes. In other words, we identify which program characteristics are associated with higher likelihood of obtaining positive employment outcomes.[104]

Data

LFS data are used for information on the employment outcomes and program characteristics of young individuals who completed a TVET program and those who did not.[105] We use the October (third quarter) round of LFS in 2018 to account for the first set of graduates of the senior high school program, which consists of a technical–vocational and livelihood (TVL) track[106] for students.[107] Our sample of interest is individuals aged 15 to 24 who are neither in school nor in training.[108] Also, we exclude individuals for whom we do not have information about their parents' education.[109] The importance of this variable is further discussed in the next section. The summary statistics of the sample are presented in Tables A8.1–A8.3 of Appendix 8.2.

The main limitations of using the LFS are the lack of information on the timing, duration, and other characteristics of the TVET program completed by the individual. The lack of information on timing and

---

[100] See Appendix 8.1 for the assumptions, functions, and step-by-step process of this estimator.
[101] This follows the suggestion of Rubin (2008). This post-estimation test was derived by Imai and Ratkovic (2014).
[102] See Appendix 8.1 for the detailed description of endogenous treatment estimators.
[103] The models are elaborated in Appendix 8.1.
[104] Aside from treatment effects estimators, Generalao (forthcoming, 2021) applies probabilistic regression techniques to determine the correlation estimates of the effects of TVET program completion on employment outcomes.
[105] Starting April 2016, the LFS adopted the 2013 Master Sample Design, with a sample size of approximately 44,000 households. In terms of generating the labor force statistics, the population projections are based on the 2010 Census of Population and Housing (PSA, 2012).
[106] The TVL track allows students to learn skills and earn requisite COCs (Certificates of Competency) and NCs (National Certificates) which might boost their career opportunities.
[107] The first set of senior high school graduates are those graduating in academic year 2017–2018. The potential youth samples in years before the implementation of the K to 12 program are substantially different from those post-implementation. Thus, we carefully restrict our analysis to those after the program and avoid comparing across years before the reform.
[108] Note that only the 2018 LFS contains information on whether the individual is currently attending a TVET program or not, and in school or not. Still, the other two rounds have information on whether he/she is currently in school or not.
[109] The relevant question for classifying an individual as a parent in the LFS does not distinguish between the father or the mother. To maximize the number of individuals in the sample, all three, including household head, are used as the bases for identifying one as a parent.

duration implies that the TVET course could have been completed at any point in the individual's life, while his or her employment status is measured at the specific point in time of the survey. Restricting the sample into this young cohort partially reduces the magnitude of this timing problem. The LFS also lacks information on program characteristics, such as type, sector, and modality, in the survey. Thus, we cannot use LFS to analyze the program characteristics of the graduates who benefitted the least or most from completing TVET. To determine these employment correlates, we alternatively use TESDA's SETG 2017 covering 2016 TVET graduates. The data collection for the SETG was done through a nationwide survey of selected TVET graduates using a structured survey instrument with clearance issued by the Philippine Statistical Authority. Specifically, the survey was conducted through either face-to-face or phone interview using a structured questionnaire.

Main Findings

Impact of TVET on Youth Employment Outcomes

Evidence that TVET causes young individuals to be part of the labor force is confirmed using the IPWRA method. Specifically, we find that, for the population of TVET graduates, the average labor force participation rate would be 76.7% in the counterfactual case of no TVET (Table 8.1). Thus, among TVET graduates, TVET completion increases the average labor force participation rate (LFPR) by an average of 6.2 percentage points. These results are intuitive because the willingness of TVET graduates to upskill and reskill through TVET implicitly suggests that they are relatively more determined and motivated to look for work and participate in the labor market than nongraduates.

Program completion has no significant positive impact on employment for young TVET graduates. When none of the individuals in the sample completes a TVET program (i.e., in the counterfactual case of no TVET), the average employment rate[110] is 83.2% (Table 8.1). The estimated average treatment effect is insignificant. This suggests that the average employment rate when all the individuals in the sample complete a TVET program is not significantly different from the counterfactual case of no TVET. This set of findings can be possibly explained by a myriad of factors. The lack of soft and technical skills among TVET graduates and the lack of recognition of certifications by employers may be the primary employment barriers, as highlighted by ADB (2020). The existence of a mismatch between the skills demanded in the labor market and the skills graduates gained from TVET is also a possibility. Chapter 10 explores the issue of mismatch among TVET graduates. Other factors relating to program-specific characteristics are discussed in the next subsection.

When evaluating the possible employment effects of TVET, we must also extend our analysis, not only in terms of improved employment rates, but also in the quality of jobs in which they are employed. One aspect of job quality is assessing whether the individual is experiencing underemployment, which in this chapter refers to time-related underemployment (the underemployed are defined as employed persons who express the desire to have additional hours of work in their present job or an additional job, or a new job with longer working hours). Other key dimensions are level of formality, working conditions, and just compensation.

The empirical results suggest that TVET does not help solve the youth underemployment problem. This is confirmed by the regression results using the IPWRA. In particular, we find that, for the population of employed TVET graduates, the average underemployment rate would be around 15% in the counterfactual case of no TVET (Table 8.1). TVET completion increases the average underemployment rate by 5.9 percentage points among TVET graduates. This can be attributed to the large proportion of enrollment in programs leading to occupations that are nonroutine manual in nature and low-paying in the Philippine labor market. One of the reasons for the

---

[110] We define employment rate as the proportion of employed persons to the total labor force, following the definition of PSA.

Table 8.1: Average Treatment Effect on the Treated of Technical and Vocational Education and Training on Employment Outcomes, 2018

Item	Labor Force	Employed	Underemployed
Average treatment on the treated	0.062***	−0.001	0.059**
	(0.021)	(0.023)	(0.027)
Potential outcomes	0.767***	0.832***	0.146***
	(0.011)	(0.009)	(0.010)

*** $p<0.01$, ** $p<0.05$, * $p<0.1$
Source: ADB estimates, using inverse-probability weighted regression adjustment (IPWRA) estimators.

influx of demand for this type of programs is the employment opportunity and corresponding relative high pay in such occupations overseas. The impacts of other program-specific characteristics on underemployment are discussed in the succeeding subsection.

Results of the test for covariate balance suggest that the employment outcomes are conditionally independent of TVET completion and justify the use of IPWRA estimator (Table 8.2). In particular, the estimates from the overidentification test imply that we do not find sufficient evidence to reject the null hypothesis that the covariates are balanced. This implies that the distributions of the covariates do not vary over treatment levels and the treatment effect estimates can be used for inference.

The Wald test statistics, following the endogenous treatment effects estimation, point to an absence of endogeneity and further validates the use of IPWRA estimators (Table 8.3). Except for the outcome variable of underemployment, which is only significant at the 10% level of significance, the results suggest that we do not find enough evidence to reject the null hypothesis of no endogeneity. This implies that the unobservable factors that determine employment outcomes are not correlated with the decision to complete a TVET program. This, ultimately, the IPWRA estimator, which gives correct standard errors, is preferred and appropriate for the all the employment outcome models.

Table 8.2: Overidentification Test for Covariate Balance

Dependent Variable	
Labor force participation	26.71
	(0.22)
Employment	22.54
	(0.43)
Underemployment	19.83
	(0.59)

The p-values of the chi-squared test statistic are in parentheses.
*** $p<0.01$, ** $p<0.05$, * $p<0.1$
Source: ADB estimates.

Table 8.3: Wald Test for Endogeneity of the Unobservable Characteristics

Dependent Variable	
Labor force participation	1.17
	(0.5571)
Employment	1.53
	(0.4663)
Underemployment	5.87
	(0.0532*)

The p-values of the chi-squared test statistic are in parentheses.
*** $p<0.01$, ** $p<0.05$, * $p<0.1$
Source: ADB estimates.

Impact of Program Characteristics on Youth Employment Outcomes

In terms of program characteristics, graduates from enterprise-based TVET programs have higher probabilities of being employed relative to community-based or mobile training programs. On the other hand, there is no significant difference between the employment outcomes of graduates of community-based and institution-based TVET programs. This affirms the recommendation of Orbeta and Esguerra (2016) of realigning training programs with the EBT modality. Except for underemployment where graduates from programs with training regulations recorded higher probabilities, there is no significant difference in terms of labor force participation and employment when comparing graduates of programs with and without training regulations. This is likely because the programs without training regulations are mostly offered on a demand basis by private TESDA technical institutions (TTIs), while those with regulations are less dynamic given that it usually takes more than a year to approve and publish a new one. In terms of sector classification, programs classified under the agricultural, forestry, and fishery sector are more likely to result in employed graduates than those under the human health/health care, tourism (hotel and restaurant), and wholesale and retail trading sectors, among others. However, programs in the teacher training or TVET sector, such as Trainers Methodology, will result in higher employment probabilities as compared to programs in the agricultural, forestry, and fishery sector (as compared to programs in the latter, there is no significant difference in terms of employment outcomes for the rest of the sectors) (Table A8.4).

In terms of individual, TVET-related characteristics, certified graduates, or those who took and passed the competency exams, have better odds of becoming employed than those who failed and did not take the exam. Scholars have higher chances of participating in the labor market and becoming underemployed than non-scholars. However, there is no significant difference between the two groups in terms of employment probabilities (Table A8.4).

The more educated the TVET graduates are, the higher the likelihood of experiencing positive employment outcomes. Among the demographic variables, educational attainment remains a consistent significant explanatory variable for understanding the employment-related correlates. In particular, those with college degrees and beyond are more likely to participate in the labor market, become employed and not underemployed relative to those with high school undergraduate and below, holding other things constant (Table A8.4).

Conclusions and Way Forward

The role of TVET in upskilling and reskilling the labor force has never been more crucial, due to the challenge of rapidly changing landscape of work brought about by Industry 4.0 and the widespread job displacement across sectors caused by COVID-19. Certain industries (i.e., tourism, transportation, etc.) and demographic groups (i.e., youth and women) have been disproportionately affected by these two phenomena. In this context, TVET has the potential to effectively facilitate the smooth transitions of workers across jobs and industries and aid in the economic recovery during and after the pandemic.

The study presented in this chapter found strong evidence of a causal impact of TVET on the labor force participation of young individuals not in school nor in training. In particular, using the IPWRA estimator, we found that TVET completion increases the average LFPR of graduates by an average of 6.2 percentage points compared to the counterfactual case (i.e., had they not completed any TVET program).

**Although the positive effects of TVET on labor force participation should be acknowledged, it is of particular interest to policy makers and stakeholders of the training system to know whether TVET leads to

employment among the youth. The treatment effect estimates from the IPWRA estimators show that TVET program completion has no significant positive impact on employment for young TVET graduates.

Looking at aspects of employment quality, we find that TVET does not help solve the problem of youth underemployment. The results suggest that even when TVET leads to employment, this is apparently more likely to be in occupations where workers still desire additional working hours, or look for an additional job or even a new job with longer hours. These findings suggest further monitoring and evaluation in terms of the nature of jobs TVET graduates take post-training. It is not enough for graduates to be employed in any type of job but ideally in occupations that they trained for. The issue of training–job mismatch must be carefully studied and addressed. Chapter 10 attempts to measure the incidence of mismatch among TVET graduates.

Identifying the type of programs that lead to positive and even poor employment outcomes will guide policy makers in crafting better polices, such as channeling the right amount of resources and coordinating with concerned stakeholders. Unsurprisingly, we found that graduates from enterprise-based TVET programs have the highest probabilities of gaining employment as compared to institution- and community-based programs. There is no significant difference in terms of employment outcomes of graduates from programs with and without training regulations. This is likely because the latter programs are mostly offered on a demand basis by private TTIs, while the former are less dynamic. In terms of sector classification, programs classified under the agricultural, forestry and fishery sector are more likely to result in employed graduates than those in programs under human health/health care, tourism (hotel and restaurant), wholesale and retail trading, and others. However, programs in the teacher training or TVET sector, such as Trainers Methodology, will result in higher employment probabilities as compared to programs in the agricultural, forestry, and fishery sector. These results should direct the attention of TESDA and other stakeholders to programs that produce graduates with poor employment outcomes. Further studies on the constraints faced by these institutions and trainees are needed.

Certified graduates or those who took and passed the competency exams have better odds of becoming employed than those who failed and did not take the exam. This affirms the importance of quality assurance post-training of TVET graduates. It also suggests that graduates' TVET certificates are being recognized by employers.

In terms of scholarship programs, the estimates suggest that scholars have a higher probability of participating in the labor market than non-scholars. This can be because of the additional effort and motivation of the recipients. These positive results could incentivize and justify increased financial assistance of the government and the private sector to trainees. However, it must be noted that there is no significant difference between the employment of scholars and non-scholars.

This study can be further extended by analyzing other key dimensions of employment quality such as level of formality, working conditions, and just compensation. In addition, the scope of the study may be expanded to include not just young individuals not in school nor in training but the entire labor force. This will only be possible, however, if data collection techniques are continually improved and expanded to include TVET dropouts. Not all LFS rounds contain information on the basic characteristics (i.e., public or private, type and level) of the TVET course taken and completed of the individual. Such data would have provided important insights on specific program characteristics and its employment correlates. Finally, inclusion of the year the individual completed his or her TVET program, if possible, would resolve the timing issue that arises when using the LFS as the primary source of data for this type of analysis.

Appendix 8.1: Empirical Methodology

Treatment Effects Estimators

The problem with using observational data is that all the potential outcomes of the same individual cannot be observed, which gives rise to the missing-data problem and thus prevents estimating individual-level effects. Potential-outcome models[111] provide a solution by specifying the potential outcomes that each individual would obtain under each treatment level, the treatment assignment process, and the dependence of the potential outcomes on the treatment assignment process. There are three assumptions that need to be satisfied before using treatment effect estimators. These are the independent and identically distributed sampling, conditional-independence, and the overlap assumption. The independent and identically distributed assumption assures that the outcome and treatment status of each i is not related to that of other individuals in the population. The sampling technique used in collecting the data to be used in our study satisfies this condition. The overlap assumption states that each individual has a positive probability of receiving treatment. Anyone from our sample can participate and complete a TVET program. Conditional independence is a strong assumption which does not need to be met if we are interested in estimating the average treatment effect on the treated (ATET). That is, estimating the impact of TVET on employment outcomes among graduates. We must only satisfy the conditional mean independence assumption, which states that, after accounting for the covariates X_i, the treatment does not affect the conditional mean of each potential outcome.

Inverse-Probability Weighted Regression Adjustment

Inverse-probability weighted regression adjustment (IPWRA) possesses a property where only one of the two models needs to be specified correctly to obtain correct estimates of the treatment effect.[112] It is a regression adjustment estimator that adopts the estimated inverse-probability weights. This puts weights on the regression adjustment equations using the propensity scores to achieve balance between treatment and comparison groups as indicated by balance in the covariates.

We use the IPWRA estimators to predict TVET program completion and employment outcomes. The following steps estimate the treatment effects:[113]

(i) Estimate the parameters of the treatment model as in Equation 1 using a logit regression.

$$P(T=1|X=x) = \Lambda(\beta_0 + \beta X + \varepsilon) \quad (1)$$

Where T is the binary treatment status of being a TVET graduate or not, X refers to a vector of controls which include educational attainment, parents' education, potential work experience, and location.

(ii) Derive the predicted value of the probability or propensity score, $\hat{p}(x)$, from the treatment model (Equation 1) and use it to compute for the inverse-probability weights, assigned to the treatment and control groups as follows:

$$w(x) = \begin{cases} 1 & \text{if } T=1 \\ \dfrac{\hat{p}(x)}{1-\hat{p}(x)} & \text{if } T=0 \end{cases} \quad (2)$$

---

[111] This is also known as the Rubin causal model and the counterfactual model. For detailed discussions, refer to Rubin (1974) and Wooldridge (2010, chap. 21).
[112] See Cattaneo (2010) for a detailed discussion.
[113] Refer to StataCorp (2015).

(iii) Fit the weighted logit regression models of the employment outcomes (Equation 3) for each treatment level using the estimated inverse-probability weights from Equation 2.

$$P(Y=1|V,T) = \Lambda(\alpha_0 + \alpha V + \mu) \quad [w(x)] \qquad (3)$$

Where Y is a vector of binary employment outcomes (e.g., employed or unemployed, underemployed or not,[114] and out of the labor force or not) of individual i and T refers to the binary treatment status of individual i as a graduate or nongraduate, and V pertains to a vector of controls including educational attainment,[115] parents' education, potential work experience and its square, marital status, and urbanity.[116]

(iv) Compute the means of the treatment-specific predicted outcomes. The differences of these averages for the subset of TVET graduates, in comparison to nongraduates, are the ATETs (Equation 4).

$$ATET = \hat{Y}_i^G - \hat{Y}_i^{NG} = \frac{1}{N_G}\sum_{i \in G} Y_i^G - \frac{1}{N_{NG}} \sum_{i \in NG} \frac{\hat{p}(X_i)}{1-\hat{p}(X_i)} Y_i^{NG} \qquad (4)$$

Where N_G is the number of TVET graduates N_{NG} the number of nongraduates.

Before inferring from the results of the treatment effects estimation, we follow the recommendation of Rubin (2008) to ensure that the treatment model balanced the covariates. This implies that the distributions of the covariates do not vary over treatment levels. To verify this, we implement an overidentification post-estimation test for balanced covariates using the Stata command, *tebalance overid,* developed by Imai and Ratkovic (2014). The null hypothesis of the test is that the covariates are balanced. Rejection of the hypothesis suggests the need to revise the model. Otherwise, we can proceed with inferring from the estimates of the treatment effects estimators.

Endogenous Treatment Effects Estimators

Suppose we suspect that the treatment assignment is correlated with the potential outcomes. In other words, enrolling and completing a TVET program is not independent of the potential employment status of the individual. This violates the conditional mean independence assumption and implies an endogeneity problem. If that is the case, we apply the endogenous treatment-effects estimators to calculate the treatment effects. It is an extension of regression adjustment estimators but relaxing the conditional mean independence assumption. Moreover, it fits our purposes given that it allows for binary outcomes and treatment variables.

To address the potential endogeneity of the treatment assignment, the residuals from the treatment model (Equation 5) will be included in the potential outcome model (Equation 6), known as the control-function approach.[117]

$$P(T=1|Z=z) = \Phi(\beta_0 + \beta Z + \mu) \qquad (5)$$

---

[114] We define underemployed as those employed persons who express the desire to have additional hours of work in their present job or an additional job, or a new job with longer working hours, following the definition of PSA.
[115] We included Grades 11 and 12 in the group of high school graduates.
[116] For a detailed theoretical discussion of doubly robust estimators, refer to section 21.3.4 of Wooldridge (2010).
[117] See Wooldridge (2010) for an elaborate and clear discussion, which includes the conditions and assumptions for the validity of the estimator.

such that $E(\mu|T) \neq 0$, suggesting endogeneity and T is the binary treatment status of being a TVET graduate or not, Z is a vector of controls such as educational attainment, parents' education, potential work experience, and location.

$$P(Y=1|W, \mu, T) = \Phi(\alpha_0 + \alpha W + \gamma\mu + \varepsilon) \ \forall \ T \in (0, 1) \qquad (6)$$

where μ is the residual from Equation 5, T is the binary treatment status of being a TVET graduate or not, Y is a vector of binary employment outcomes (e.g., employed or unemployed, underemployed or not, and out of the labor force or not), and W pertains to the set of controls which include educational attainment, parents' education, potential work experience and its square, marital status, and urbanity.

It must be noted that the bases of the control function estimator are Equation 5, endogeneity, $E(\mu | T) \neq 0$, and independence of the ε with Z. Using probit models for both the treatment assignment and potential outcomes, we estimate Equations 5 and 6 using the endogenous treatment-effects estimators and calculate the treatment effects (Equation 7). The main difference between Equation 4 and Equation 7 is the specification of the outcome models where they are derived from, which are Equation 3 and Equation 6, respectively. The former allows for endogeneity, while the latter uses inverse probability weights.

$$ATET = \hat{Y}_i^G - \hat{Y}_i^{NG} \qquad (7)$$

Where N_G is the number of TVET graduates N_{NG} the number of nongraduates.

Finally, to verify endogeneity, we perform a post-estimation test, a Wald test, which determines whether the estimated correlations between our two models are significantly different from zero, which is possible given the control-function approach of the estimator.

Probabilistic Regression Techniques

To measure the impact of TVET program characteristics on employment outcomes, we would ideally run an experimental design, by, for instance, performing randomized control trials to control for selection bias and establish causality. However, the lack of data and resource constraints only allow for the use of probabilistic regression techniques. We define three sets of employment outcomes of TVET graduates, labor force participation, employment, and underemployment status. We specify the models for each outcome as:

$$Y_{iEMP} = \alpha_0 + \alpha_1 T_i + \alpha X_i + \gamma W_i + \varepsilon_i \qquad (8)$$

where Y_{iEMP} is the dichotomous dependent variable pertaining to either labor force participation, employment or underemployment status; T_i refers to the binary treatment variable of interest of i (whether he/she completed a TVET program or not); X_i is a vector of observed characteristics such as educational attainment, sex, marital status, location, potential work experience, and its square; W_i is a vector of program-specific characteristics such as training modality, registration status, and sector of the TVET program, and individual-specific, TVET-related behavior and status (e.g., taking, passing, or failing the competency exam and scholarship status); and ε_i is the residual of the estimation or the error term, which captures the unobserved characteristics (e.g., effort, motivation, and perception of employers).

Appendix 8.2: Summary Statistics

Table A8.1: Summary Statistics of the Sample, 2018

Variable	2018 (%)
TVET status	
Nongraduate	94.0
Graduate	6.0
Educational attainment	
High school undergraduate and below	36.0
High school graduate	30.2
Some college and post-secondary education	18.3
College and beyond	15.5
Sex	
Female	41.2
Male	58.8
Age	20.9
Marital status	
Single	83.4
Married	15.6
Others	1.1
Number of observations	11,821

TVET = technical and vocational education and training.
Note: The estimates are weighted using survey weights.
Source: ADB estimates.

Table A8.2: Employment Status by Selected Demographic Groups, 2018

Variable	Unemployed	Employed	Not Part of the Labor Force (%)
TVET status			
Nongraduate	11.5	58.9	29.6
Graduate	14.1	68.5	17.4
Educational attainment			
High school undergraduate and below	7.9	61.0	31.1
High school graduate	12.5	57.4	30.1
Some college and post-secondary education	14.2	56.7	29.1
College and beyond	16.0	63.3	20.7
Sex			
Female	11.8	47.2	41.0
Male	11.6	68.0	20.4
Marital status			
Single	13.2	59.1	27.8
Married	4.4	61.3	34.3
Others	2.4	64.0	33.6

TVET = technical and vocational education and training.
Note: The estimates are weighted using survey weights.
Source: ADB estimates.

Table A8.3: Underemployment Status by Selected Demographic Groups, 2018

Variable	Not underemployed (%)	Underemployed (%)
TVET status		
Nongraduate	85.4	14.6
Graduate	80.1	19.9
Educational attainment		
High school undergraduate and below	81.3	18.7
High school graduate	83.5	16.5

Table A8.3: *continued*

Variable	Not underemployed (%)	Underemployed (%)
Some college and post-secondary education	88.4	11.6
College and beyond	92.4	7.6
Sex		
Female	90.3	9.7
Male	82.5	17.5
Marital status		
Single	86.1	13.9
Married	79.5	20.5
Others	84.3	15.7

TVET = technical and vocational education and training.
Note: The estimates are weighted using survey weights.
Source: ADB estimates.

Appendix 8.3: Average Marginal Employment Effects

Table A8.4: Average Marginal Employment Effects of Demographic and Program-Specific Characteristics, 2017 Graduate Tracer Study

Variables	Labor Force Participation Coef.	Std.Err.	Employment Coef.	Std.Err.	Underemployment Coef.	Std.Err.
Sex (Base=Female)	0.035**	(0.014)	0.023	(0.017)	0.017	(0.022)
Potential work experience	0.021***	(0.002)	0.009***	(0.002)	−0.000	(0.002)
Potential work experience squared	−0.041***	(0.004)	−0.014***	(0.005)	−0.004	(0.006)
Educational attainment (Base=high school undergraduate and below)						
High school graduate	0.198***	(0.019)	−0.037	(0.026)	−0.018	(0.035)
Some college or post-secondary degree	0.223***	(0.021)	0.011	(0.029)	−0.028	(0.038)
Bachelor's degree or higher	0.379***	(0.022)	0.142***	(0.027)	−0.073*	(0.039)
Marital status (Base=Single)						
Married	0.007	(0.019)	0.060***	(0.021)	0.036	(0.027)
Others	0.005	(0.039)	0.077*	(0.043)	0.076	(0.054)
Region (Base=NCR)						
Region I - Ilocos Region	−0.115***	(0.029)	0.063**	(0.031)	0.171***	(0.044)
Region II - Cagayan Valley	0.003	(0.027)	0.001	(0.032)	0.214***	(0.044)
Region III - Central Luzon	−0.087***	(0.026)	−0.079**	(0.031)	0.122***	(0.041)
Region IVA - CALABARZON	0.011	(0.025)	−0.071**	(0.029)	−0.026	(0.038)
Region V- Bicol	−0.008	(0.031)	0.011	(0.035)	0.106**	(0.046)
Region VI - Western Visayas	−0.073**	(0.029)	−0.050	(0.035)	0.246***	(0.045)
Region VII - Central Visayas	−0.147***	(0.026)	−0.090***	(0.033)	0.060	(0.042)
Region VIII - Eastern Visayas	−0.026	(0.034)	−0.177***	(0.045)	0.097*	(0.059)
Region IX - Zamboanga Peninsula	−0.137***	(0.034)	−0.167***	(0.045)	0.101*	(0.060)
Region X - Northern Mindanao	−0.055	(0.051)	−0.082	(0.056)	0.135*	(0.071)
Region XI - Davao	−0.103***	(0.034)	0.190***	(0.026)	−0.044	(0.044)
Region XII - SOCCSKSARGEN	−0.010	(0.030)	−0.217***	(0.038)	0.283***	(0.053)
Cordillera Administrative Region	0.026	(0.038)	0.052	(0.041)	0.186***	(0.060)
Autonomous Region in Muslim Mindanao	−0.014	(0.034)	−0.032	(0.039)	0.282***	(0.050)
Region XIII - Caraga	0.018	(0.071)	−0.324***	(0.093)	0.203*	(0.111)
Region IVB - MIMAROPA	0.092***	(0.030)	0.038	(0.033)	0.172***	(0.044)
Scholar (Base=non-scholar)	0.066***	(0.015)	−0.015	(0.018)	0.067***	(0.022)
Competency status (Base=Did not take)						
Failed	−0.087**	(0.038)	0.053	(0.047)	−0.167***	(0.049)
Passed	0.027	(0.016)	0.052**	(0.020)	−0.019	(0.027)

Table A8.4: *continued*

Variables	Labor Force Participation		Employment		Underemployment	
	Coef.	Std.Err.	Coef.	Std.Err.	Coef.	Std.Err.
Training modality (Base=Community-based or mobile)						
Enterprise-based	0.138***	(0.033)	0.101***	(0.037)	−0.051	(0.053)
Institution-based	0.029	(0.020)	0.041	(0.025)	0.010	(0.032)
With Training Regulations (Base=no technical regulation or unregistered)	−0.014	(0.020)	0.014	(0.026)	0.079**	(0.033)
Sector of the program (Base=Agriculture, Forestry and Fishery)						
Automotive and Land Transportation	0.001	(0.034)	−0.035	(0.045)	0.014	(0.057)
Construction	0.030	(0.041)	−0.067	(0.055)	0.030	(0.066)
Decorative Crafts	−0.108	(0.244)	–	–	–	–
Electrical and Electronics	−0.008	(0.032)	−0.032	(0.043)	0.061	(0.058)
Entrepreneurship	0.054	(0.045)	0.052	(0.053)	0.201***	(0.074)
Furniture and Fixtures	−0.066	(0.136)	–	–	0.128	(0.315)
Garments	0.086**	(0.043)	0.011	(0.055)	0.065	(0.078)
Heating, Ventilation, Air-conditioning, and Refrigeration	−0.046	(0.077)	−0.068	(0.084)	0.068	(0.122)
Human Health/Health Care	0.005	(0.037)	−0.112**	(0.049)	0.092	(0.062)
Information and Communication Technology	−0.023	(0.035)	−0.049	(0.049)	−0.006	(0.064)
Language	0.044	(0.058)	0.025	(0.066)	0.165*	(0.088)
Logistics	–	–	–	–	0.157	(0.349)
Maritime	0.047	(0.109)	−0.031	(0.141)	0.334*	(0.198)
Metals and Engineering	0.072**	(0.034)	−0.021	(0.046)	0.005	(0.059)
Processed Food and Beverages	0.003	(0.038)	−0.072	(0.051)	0.136**	(0.065)
Social, Community Development, and Other Services	0.016	(0.035)	−0.026	(0.045)	0.069	(0.060)
TVET	0.185*	(0.107)	0.131*	(0.077)	−0.106	(0.087)
Tourism (Hotel and Restaurant)	−0.041	(0.029)	−0.087**	(0.042)	0.058	(0.054)
Wholesale and Retail Trading	−0.084	(0.089)	−0.244**	(0.122)	0.047	(0.168)
Others	−0.039	(0.033)	−0.078*	(0.047)	0.056	(0.058)
Observations	6,629		4,187		3,063	

*** $p<0.01$, ** $p<0.05$, * $p<0.1$

CALABARZON = Cavite, Laguna, Batangas, Rizal, and Quezon; MIMAROPA = Occidental Mindoro, Oriental Mindoro, Marinduque, Romblon, and Palawan; NCR = National Capital Region; SOCCSKSARGEN = South Cotabato, Cotabato, Sultan Kudarat, Sarangani and General Santos; TVET = technical and vocational education and training.

Note: The estimates are weighted using survey weights.

Source: ADB estimates.

9. Returns to Technical and Vocational Education and Training in the Philippines

Estimating the returns to TVET is important for individuals, businesses, and policy makers. For individuals it is particularly helpful in deciding between pursuing vocational training or employment. There are financial costs to pursuing vocational training, as well as opportunity costs for the time spent in training. The high costs of tertiary education may discourage its pursuit, with the lower cost and shorter duration of TVET making it a viable alternative. In the Philippines, a large majority of tertiary school-age population does not pursue post-secondary or tertiary education. Only one-third is enrolled in tertiary, largely academic education, while only 10% is enrolled in post-secondary non-tertiary education. To understand the low enrollment in post-secondary education, it is helpful to determine its profitability.

This chapter aims to determine the private rates of return to TVET at the upper secondary, post-secondary, and tertiary levels. It provides an overview of the methodological approach and data sources, and presents main findings and conclusion to the assessment.

Methodological Approach

This assessment uses the human capital earnings function, or Mincerian equation,[118] as the benchmark model. It relates the logarithm of current earnings to years of schooling and years of work experience, where the coefficient of schooling approximates the rate of return to a year of schooling. The basic model is augmented by controlling for observed characteristics including sex, urbanity, region, industry, occupation, class of work and nature of employment. Rates of return to various levels of education, various tracks of upper secondary education, various fields of post-secondary non-tertiary and short-cycle tertiary education, and various levels of higher education are also estimated.[119] Notwithstanding the correction of bias due to the omission of observable characteristics, estimated rates of return may still suffer from selection bias as wages are only observed among those in the labor force, those who are employed, and those in particular classes of work.[120]

To correct for selection bias, a Heckman (1979) model is fitted on the various equations to account for factors that affect labor force participation, employment, and work for pay. Given the correction for selection bias, the Heckman model is the preferred model among these three approaches. Appendix 9 elaborates on the various models. The key variables in these models are as follows:

- **Earnings** (in logarithm) is the dependent variable and is measured in terms of hourly wage. Hourly wage is computed as basic pay per day divided by the normal number of hours worked per day.

---

[118] J. Mincer. 1974. *Schooling, Experience, and Earnings* (Human Behavior and Social Institutions 2). Cambridge, MA: National Bureau of Economic Research.
[119] The April 2019 LFS round identifies highest educational attainment by level, broad field, and specific qualification including TESDA National Certificate following the Philippine Standard Classification of Education.
[120] Wages are observed only for workers in government, private establishments, private households, and workers with pay in family-owned businesses. Wages are not observed for the self-employed, employers, and workers without pay in family-owned businesses.

- **Education** represents the level of education and **schooling** is the total number of years of schooling for various education levels: 0 for no education, 1 for early childhood, 6 for primary, 10 for lower secondary, 12 for upper secondary, 11 for post-secondary non-tertiary, 12 for short-cycle tertiary, 14 for bachelor's, 16 for master's, and 18 for doctorate. Incomplete schooling at various levels is also accounted for. The interaction between education level and years of schooling allows the estimation of rates of return across levels of education.
- **Work experience** is approximated by age minus years of schooling and age at start of schooling. Using experience is preferable to age as the latter would lead to a partial omission of schooling and therefore an underestimate of the rate of return (footnote 118).
- **Upper secondary education** includes Grade 11 and Grade 12. It has four **tracks**: academic, arts and design, sports, and technology and livelihood.
- **Post-secondary non-tertiary education** includes TESDA National Certificate (NC) qualifications, other TVET courses, and incomplete qualifications.
- **Short-cycle tertiary education** includes complete and incomplete cycles. Both of these have the following **broad fields:** generic programs and qualifications; education, arts and humanities; social sciences, journalism, and information; business, administration, and law; natural sciences, mathematics, and statistics; information and communication technologies; engineering, manufacturing, and construction; agriculture, forestry, fishery, and veterinary; health and welfare; and services.
- **Tertiary or higher education** includes complete or incomplete bachelor, master's, and doctorate degrees.

There are various problems in estimating returns to schooling.

Box 9.1 provides an overview of these problems and the approaches used in the literature to address them.

Box 9.1: Accounting for Ability Bias

There are several problems in estimating returns to schooling, including omitted or unobserved ability bias, measurement error, and the endogeneity of schooling.[a] The omission of ability leads to overestimation of returns to schooling as ability is positively related to both schooling and wages. To address this, Griliches (1977) suggests the inclusion of a measure of ability such as IQ or test scores, or using siblings as instrument variables. A positive measurement error would lead to an underestimation of returns to schooling.

Schooling may be endogenous as it depends on individual or family decisions. This may lead to a positive bias in returns to schooling if more able individuals acquire more schooling or incur lower costs. To address this, Griliches (1977) suggests the use of simultaneous equations models. Instrumental variable (IV) regression is also standard solution to the endogeneity problem (Card, 1999: Card, 2001). It involves finding an instrument that affects education but not ability or the error term in the wage equation.[b]

Various instruments have been used in the literature. Angrist and Krueger (1991) used quarter of birth, as it determines when an individual starts schooling. They found more schooling and more graduates (in high school) and higher wages among individuals born in later quarters of the year. However, they found that returns to schooling using IV regression are not significantly different from ordinary least squares (OLS) estimates. Card (1993) used college proximity as an instrument, arguing that it increases the benefits and reduces the costs of schooling. His IV regression increased returns to schooling by 25%–60% over the OLS estimates.

[a] Z. Griliches. 1977. Estimating the Returns to Schooling: Some Econometrics Problems. *Econometrica* 45(1): 1–22.
[b] See Card (1999) and Card (2001).
Source: Authors.

The data used in this study are from the April 2019 round of the LFS. The LFS is a quarterly nationwide survey of households conducted by the Philippine Statistics Authority (PSA) aimed at gathering demographic and socioeconomic data on the population. The April 2019 survey round has a sample size of 117,728 individuals, representing a total population of around 107.86 million.

The Returns to TVET

This section highlights the returns to TVET at the upper secondary, post-secondary, and tertiary levels. Previous literature on returns to TVET is presented in Box 9.2. For its own estimates, this study uses the Mincer equation as benchmark and then accounts for observed characteristics, and finally corrects for selection bias using the Heckman model.[121] Presented in this section are descriptive statistics, estimates of returns to average schooling, and the Heckman selection model results. Then, the rates of return are estimated by education level—at upper-secondary level and by track—for post-secondary TVET, post-secondary TVET by field, short-cycle tertiary education, short-cycle tertiary education by broad field, and tertiary education by level.

Box 9.2: Returns to Technical and Vocational Education and Training in Related Literature

Most studies on returns to education estimate returns to average schooling or compare returns to primary, secondary, and tertiary education. Not many studies estimate returns to technical and vocational education and training (TVET). For those that do, the following are the general findings:

Secondary Technical versus Other Track

- Psacharopoulos and Patrinos (1993) studied the profitability of secondary technical-vocational education in Latin America. They found higher gross earnings as well as private returns for vocational school graduates in 7 out of 11 countries, the latter ranging from 8.5% in Bolivia to 26.8% in Honduras. Vocational returns are lower in Argentina and Chile, but still respectable. Returns to vocational education in the Dominican Republic and Peru, however, are negative.

- Sakellariou (2006) compared the returns to general and technical-vocational education in Singapore using data from the mid-1998 labor force survey. Using ordinary least squares (OLS) estimates, Sakellariou found returns to vocational education of 11% per year of schooling compared to 12% for general education. Comparing returns across education levels, Sakellariou found that returns to vocational education are comparable to those for general education at secondary level. For secondary education, the return to vocational education for males is 40.4% compared to 43% for general education. For females, the return to vocational education is 68.3% compared to 52.8% for general education.

- The Organisation for Economic Co-operation and Development (OECD) (2018) found that, in Thailand, workers who did not pursue higher education, but pursued upper secondary vocational training, earned more than those who pursued upper secondary general education. Returns to secondary vocational training are more than 20 percentage points above those for general education across all regions. This indicates that demand for these workers is higher and that they are more productive and useful to the regional economy.

---

[121] J. Heckman. 1979. Sample Selection Bias as a Specification Error. *Econometrica (The Econometric Society)* 47(1): 153–61.

Box 9.2: *continued*

Post-Secondary Vocational versus General, Secondary

- Sakellariou (2006) found returns to post-secondary vocational education in Singapore to be comparable to those for general education. The return to vocational education for males is 39% compared to 32.5% for general education. For females, the return to vocational education is 48.5% compared to 35.3% for general education.

Tertiary-Level TVET versus Academic Track

- In Singapore, Sakellariou (2006) found that returns to vocational education at tertiary level (33.9% for males, 8.4% for females) are lower than those for general education (67.1% for males, 58.7% for females).

- Tan and Nam (2012) reviewed the pattern of earnings in developing countries. They found that earnings for TVET are better than those for academic programs in Israel (1983), Thailand (1989–95), Egypt (1998), Singapore (1998), and Sri Lanka (2002). On the other hand, they found that earnings for TVET are lower than those for academic programs in Suriname (1990, 1992, 1993); Rwanda (1999–2001); and Pakistan (2004).

Source: Compiled by the authors.

Descriptive Statistics

Of the 107 million population (as of the April 2019 LFS), over 69 million are economically active. The distribution of educational attainment among the economically active is shown in Table 9.1. Of special interest for this study are those whose highest educational attainment pertains to TVET, i.e., upper secondary (particularly those in technology and livelihood track), post-secondary non-tertiary, and short-cycle tertiary. Together, this group comprises one-eighth of the economically active population.

Almost 6% of the economically active population have upper secondary education. Among these, almost 14% took TVET (Technology and Livelihood track), with close to 8% completing Grade 12, and a little over 6% completing Grade 11. The large majority (over 80%) took the academic track, a little over half of whom completed

Table 9.1: Sample and Population Distribution by Education Level

Education Level	Sample	Population	Share
No schooling	1,587	8,72,241	1.30%
Early childhood	31	16,012	0.00%
Primary	22,548	1,35,00,000	19.50%
Lower secondary	46,745	3,01,00,000	43.60%
Upper secondary	6,470	40,65,496	5.90%
Post-secondary non-tertiary	3,492	20,21,633	2.90%
Short-cycle tertiary	3,646	24,79,076	3.60%
Bachelor	24,795	1,57,00,000	22.70%
Master	450	2,25,038	0.30%
Doctoral	138	86,676	0.10%
Total	**1,09,902**	**6,90,66,172**	**100.00%**

Source: Philippines Labor Force Survey, April 2019.

Grade 11 and the other half completing Grade 12. Almost 5% took the Arts and Design track, with 3% completing Grade 12 and almost 2% completing Grade 11. The remaining 1% took the Sports track, 0.6% completing Grade 12, and 0.4% completing Grade 11.

Almost 3% of the economically active have post-secondary, non-tertiary education. Of these, over 21% have completed TESDA NCs, almost 38% have completed other TVET courses, and 41% have incomplete TVET courses. Among those with TESDA NCs, almost two-thirds (65.3%) took engineering, manufacturing, and construction, followed by services (17.8%), and business administration and law (9.6%). The least-represented qualifications are health and welfare (1.7%); arts and humanities (2.6%); and agriculture, forestry, fisheries, and veterinary (2.9%).

Almost 4% of the economically active have short-cycle tertiary education. These are dominated by graduates (89.4%), with the remaining 10.6% being undergraduates. Among the graduates, the largest group (28.7%) took the engineering, manufacturing, and construction field; followed by those who took up services (19%), business, administration, and law (18.6%), and information and communication technologies (16.8%). Health and welfare was taken by 9.4%, while the rest of the fields have less than 3% shares, with natural sciences, mathematics, and statistics; generic programs; and arts and humanities having the lowest shares.

Returns to Average Schooling

The basic Mincerian model puts the average rate of return to schooling for the Philippines at 9.5%. This average rate of return is somewhat higher than the world average of 8.8% as well as that for East Asia and the Pacific (8.7%) for 1950–2014.[122] It is also a bit higher than the averages for low-income countries (9.3%) and middle-income countries (9.2%). This may be attributed to the larger variation in earnings and schooling in the country, especially across industries and occupations. This is confirmed by the large reduction in returns when controlling for industry and occupation. Variations by urbanity, region, and class of work also help account for the high returns in the basic Mincerian model.

Controlling for urbanity, region, industry, occupation, and class of work decreases the average return to schooling. Results of OLS regression with stepwise inclusion of controls are presented in Figure 9.1 The chart shows the coefficient for schooling (and experience) with the cumulative addition of the various control variables. For all models, the coefficient of schooling is significant at 0.1%. The goodness-of-fit of the model improves with the addition of each control, with the adjusted R-squared increasing from 24.5% to 47.9%.

The addition of controls lowers the average rate of return significantly. Adding the urban dummy decreases the rate of return to 9%. This means that the omission of the urban dummy overestimates returns to schooling as it captures the higher wages and higher schooling in urban areas. On the other hand, adding a dummy variable for males increases the rate of return to schooling to 9.6%. This means that omitting sex underestimates the rate of return, as it captures the lower schooling among males, although males have higher wages. Including regional dummies decreases returns to 9.3%, meaning that the omission of region overestimates the rate of return, as it captures the higher wages and schooling in NCR.

---

[122] G. Psacharopoulos and H. A. Patrinos. 2018. Returns to Investment in Education: A Decennial Review of Global Literature. *Policy Research Working Paper* 8402. Washington, DC: World Bank.

Figure 9.1: Stepwise Regression Coefficients, Returns to Education

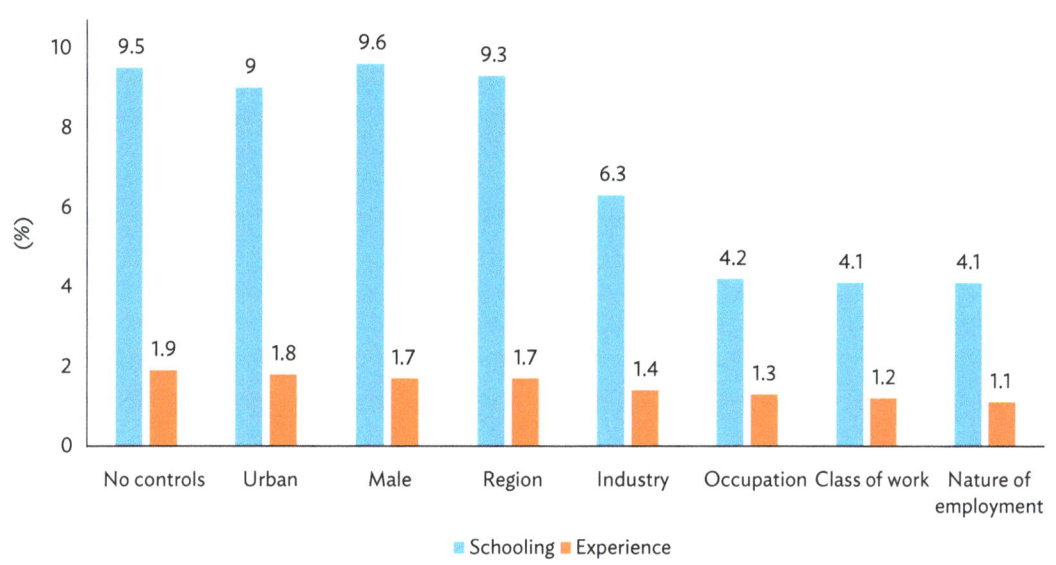

Source: ADB estimates.

Including industry dummies accounts for the greatest decrease in the rate of return, by almost a third. The omission of industry, in particular, overestimates the rate of return as this variable captures the higher wages and schooling in most industries relative to agriculture, forestry, and fishing. Including occupational dummies further decreases the rate of return to schooling by over 1 percentage point. This means that the omission of occupation overestimates returns as it captures the higher schooling in the armed forces compared to most occupations. The inclusion of class of work only slightly decreases the rate of return, while including nature of employment does not change the rate of return.

Correcting for Selection Bias in Labor Force Participation, Employment, and Paid Employment

Estimated rates of return may suffer from selection bias as wages are only observed among those in the labor force, those who are employed, and those in particular classes of work. To correct for selection bias, a two-stage Heckman (1979) model is fitted on the various equations to account for factors that affect labor force participation, employment, and work for pay. The first stage is a probit model relating the probability of labor force participation, employment and working for pay to sex, age, marital status, and number of children. The second stage is the wage equation including the inverse mills ratio (derived from the first stage) whose significance indicates selection bias in the least squares estimates. The regression results of the Heckman selection models are given in Table A9.1. The coefficient of the inverse mills ratio (lambda) is significant in all three models, indicating selection bias in the OLS estimates.

Older men and women, and women with more children are less likely to participate in the labor force. Accounting for selection in labor force participation increases returns to schooling. In the first model, the first stage relates labor force participation to sex, age, marital status, number of children, and interactions between the first variable with the latter three.[123] The results show that males are more likely than females to participate in the labor force. However, older individuals are less likely than younger individuals to participate, both for males and females. Married individuals are more likely to participate in the labor force; this is true for both sexes. Males with more children are more likely to participate in the labor force while females with more children are less likely to participate. The second stage shows higher returns to schooling (9.9%) compared to the OLS model. This means that the OLS regression underestimates returns to schooling because of the selection of certain individuals out of the labor force: older men and women, and women with more children.

For those in the labor force, older men and women with more children are less likely to be employed. Accounting for employment selection decreases returns to schooling. The first stage of the second model relates employment to the same independent variables as in the first model. The results are very similar to the first model, except that older females tend to be employed more than younger females. The second stage shows lower returns to schooling (9.3%) compared with the OLS estimate. This suggests that OLS regression overestimates returns to schooling as it captures the higher employment of older men.

Among those employed, younger men, older women, married women, and women with more children are less likely to work with pay. Accounting for selection in paid employment shows the highest returns to schooling. The first stage of the third model relates whether an employee receives wages/works for pay to the same independent variables as in the previous models. Young men are less likely to be paid than young women for their work. However, older men are more likely to be paid than younger men, while older women are less likely to be paid than younger women. Married men are more likely to work for pay than unmarried men, while married women are less likely to work for pay than unmarried women. Men with more children are more likely to work for pay than men with less children, whereas women with more children are less likely to work for pay. The second stage shows the highest returns to schooling (10.1%), indicating that the OLS estimate is downward biased given the unreported earnings of younger men, older women, married women, and women with more children.

Selection bias is reduced when accounting for various observed characteristics. Using the Heckman selection model with controls yields the results in Table A9.2. The coefficient of the inverse mills ratio is significant only for the models selecting for labor force participation and employment. There is no selection bias based on reported earnings, after controlling for the various observed characteristics. The first model accounting for labor force participation yields the same returns as the OLS. The second and third models accounting for employment and reported earnings, respectively, show only slightly lower returns than the OLS. This means that, after accounting for observed characteristics, there is little bias left.

Returns by Education Level

Returns to various levels of education are mostly positive and generally increasing. Returns to education are positive for most levels except for early childhood education where the rate of return is insignificant. The preferred Heckman selection model estimates (Figure 9.2) show returns to education decreasing from 2% for primary education to 1.7% for lower secondary level. Returns rise back to 2% for upper secondary education (including technology and livelihood track), and increase further to 2.7% for post-secondary non-tertiary TVET and to 2.9% for short-cycle tertiary TVET. Returns to tertiary education are highest at 3.8%

---

[123] This follows Congressional Budget Office (2018).

Figure 9.2: Returns to Education by Level (No Schooling As Reference)

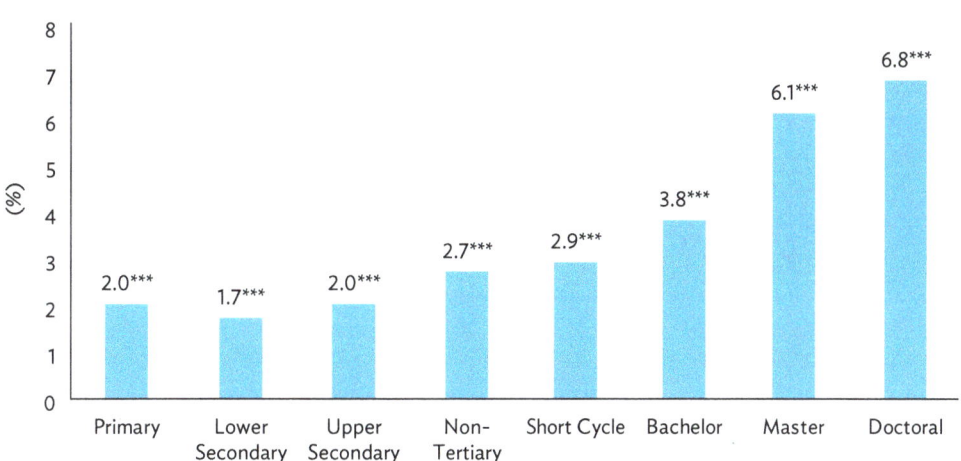

* p<0.05, ** p<0.01, *** p<0.001
Source: ADB estimates.

for bachelor, 6.1% for master, and 6.8% for doctorate degrees. Selection bias correction puts the Heckman estimates somewhat higher for primary education and master's education, and lower for lower secondary education, post-secondary non-tertiary education, bachelor's, and doctoral degrees, than for the least square estimates (Table A9.3).

The trends are consistent with global trends of higher returns to primary over secondary education and the recent increase in returns to higher education. Private returns to primary education levels have been the highest until recently.[124] Private returns to higher education have been increasing in recent decades (footnote 122). Considering public subsidy of education, however, may lower social returns to higher education below those of secondary education, revealing diminishing returns to education (footnote 124). The high returns to primary education are due to the jump in productivity from literacy and numeracy and its relatively low cost. On the other hand, the cost of education increases in secondary and tertiary education.

The likelihood of participating in the labor force depends on age, whether the person is studying, marital status, relationship to the household head, number of children, and educational attainment. The first stage of the Heckman selection model (Table A9.4) shows that those in their golden years (ages 50–64) and especially those of old age (age 65 up) are less likely to participate in the labor force than young adults (ages 15–29). Those studying are less likely to participate in the labor force than those not studying. Those who are married and widowed are less likely to participate in the labor force than those who are single. Household heads are more

---

[124] G. Psacharopoulos. 1985. Returns to Education: A Further International Update and Implications. *Journal of Human Resources* 20(4): 583–604.

likely to participate in the labor force than other members of the family. Those with more children are less likely to participate in the labor force. Those with more schooling /higher education levels are more likely to participate in the labor force than those with no education.

Returns to Upper Secondary Education

Returns to upper secondary education are positive for the completion of the academic track, negative for incomplete academic track and technology and livelihood track, and insignificant for others. The results of the Heckman selection model are shown in Figure 9.3. The rate of return to complete upper secondary education is only significant for the academic track, with returns of 3.9%. The rates of return to completion of the technology and livelihood, arts and design, and sports tracks are insignificant. The rates of return to incomplete secondary education are only significant for the academic and technology and livelihood tracks. However, the returns are negative, −8.2% for the academic track and −13.1% for the technology and livelihood track. These mean that those who do not complete the academic and technology and livelihood tracks earn 8.2% and 13.1%, respectively, less than those who only completed lower secondary education. Returns to incomplete arts and design and sports track are insignificant. The insignificance of returns to arts and design, and sports tracks may be due to the limited samples for these. Comparative returns using the basic Mincerian model and the augmented model with controls are given in Table A9.5.

Figure 9.3: Returns to Upper Secondary Education by Track
(Lower High School Graduate As Reference)

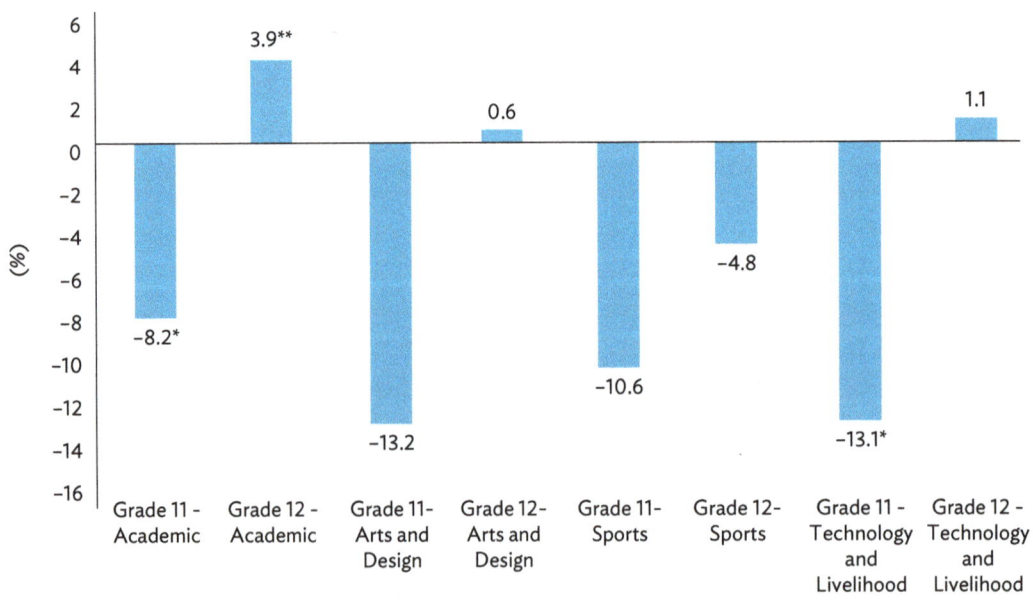

* p<0.05, ** p<0.01, *** p<0.001

Source: ADB estimates.

Returns to Post-Secondary TVET

Returns to post-secondary, non-tertiary TVET can vary depending on the duration of the training. Assuming 1 year to complete a qualification[125] and 6 months for incomplete participation, returns to post-secondary TVET are estimated at 15.9%, with the preferred Heckman model and is comparable to returns at the tertiary level, even at the post-graduate level. Using actual duration for each qualification, the estimated returns increase to 40%. This is comparable to that estimated by Sakellariou (2006) for Singapore (39% for males, 49% for females). Given the substantial returns to post-secondary non-tertiary TVET, there is arguably a gross private underinvestment in this education in terms of attendance, considering that enrollment at this level is less than one-third of that in tertiary education. As for public investment, this will be assessed in the subsequent chapter on the TESDA scholarship.

There are substantial returns to TVET at the post-secondary non-tertiary level, both for complete and incomplete participation (Figure 9.4). Among TVET graduates, returns are higher for TESDA NCs compared to other TVET courses. The Heckman selection model yields returns to TESDA NCs of 57%, while returns to other

Figure 9.4: Returns to Post-Secondary Non-Tertiary Education (Lower Secondary Graduates As Reference)

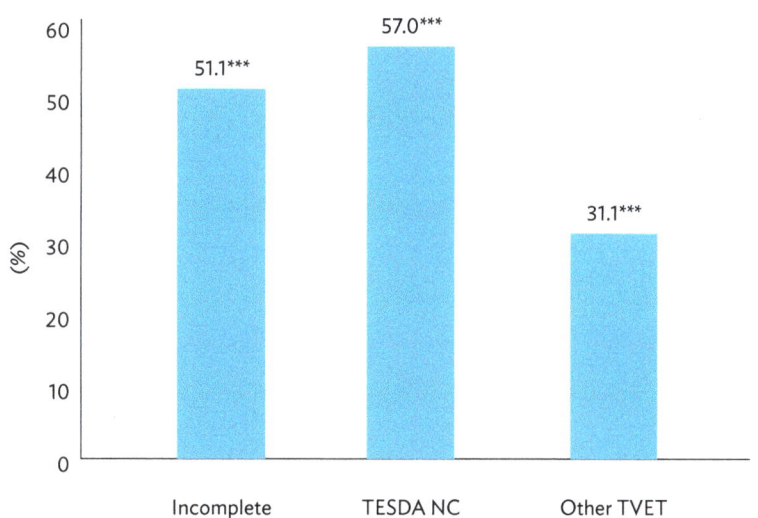

TESDA NC = Technical Education and Skills Development Authority National Certification, TVET = technical and vocational education and training.

* $p<0.05$, ** $p<0.01$, *** $p<0.001$

Source: ADB estimates.

---

[125] United Nations Educational, Scientific, and Cultural Organization - International Centre for Technical and Vocational Education and Training (UNESCO-UNEVOC). 2016. *Measuring the Return on Investment in TVET*. Bonn: UNESCO-UNEVOC.

TVET courses are 31%. Returns to incomplete participation decrease to 51%. Returns to TESDA NCs are higher, while the returns to other TVET courses and incomplete participation are lower than the least squares estimates with controls (Table A9.6). These suggests negative selection bias for TESDA NCs and positive selection bias for other TVET courses and incomplete participation.

Returns to Post-Secondary TVET by Field

Returns to TESDA National Certificates vary by field and are highest for services, health and welfare, and arts and humanities. As shown in Figure 9.5, the preferred Heckman model reveals that returns to TESDA NCs are highest for services (90.5%), followed by education and welfare (87.2%), and arts and humanities (81%). Engineering, manufacturing, and construction have the lowest returns (45.5%) followed by business, administration, and law (46.3%). The low returns to these courses might indicate oversupply of graduates at post-secondary and tertiary levels, given that most post-secondary TVET graduates took these courses. Engineering, manufacturing, and construction alone comprises almost two-thirds of the

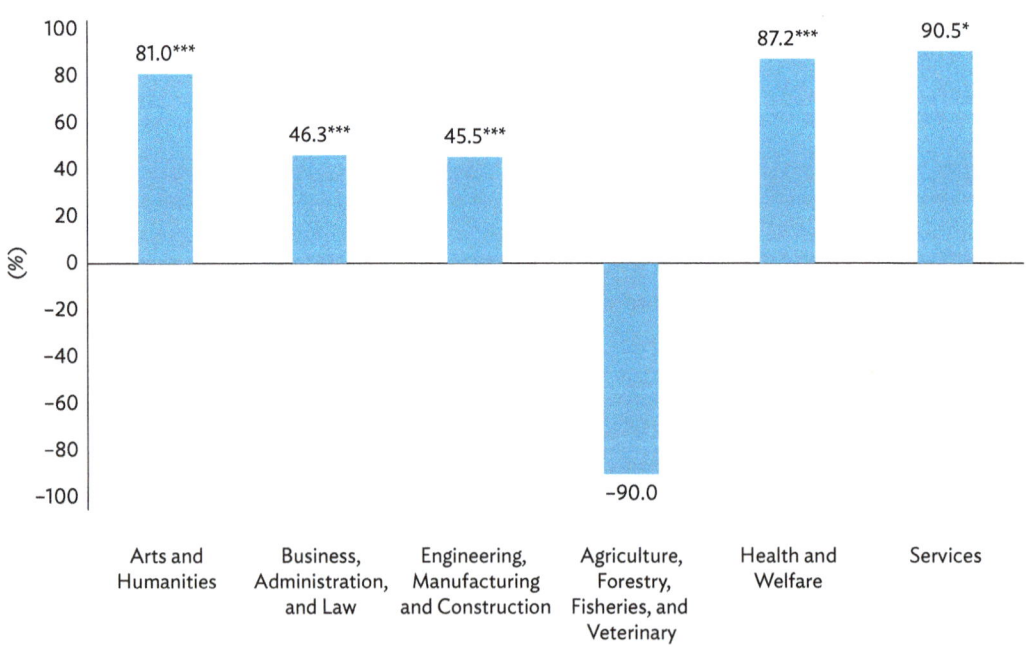

Figure 9.5: Returns to Technical Education and Skills Development Authority National Certificates by Field (Lower Secondary Graduates As Reference)

* $p<0.05$, ** $p<0.01$, *** $p<0.001$
Source: ADB estimates.

qualifications of TESDA NC holders. Returns to TVET in agriculture, forestry, fisheries, and veterinary are not significantly different from those of high school graduates. The Heckman estimates are mostly lower than the least squares estimates, with controls suggesting positive selection bias in the latter. However, the estimates for arts and humanities and agriculture, forestry, fisheries, and veterinary are higher than the least squares estimate indicating negative selection bias. Comparative returns using the Mincerian and with controls are given in Table A9.7.

Returns to Short-Cycle Tertiary TVET

There are respectable returns to short-cycle tertiary TVET, both for completion and incomplete participation. Figure 9.6 shows the Heckman model estimates of returns to short-cycle tertiary TVET. Accounting for selection bias reveals returns to short-cycle tertiary education graduates of almost 11%. This is higher than the returns to tertiary-level TVET estimated by Sakellariou (2006) for females in Singapore (8.4%), but way below that for males (33.9%). It is comparable to, even somewhat higher than, the rate of return to a bachelor's degree (10.5%). The estimate for incomplete participation is also significant (at 5% confidence level) with estimated return of 7.7%. The estimated returns are higher than those in least squares model with controls suggesting that negative selection in the least squares estimates.

Figure 9.6: Returns to Short-Cycle Tertiary Education (Lower Secondary Graduate As Reference)

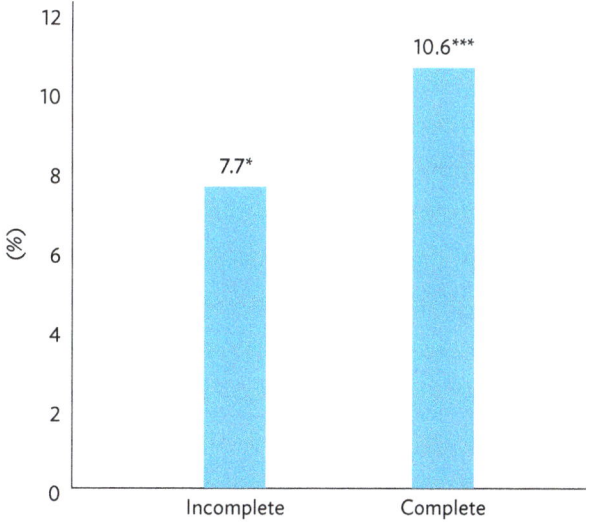

* $p<0.05$, ** $p<0.01$, *** $p<0.001$
Source: ADB estimates.

Returns to Short-Cycle Tertiary Education by Broad Field

Returns to short-cycle tertiary education vary by field. Significant estimates range 9%–19% in the Heckman selection model (Figure 9.7). Returns are highest for health and welfare (18.5%); social sciences, journalism, and information (13.9%); and education (11.3%). Returns are lowest for engineering, manufacturing, and construction (8.6%); agriculture, forestry, fisheries, and veterinary (8.7%); and services (10.2%). Returns to generic programs and qualifications and arts and humanities are insignificant.

Figure 9.7: Returns to Short-Cycle Tertiary Education by Field (Lower Secondary Graduate As Reference)

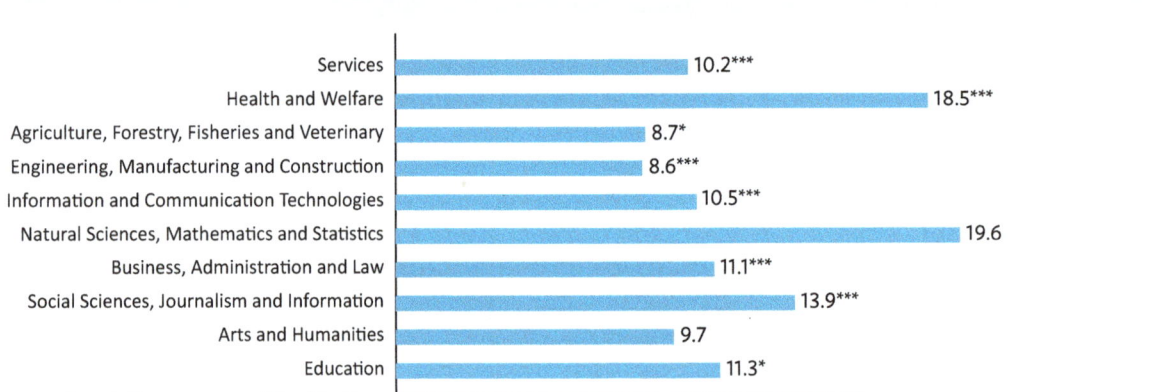

* $p<0.05$, ** $p<0.01$, *** $p<0.001$
Source: ADB estimates.

Returns to Tertiary Education

Returns to tertiary education are significantly positive for bachelor's, master's, and doctorate levels, both for completion and incomplete participation.[126] Returns generally increase by level, being lowest for incomplete bachelor's, and increasing with completion and advanced studies. Returns to incomplete bachelor's education are at 6%, with those for complete bachelor's rising to 10.5% (Figure 9.8). Returns increase with master's education to 15.1% for incomplete master's and 13.9% for complete master's education. Returns for doctorate education are 14.9% for incomplete and 13.7% for complete. Comparative estimates for the Mincerian model and the augmented model with controls are given in Table A9.9. The Heckman model estimate for incomplete bachelor's is slightly lower than the estimate from least squares model with controls, suggesting positive selection bias in the latter. On the other hand, the Heckman model estimate for complete bachelor's is slightly higher and for master's education is substantially higher than the OLS estimate, suggesting negative selection bias in the least squares estimate.

---

[126] Incomplete participation is defined as not having completed the course, and applies to current students and those who dropped out.

Figure 9.8: **Returns to Tertiary Education (Lower Secondary Graduate As Reference)**

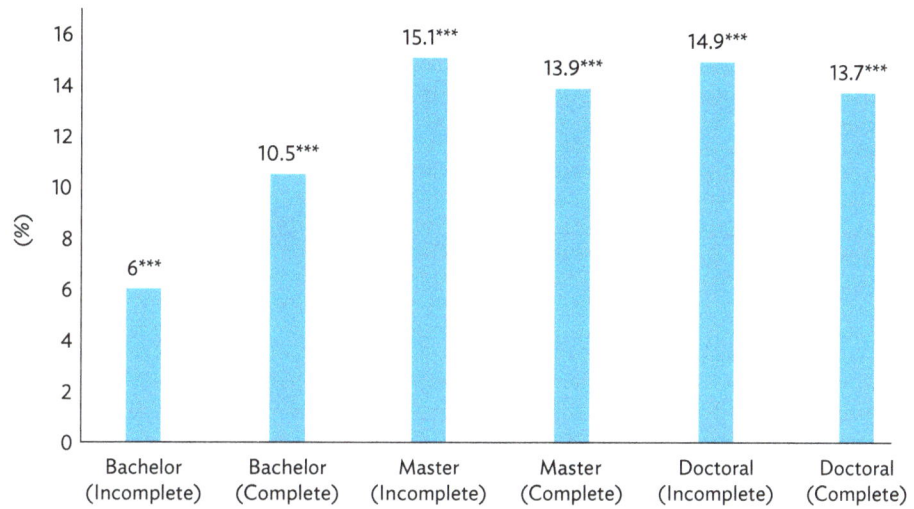

* p<0.05, ** p<0.01, *** p<0.001
Source: ADB estimates.

Conclusions

The basic estimate of average rate of return to schooling in the Philippines is comparable to the global and regional average. In fact, it is slightly higher, which may be due to larger variation in earnings and schooling in low-income countries, especially across industries and occupations. This is confirmed by the large reduction in the rate of return when controlling for industry and occupation. Variations by urbanity, region, and class of work also help account for the high returns in the basic Mincerian model.

Notwithstanding the relatively high returns to schooling in the country, returns appear to be underestimated due to selection bias, with some older men and women, and women with more children, selected out of the labor force; older men and women with more children selected out of employment; and young men, older women, and married women and women with more children selected out of paid work. Had they not been constrained from joining the labor force or from paid work, these groups would earn higher earnings than average and drive up the returns to schooling. The selection bias in labor force participation remains even after accounting for the effect of locational and occupational characteristics. The bias in paid work/reported earnings, however, disappears when including the controls. This means that particular industries, occupations, and classes of work are prone to experiencing unpaid work, such as agriculture/farming and family-owned business.

Returns to various levels of education are mostly positive and generally increasing. While returns to early childhood education are insignificant, returns to most levels of education are significantly positive. Returns to education decrease from primary to lower secondary levels, but increase at upper secondary level up to tertiary level.

Returns to TVET at the upper secondary level are not significant for completion and even negative for incomplete participation (i.e., non-completion the full duration of the course), while the return to upper secondary academic track completion is around 4% (the first-ever evaluation of returns to the K to 12 program).

Nevertheless, there are substantial returns to TVET at post-secondary non-tertiary level. Assuming a 1-year duration for a certificate places average returns at 16%, comparable to returns to tertiary education even at post-graduate level. Moreover, given the shorter actual training durations, average returns to post-secondary TVET are even higher at 40%, with returns to TESDA national certificates at 57% and to other TVET courses at 31%. Given the substantial returns to post-secondary non-tertiary TVET, there is arguably a gross private underinvestment in this education in terms of attendance, considering that enrollment at this level is less than one-third of that in tertiary education.

Across TESDA qualifications, returns are highest for services, education and welfare, and arts and humanities; lowest for engineering, manufacturing, and construction, and business, administration, and law; and insignificant for agriculture, forestry, fisheries, and veterinary. The low returns to engineering, manufacturing, and construction, and business, administration, and law might indicate an oversupply of graduates at the post-secondary as well as tertiary levels, given that most post-secondary TVET graduates took these courses. Engineering, manufacturing, and construction alone comprises almost two-thirds of the qualifications of TESDA NC holders.

There are also respectable returns to short-cycle tertiary level TVET, both for completion and incomplete participation. Across fields, returns are highest in health and welfare followed by social sciences, journalism and information, and education. Engineering, manufacturing, and construction has the lowest positive returns followed by agriculture, forestry, fisheries, and veterinary and services. Between these are business, administration, and law, and information and communication technologies. Returns to generic programs and arts and humanities are not significant.

To our knowledge, this is the first study to estimate returns to TVET in the Philippines and to estimate returns at various levels and for various fields. It has done so by accounting for various observed characteristics, as well as correcting for unobserved selection bias, thereby providing reasonably unbiased estimates. Nevertheless, further analysis can be done in the future to address other issues such as the endogeneity of schooling and unobserved ability bias. The former can be addressed by using instrumental variable regression, while the latter can be addressed by comparing returns between twins/siblings using fixed-effects estimation.

Appendix 9: Empirical Methodology and Summary Results

The approach begins with the basic human capital earnings function that relates wage to schooling and experience; this serves as a benchmark model. We then add controls in a stepwise manner to determine how returns to schooling changes with each control, from demographic, to geographic and occupational characteristics. This model is as follows:

$$lnwage = \beta_1 + \beta_2 Sch + \beta_3 Exp + \beta_4 Exp^2 + X\beta + \varepsilon \tag{1}$$

Where *lnwage* log hourly wage, *Sch* is years of schooling; *Exp* is years of work experience; and *X* is a vector for various control variables: urbanity, sex, region, industry, occupation, class of work, and nature of employment. The coefficient of schooling, β_2, is the coefficient of interest and represents the rate of return to schooling.

For the control variables, dummy variables are created for male, urban, 17 regions with reference to NCR; 19 industries (2009 Philippine Standard Occupational Classification Sections) with reference to agriculture, forestry, and fishing; 9 occupations (2012 PSOC Major Groups) with reference to the armed forces; 6 classes of work[127] with reference to government employees; and nature of employment[128] with reference to permanent job.

Notwithstanding the correction of bias due to the omission of observable characteristics, the estimated rate of return may still be suffering from selection bias as wages are only observed among a subset of those in the labor force and those who are employed. To address selection bias, we use a two-stage Heckman (1979) selection model. The first stage fits a probit model that relates the probability of participating in the labor force to a vector of independent variables *w* which includes sex, age, marital status, and number of children.[129]

$$P(LFP) = \Phi(\alpha_1 + \alpha_2 w_i + u_i) \tag{2}$$

The second stage is the wage equation plus a new variable known as the inverse mills ratio (λ_i) derived from the first stage. The inverse mills ratio allows the wage equation to account for factors that influence labor force participation, employment, and reported earnings so that conditioning on it makes the sample approximate a randomly selected sample.

$$lnwage = \beta_1 + \beta_2 Sch + \beta_3 Exp + \beta_4 Exp^2 + X\beta + \beta_\lambda \lambda_i + \varepsilon \tag{3}$$

A significant coefficient for the inverse mills ratio means that there is selection bias in the least squares results. Given the focus on TVET, return to schooling is then estimated for TVET graduates relative to high school graduates by relating wage to years of schooling in TVET.

$$lnwage = \beta_1 + \beta_2 TVETSch + \beta_3 Exp + \beta_4 Exp^2 + X\beta + \varepsilon \tag{4}$$

Where *TVETSch* is years of schooling for TVET qualifications. An extended earnings function is then fitted by interacting TVET schooling with specific qualifications (National Certificates) to determine returns to schooling for various TVET courses.

$$lnwage = \beta_1 + \sum_{i=2}^{i=20} \beta_i (Qualif_i * Sch) + \beta_{21} Exp + \beta_{22} Exp^2 + X\beta + \varepsilon \tag{5}$$

Where *Qualif* is a series of dummy variables for various TVET qualifications with secondary education as reference.

---

[127] Includes private households, private establishments, self-employed, employer, family-owned business with pay, and family-owned business without pay.
[128] Short-term and different employer.
[129] This follows Congressional Budget Office (2018).

Table A9.1: Heckman Selection Model, Without Controls

	(1) Ln Wage	(2) Ln Wage	(3) Ln Wage
SECOND STAGE			
Schooling	0.0987	0.0934	0.101
	(108.74)***	(99.24)***	(95.67)***
Experience	0.0152	0.0153	0.0267
	(20.69)***	(16.08)***	(27.05)***
Experience squared	−0.000162	−0.000194	−0.000249
	(−11.83)***	(−12.88)***	(−18.45)***
Constant	2.853	2.826	2.803
	(196.01)***	(117.75)***	(171.02)***
FIRST STAGE	Labor force	Employed	With pay
Male	0.5	0.419	−0.412
	(20.36)***	(6.74)***	(−11.60)***
Age	−0.006	0.0258	−0.029
	(−15.96)***	(16.66)***	(−48.18)***
Male*age	−0.00885	−0.0171	0.00668
	(−14.32)***	(−8.94)***	(8.44)***
Married	0.153	0.379	−0.251
	(11.50)***	(10.65)***	(−14.32)***
Male*married	1.091	0.181	0.248
	(48.81)***	(3.96)***	(10.58)***
Number of children	−0.0855	−0.0387	−0.0832
	(−17.97)***	(−3.43)***	(−13.59)***
Male*number of children	0.0939	0.0325	0.0378
	(13.28)***	(2.27)*	(4.95)***
Constant	−0.264	0.399	1.495
	(−15.44)***	(8.07)***	(52.13)***
mills			
lambda	−0.194	−0.319	−0.449
	(−24.62)***	(−6.10)***	(−11.19)***
N	82547	39857	68260

* $p<0.05$, ** $p<0.01$, *** $p<0.001$
Note: t statistics in parentheses.
Source: ADB estimates.

Table A9.2: Heckman Selection Model, With Controls

	(1) Ln Wage	(2) Ln Wage	(3) Ln Wage
SECOND STAGE			
Schooling	0.0405	0.0389	0.0403
	(40.07)***	(37.45)***	(36.88)***
Experience	0.0102	0.0071	0.0108
	(15.87)***	(8.75)***	(12.95)***
Experience squared	−0.000125	−0.000101	−0.000144
	(−10.68)***	(−7.90)***	(−12.47)***
Constant	3.799	3.836	3.695
	(78.02)***	(76.31)***	(77.52)***
FIRST STAGE	Labor force	Employed	With pay
Male	0.5	0.419	−0.412
	(20.36)***	(6.74)***	(−11.60)***
Age	−0.006	0.0258	−0.029
	(−15.96)***	(16.66)***	(−48.18)***
Male*age	−0.00885	−0.0171	0.00668
	(−14.32)***	(−8.94)***	(8.44)***
Married	0.153	0.379	−0.251
	(11.50)***	(10.65)***	(−14.32)***
Male*married	1.091	0.181	0.248
	(48.81)***	(3.96)***	(10.58)***
Number of children	−0.0855	−0.0387	−0.0832
	(−17.97)***	(−3.43)***	(−13.59)***
Male*number of children	0.0939	0.0325	0.0378
	(13.28)***	(2.27)*	(4.95)***
Constant	−0.264	0.399	1.495
	(−15.44)***	(8.07)***	(52.13)***
Mills			
Lambda	−0.0826	−0.369	0.0283
	(−8.28)***	(−8.27)***	−0.89
N	82,547	39,857	68,260

* $p<0.05$, ** $p<0.01$, *** $p<0.001$
Note: t statistics in parentheses.
Source: ADB estimates.

Table A9.3: Returns to Education by Level

Item	Mincerian		With Controls		Heckman	
	Coef.	Robust S.E.	Coef.	Robust S.E.	Coef.	Robust S.E.
Early childhood	0.202	0.111	0.063	0.082	0.143	0.18
Primary	0.052	0.004***	0.019	0.004***	0.02	0.003***
Lower secondary	0.047	0.002***	0.018	0.002***	0.017	0.002***
Upper secondary	0.04	0.003***	0.02	0.003***	0.02	0.002***
Non-tertiary	0.062	0.003***	0.028	0.002***	0.027	0.002***
Short cycle	0.063	0.002***	0.029	0.002***	0.029	0.002***
Bachelor's	0.08	0.002***	0.038	0.002***	0.038	0.001***
Master's	0.104	0.002***	0.055	0.003***	0.061	0.002***
Doctorate	0.111	0.005***	0.07	0.005***	0.068	0.003***
Experience	0.02	0.001***	0.012	0.001***	0.013	0.001***
Experience squared	0	0.000***	0	0.000***	0	0.000***
Constant	3.035	0.024***	4.48	0.083***	4.356	0.047***
lambda					0.028	0.008***
N	36,462		36,462		82,508	
Adj. R-sq	0.2973781		0.4903848			

* $p<0.05$, ** $p<0.01$, *** $p<0.001$
Note: t statistics in parentheses.
Source: ADB estimates.

Table A9.4: First Stage Probit Regression: Heckman Model with Labor Force Participation Selection

Item	Coef.	Std. Err.
Studying	−2.027	0.022***
30–49	0.255	0.015***
50–64	−0.33	0.020***
65 up	−1.81	0.029***
Male	0.816	0.013***
Married	−0.104	0.020***
Widowed	−0.308	0.032***
Divorced/separated	0.012	0.038
Wife/spouse	−0.72	0.018***
Son/daughter	−0.373	0.022***
Brothers/sisters	−0.43	0.040***
Son/daughter-in-law	−0.411	0.031***
Grandchildren	−0.565	0.042***

Table A9.4: *continued*

Item	Coef.	Std. Err.
Father/mother	−0.704	0.065***
Other relative	−0.42	0.033***
Boarder	−0.37	0.26
Domestic helper	7.948	.
Non-relative	0.056	0.074
Number of children	−0.028	0.004***
ECE	0.05	0.307
Primary	0.858	0.048***
Lower secondary	0.874	0.048***
Upper secondary	0.783	0.056***
Non-tertiary	0.99	0.055***
Short cycle	0.961	0.055***
Bachelor's	1.231	0.048***
Master's	1.94	0.090***
Doctorate	1.823	0.146***
Constant	−0.606	0.053***
Mills		
Lambda	0.028	0.008***
N	82,508	

ECE = early childhood education.
* p<0.05, ** p<0.01, *** p<0.001
Source: ADB estimates.

Table A9.5: Returns to Upper Secondary Education by Track

	Mincerian		With Controls		Heckman	
Item	Coef.	Robust S.E.	Coef.	Robust S.E.	Coef.	Robust S.E.
Grade 11 - Academic Track	−0.136	0.058*	−0.098	0.055	−0.082	0.032*
Grade 12 - Academic Track	0.014	0.023	0.035	0.02	0.039	0.014**
Grade 11 - Arts and Design Track	−0.2	0.137	−0.09	0.134	−0.132	0.131
Grade 12 - Arts and Design Track	−0.058	0.094	−0.034	0.073	0.006	0.062
Graded 11 - Sports Track	−0.134	0.156	−0.102	0.075	−0.106	0.228
Grade 12 - Sports Track	−0.089	0.186	−0.041	0.095	−0.048	0.088
Grade 11 - Technology and Livelihood Track	−0.1	0.123	−0.082	0.094	−0.131	0.066*

continued on next page

Table A9.5: continued

Item	Mincerian Coef.	Mincerian Robust S.E.	With Controls Coef.	With Controls Robust S.E.	Heckman Coef.	Heckman Robust S.E.
Grade 12 - Technology and Livelihood Track	0.013	0.036	0.04	0.027	0.011	0.022
Experience	0.019	0.002***	0.013	0.002***	0.012	0.001***
Experience Squared	0	0.000***	0	0.000***	0	0.000***
Constant	3.542	0.022***	4.439	0.222***	4.304	0.092***
Lambda					0.031	0.011**
N	11,555		11,555		57,611	
Adj. R-sq	0.0278222		0.3342931			

* $p<0.05$, ** $p<0.01$, *** $p<0.001$

Source: ADB estimates.

Table A9.6: Returns to Post-Secondary Non-Tertiary Technical and Vocational Education and Training

Item	Mincerian Coef.	Mincerian Std. Err.	With Controls Coef.	With Controls Std. Err.	Heckman Coef.	Heckman Std. Err.
TESDA NCs	0.842	0.122***	0.542	0.099***	0.57	0.080***
Other TVET	0.753	0.160***	0.543	0.132***	0.511	0.095***
Incomplete	0.397	0.105***	0.353	0.087***	0.311	0.051***
Experience	0.02	0.002***	0.013	0.002***	0.011	0.001***
Experience squared	0	0.000***	0	0.000***	0	0.000***
Constant					−7.486	0.051***
Lambda					0.041	0.012***
N	12,086		12,086		58,141	
Adj. R-sq	0.0310402		0.3443393			

NC = national certificate, TESDA = Technical Education and Skills Development Authority, TVET = technical and vocational education and training.

* $p<0.05$, ** $p<0.01$, *** $p<0.001$.

Source: ADB estimates.

Table A9.7: Returns to Post-Secondary Non-Tertiary Technical and Vocational Education and Training by Field

Item	Mincerian		With Controls		Heckman	
	Coef.	Robust S.E.	Coef.	Robust S.E.	Coef.	Robust S.E.
Arts and humanities	0.685	0.296*	0.709	0.334*	0.81	0.225***
Business, administration, and law	0.959	0.216***	0.541	0.182**	0.463	0.134***
Engineering, manufacturing, and construction	0.864	0.165***	0.533	0.118***	0.455	0.129***
Agriculture, forestry, fisheries, and veterinary	−2.036	0.886*	−1.433	0.722*	−0.9	0.541
Health and welfare	1.142	0.213***	1.155	0.261***	0.872	0.264***
Services	1.047	0.375**	0.904	0.306**	0.905	0.380*
Experience	0.019	0.002***	0.013	0.002***	0.012	0.001***
Experience squared	0	0.000***	0	0.000***	0	0.000***
Constant	3.541	0.023***	4.503	0.217***	4.346	0.090***
Lambda					0.044	0.012***
N	11299		11299		57355	
Adj. R-sq	0.0278941		0.3402357			

* $p<0.05$, ** $p<0.01$, *** $p<0.001$
Source: ADB estimates.

Table A9.8: Returns to Short-Cycle Tertiary Technical and Vocational Education and Training

Item	Mincerian		With Controls		Heckman	
	Coef.	Std. Err.	Coef.	Std. Err.	Coef.	Std. Err.
Incomplete	0.098	0.062	0.064	0.05	0.077	0.033*
Complete	0.144	0.010***	0.099	0.010***	0.106	0.006***
Experience	0.02	0.002***	0.013	0.002***	0.011	0.001***
Experience squared	0	0.000***	0	0.000***	0	0.000***
Constant					−7.47	0.041***
Lambda					0.038	0.012**
N	12,394		12,394		58,449	
Adj. R-sq	0.0492257		0.3475828			

* $p<0.05$, ** $p<0.01$, *** $p<0.001$
Source: ADB estimates.

Table A9.9: **Returns to Tertiary Education by Level**

Item	Mincerian		With Controls		Heckman	
	Coef.	Robust S.E.	Coef.	Robust S.E.	Coef.	Robust S.E.
Bachelor's (Incomplete)	0.116	0.007***	0.064	0.007***	0.06	0.005***
Bachelor's (Complete)	0.179	0.003***	0.104	0.004***	0.105	0.002***
Master's (Incomplete)	0.2	0.020***	0.108	0.016***	0.151	0.011***
Master's (Complete)	0.199	0.006***	0.124	0.006***	0.139	0.005***
Doctorate (Incomplete)	0.209	0.023***	0.15	0.019***	0.149	0.019***
Doctorate (Complete)	0.191	0.012***	0.14	0.012***	0.137	0.006***
Experience	0.025	0.002***	0.017	0.001***	0.016	0.001***
Experience squared	0	0.000***	0	0.000***	0	0.000***
Constant	3.473	0.016***	4.733	0.101***	4.58	0.054***
Lambda					0.041	0.011***
N	22,162		22,162		68,213	
Adj. R-sq	0.3154061		0.5153823			

* $p<0.05$, ** $p<0.01$, *** $p<0.001$

Source: ADB estimates.

10. Measuring Training–Job Mismatch

Failure of skills supply to keep up with, and adapt to, rapidly evolving demand can exacerbate existing mismatches. Policies geared toward matching the expected and actual post-training occupations of graduates have been hampered by inadequate labor market information systems and limited technical capacity, among other factors.[130] The lack of available data for researchers and policy makers is an additional constraint in undertaking research and evaluations around skills mismatch, compromising the scope for evidence-based policy making to help close skills gaps.

This chapter investigates the effectiveness of TVET programs in terms of matching the expected and actual post-training occupations of graduates. In other words, it attempts to measure the extent of the transferability of the skills acquired in TVET to the labor market. This chapter extends the analysis of Generalao (2019a), which estimates the level of training–job mismatch among 2014 TVET graduates to multiple years. It provides an overview of the concept of skills mismatch and presents the methodological approach employed as well as the main findings and conclusion to the analysis of skills mismatch.

Defining Mismatch

There are a range of different interpretations for what mismatch constitutes and therefore how mismatches are measured. McGuinness et al. (2017) cite the lack of specificity in the definition of mismatch as a contribution to ineffective policies to address skills mismatches. Palmer (2018)[131] provides a general definition of skills mismatch as the "lack of matching between the skills that are available in (or supplied to) the labor market and the skills that are in demand in the labor market."

Two broad categorizations of mismatch can be outlined in recent literature: vertical and horizontal mismatch.[132] According to McGuinness et al. (2017), vertical mismatch refers to whether an individual is over- or under-qualified or -educated for a job. An individual is over- (under-) qualified if he or she holds a higher (lower) qualification than what the job requires, while is considered over- (under-) educated if his or her years of schooling are more (less) than what is required of his or her current occupation (Table 10.1). Horizontal mismatch refers to where an individual's field or education is inappropriate for the job. Additional concepts include skills gaps, which refers to the extent to which workers lack the skills needed to do the job, and skill obsolescence (i.e., when the skills of an individual become obsolete in the market because of technological changes or the depreciation of certain skills).

---

[130] Palmer (2018) summarizes the findings of Handel (2017a), Kupets (2017), and McGuinness et al. (2017) on key issues about skill mismatches in low- and middle-income countries. Handel (2017b) notes how raising the education levels which produces more tertiary education graduates in the context of high levels of overeducation aggravates the situation.
[131] See page 10 of Palmer (2018).
[132] Palmer (2018) also described the definitions and implications of jobs and skills mismatch in the informal economy. A review of some effective policies mitigating the impact of skills mismatch is also discussed.

Table 10.1: Types of Skills Mismatch

Type	Definition
Overqualification or overeducation (underqualification or undereducation)	Workers hold a higher (lower) qualification or have more (less) years of education than the job requires
Overskilling (underskilling)	Workers possess more (less) skills than their current job demands
Horizontal mismatch	Workers, typically graduates, are employed in an occupation that is unrelated to their principal field of study
Skill obsolescence	Workers' skills have become physically or economically obsolete or underutilized
Skill gap	Workers lack the skills necessary to perform their current job
Skill shortage (surplus)	Demand (supply) for a particular skill exceeds the supply (demand) of people with that skill resulting to unfilled or hard-to-fill vacancies (overflow)

Sources: S. McGuinness, K. Pouliakas, and P. Redmond. 2017. How Useful Is the Concept of Skills Mismatch? In *Skills and Jobs Mismatches in Low- and Middle-Income Countries*, edited by Paul Comyn and Olga Strietska-Ilina, 5–34. Geneva: International Labour Office; ILO. 2013. *Global Employment Trends for Youth 2013: A Generation at Risk*. Geneva.

The Philippines' Department of Labor and Employment-Bureau of Local Employment (DOLE-BLE) also recognizes mismatches on a regional and sector basis.[133] Alongside skills and qualifications mismatches that loosely align with those outlined, the DOLE-BLE also categorizes a type of mismatch based upon the matching of potential employees in locations and economic sectors with job vacancies. While qualification and education mismatches reflect differences between the output of education and training systems and labor market needs as well as information asymmetry, regional and sector mismatches can also be associated with the cost of moving from one geographic area or sector to another.

Several studies and statistics by the DOLE-BLE and the Philippine Statistics Authority (PSA) provide evidence of skill shortages and surpluses in the labor market. For instance, the presence of hard-to-fill jobs and positions is a manifestation of skill shortages in the labor force. However, the literature on measuring the level of skill mismatches in the Philippines remains limited.[134] The most recent study, Epetia (2018), classifies Filipino college graduates in non-college jobs as being overeducated, and accordingly estimates that about one-third of college graduates are overeducated.

Corresponding to the definitions used, there are different approaches available for measuring mismatches. Table 10.2 outlines the different approaches used in the literature in estimating the level of skills mismatch. McGuinness et al. (2017) elaborate on the intricacies of each approach and point out its advantages, as well as its drawbacks and limitations. They note that, in the most-estimated measure, i.e., overqualification or overeducation, the subjective and empirical methods resulted in conflicting and inconsistent results. Human resource specialists conduct direct assessment to identify cases of overskilling (underskilling). Self-assessment

---

[133] BLE-DOLE. 2012. *Job-Skill Mismatch: Is there an Effective and Quick Solution?* Presentation. https://www.britishcouncil.ph/sites/default/files/ruth_r_rodriguez_skills_job_mismartch.pdf (accessed 11 December 2020).
[134] See Perlman (1978), CHED et al. (mimeo), Smith and Domingo (1977), and Mehta et al. (2011).

Table 10.2: Measures of Skills Mismatch

Type	Approach
Overqualification or overeducation (underqualification or undereducation)	Subjective method through worker self-assessment surveys
	Normative method by matching using ISCO and ISCED
	Empirical method or the statistical or the realized matches method
	Job evaluation method conducted by professional job analysts
Overskilling (underskilling)	Direct assessment by human resource specialists
Horizontal mismatch	Subjective worker self-assessment surveys
	Independent comparisons of a field of study variable with occupation codes
Skill obsolescence	Subjective worker self-assessment surveys
Skill gap	Employers' perception surveys
Skill shortage (surplus)	Employers' surveys on job vacancies

ISCED = International Standard Classification of Education, ISCO = International Standard Classification of Occupations.
Source: S. McGuinness, K. Pouliakas, and P. Redmond. 2017. How Useful Is the Concept of Skills Mismatch? In *Skills and Jobs Mismatches in Low- and Middle-Income Countries,* edited by Paul Comyn and Olga Strietska-Ilina, 5–34. Geneva: International Labour Office.

surveys can be given to workers to estimate overqualification, horizontal mismatch, and skill obsolescence. On the other hand, skills gaps, skill shortages, or surplus can be estimated through surveys of firms and businesses.

This study focuses on measuring the level of horizontal mismatch among TVET graduates, which we call training–job mismatch. Mismatch defined as such will be measured using two different approaches. The main approach introduces a novel way of measuring skills mismatch, an occupational distance measure defined in Generalao (2020) as proxy for training–job mismatch, and using a task-based framework to estimate the level of skill transferability across occupations. For comparison, the study also presents a simple matching technique which directly compares the expected occupation and the actual post-training occupation of the graduate. This is similar to the traditional approach of independently comparing fields of study and occupational codes. This approach allows us to determine whether the graduates use the skills they learned from training in the specific expected occupations of the program they completed.[135]

The task-based framework treats occupations or jobs as bundles of tasks rather than as discrete categories. The use of the task-based approach stems from the idea that only specific tasks of occupations and not the occupation itself are being changed by technological improvements.[136] In this context, skills are task-specific, rather than occupation-specific, and may be transferable across occupations. Thus, one can build an occupational distance measure, which measures how similar two occupations are in terms of their task content or task profiles. In the context of Industry 4.0, which is rapidly changing the labor market environment by changing how specific tasks are performed, flexibility among the labor force in terms of their skill set has been growing in importance.

---

[135] Ideally, the mismatch issue is treated in a dynamic sense where trainees are still finding their way in the labor market and employers only deal with those who are applying for available jobs. Due to the lack of data, the methodology used in this study treats mismatch as static in nature, which is one of its shortcomings.

[136] D.H. Autor, F. Levy, and R. J. Murnane. 2003. The Skill Content of Recent Technological Change: An Empirical Exploration. *Quarterly Journal of Economics* 118(4): 1279–333.

Methodological Approach

The task-based approach differs from simple matching techniques based on occupational group and associated skill levels. Based on the task-based framework, we use a novel approach, creating a proxy of training–job mismatch that uses the notion of occupational distance applied to bundles of jobs to assess the difference, or mismatch according to tasks learned in their course or program and those used in their occupation. It differs from standard matching approaches such as simple matching techniques based on occupational groups and associated skill levels. For comparative purposes, the study conducts and presents the findings of a simple matching technique before applying the task-based framework. The approaches for the simple matching technique and task-based framework are presented as follows, along with an overview of the data used in the study.

Simple Matching Technique

Simple matching techniques match and compares the expected and actual post-training occupation of the TVET graduate. The expected occupation of a TVET program comes from its publicly available training regulation. It is explicitly stated in each training regulation that a graduate from a particular program is competent enough to be employed in the stated expected occupation. Tracer studies provide the information on the actual post-training occupation of the graduate.

One approach is to use "occupational group mismatch," which assesses a graduate's occupation against the expected occupation of their training. This is done in terms of its Philippine Standard Occupational Classification (PSOC)[137] at the 1-digit level, or at the major occupational grouping. For instance, an individual who completed his Shielded Metal Arc Welding NC II program is expected to be employed as a welder, which belongs to the major occupational group of craft and related trades workers. If the same individual is currently a garbage collector, an elementary occupation, then he is experiencing training–job mismatch. But if he is working as a carpenter then he is considered to be training–job matched. This is a lenient definition of mismatch (see findings in Box 10.1).

Another approach is to use "skill group mismatch," which assesses the associated skill levels of graduates' occupation against the expected occupation of their training. This is done in terms of the International Standard Classification of Occupations (ISCO) and associated skill levels. Note that for each PSOC 1-digit level (10 groups), there is a corresponding skill level (4 levels).[138] For example, if an individual completes a Food and Beverage NC II program, he expects to be employed as a waiter, which is at skill level 2. However, if the same individual is currently a mining laborer, an occupation classified as skill level 1, then he experiences skill group mismatch.

Task-Based Framework

The main methodology presented in this paper adopts a task-based framework as the basis for estimating training–job mismatch. The task-based framework treats occupations or jobs as bundles of tasks rather than as discrete categories. The use of the task-based approach stems from the idea that only specific tasks of occupations and not the occupation itself are being changed by technological improvements (footnote 136). In this context, skills are task-specific, rather than occupation-specific, and may be transferable across occupations. Thus, one can build an occupational distance measure, which shows how similar two occupations are in terms of their task content or task profiles. Like the simple matching technique, the approach compares the expected occupation of the TVET program and the current occupation of the individual. There are four main steps in our

---

[137] PSA. 2014. *2012 Philippine Standard Occupational Classification*. Quezon City..
[138] See ILO (2012) for the full list.

analysis: assigning task profiles, obtaining the occupational distance, occupational direction, and weighting. The approach follows that of Generalao (2020).

- **Step 1 of the task-based framework is to construct or apply task profiles of occupations.** This paper uses the task profiles of Generalao (2019b), which maps tasks to occupations in the Philippines. The source of the task characteristics of occupations is ISCO-08. Each task is classified into a task-type (e.g., nonroutine analytical, routine manual, etc.) using keywords from the task-based literature, resulting in occupational task profiles. The task profiles provide factor scores, which represent the occupation's relative intensity with respect to each task type and are used to derive the occupational distance and direction measures. Specifically, factor scores are normalized task scores, which serve as inputs to the distance and direction formulas described as follows.[139]
- **Step 2 is to measure similarity between occupations according to their task composition and skill transferability between occupations.** Comparing occupations in terms of their task contents allows us to measure the similarity among pairs of occupations, and therefore to understand the level of skill transferability between occupations. That is, the "closer" two occupations are in terms of distance, the more transferable the skills associated with these occupations (i.e., the lower are the barriers to occupational mobility). The distance is defined using the Euclidean distance formula as in Robinson (2018).
- **Step 3 applies a direction measure to ascertain whether the distance measure corresponds to an increase or decrease in skill levels.** The sign of the direction measure provides the information about upskilling or downskilling between two occupations. The sign of the direction measure is positive when the move represents upskilling and negative for downskilling. If the direction measure is zero, then the occupational move is considered a lateral occupational move.[140]
- **Step 4 assigns weights to each task according to the relative importance in predicting wages.** This is consistent with the approach of Robinson (2018) and Generalao (2020). This step assumes that the skills needed for the performance of certain tasks are more complex and productive than others, and are therefore usually met with a higher monetary reward (i.e., wage). To account for the sample selection bias caused by the likelihood of employment, weights are derived using a maximum likelihood Heckman sample selection model to estimate the effects of task scores on wages. The weights are derived from the coefficient estimates of this Heckman sample selection regression.[141]

The overall occupational distance measure is the combination of the steps and indicates whether a graduate is experiencing training–job mismatch and its extent. A value close to zero indicates that the occupations we are comparing are very similar; in effect, their associated skills are highly transferable. If the value is exactly zero, then the two occupations are exactly similar in terms of their task contents. The farther the value is from zero, the less transferable, and thus less useful, are the skills acquired via a current occupation. Individuals who are currently working in occupations that are very similar to what was expected from their training program are not considered to be experiencing training–job mismatch. We categorize values which fall under the threshold range of (–0.01, 0.01) as the training–job match level.[142] Otherwise, the individual is experiencing training–job mismatch, which can be measured by its difference from the cut-off points. Box 10.1 provides an example.

---

[139] For a detailed methodology of the task profiling process, see Generalao (2019b).
[140] This follows the steps outlined in Generalao (2020).
[141] For more details on the methodology, see Generalao (2020).
[142] The initial choice for the match is zero as in Generalao (2020). But to account for the possible encoding errors and inaccuracies, we consider a threshold that is non-zero but as close to zero as possible. Different bands were considered in the process and the results are presented in Generalao (forthcoming, 2021).

> **Box 10.1: Example of Simple Matching Technique versus Occupational Distance Scoring**
>
> The table presents examples of individual graduates, the programs they have completed, and their level of training–job mismatch in relation to their current occupation. In this example, a graduate of a Programming National Certificate (NC) IV program, who is currently a factory worker, experiences significant training–job mismatch, as denoted by a score of –1.18. The negative value also reflects a position requiring less qualification than what was trained for. This represents inefficient resource allocation, including human resources in terms of skills allocation, as well as time and financial resources spent on the program. Elsewhere, a Shielded Metal Arc Welding (SMAW) NC II graduate who is presently working as an on-call welder, applies the skills they learned in the program and thus enjoys training–job matching. In this case, the occupational distance score is zero, representing zero mismatch.
>
> **Examples of Occupational Distance Measure as Proxy to the Level of Training–job Mismatch**
>
> | TVET Program | Expected Occupation of the Training Program | Current Occupation of the Trainee | Occupational Distance = Training–Job Mismatch Level |
> |---|---|---|---|
> | Shielded Metal Arc Welding (SMAW) NC II | Welders and flame cutters | On-call welder | 0 |
> | Programming NC IV | Web and multimedia developers | Factory worker | –1.18 |
> | Housekeeping NC II | Domestic helpers and cleaners | Assistant accountant | 0.77 |
>
> NC = national certificate, TVET = technical and vocational education and training.
> Source: ADB estimates.

Data Used in the Methodology

The assessment uses the individual graduate tracer surveys of TESDA or the Study on the Employability of TVET Graduates (SETG) 2014, 2015, and 2018. There is no available survey for 2016, while the 2017 SETG contains insufficient information needed for our analysis. To be more specific, the 2017 SETG did not record occupational information at the 4-digit PSOC level, which is needed for the second approach described as follows. The data collection was done through a nationwide survey of selected TVET graduates using a structured survey instrument with clearance issued by the PSA. Specifically, the survey was conducted through either face-to-face or phone interview using a structured questionnaire.

Each survey contains detailed information of TVET graduates who are tracked after undertaking a TVET program in the previous year. That is, 2018 SETG contains occupational and program characteristics of 2017 TVET graduates. This information includes demographic characteristics such as age and sex, employment-related outcomes such as employment status and wages before and after training, and characteristics of the training program or programs the individual completed. We restrict our sample to graduates from programs with national certification and with publicly available training regulations[143] and those who are employed at the time of the survey. These strict restrictions allow more accurate identification of the expected occupation of the training as contained in each training regulation. Table 10.3 describes the number of respondents, the size of the labor force, and the corresponding selected sample for each year.

---

[143] A training regulation serves as the basis for the competency assessment and certification, registration and delivery, development of curriculum, and assessment instruments of a training program. See TESDA (2018d) for the complete list.

Table 10.3: Sample Identified from the Individual Graduate Tracer Surveys, 2013–2014 and 2017

Year Graduated	Number of Respondents	Labor Force	Sample Number of Individuals	Sample Number of Programs
2013	12,432	8,471	2,255	93
2014	9,924	6,536	2,194	83
2017	6,933	4,380	1,064	99

Source: ADB estimates.

Main Findings

Simple techniques expose high mismatch using occupational matching and slightly lower mismatch using skill equivalence, suggesting task-specific skills are transferable across occupations. As detailed in the methodology section, a simple matching technique using occupational groups suggests elevated mismatches, at 81.7% in 2013, 58.8% in 2014, and 69.9% in 2017 (Figure 10.1). However, when shifting to a simple matching technique using skills groups, the mismatches are lower, at 58.2% in 2013, 42.2% in 2014, and 47.6% in 2017. This supports the notion that task-specific skills may be transferred to other occupations, and is an encouraging case for using an occupational distance measure as a proxy to the training–job mismatch level.

Figure 10.1: Mismatch Rates Using Simple Matching Technique, 2013, 2014, and 2017 Graduates

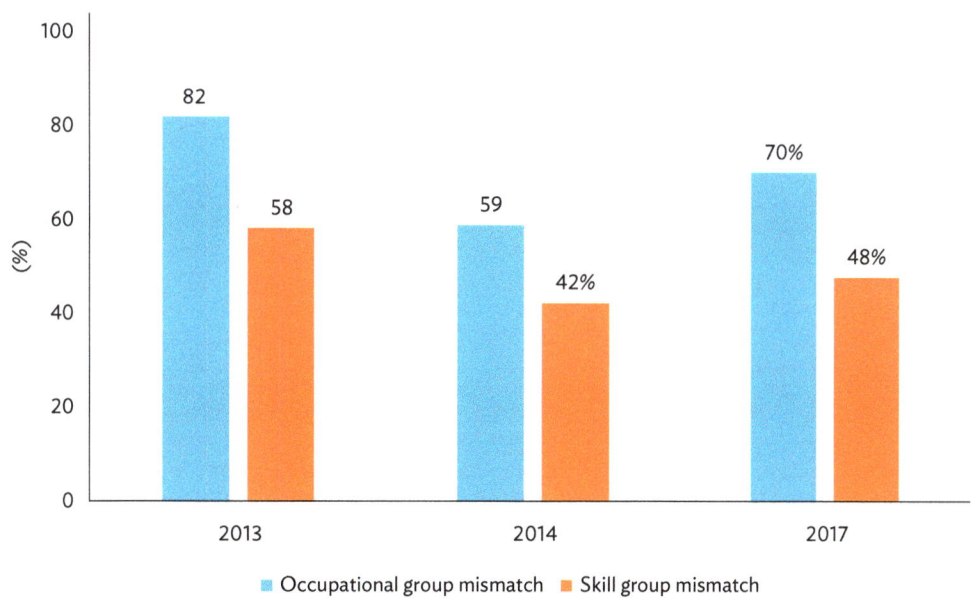

Source: ADB estimates.

Using the occupational distance measure, matching rates increased from 2013 to 2017, but results still suggest that most trainees were not in matched occupations. Findings suggest a slight increase in matched rates, i.e., where a trainee is in an occupation that matches the expected occupations from the program, from 2013 to 2014, and to 2017. These increased from 32.3% to 35.6%–36%, respectively (Figure 10.2). Despite this positive trend, nearly two-thirds of TVET graduates still experience training–job mismatch or work in occupations that are not similar to the expected occupation of their training program.

TVET programs with the highest matching rates were those with nonroutine manual task-specific skills, highlighting the comparative advantage of TVET in technical and manual skills. Figure 10.3 highlights the TVET programs which had the highest rates of matching graduates to their expected post-training occupations. All these programs provide training for mostly nonroutine manual task-specific skills.

The largest share of mismatched occupations is in occupations requiring higher skills than graduates were trained for, suggesting a shortage of skills in these occupations relative to market demand. These are the underskilled and comprise the largest share of TVET graduates, as depicted in Figure 10.2. Figure 10.4 provides a selection of TVET programs that had the highest rates of underskilled occupations. There are a few possible explanations, including the pursuance of practical skills such as baking and cooking, by individuals who already have high educational credentials, or the possibility of low-skill but higher-paying work opportunities outside the country. Specific TVET programs such as Housekeeping NC II, Computer Systems Servicing NC II, and Consumer Electronics Servicing NC II are associated with occupations with high demand abroad. However, caution must be exercised in making such conclusions given the small proportion of trainees tracked and identified working abroad after training.

Figure 10.2: Share of Trainees Matched, Underqualified, or Overqualified, 2013, 2014, and 2017

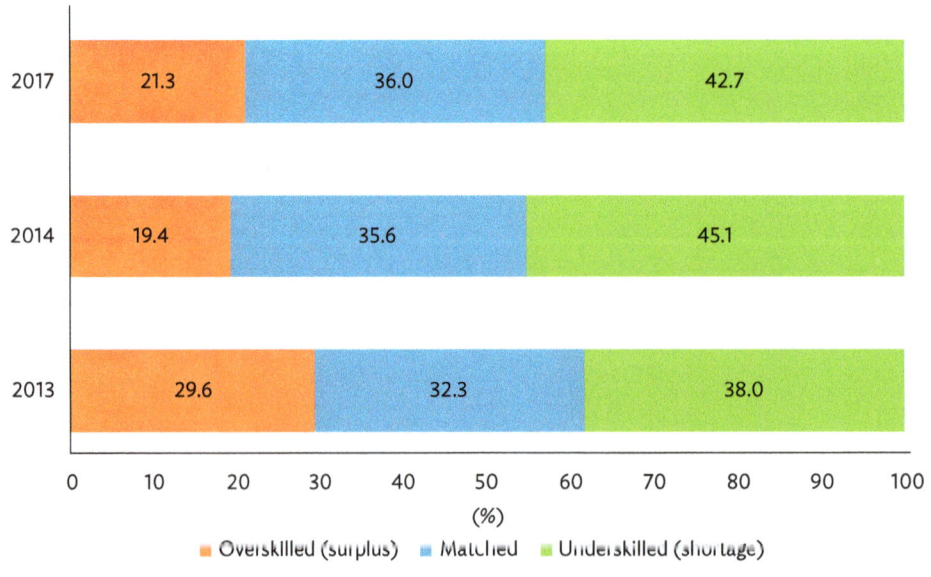

Source: ADB estimates.

Figure 10.3: Share of Trainees Matched with Expected Occupation, Top 10 Programs

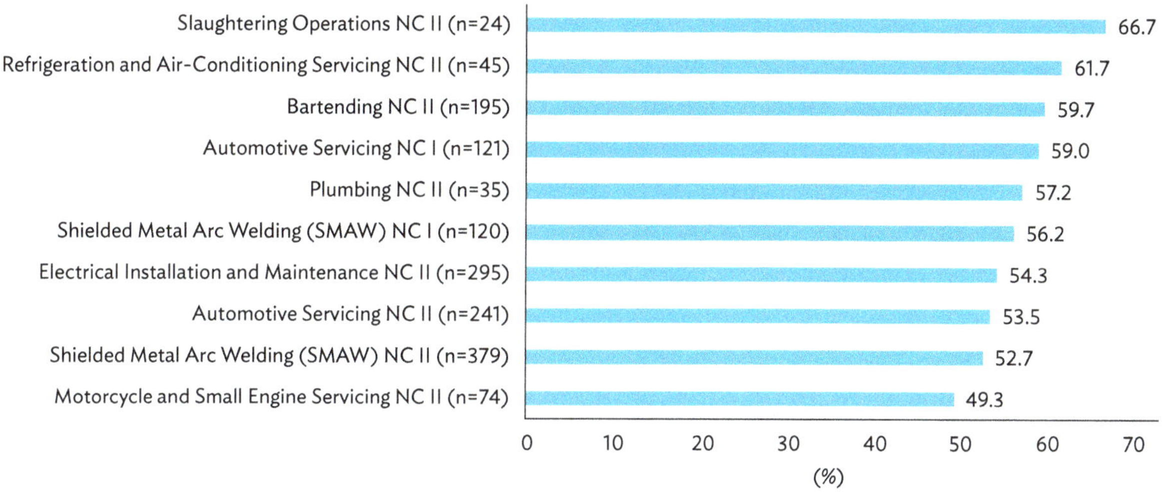

Program	%
Slaughtering Operations NC II (n=24)	66.7
Refrigeration and Air-Conditioning Servicing NC II (n=45)	61.7
Bartending NC II (n=195)	59.7
Automotive Servicing NC I (n=121)	59.0
Plumbing NC II (n=35)	57.2
Shielded Metal Arc Welding (SMAW) NC I (n=120)	56.2
Electrical Installation and Maintenance NC II (n=295)	54.3
Automotive Servicing NC II (n=241)	53.5
Shielded Metal Arc Welding (SMAW) NC II (n=379)	52.7
Motorcycle and Small Engine Servicing NC II (n=74)	49.3

NC = National Certificate.
Note: Selected programs exclude those with fewer than 20 graduates in the sample. Pooled data for 2013, 2014, and 2017.
Source: ADB estimates.

Figure 10.4: Share of Trainees Unmatched with Expected Occupation and in Occupations with Higher Qualification Requirements

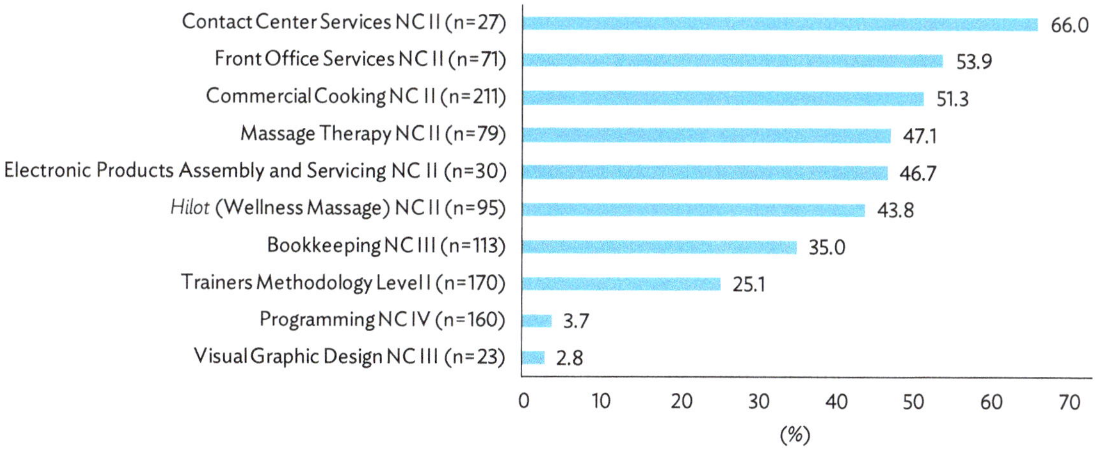

Program	%
Contact Center Services NC II (n=27)	66.0
Front Office Services NC II (n=71)	53.9
Commercial Cooking NC II (n=211)	51.3
Massage Therapy NC II (n=79)	47.1
Electronic Products Assembly and Servicing NC II (n=30)	46.7
Hilot (Wellness Massage) NC II (n=95)	43.8
Bookkeeping NC III (n=113)	35.0
Trainers Methodology Level I (n=170)	25.1
Programming NC IV (n=160)	3.7
Visual Graphic Design NC III (n=23)	2.8

NC = National Certificate.
Note: Selected programs exclude those with fewer than 20 graduates in the sample. Pooled data for 2013, 2014, and 2017.
Source: ADB estimates.

Occupations requiring lower skills than graduates were trained for, suggests a surplus of skills in these occupations relative to market demand. These are the overskilled. Figure 10.5 highlights the programs with the highest shares of graduates in occupations with lower skill requirements than graduates trained for. The list features programs which require complex task-specific skills, including Visual Graphic NC III, Programming NC IV, and Bookkeeping NC III. Trainees who completed these programs were not able to apply the high level of skills they gained from their training in their current occupation. This can possibly be explained by the lack of employment opportunities or limited demand for these occupations, despite the programs undergoing market demand processes.

The distance between the expected and post-training occupations are compared for different groups, by sex, educational level, region, type of provider, and scholarship program, with mixed findings. Using a logit regression,[144] the likelihood of experiencing training–job match in terms of program and individual graduate characteristics is assessed. The estimates show that those who are more educated are more likely to experience training–job mismatch relative to those who are less educated (noting that this finding was strongest and significant for 2014 and 2017 data only) (Table A10.1). This supports the hypothesis of highly educated graduates enrolling and completing programs out of interest, to acquire additional skills or to target opportunities overseas. It also aligns with the high proportion of overeducated college graduates in the

Figure 10.5: Share of Trainees Unmatched with Expected Occupation and in Occupations Requiring Lower Qualifications

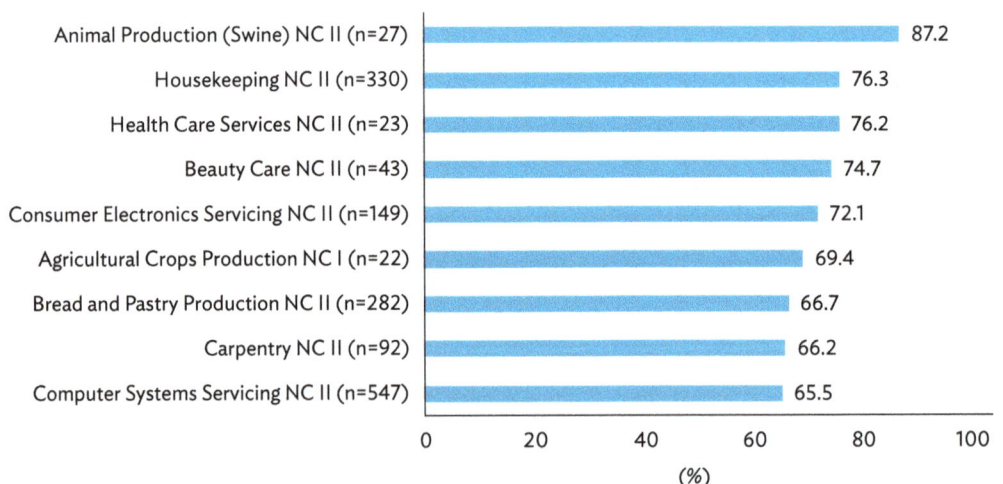

NC = National Certificate.
Note: Selected programs exclude those with fewer than 20 graduates in the sample. Pooled data for 2013, 2014, and 2017.
Source: ADB estimates.

---

[144] The model specification is described in Appendix 10. The distributions, correlates, and policy implications of the continuous mismatch measure are elaborated in Generalao (forthcoming, 2021).

Philippines estimated by Epetia (2018). Other data were more mixed. Male individuals have higher chances of working in occupations similar to what they trained for, and graduates from NCR are more likely to enjoy training–job match relative to some other regions.

Conclusions

This chapter examined the effectiveness of training programs in providing individuals with skills that are relevant and useful in the labor market. The two methodologies applied to 2013, 2014, and 2017 TVET graduates resulted in different mismatch rates. The first technique of simple matching, which assumes that skills are not transferable across occupations, recorded alarmingly high mismatch rates, ranging from 60% to 82%. The second methodology makes use of the task-based framework and assumes that task-specific skills are transferable across occupations. This study follows the methodology of Generalao (2020) in building an occupational distance measure to estimate the level of transferability across occupations. Using the distance measures as a proxy for training–job mismatch, this study finds that, among the employed TVET graduates, only about one-third are successfully matched with the expected post-training occupation of their program. That is, the matching rates are 64%–68% in covered in the study, which are somewhat higher as compared to the matching rates recorded using the first methodology.

The results allow identification of training programs that are most effective, suggesting successful programs in terms of training–job match are mostly nonroutine manual in nature. Correlates of the training–job mismatch are also determined using logit regressions. In summary, male and less-educated individuals are less likely to experience training–job mismatch. For the other variables, there have been mixed results for different years. In terms of the impact of scholarships, there is no significant difference between those TVET scholars and non-scholars in terms of training–job mismatch rates.

These findings re-emphasize the importance of anticipating skills demand, to the extent possible, in order to ensure better targeting of TVET programs and greater efficiency of skills supply, limit mismatch, and improve labor market outcomes. Understanding the sectoral and industry demands requires stronger and more effective collaborations and partnerships among key stakeholders such as industry, government, academe, and civil society. Although improving employability and matching rates is needed, the quality of employment must be raised, especially in largely informal economies like the Philippines. Employment in low-paying and low-productivity jobs should be addressed by introducing skills policies that would complement other policies in expanding and improving the available opportunities for these workers.

Appendix 10: Summary Results

We estimate the model using a logit regression to determine who are likely to be experiencing training–job match in terms of program and individual graduate characteristics.

$$match\ h_i = \beta_0 + \beta X + \gamma W + \varepsilon_i \tag{1}$$

Where *match* refers to whether the individual is experiencing training job match or not; *X* is a vector for demographic characteristics such as highest educational attainment, sex, region, and age; *W* is a vector for TVET-related characteristics such as the type of scholarship received by the graduate and the type of training modality; and ε pertains to the error term.

Table A10.1: Coefficient Estimates from the Logit Regression, 2013–2014 and 2017 Technical and Vocational Education and Training Graduates

Variable	2013 Coef.	2013 Std.Err.	2014 Coef.	2014 Std.Err.	2017 Coef.	2017 Std.Err.
Educational Attainment (Base = College graduate and beyond)						
College Undergraduate	0.07	–0.21	0.556**	–0.23	0.858***	–0.25
Tech-Voc Graduate and Undergraduate	0.09	–0.26	0.497*	–0.27	0.882***	–0.30
High School Graduate and Undergraduate	–0.07	–0.18	0.870***	–0.18	1.334***	–0.36
Elementary Graduate and Below	–0.15	–0.47	1.881***	–0.51	2.680**	–1.11
Sex (Base = Female)	0.508***	–0.10	0.631***	–0.13	0.551***	–0.21
Age	–0.05	–0.03	0.148***	–0.04	–0.03	–0.06
Age2	0.06	–0.05	–0.195***	–0.06	0.02	–0.08
Region (Base = National Capital Region)						
CAR	0.02	–0.30	–0.45	–0.33	–0.21	–0.57
Region I	0.38	–0.26	–0.531*	–0.28	0.23	–0.61
Region II	0.724**	–0.31	–0.37	–0.31	0.01	–0.48
Region III	0.35	–0.23	–0.743***	–0.21	–0.14	–0.51
Region IV-A	0.387*	–0.22	–1.390***	–0.39	–0.67	–0.46
Region IV-B	0.988***	–0.28	–1.230***	–0.35	–1.147**	–0.52
Region V	0.27	–0.27	–0.715**	–0.33	–0.05	–0.44
Region VI	0.50	–0.54	–0.22	–0.25	–0.42	–0.42
Region VII	0.39	–0.24	–0.734**	–0.33	–0.25	–0.46
Region VIII	0.36	–0.28	–0.608*	–0.33	–0.974**	–0.47
Region IX	–0.13	–0.39	–0.577*	–0.34	–1.400**	–0.59
Region X	0.723***	–0.27	–1.364***	–0.33	–0.49	–0.54
Region XI	0.36	–0.29	–0.732***	–0.28	–0.10	–0.48
Region XII	0.16	–0.30	0.46	0.32	0.59	–0.47
Caraga	0.906**	–0.36	–0.36	–0.45	–1.369**	–0.55
ARMM	1.028***	–0.27	–3.199***	–1.11	–1.486*	–0.86

Table A10.1: *continued*

Variable	2013		2014		2017	
	Coef.	Std.Err.	Coef.	Std.Err.	Coef.	Std.Err.
Type of Training Provider *(Base = Institution-based)*						
Enterprise-based	−0.43	−0.33	0.78	−0.53	0.47	−0.44
Community-based	−0.28	−0.27	−0.47	−0.29	−0.564*	−0.30
Scholarship (Base = Non-scholar)						
TWSP	−0.231*	−0.13	0.08	−0.16	0.26	−0.42
PESFA	0.01	−0.28	−0.42	−0.30	−0.08	−0.25
STEP	–	–	−0.40	−0.57	−0.67	−0.49
Others	0.15	−0.15	0.13	−0.21	0.39	−0.32
Constant	−0.60	−0.59	−3.454***	−0.72	−0.21	−1.07
Number of observations	2,279		2,100		848	

*** $p<0.01$, ** $p<0.05$, * $p<0.1$

ARMM = Autonomous Region of Muslim Mindanao, CAR = Cordillera Administrative Region, PESFA = Private Education Student Financial Assistance, STEP = Special Training for Employment Program, TVET = technical and vocational education and training, TWSP = Training for Work Scholarship Program.

Note: All models are weighted by sampling weights.

Source: ADB estimates.

11. Impact of the Technical Education and Skills Development Authority Scholarships

Scholarship programs of the Technical Education Skills and Development Authority (TESDA) fall under its strategy to "expand TVET capacity in key growth areas and to address the growing demand for skilled labor."[145] TESDA's scholarships are aimed at improving both productivity and equity. On one hand, emerging industries or key employment generators are being promoted; on the other, disadvantaged sectors and special clients are being targeted as priority beneficiaries. There is a need to examine whether both goals are being achieved or whether one is progressing at the expense of the other.

This chapter evaluates three of the four major scholarship programs offered by TESDA. The major scholarship programs offered by TESDA: Training for Work Scholarship Program (TWSP), Special Training for Employment Program (STEP), Private Education Student Financial Assistance (PESFA), and a scholarship under the Universal Access to Quality Tertiary Education Act (UAQTEA). Each has different objectives and focal areas. It presents the findings of an evaluation of the first three of these scholarships (excluding UAQTEA, which was implemented starting only in 2018) on completion, assessment, competency, and national certification rates.

Also provided in this chapter is an overview of the different scholarships under evaluation and evaluation design and methodology, including rationale for approaches and data sources. The main findings and conclusions from these evaluations are also included.

Overview of TWSP, STEP, and PESFA Scholarship Programs

Three scholarships are assessed in this evaluation, TWSP, STEP, and PESFA, all of which have a common goal (Box 11.1), but each has its own purpose and outputs:

- **TWSP is aimed at improving productivity or efficiency and shaped around addressing global competitiveness and job readiness.** The purpose of the TWSP scholarship is to enhance access to TVET training. The TWSP scholarship covers the skills training and assessment fees.
- **STEP is aimed at addressing social equity and reducing poverty in the informal sector.** The purpose is to promote employment through entrepreneurship and service activities by providing short-term, community-based training. On top of skills training and assessment fees, STEP covers the entrepreneurship training fee, and provides a training allowance and a starter toolkit.
- **The goal of PESFA is to boost manufacturing toward rapid, inclusive, and sustainable economic growth.** The purpose is to enhance industrial competitiveness through improving labor competency and productivity

---

[145] TESDA. 2018b. Strategic Direction. In *National Technical Education and Skills Development Plan 2018–2022*. Taguig.

> **Box 11.1: Technical Education and Skills Development Authority Scholarship Targets**
>
> - The National Technical Education and Skills Development Plan (NTESDP) targets an employment rate for technical and vocational education and training (TVET) graduates of 67.3% and a certification rate of 85% for 2018.
>
> - The overall target for the number of TVET enrollees is 2.41 million for 2018, while the target for the number of TVET graduates is 2.17 million, or a completion rate of 89.9%.
>
> - The target number of graduates under the Training for Work Scholarship Program is 222,633 and under the Private Education Student Financial Assistance (PESFA) it is 10,000. These are exactly 90% of the target beneficiaries for the year. No target is specified for the Special Training for Employment Program (STEP).
>
> Source: TESDA. 2018b. Strategic Direction. *In National Technical Education and Skills Development Plan 2018-2022*. Taguig.

by assisting "marginalized but deserving students" and private technical–vocational institutions (TVIs). PESFA provides training allowance and book allowance apart from covering the training and assessment fees.

The TWSP accounts for the largest share of target beneficiaries, but the introduction of the UAQTEA has lowered the target beneficiaries under the other scholarship programs. As shown in Figure 11.1, the TWSP has the largest number of target beneficiaries, at nearly 250,000 in 2018, accounting for the majority of the scholarships' target beneficiaries until the UAQTEA was introduced in 2018 (with 170,000 target beneficiaries).

Figure 11.1: TWSP, STEP, and PESFA Target Beneficiaries, 2014-2018

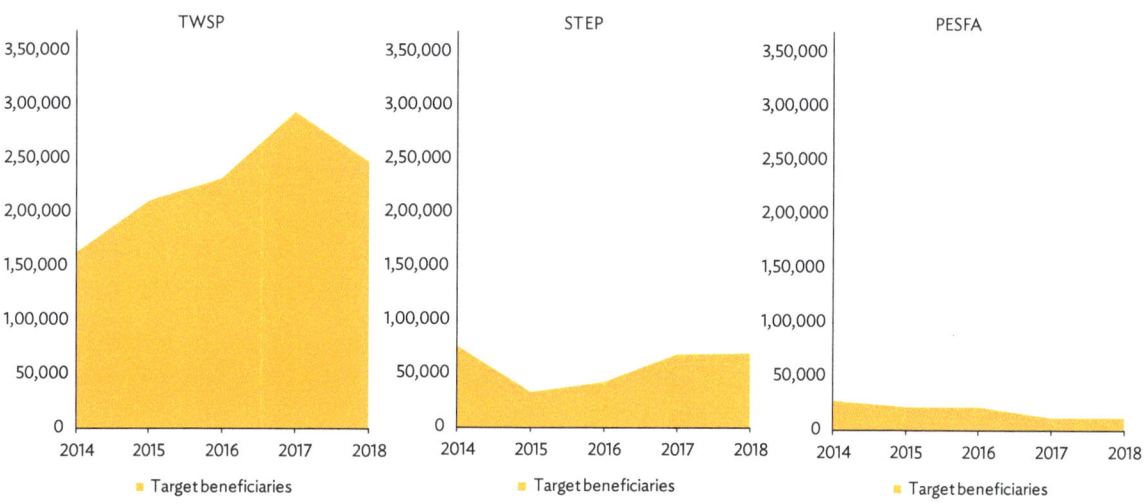

PESFA = Private Education Student Financial Assistance, STEP = Special Training for Employment Program, TWSP = Training for Work Scholarship Program.
Source: Scholarship Programs, fiscal years 2014 to 2019 Scholarship Programs, Technical Education and Skills Development Authority.

Both PESFA and STEP have exhibited decreasing numbers of target beneficiaries since 2014, although STEP has increased its number of target beneficiaries in 2019 to 75,000.

Total budget allocation has varied between scholarship programs from 2014 to 2018. The TWSP's budget nearly doubled in nominal terms from P1.4 billion in 2014 to P2.8 billion in 2018, while STEP's budget has decreased from P1.0 billion in 2014 to P900,000 in 2018 (dipping to P400,000 in 2015), as shown in Figure 11.2. Meanwhile, PESFA's budget has remained unchanged at P200,000 per year from 2014 to 2018. All the scholarships' budgets were dwarfed by UAQTEA's budget of P6.9 billion in 2018, but this decreased to P3.9 billion in 2019.

Enrollment has been increasing in recent years for most scholarship programs. As shown in Figure 11.3, TWSP enrollment has increased from around 206,000 in 2014 to nearly 350,000 in 2018. The enrollment for 2018 was 27% higher than the target beneficiaries. After the drop in STEP enrollment in 2015 to 20,500, it has steadily increased to 68,000 in 2018, while PESFA enrollment has decreased from 28,000 in 2014 to around 20,000 in 2018. The PESFA decrease is likely to be due to the increase in cost per student from around P7,000 in 2014 to around P9,500 in 2018. Despite this, PESFA enrollment has been higher than target beneficiaries. STEP enrollment has been below or close to the target beneficiaries since 2014. For comparative purposes, UAQTEA's enrollment was only 35% of the target beneficiaries in 2018.

Graduation rates were high for all three scholarships in 2018, exceeding graduation rates for those without scholarships. As shown in Figure 11.3, for all scholarships, graduation rates are high (i.e., where the gap between graduates and enrollees is smallest), some exceptions exist around 2014 for TWSP and 2015 for PESFA; however,

Figure 11.2: TWSP, STEP, and PESFA Total Budget Allocation, 2014–2018

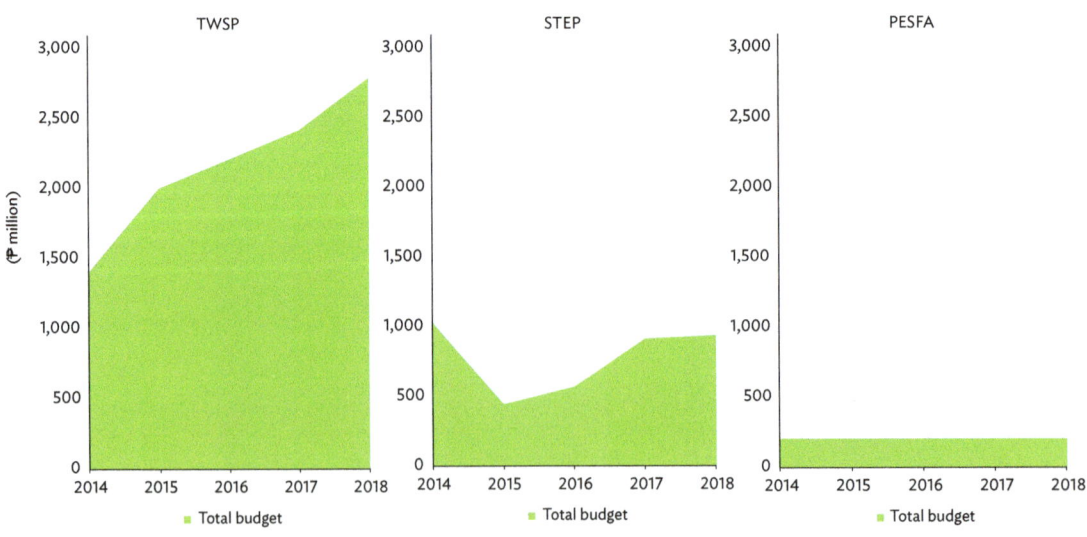

PESFA = Private Education Student Financial Assistance, STEP = Special Training for Employment Program, TWSP = Training for Work Scholarship Program.
Source: Scholarship Programs, fiscal years? 2014 to 2019 Scholarship Programs, Technical Education and Skills Development Authority.

Figure 11.3: TWSP, STEP, and PESFA Total Enrollment and Graduation, 2014–2018

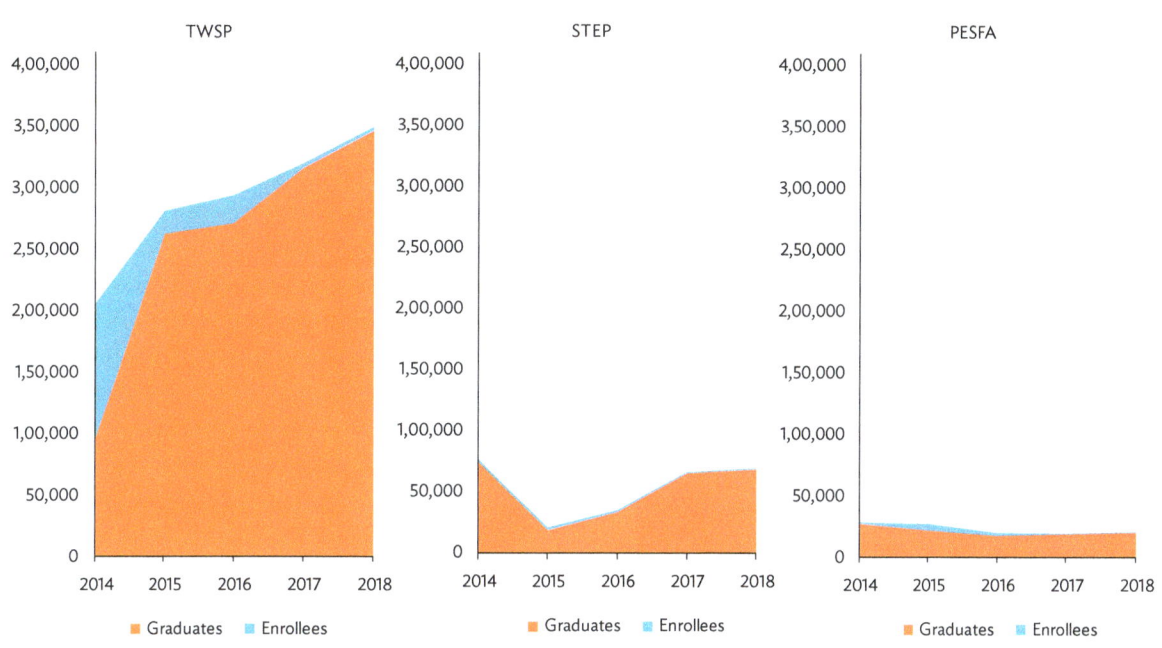

PESFA = Private Education Student Financial Assistance, STEP = Special Training for Employment Program, TWSP = Training for Work Scholarship Program.
Source: Scholarship Programs, FYs 2014 to 2019 Scholarship Programs, Technical Education and Skills Development Authority.

in 2018, graduation rates were estimated at around 98%–99% for all three scholarships. This compares to 96.5% for all trainees, suggesting lower graduation rates for those without scholarships.

Labor force participation rates (LFPRs) are higher among non-scholars, but employment rates are higher among scholars. LFPRs for all TVET graduates were estimated at 72.3% in 2017 (Figure 11.4). LFPRs were marginally higher for non-scholars than scholars, at 75% to 73.4%, respectively. Among the three scholarships, the highest LFPR was exhibited by those in the TWSP (73.9%), followed by STEP (70.1%), and PESFA (69%). However, the employment rate is higher among those who availed of scholarships (70.9%) compared to those who did not (65.3%). Employment rates for 2017 vary across scholarships, with PESFA having the highest employment rate at 77%. The employment rate among the TWSP scholars is 71%, while for STEP scholars, it is 68%.

However, not all who participate in the labor force have jobs, and unemployment rates and employment-to-population ratios tell a different story. Unemployment rates are highest for non-scholars at 34.7%, compared to 29.1% of scholars. There is also a higher employment-to-population ratio for scholars at 52%, compared to 48.9% for non-scholars. Despite having the lowest labor force participation rate, PESFA scholars exhibited the highest employment-to-population ratios of the three scholarships, at 53.1% (and lowest unemployment rate of 23%), followed by the TWSP at 52.4% (and unemployment rate of 29%) and STEP at 47.7% (and unemployment rate of 32%).

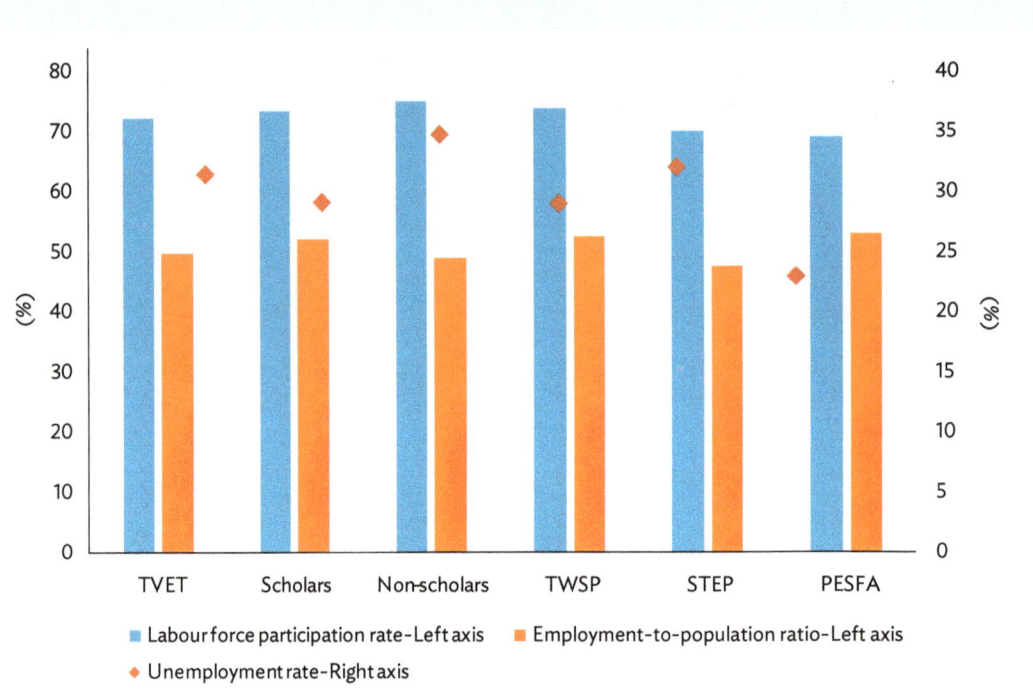

Figure 11.4: Selected Labor Market Indicators for Technical and Vocational Education and Training Graduates, 2017

PESFA = Private Education Student Financial Assistance, STEP = Special Training for Employment Program, TWSP = Training for Work Scholarship Program, TVET = technical and vocational education and training.
Source: Technical Education and Skills Development Authority. 2019c. *2018 Study on the Employment of TVET Graduates Full Report*. Taguig.

Evaluation Design and Methodology

Evaluating the impact of a scholarship on labor outcomes involves establishing that the program alone is responsible for those outcomes. The impact of the program on an outcome is the difference between the outcome with the program and the outcome without the program for the beneficiaries. In the case of scholarships, the impact on trainees' incomes is the difference in their income after receiving the scholarship and their income at the same point in time had they not received the scholarship. However, since we cannot measure these two alternative states for the same group at the same time, we compare the outcomes for those with the scholarship (treatment group) with those of an identical comparison group who did not receive the scholarship. To be valid, a comparison group should have similar characteristics as the treatment group, without the program. These common characteristics include sex, age, education, marital status, and region, and are discussed further in the evaluation methods below.

In choosing the appropriate impact evaluation method, we rely on the operational rules of the program. A valid comparison group can be identified if the operational rules are equitable, transparent, and accountable.[146] Operational rules are equitable if everyone has an equal chance of benefiting from the program, or there are clear

---

[146] Gertler, Paul, Sebastian Martinez, Patrick Premand, Laura Rawlings, and Christel Vermeersch. 2016. *Impact Evaluation in Practice*. Washington, DC: The World Bank.

criteria for prioritizing those eligible, transparent assignment rules are publicly available and their enforcement can be externally validated. TWSP, STEP, and PESFA appear to meet these criteria, albeit with the availability of Qualification Maps to the public and the enforcement of relevant guidelines yet to be externally validated, performance of relevant distribution bodies (provincial and regional offices) assessed, and implementation of selection rules and criteria further verified.

A valid comparison group depends on the key operational rules of the program, including specification of program benefits, financing and distribution, and selection of beneficiaries. Key operational rules involve questions on the available resources, the eligibility criteria, and the timing of implementation.[147] The question of available resources concerns whether the program has enough resources to allow full or limited coverage of eligible beneficiaries (Box 11.2). In each scholarship program, coverage is considered highly limited compared to the target population and the absorptive capacity of TVIs. Each scholarship program has a set of eligibility criteria at the following levels: qualifications, region/province, TVIs, and beneficiaries. Timing of implementation concerns whether the enrollment of beneficiaries can be done all at once or phased over time.

Qualification assignment is based on industry priorities and qualification levels, among other criteria. The TWSP covers 249 qualifications in priority industries/key economic generators: agri-fishery/agri-business/agro-industrial, tourism, information technology-business process management (IT-BPM), semiconductors and electronics, automotive, other priority manufacturing industries, logistics, general infrastructure, and new and emerging sectors. Priority is also given to higher level qualifications (NC III/IV, PQF Level IV) and Training Methodology levels I and II. STEP covers 52 qualifications included in the 2018 STEP TVET Programs Coverage and Schedule of Costs.[148] PESFA covers 218 single qualifications and four pairs of bundled qualifications.[149] Most eligible qualifications are NC II and aforementioned; many NC I qualifications are not eligible. The distributions of eligible qualifications for the three scholarships are shown in Table 11.1.

Table 11.1: **TWSP, STEP, and PESFA Distribution of Qualifications by Industry, 2018**

Industry	TWSP	STEP	PESFA
Agriculture and Fishery	19	6	16
Automotive	34	9	32
Construction	44	9	40
Metals and Engineering	28	1	19
Heating, Ventilation, Air-conditioning, and Refrigeration	5	1	5
Utilities	6	0	6
Electronics	11	4	12
Footwear and Leather Goods	1	0	1
Furniture and Fixtures	1	1	1
Garments	3	2	3
Processed Food and Beverages	6	3	5
Pyrotechnics	1	0	1
Information and Communication Technology	20	0	21
Tourism (Hotels and Restaurants)	18	5	18

continued on next page

---

[147] P Gertler et al. 2016. *Impact Evaluation in Practice.* Washington, DC.
[148] TESDA Circular No. 6. 2018. 2018 Special Training for Employment Program (STEP) TVET Programs Coverage and Schedule of Cost. Taguig.
[149] PESFA's bundled qualifications comprise one pair of qualifications each for Metals and Engineering; Heating, Ventilation, Air-conditioning, and Refrigeration; Automotive; and Electronics.

Table 11.1: *continued*

Industry	TWSP	STEP	PESFA
Land Transportation	3	0	3
Wholesale and Retail Trading	1	0	1
Health, Social, and Other Community Development Services	15	11	32
Visual Arts	2	0	2
TVET	8		
Language and Culture	8		

PESFA = Private Education Student Financial Assistance, STEP = Special Training for Employment Program, TWSP = Training for Work Scholarship Program, TVET = technical and vocational education and training.
Note: PESFA list refers to single qualifications only.
Source: 2018 TWSP TVET Programs Coverage and Schedule of Cost, 2018 STEP TVET Programs Coverage and Schedule of Cost, 2018 PESFA Schedule of Costs per Single Qualifications.

In addition, the TWSP and STEP follow guidelines for allocation of scholarships by region/province and TVIs. Regions and provinces are guided by the Scholarship Allocation Plan, based on absorptive capacities of TVIs and priority skills identified in the regional/provincial Technical Education and Skills Development (TESD) Plan and Barangay Skills Needs Survey. Scholarship allocation has three stages: (i) Central Office approval of regional office's budget allocation, (ii) regional office scholarship budget distribution to provincial offices, and (iii) TVI implementation of training programs. Provincial offices allocate scholarships to TVIs based on their qualifications map identifying their proposed training programs, number of slots, trainers, and other relevant information. Regional offices approve the qualifications maps, subject to the review of eligibility requirements and selection criteria for TVIs. TVIs are selected based on their absorptive capacity, utilization rate, and employment rate. Priority in the allocation of grants is also given to TVIs with system for TVET accreditation and recognition-rated programs, those accredited by the Asia Pacific Accreditation and Certification Commission, and ISO-certified and Philippine Quality Awards recipients.

Box 11.2: Eligibility Criteria for Beneficiaries

- **Training for Work Scholarship Program (TWSP):** Beneficiaries are based on basic qualifications and on the industry/community they belong to. Beneficiaries must be Filipino citizens, and at least 18 years old at the time he/she finishes the training program. Target beneficiaries are those who belong to a list of industries and communities/special clients. There is no explicit scoring/ranking system in the selection/admission of scholars.

- **Special Training for Employment Program (STEP):** Beneficiaries are Filipino citizens who are at least 15 years old at the start of the training program and not simultaneously holding other government scholarship or subsidy. STEP also has no explicit selection score, ranking, and cut-off.

- **Private Education Student Financial Assistance (PESFA):** Beneficiaries are Filipino citizens who have completed at least high school and at least 15 years old at the start of the training program. Beneficiaries should have a family income no higher than ₱300,000 per year. Given this, family income can be ranked across beneficiaries with the cut-off used to distinguish between eligible and non-eligible trainees.

Source: Technical Education and Skills Development Authority (TESDA) Omnibus Guidelines for 2018 TWSP and STEP, TESDA Implementing Guidelines for 2018 PESFA.

For all three scholarships, timing of implementation is such that TVIs can proceed with their training programs as soon as their qualification maps are approved by the regional director and they have submitted a notarized affidavit of undertaking. The provincial offices and TVIs then conduct the training induction program. The regional offices submit the approved qualification maps and notarized affidavit of undertaking to the central Scholarship Management Office, which then issues a scholarship grant certificate to the TVIs through the regional offices and provincial offices. TESDA scholarships are not randomly assigned. Potential scholars choose to enroll in TVET and apply for scholarships. The method chosen for evaluating programs with voluntary enrollment is instrumental variables (IVs). It uses an external factor to determine program participation. In this context, an IV is something external to an individual's decision that affects his or her participation, but is not related to his or her characteristics.

The impacts of the scholarships are assessed on six outcomes: completion rate, assessment rate, certification rate, national certification rate, employment rate, and earnings. Completion rate is the proportion of trainees whose training status indicates they have "completed" the training as opposed to those who "dropped out" have "not completed," or have been "removed." Assessment rate is the proportion of those who completed their training who underwent an assessment. Certification rate is the proportion of those assessed whose result indicated "competent" as opposed to "not yet competent." National certification rate is the proportion of trainees assessed to be competent and obtained a national certificate (NC) as opposed to a certificate of competency (COC). Employment rate is the proportion of employed graduates out of those in the labor force. Earnings is the gross monthly income of the employed graduates.[150]

The evaluation methodology is composed of three models: linear probability model (LPM), propensity score matching (PSM), and IV regression. The specification of the models is given in Appendix 11. The benchmark LPM model relates the outcome of interest to scholarship receipt and other independent variables (sex, age, education, marital status and region; additional variables for the employment and earnings equations include delivery mode, program registration, internship/on-the-job training, competency/certification). The LPM estimates are unbiased,[151] efficient with the use heteroskedasticity-robust standard errors, and are easy to interpret.[152] The coefficient estimates for the scholarships are simply the differential rates of completion, assessment, certification, national certification, and employment, and earnings differential for scholars relative to non-scholars.

However, the LPM estimates may be subject to selection bias as scholarship assignment is not random but subject to purposive assignment or self-selection. For instance, the TWSP prioritizes program assignment to key employment-generating industries and special communities/clients. Scholars may also self-select based on observed as well as unobserved characteristics. If unobserved characteristics are correlated with receipt of the scholarship, the estimate of the effect of scholarship will be biased.

To correct for selection bias based on observable characteristics, the PSM is used. The PSM creates a comparison group based on the probability of receiving a scholarship using data on observed

---

[150] The definitions of the outcomes are generally consistent with TESDA's formula: Completion rate = graduates/enrolled x 100; Certification rate = certified/assessed x 100 Note: certified includes both those who have assessed as COC and for full qualification. However, TESDA defines national certification rate over those assessed while we defined it over those certified. Nevertheless, this should not matter as the focus is on impacts rather than levels.
[151] While the disturbances are not normally distributed but follow a Bernoulli distribution, the estimates remain unbiased.
[152] While the error variance is heteroskedastic, making the estimates inefficient, this can be addressed by using heteroskedasticity-robust standard errors (Wooldridge 2002). Third, the use of LPM is even more justified when the regressors are discrete. For categorical variables with mutually exclusive and exhaustive categories, the estimated probabilities are simply the average outcomes for the different categories; and the predicted outcomes are always within bounds (i.e., between 0 and 1).

characteristics. Scholarship recipients and non-recipients are matched based on this probability or propensity score. The average difference in the outcomes of these two groups is the average treatment effect of the scholarship.

To correct for selection bias based on unobserved characteristics that vary with time, IV regression is used. IV estimation is done in two stages. In the first stage, we regress scholarship receipt on the instruments and other independent variables. Candidate instruments considered are eligibility criteria that affect scholarship receipt (i.e., eligible qualifications/NCs, NC level, age, whether TVIs have STAR-rate programs or APACC-accreditation, whether trainee is a high school graduate, income before training—whichever applies to the particular scholarship), but not the outcome. The instruments are tested for exogeneity using the Sargan NR-square test and for relevance using the Anderson LR test. In the second stage, we regress the outcome of interest on the predicted value of the scholarship receipt from the first stage regression along with other independent variables. Scholarship receipt is then tested for endogeneity using the Wu-Hausman F test. If scholarship receipt is endogenous, the IV estimates are used. Otherwise, if scholarship receipt is exogenous, the PSM estimates are adopted. It is important to note that while eligible qualifications are considered exogenous to scholarship receipt a priori, it might not be exogenous to the choice of qualification. However, this determination is outside the scope of this study.

Data used in the evaluation are drawn from the TESDA Trainee Management Information System (T2MIS); the TWSP, STEP, and PESFA program coverage; and the Study on the Employment of TVET Graduates (SETG) 2018 survey. The T2MIS datasets include the enrollment dataset by region for 2018 and the certification dataset by region for 2018 and 2019. The enrollment data set includes data on completion, types of scholarship, region, sector, sex, age, civil status, and education, and type of client. The certification data set includes data on assessment, competency, and certification (COC or NC). The enrollment data set is merged with the certification datasets. The final data set includes 937,323 observations, 863,195 with training status (completed or not), 850,618 of whom completed their training, 687,293 were assessed, 637,794 obtained certification (COC and NC), and 544,091 obtained National Certificates. The TWSP, STEP, and PESFA program coverage identifies the eligible qualifications. The SETG survey includes data on employment and earnings of TVET graduates.

Findings

The following are the results of the preferred models based on the endogeneity tests. The tests show that the TWSP and STEP scholarships are endogenous in all equations: completion, assessment, competency certification, and national certification. On the other hand, PESFA is endogenous in the assessment and national certification equations, but exogenous in the completion and competency certification equations. Accordingly, IV regression results are reported for the TWSP and STEP for completion, assessment, competency certification and national certification, and for PESFA for assessment and national certification outcomes. On the other hand, the PSM results are reported for PESFA for completion and competency certification outcomes. Factors associated with the receipt of scholarship are presented in Box 11.3.

Impact of Scholarships on Technical and Vocational Education and Training Completion

Completion rates for STEP and PESFA scholars are higher than non-scholars, while completion rates for the TWSP scholars are lower than non-scholars. Figure 11.5 shows that completion rates for STEP scholars are 1 percentage point higher than those for non-scholars (96.8%), while completion rates for PESFA scholars are 1.9 percentage points higher than non-scholars (96.7%). On the other hand, completion rates for the TWSP scholars are 2.5 percentage points lower than non-scholars (98.9%). These may be attributed to the provision of training allowance. The P60 daily allowance may be encouraging attendance and therefore completion as it can cover transportation to and from the training center and a meal or snacks.

Box 11.3: Factors Associated with Receipt of Scholarship

The results of the first stage of propensity score matching (PSM) show how various characteristics (region, sector, sex, age, civil status, and education) affect scholarship receipt:

- **Region:** The estimates across regions show that trainees in most other regions are less likely to receive the Training for Work Scholarship Program (TWSP) scholarships than those in the National Capital Region (NCR). Only a few regions, Western Visayas, Northern Mindanao, and Autonomous Region Muslim Mindanao (ARMM), are more likely receive the TWSP scholarships than the NCR. More regions are more likely to receive STEP scholarships than the NCR including Occidental Mindoro, Oriental Mindoro, Marinduque, Romblon, and Palawan (MIMAROPA); Bicol; Western Visayas; Central Visayas; Northern Mindanao; Davao; and ARMM. For Private Education Student Financial Assistance (PESFA) scholarships, all other regions are more likely to receive them than the NCR.

- **Sex:** Scholarship receipt by sex shows that males are equally likely to receive the TWSP scholarships as females. However, males are less likely to receive STEP and PESFA scholarships than females.

- **Age:** For the TWSP, findings are consistent with the qualification that the TWSP scholars must be 18 years old by the end of the training. For STEP, however, trainees 25 years old and over are more likely to receive STEP scholarships than trainees below age 15, but trainees aged 15–25 are less likely to receive STEP scholarships. This is inconsistent with the requirement that STEP beneficiaries must be at least 15 years old at the start of the training. For PESFA, trainees ages 15–24 and 45–54 are equally likely to receive PESFA scholarships as trainees below age 15. This is inconsistent with the requirement that beneficiaries must be at least 15 years old at the start of the training. However, part of these inconsistencies may be due to measurement error, as some trainees are too young to undertake any training.

- **Marital status:** Married trainees and widows/widowers are more likely to receive the TWSP, STEP, and PESFA scholarships than single trainees. Separated/divorced/annulled trainees are more likely to receive the TWSP and STEP scholarships than single trainees, but are equally likely to receive PESFA scholarships. Trainees with common law/live-in partners are equally likely as single trainees to receive the TWSP and STEP scholarships, but less likely to receive PESFA scholarships.

- **Education:** Trainees with no grade completed are more likely to receive the TWSP scholarships than those with incomplete elementary to college education and doctorate education. However, college graduates and those with master's degrees are equally likely to receive the TWSP scholarships as those with no education, perhaps due to better knowledge of the training and scholarship opportunities. Trainees with no education are also more likely to receive STEP scholarships than those with education, except elementary graduates, who are equally likely to receive STEP scholarships. Trainees with partial elementary, high school, and post-secondary non-tertiary/technical and vocational education are less likely to receive PESFA scholarships than trainees with no education. However, trainees with high school graduate and college graduate education are more likely to receive PESFA scholarships. This is consistent with the guidelines requiring beneficiaries to be at least high school graduate.

Source: Authors.

The foregoing results are based on the IV regression estimates for the TWSP and STEP, and the PSM estimates for PESFA. IV estimates are appropriate for the TWSP and STEP given the endogeneity of scholarship receipt while the TWSP estimates are more appropriate for PESFA given the exogeneity of scholarship receipt. The TWSP receipt is positively related to the eligibility of the qualifications, but is negatively related to whether the trainee is a special client; the latter is inconsistent with policy. STEP receipt is positively related to the eligibility of the qualifications and to whether the trainee is age 15 and above, consistent with policy.

Figure 11.5: Impact of Scholarships on Completion—TWSP, STEP, and PESFA

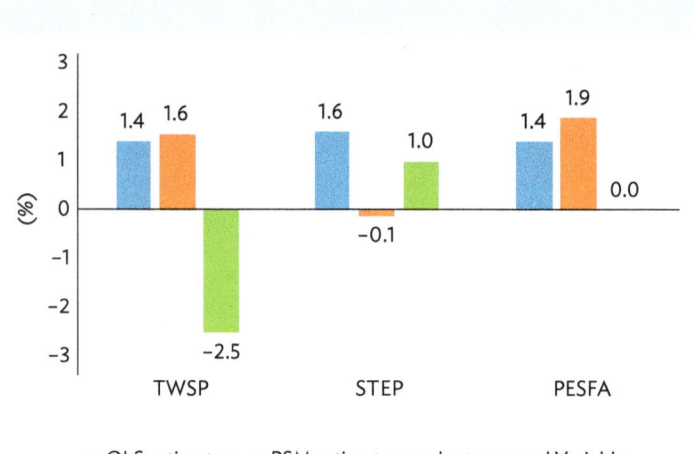

OLS = ordinary least squares, PESFA = Private Education Student Financial Assistance, PSM = propensity score matching, STEP = Special Training for Employment, TWSP = Training for Work Scholarship Program.
* p<0.05, ** p<0.01, *** p<0.001
Source: ADB estimates.

Impact of Scholarships on TVET Assessment

Assessment rates for the TWSP and STEP scholars are substantially higher than those for non-scholars, but in the case of PESFA scholars, they are not significantly different from those of non-scholars. Figure 11.6 shows that the assessment rate for the TWSP scholars is 61.4 percentage points higher than those for comparable non-scholars (2%). The assessment rate is universal (100%) for STEP scholars and nil for comparable non-scholars. The assessment rate for PESFA scholars is not significantly different from that for non-scholars (57.1%). The considerable impacts of the TWSP and STEP on assessment may be attributed to the scholarships' coverage of the assessment fees. It may also be attributed to the fact that "competency assessment is mandatory for qualifications with Training Regulations (TRs) with Competency Assessment Tools (CATs)."[153] It might also be due to possible sanctions for scholars who fail to get assessed. Anecdotal evidence suggests that scholars are liable for the full training cost if they do not attend the assessment. While this is not TESDA policy, TVIs may have an incentive to impose this condition on their trainees.

The foregoing results are based on the IV regression estimates for the TWSP, STEP, and PESFA. The IV estimates are appropriate for all three given the endogeneity of scholarship receipt. TWSP receipt is positively related to the eligibility of the qualifications and whether the trainee is Filipino, consistent with policy. STEP receipt is positively related to the eligibility of the qualifications and whether the trainee is age 15 and above, consistent with policy. Only income is the relevant instrument for PESFA receipt and is negatively related to income, consistent with policy.

---

[153] TESDA Circular No. 3. 2018. Omnibus Guidelines for 2018 Training for Work Scholarship Program (TWSP) and Special Training for Employment Program (STEP). Taguig City.

Figure 11.6: Impact of Scholarships on Assessment—TWSP, STEP, and PESFA

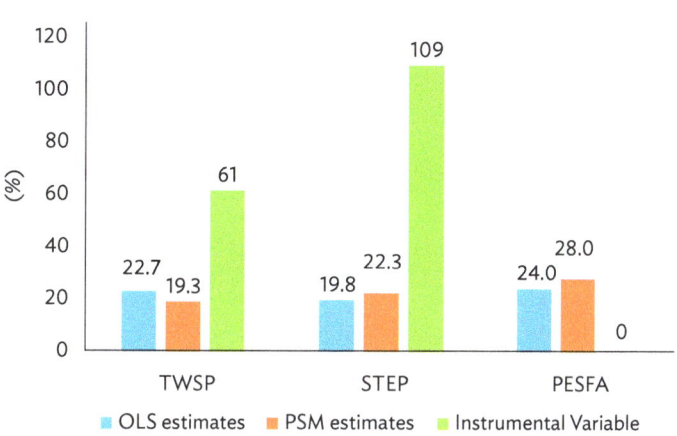

OLS = ordinary least squares, PESFA = Private Education Student Financial Assistance, PSM = propensity score matching, STEP = Special Training for Employment, TWSP = Training for Work Scholarship Program.
* $p<0.05$, ** $p<0.01$, *** $p<0.001$
Source: ADB estimates.

Impact of Scholarships on TVET Competency or Certification Rate

Scholarship has a positive impact on competency or certification rate for STEP scholars, negative impact for the TWSP scholars, and no impact for PESFA scholars. Figure 11.7 shows that the certification rate for STEP scholars is 2.7 percentage points higher than that for comparable non-scholars (97.3%), while the certification rate for the TWSP scholars is 25.5 percentage points lower than that for non-scholars (100%). The certification rate for PESFA scholars is not significantly different from that of non-scholars (90.6%). The positive impact for STEP scholars may be attributed to the provision of supplemental entrepreneurship training which may reinforce the skills learned during the training. STEP courses are also relatively short so recall of skills is relatively easier during the assessment. The effect of the tool kit provision is ruled out as their procurement and distribution had a problem during the subject year. If any, this should have a negative effect on the certification rate.

The foregoing results are based on the IV regression estimates for the TWSP and STEP, and the PSM estimates for PESFA. IV estimates are appropriate for the TWSP and STEP given the endogeneity of scholarship receipt, while PSM estimates are more appropriate for PESFA given the exogeneity of scholarship receipt. TWSP receipt is positively related to whether the trainee is Filipino, age 18 and above, the eligibility of the qualifications, and higher-level qualifications, consistent with policy. However, it is negatively related to whether the trainee is a special client, inconsistent with policy. STEP receipt is positively related to whether the trainee is Filipino, aged 15 and above, the eligibility of the qualifications, and whether the trainee is a special client.

Impact of Scholarships on TVET National Certification

National certification rates are lower for the TWSP, STEP, and PESFA scholars than those for comparable non-scholars. Figure 11.8 shows that the national certification rate for the TWSP scholars is 22.2 percentage points

Figure 11.7: Impact of Scholarships on Competency—TWSP, STEP, and PESFA

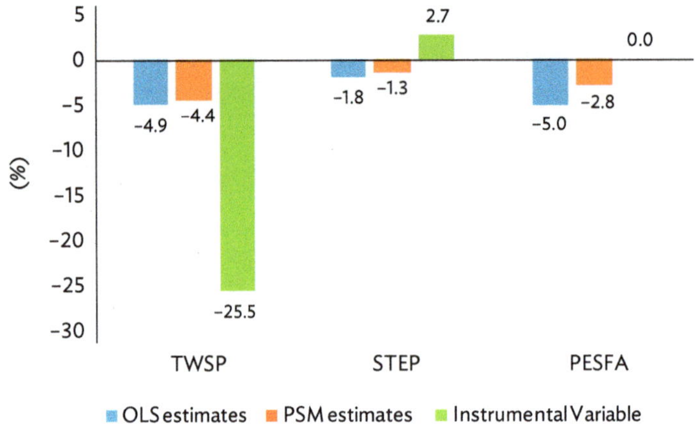

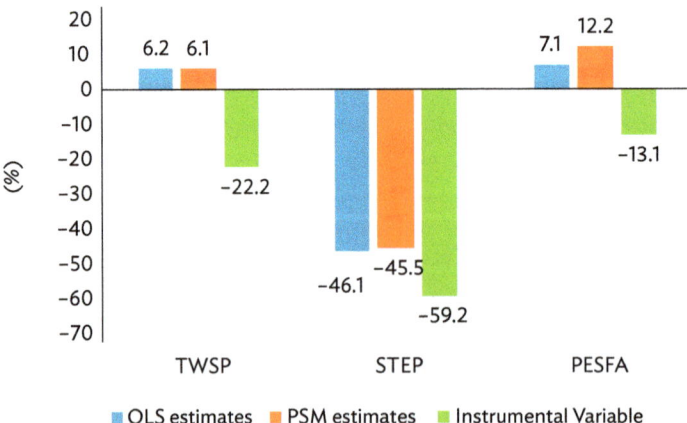

OLS = ordinary least squares, PESFA = Private Education Student Financial Assistance, PSM = propensity score matching, STEP = Special Training for Employment, TWSP = Training for Work Scholarship Program.
* $p<0.05$, ** $p<0.01$, *** $p<0.001$
Source: ADB estimates.

Figure 11.8: Impact of Scholarships on National Certification—TWSP, STEP, and PESFA

OLS = ordinary least squares, PESFA = Private Education Student Financial Assistance, PSM = propensity score matching, STEP = Special Training for Employment, TWSP = Training for Work Scholarship Program.
* $p<0.05$, ** $p<0.01$, *** $p<0.001$
Source: ADB estimates.

lower than that for comparable non-scholars (76.6%). The negative impact for STEP scholars is even bigger, 59.2 percentage points below that for non-scholars (86%). National certification rate for PESFA scholars is 13.1 percentage points lower than that for non-scholars (83.7%). These results indicate that the scholarships do not improve national certification rates, apart from scholars' innate abilities. This may be due to the absence of program incentives to obtain national certification or sanction for failure to do so. This needs to be addressed in future scholarship rounds in order to better promote national certification.

The foregoing results are based on the IV regression estimates for TWSP, STEP, and PESFA. The IV estimates are appropriate for all three given the endogeneity of scholarship receipt. TWSP receipt is positively related to the eligibility of the qualifications and to whether the trainee is Filipino, consistent with policy. STEP receipt is positively related to the eligibility of the qualifications, consistent with policy. PESFA receipt is positively related to the eligibility of the qualifications and negatively related to income, consistent with policy.

Disadvantage and Ability among Scholars

TWSP and PESFA scholars are generally more disadvantaged than non-scholars, whereas STEP scholars are more advantaged than non-scholars. The TWSP scholars are generally more disadvantaged than nonscholars. The LPM estimate of impacts are underestimated relative to the PSM estimate indicating negative selection of TWSP scholars in terms of observable characteristics.[154] However, TWSP scholars who complete their training are more advantaged. This suggests that some disadvantage remains to be addressed to further promote completion. This may be related to the absence of training allowance for TWSP scholars. PESFA scholars are also more disadvantaged than non-scholars. On the other hand, STEP scholars are generally more advantaged than non-scholars.[155] This difference may be due to the fact that, while the TWSP and PESFA beneficiaries are largely selected by TESDA, STEP beneficiaries are largely selected by legislative sponsors. However, those with higher outcomes—those who are assessed, gain competency, and obtain national certification—are more disadvantaged. This indicates moral hazard among scholars who do not complete their course or go for assessment. Some scholars may be enjoying the benefits of the scholarship without full commitment to completing the course or obtaining certification, given their relative advantage. This suggests the need for a more careful screening of STEP scholars to make sure scarce government subsidy goes to the needy.

TWSP and PESFA scholars are generally more able than non-scholars, but STEP scholars are generally less able than non-scholars. TWSP scholars are generally more able than non-scholars. The PSM estimate of impacts are overestimated relative to the IV estimate indicating positive selection of TWSP scholars in terms of unobservable characteristics.[156] However, TWSP scholars who complete their training are less able. PESFA scholars are also generally more able than non-scholars. However, those who obtain certificates of competency, but not national certificates, are less able. STEP scholars are generally less able, except for those who obtain NCs.

The difference in ability among scholars may be related to differences in the eligible qualifications, prior education, and prior training. TWSP and PESFA offer scholarships for a wider range of qualifications that allows the participation of more able beneficiaries, even among the disadvantaged for TWSP, and given the high school requirement for PESFA. On the other hand, STEP qualifications are fewer and may be confined to

---

[154] For instance, the OLS estimate of the impact of TWSP on completion rate is 0.2 percentage points less than the PSM estimate. This indicates a negative bias in the OLS estimates implying disadvantage based on observed characteristics (i.e., sex, age, education, marital status, and region).
[155] In this case, the OLS estimates are higher than the PSM estimates, suggesting positive bias, which is taken to mean advantage in observed characteristics.
[156] For instance, the PSM estimate of the impact of TWSP on completion rate is 1.6% compared to IV estimate of -2.5%. This indicates a positive bias in unobserved characteristics in the PSM estimates, implying greater unobserved "ability".

the less able. Educational attainment is higher among TWSP and PESFA scholars than among STEP scholars; 93% of TWSP scholars and 96% of PESFA scholars have at least completed high school education, whereas only 82% of STEP scholars have. More TWSP and PESFA scholars also have previous competency (NC I); 93.5% of TWSP scholars and 99.7% of PESFA scholars are taking up NC II or higher training compared to 85.8% of STEP scholars.

In general, TWSP and PESFA generally caters to more disadvantaged but more able beneficiaries. This is consistent with the goals of social equity and competitiveness enshrined in the NTESDP. Moreover, PESFA caters to "deserving underprivileged students" consistent with its enabling law, the Government Assistance to Students and Teachers in Private Education Act. In contrast, STEP beneficiaries tend to be more advantaged and less able.

Eligibility Criteria as Valid Instruments

The criteria for qualifying for scholarships are generally valid instruments in estimating the effects of scholarship receipt on various outcomes. Consistent with the guidelines, being Filipino is positively related to receipt of TWSP and STEP scholarships, but is not relevant to receipt of PESFA scholarship. This suggests leakages to non-Filipino trainees, which need to be addressed. Out of 620 non-Filipino trainees, 5% received PESFA scholarship, and the proportion of Filipino trainees who received a PESFA scholarship is not significantly different. For outcomes where it is relevant, age is positively related to receipt of all scholarships. Members of the target industries/communities/special clients are more likely to receive STEP scholarships, but are less likely to receive TWSP scholarships. Again, these indicate leakages to non-target beneficiaries. However, these are quite contrary to selection bias based on sex, age, education, marital status, and region. Trainees who are taking qualifications covered by the scholarship programs are more likely to receive the scholarship. Where relevant, trainees taking a higher qualification are more likely to receive the TWSP scholarships. Contrary to policy, being a high school graduate is not related to the receipt of PESFA scholarships. This means that some scholarships leak to non-high school graduates. This may be affecting the performance outcomes of the scholarship. However, those with higher salaries are less likely to receive PESFA scholarships, making these scholarships more equitable.

Impact of Scholarships on Employment

TWSP has a positive impact on employment but STEP and PESFA do not. The employment rate among the TWSP scholars is 72.9%, while that for comparable non-scholars is not significant (Figure 11.9). The employment rate for STEP scholars is not significantly different from that of comparable non-scholars, which is 73.2%. The employment rate of PESFA scholars is likewise not significantly different from that of comparable non-scholars at 66.7%.

The foregoing results are based on the IV regression estimates for TWSP and PSM estimates for STEP and PESFA. The IV estimates are appropriate for TWSP given the endogeneity of TWSP receipt, while PSM estimates are more appropriate for STEP and PESFA given the exogeneity of scholarship receipt. TWSP receipt is significantly related to the eligibility of the qualifications and are greater among higher level qualifications, consistent with policy.

Impact of Scholarships on Earnings

TWSP and PESFA have no impact on scholars' earnings, while STEP has a negative impact on scholars' earnings. TWSP scholars' earnings are not significantly different from that of comparable non-scholars, which averages P12,747 a month. PESFA scholars' earnings are likewise not significantly different from those of comparable non-scholars, which amounts to an average of P11,270 a month. On the other hand, STEP scholars' earnings are 22% lower than those of comparable non-scholars (P10,241), placing them at P8,204 a month.

These results (presented in Figure 11.10) are based on PSM estimation as the IV estimates are inappropriate given the exogeneity of scholarship receipt.

Figure 11.9: Employment Rates for Scholars and Non-Scholars

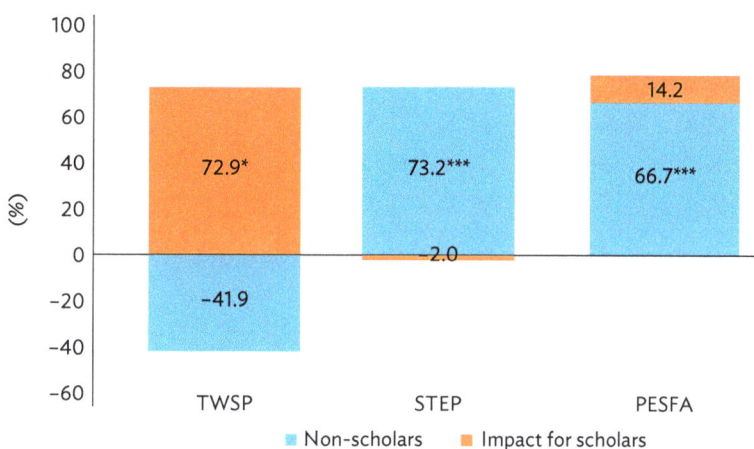

PESFA = Private Education Student Financial Assistance, SETG = Study on the Employment of TVET Graduates, STEP = Special Training for Employment, TVET = technical and vocational education and training, TWSP = Training for Work Scholarship Program.
*** p<0.01, ** p<0.05, * p<0.1. Significance levels are different from those in the completion, assessment, competency certification, and national certification outcomes as the SETG survey has a limited sample compared to the T2MIS.
Source: ADB estimates.

Figure 11.10: Monthly Earnings for Scholars and Non-Scholars

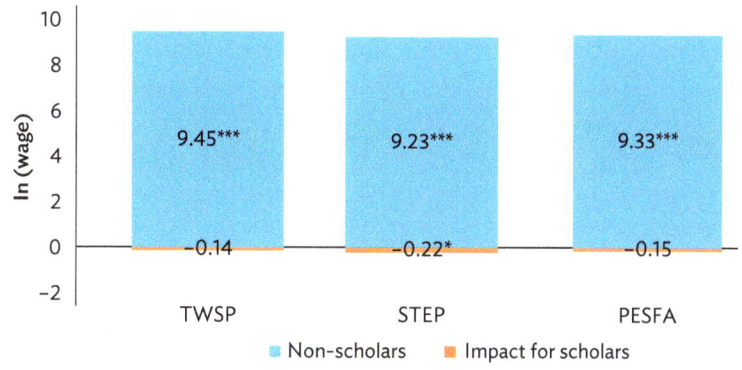

PESFA = Private Education Student Financial Assistance, SETG = Study on the Employment of TVET Graduates, STEP = Special Training for Employment, TVET = technical and vocational education and training, TWSP = Training for Work Scholarship Program.
*** p<0.01, ** p<0.05, * p<0.1. Significance levels are different from those in the completion, assessment, competency certification, and national certification outcomes as the SETG survey has a limited sample compared to the T2MIS.
Source: ADB estimates.

Conclusions

TESDA's scholarships are most effective for achieving higher completion and assessment rates for scholars; however, they are less effective at improving competency and national certification. Using appropriate econometric techniques to address beneficiary selection bias both observed and unobserved, this chapter finds positive impacts on completion rates for STEP and PESFA scholars, which may be attributed to the provision of training allowances to STEP and PESFA scholars. It also finds positive impacts on assessment rates for the TWSP and STEP scholars. This may be attributed to the coverage of assessment fees and the mandatory assessment for qualifications with training regulation and competency assessment tools. Trainees might also be compelled to undergo assessment under the threat of being held liable for the full training cost for failure to do so. The study also finds a positive impact on competency certification rates among STEP scholars, but not for the TWSP and PESFA scholars. This may be due to the provision of supplemental entrepreneurship training, which may reinforce the skills learned during the training. STEP courses are also relatively short, so recall of skills is relatively easier during the assessment. However, the study finds negative impact on national certification rates for the TWSP, STEP and PESFA scholars alike. This may be due to the absence of program incentives to obtain national certification or sanction for failure to do so. This needs to be addressed in future scholarship rounds in order to better promote national certification.

TWSP and PESFA scholars are generally more disadvantaged than non-scholars, whereas STEP scholars are more advantaged than non-scholars. TWSP scholars are generally more disadvantaged than non-scholars except those who complete their training suggesting that some disadvantage remains to be addressed to further promote completion, such as the provision of training allowance for the TWSP scholars. PESFA scholars are also more disadvantaged than non-scholars. On the other hand, STEP scholars are generally more advantaged than non-scholars, perhaps because STEP beneficiaries are largely selected by legislative sponsors. However, STEP scholars who achieve higher outcomes—those who are assessed, gain competency, and obtain national certification—are more disadvantaged. This further indicates a potential moral hazard among some scholars who fail to complete their course, undergo assessment, or achieve certification, enjoying the benefits of the scholarship without seriously aiming for completion or certification, given their relative advantage. This suggests the need for a more careful screening of STEP scholars to make sure scarce government subsidy goes to the needy.

TWSP and PESFA scholars are generally more able than non-scholars, but STEP scholars are generally less able than non-scholars. TWSP scholars are generally more able than non-scholars except those who complete their training. PESFA scholars are also generally more able than non-scholars except those who obtain certificates of competency. STEP scholars are generally less able except for those who obtain NCs.

The difference in ability among scholars may be related to differences in the eligible qualifications, prior education, and prior training. TWSP and PESFA offer scholarships for a wider range of qualifications that allows the participation of more able beneficiaries, and given the high school requirement for PESFA. On the other hand, STEP qualifications are fewer and may be confined to the less able. Educational attainment is higher among TWSP and PESFA scholars than among STEP scholars. More TWSP and PESFA scholars also have prior competencies.

In general, TWSP and PESFA generally caters to more disadvantaged but more able beneficiaries. This is consistent with the goals of social equity and competitiveness enshrined in the NTESDP. Moreover, PESFA caters to "deserving underprivileged students" consistent with its enabling law, the GASTPE Act. In contrast, STEP beneficiaries tend to be more advantaged and less able.

TWSP has a positive impact on employment but STEP and PESFA do not. The employment rate among TWSP scholars is higher than that for comparable non-scholars, while the employment rates for STEP and PESFA scholars are not significantly different from those of comparable non-scholars.

TWSP and PESFA have no impact on scholars' earnings, while STEP has a negative impact on scholars' earnings. TWSP and PESFA scholars' earnings are not significantly different from those of comparable non-scholars. On the other hand, STEP scholars' earnings are lower than that comparable non-scholars.

The foregoing results suggest that TESDA's scholarships largely satisfy social equity objectives regarding the selection of disadvantaged beneficiaries, especially among TWSP and PESFA scholars. They have also partly achieved the objective of competitiveness with the selection of more able beneficiaries especially among TWSP and PESFA scholars. While STEP scholars tend to be more advantaged and less able, the scholarship's incentives have been able to achieve impacts in most TVET outcomes: in completion, assessment, and competency certification, except in national certification, which it was not designed for anyway. This proves that incentives are effective in influencing behavior; as such, they need to be designed appropriately to achieve desired outcomes.

Notwithstanding the selection of able beneficiaries, especially among TWSP and PESFA scholars, the scholarships need much more improvement in promoting competitiveness and productivity given the limited impact on graduates' employment and largely insignificant impact on graduates' earnings. In this regard, the scholarships should consider providing placement services for their graduates, linking their graduates to competitive employers, thereby achieving graduate employability and productivity, and supporting industry demands.

The criteria for qualifying for scholarships are generally valid instruments in estimating the effects of scholarship receipt on various outcomes. Consistent with the guidelines, being Filipino is positively related to receipt of TWSP and STEP scholarships, but is not relevant to receipt of PESFA scholarship. This suggests leakages to non-Filipino trainees, which need to be addressed. Fully 5% of non-Filipino trainees received a PESFA scholarship, and the proportion of Filipino trainees who received is not significantly different. For outcomes where it is relevant, age is positively related to receipt of all scholarships. Members of the target industries, communities, or special clients are more likely to receive STEP scholarships, but are less likely to receive TWSP scholarships. Again, these indicate leakages to nontarget beneficiaries. However, these are quite contrary to selection bias based on sex, age, education, marital status, and region. Trainees who are taking qualifications covered by the scholarship programs are more likely to receive the scholarship. Where relevant, trainees taking a higher qualification are more likely to receive TWSP scholarships. Contrary to policy, being a high school graduate is not related to the receipt of PESFA scholarships. This means that some scholarships leak to non-high school graduates. This may be affecting the performance outcomes of the scholarship. However, those with higher salaries are less likely to receive PESFA scholarships, making them more equitable.

Appendix 11: Empirical Methodology

Ordinary Least Squares

A basic approach to impact evaluation would use an ordinary least squares (OLS) model to determine the effect of scholarship on outcomes:

$$Y_i = \alpha S_i + \beta X_i + \varepsilon_i$$

where Y_i is the outcome, S_i is categorical variable equal to 1 for scholars and 0 for non-scholars, X_i is a vector of observed characteristics, and ε_i is the error term that captures unobserved characteristics. The OLS model serves as a benchmark for comparison purposes. In the context of a binary regression, the OLS is known as a linear probability model (LPM). The LPM estimates are unbiased, efficient with the use heteroskedasticity-robust standard errors, and are easy to interpret. While the disturbances are not normally distributed but follow a Bernoulli distribution, the estimates remain unbiased (Gujarati, 2003). Second, while the error variance is heteroskedastic, making the estimates inefficient, this can be addressed by using heteroskedasticity-robust standard errors (Wooldridge, 2002). Third, the use of LPM is even more justified when the regressors are discrete. For categorical variables with mutually exclusive and exhaustive categories, the estimated probabilities are simply the average outcomes for the different categories; and the predicted outcomes are always within bounds (i.e., between 0 and 1). The coefficient estimates for the scholarships are simply the differential rates of completion, assessment, competency, certification, and employment, and earnings differential for scholars relative to non-scholars.

However, LPM estimates may be subject to selection bias as scholarship assignment is not random, but subject to purposive assignment or self-selection. For instance, the TWSP prioritizes program assignment to key employment-generating industries and special communities/clients. Scholars may also self-select based on observed as well as unobserved characteristics. If unobserved characteristics are correlated with receipt of the scholarship, i.e., $Cov(S, \varepsilon) \neq 0$, the estimate of the effect of scholarship, α, will be biased.

Propensity Score Matching

To correct for selection bias based on observable characteristics, propensity score matching (PSM) may be used. PSM creates a comparison group based on the probability of receiving a scholarship using data on observed characteristics. Scholarship recipients and non-recipients are matched based on this probability or propensity score. The average difference in the outcomes of these two groups is the average treatment effect of the scholarship.

To be valid, the PSM must satisfy two conditions: conditional independence and substantial common support. The assumption of conditional independence means that expected outcomes are independent of treatment conditional on the observed characteristics.

$$Y_i \perp T_i | X_i$$

Substantial common support means that scholars can be matched with non-scholars on the observed characteristics across the range of the probability distribution.

$$0 < P(T_i = 1|X_i) < 1$$

The first step of the PSM is to model scholarship receipt as a function of observed characteristics using a probit or logit model.

$$P(S_i) = \phi X_i + u_i$$

We then derive the predicted value of the probability or propensity score, $\hat{P}(S_i)$, from the model.

Second, we determine the common support where the probability distributions for the scholars and non-scholars overlap. Observations outside the common support, i.e., scholars or non-scholars without a match, may have to be dropped.

Third, scholars are matched with non-scholars using any of several matching techniques. Finally, the average treatment effect is estimated as the average difference in the outcomes between scholars and non-scholars in the common support:

$$TOT = \frac{1}{N_S}\left[\sum_{i \in S} Y_i^S - \sum_{j \in N} \omega(i,j) Y_j^N\right]$$

Where N_s is the number of scholars i, $\omega(i,j)$ is the weight of the aggregated outcomes of non-scholars j.

To implement PSM, we use the Stata command *psmatch2.ado* developed by Leuven and Sianesi (2003).

Instrumental Variable Regression

The IV regression approach corrects for selection bias based on unobserved characteristics that vary with time. Recall from the OLS equation that $Cov(S, \varepsilon) \neq 0$. To address this, we use an instrument Z that is correlated with the receipt of scholarship ($Cov(Z, T) \neq 0$) but not correlated with the error term ($Cov(Z, \varepsilon) = 0$).

The first stage is given by the following equation:

$$S_i = \gamma Z_i + \phi X_i + u_i$$

Where S_i is receipt of the scholarship, Z_i is the instrumental variable, and X_i is a vector of independent variables. For the TWSP, the instruments chosen are whether the qualification taken is under the priority sectors and key employment generators identified by TESDA,[157] whether the trainee is a member of TESDA's special communities or clients (footnote XXX), whether the training is for a higher qualification (NC III or IV), and whether the trainee is 18 years old and above. For STEP, the instruments are whether the qualification undertaken is included in the 2018 STEP Programs Coverage, whether the trainee is a member of TESDA's special communities/clients, and whether the trainee is 15 years old and above, according to TESDA Circular

---

[157] The priority sectors are agriculture, fishery, and forestry; automation; electronics; construction; information and communication technology; and tourism. See TESDA (2018a).

No. 3. For PESFA, the instruments are completion of secondary education, whether the trainee is 15 years old and above, and monthly wage.[158] The independent variables include region, sector, sex, age, civil status, and education.[159] For all three scholarship, additional instruments considered are whether TVIs have STAR-rate programs or APACC-accreditation.

The second stage is as follows:

$$Y_i = \alpha \hat{S}_i + \beta X_i + \varepsilon_i$$

Where Y_i is the outcome variable, $\hat{S}_i$ is the likelihood of scholarship receipt from the first-stage regression, and X_i is as in the first stage. The coefficient of $\hat{S}_i$

$$\alpha = \frac{Cov(Y_i, Z_i)}{Cov(S_i, Z_i)}$$

no longer suffers from the correlation between receipt of the scholarship and unobserved characteristics.

To test the exogeneity of the instruments, we use the Sargan N*R-square test or Hansen J Statistic—for generalized method of moments estimation (footnote 179). Under the null hypothesis that the instruments are uncorrelated with the error term, a significant Chi-square statistic indicates some or all of the instruments are not exogenous. To test which instruments are correlated with the error term, we use the difference-in-Sargan or C statistic test. The C statistic is the difference in the Hansen J or Sargan statistics of the regression with all the instruments and the regression excluding suspect instruments. Under the null hypothesis that the suspect instruments are uncorrelated with the error term, a significant Chi-square statistic indicates that the suspect instruments are not exogenous. To test the relevance of the instruments, we use the Anderson LR test. Under the null hypothesis that the suspect instrument is redundant, a significant Chi-square statistic indicates that the instrument is relevant.

To test the endogeneity of scholarship receipt, and the appropriateness of IV regression over OLS regression, we use the Wu-Hausman F test or Durbin-Wu-Hausman Chi-square test.[160] Under the null hypothesis that it is appropriate to use OLS estimation, a significant F or Chi-square statistic indicates inconsistent OLS estimates and the endogeneity of scholarship receipt.

To implement the foregoing methodology, we use data from the TESDA Trainee Management Information System.[161] The data sets include enrollment by region for 2018 and certification by region for 2018 and 2019. The enrollment data sets include data on completion, types of scholarship, region, sector, sex, age, civil status, education, and type of client. The certification data sets include data on assessment, competency certification, and national certification. The enrollment data sets are appended across regions and merged with the certification datasets also appended across regions. The final data set includes 937,323 observations,

---

[158] TESDA Circular No. 28. 2018. Implementing Guidelines for 2018 Private Education Student Assistance (PESFA). Taguig City.
[159] These include regional dummies (the NCR as reference), a male dummy, civil status (dummies for married, common-law, widow/er; single as reference), education dummies (elementary non-graduate, elementary graduate, high school non-graduate, high school graduate, post-secondary non-tertiary technical vocational non-graduate, post-secondary non-tertiary technical vocational graduate college non graduate, college graduate, master's, and doctorate; no grade as reference), and employment status (underemployed, self-employed, wage-employed; unemployed as reference).
[160] C. F. Baum. 2006. *An Introduction to Modern Econometrics Using Stata*. College Station, Texas: Stata Press.
[161] TESDA. TESDA Trainee Management Information System (T2MIS). Taguig.

863,195 with training status (completed or not), 850,618 of whom completed their training, 687,293 were assessed, 637,794 obtained competency (COC and NC), and 544,091 with NCs. To evaluate the impacts of the scholarships on employment and earnings, we use data from the Study on the Employment of TVET Graduates (SETG) 2018 survey. The survey has a sample size of 3,772, of whom 2,696 were in the labor force, and 1,853 were employed and have earnings.

With family income as a selection criterion for PESFA that can be ranked and given the specified threshold, it would have been preferable to use regression discontinuity to evaluate PESFA. However, given the substantial overlap in the distribution of income between scholars and scholars, a consistent ranking of income was not feasible. In lieu of regression discontinuity, we use the same techniques as those used for TWSP and STEP, and use income as an instrument in the IV regression for PESFA.

Strengthened linkages. Industry collaboration is helping enhance the relevance of demand-driven TVET.

PART IV
CONCLUSIONS AND RECOMMENDATIONS

Part IV of the TVET sector study provides an overview of what is needed for successful TVET provision, followed by conclusions and associated recommendations. Chapter 12 provides an overview of "what works" for TVET, drawing from ADB's experience and international literature, identifying a number of core areas for successful TVET provision. Chapter 13 provides an overview of key conclusions and associated recommendations based on findings from this report.

12. What Works for Technical and Vocational Education and Training: Review of International Experience

Many TVET systems worldwide are not adequately equipped to respond to the technological change resulting from Industry 4.0. In several countries, education outcomes and employers' needs are still disconnected. This finding is consistent with feedback from employers on the difficulty of recruiting workers with the required skills.[162] Skills mismatch or skills gaps require reforming TVET systems and redefining the role of TVET in bridging the divide between the supply and the demand of skills. However, there is a lack of linkages between TVET and industry, particularly with limited involvement of employers in setting of standards and articulation of skills needs. This can lead to a lack of engagement in delivery of training (from providing internships to participation in apprenticeship schemes) and minimal involvement in assessment and certification.

Vocational skills can be a driver for growth and employment, but TVET systems need to reform in order to empower human capital development. Inadequate, obsolete equipment, low quality of physical facilities, and weak institutional management contribute to low training quality. There needs to be capacity for teachers to provide demand-driven and practice-oriented training using technology and preparing students for the requirements of the future labor market. Another challenge is that students, parents, policy makers, and other stakeholders often view TVET as a second-best choice to a university degree, which leads to low TVET enrollment. Fragmentation and underfinancing can pose additional challenges. In many countries, a low level of foundational skills due to weak primary and secondary education systems also leads to challenges in learning for TVET. There is also the ongoing challenge of equal access to TVET (participation of women, disabled, ethnic minorities, out-of-school youth, etc.) that needs to be addressed.

TVET reforms in ADB developing member countries (DMCs) tackle a variety of challenges aiming at the transformation of largely supply-driven, underfinanced, undermanaged, and fragmented systems. Weak private sector involvement in defining occupational standards, developing curricula, provision of training, and assessment and certification, as well as inadequate, obsolete equipment, low quality of physical facilities, and weak institutional management are important areas for improvement. To strengthen the capacities of teachers to provide demand- and practice-oriented training using modern technology is another priority area for many DMCs. At the same time, reform efforts aim at improving limited enrollment in the TVET systems, and at addressing the underrepresentation of women and disadvantaged groups in TVET.

Learning from international experiences and good practices can help inform design of TVET systems. Context-specific solutions are required, which are informed by experiences and evidence from other countries. TVET systems cannot be reformed in isolation, and complex economic, labor market, and education sector challenges are not solved by improvements in the TVET system alone. Holistic reform efforts are required that take into account economic development and labor market dynamics in specific sectors as well as changes in the

---

[162] Manpower Group. 2015. *2015 Talent Shortage Survey*. Milwaukee.

overall education sector. This chapter presents key characteristics of a successful TVET system, drawing from the current state of knowledge and lessons learned from ADB TVET projects around the world, shaped around six common key strategies for TVET success:

- Plan, design, and deliver in line with national strategies
- Collaborate with industry for relevant, demand-driven training
- Continually adjust for lifelong learning
- Ensure accessibility and inclusion
- Invest in TVET teacher training
- Support governance, management, and quality assurance

Plan, Design, and Deliver in Line with National Strategies

Successful TVET is aligned with the national vision and direction of a country's development. TVET requires a coordinated effort and collaboration between various government functions. In many countries, fragmentation of responsibilities between ministries and agencies generates uncoordinated efforts with heavy bureaucracy, slow decision-making, and inability to address current and emerging training demands. Government functions such as economic planning, public investments, business and industry development, labor, and education all heavily influence how TVET systems should transform in order to best support economic strategies and human capital development. There needs to be strong mechanisms for coordination, information exchange, and dialogue between these government functions for the TVET system to be aligned with national development strategies and adaptive to changing demands.

With clarity of the national direction, strong partnerships between public and private stakeholders are possible and necessary. The cooperation between government, training providers and public and private employers, business membership organizations, and chambers and clusters of entrepreneurs is pivotal for demand-driven TVET. If linkages are weak, it is more likely that TVET policy will not achieve its full potential. As underlined by University College London: "TVET systems must increase their partnership with employers to ensure appropriate forms of learning and access to world-class skills to promote new and continuing employment suitable for a high-skill economy and newly emerging forms of employment."[163] For public–private partnerships in TVET, a balanced approach is needed to provide portable skills leading to long-term employability, alongside addressing short-term industry skills gaps.

Employers' engagement is critical throughout the entire process of TVET. This includes in defining skills requirements and standards, designing curriculum and assessment procedures, training delivery, job placements, and quality improvements and refinements of programs (Box 12.1). In actual training delivery, the capacity and willingness from companies to facilitate internships, industry immersions, apprenticeships, and different forms of on-the-job training are necessary for skills application in real working environments, leading to greater work readiness and employability of the students. Close cooperation between TVET institutes and companies also generates valuable opportunities for companies to learn pedagogical and didactical practices from the education sector and gives TVET teachers and managers exposure to current trends and technology usage in the private sector.

---

[163] Bandura, Romina, and Paul Grainger. 2019. *Rethinking Pathways to Employment: Technical and Vocational Training for the Digital Age*. Policy Brief. University College London: Center for Strategic and International Studies.

> **Box 12.1: Active Employers' Engagement in German Technical and Vocational Education and Training Systems**
>
> In Germany, a long-standing dual system continues to be upheld by industry associations, unions, politicians, and vocational specialists. The wide acceptance of the technical and vocational education and training (TVET) system is largely dependent on the fact that enterprises play an active role in the definition of occupational profiles, the delivery of training at the workplace, and in assessment and certification. As occupational change becomes more pronounced and rapid, the dual system must respond appropriately with new occupations and competencies; however, the dual system appears to be holding up well. Indeed, as university education no longer guarantees a job, a return to technical–vocational in nontraditional areas such as cybersecurity, data analytics, and so on, is growing. In the German dual system, occupational profiles are currently being updated to respond to digital change. New regulations for metal working and electrical occupations came into effect in 2018: "Digitalization of work, data protection and information security have all now become integral components of training. Various optional additional qualifications will also enable companies occupying different positions within the digitalization process to take a targeted approach to establishing competencies in order to embrace the digital shift."
>
> Source: Federal Institute for Vocational Education and Training (BIBB). 2018. *Metal Working and Electrical Occupations Structured in a Future-Proof Way.* 19 June. https://www.bibb.de/en/pressemitteilung_81176.php (accessed 11 December 2020).

Collaborate with Industry for Relevant, Demand-Driven TVET

TVET systems need to anticipate the future needs of manpower in current and emerging sectors in the economy in order to be able to offer demand-driven training opportunities. The importance of understanding economic direction, investment policy, industrial policy, as well as innovation trends and productivity is critical in this regard (Box 12.2). With rapid changes and disruptions in the world of work, manpower planning and skills forecasting is an increasingly challenging task. TVET system governing bodies and providers must put continuous efforts in identifying employment growth sectors and emerging skills demands. Mechanisms to capture, analyze, and present skills supply and demand data are critical for TVET planning; however, equally important is a structured dialogue between educators, the business community, and civil society to identify and understand trends and developments critical to TVET planning and delivery.

Partnerships between training providers and employers are critical and employers should be actively engaged in design, delivery, and assessment of training. Learning content and methodologies must be oriented to the demands of the labor market. A condition for excellent TVET is the need for a clear line of sight between the learning environment and the work environment;[164] although work-based learning is an avenue to reskill vulnerable groups and upskill older workers, it is vital that it is not restricted to, or identified with, underperforming groups. Work-based learning is important not only for manual or low-skilled occupations, but plays a significant role in the new middle- and high-level skilled occupations (footnote 163).

Industry can be invested in TVET as members of institution governing councils, advisory committees, or sector skill councils. However, experience shows that without a clear mandate, roles and responsibilities, targets, funding

---

[164] Commission on Adult Vocational Teaching and Learning (CAVTL). 2013. *It's About Work... Excellent Adult Vocational Teaching and Learning.* England: Learning and Skills Improvement Service (LSIS).

mechanisms, and capacities, sector skills councils run the risk of failing, instead of creating a demand-driven system.[165] The role of the industry should not be limited to an advisory role. ADB supports DMCs in engaging companies and industry associations in all steps of TVET from the definition of occupational/competency standards and the development of curricula to the provision of training. Training phases at TVET institutes are combined with work-based learning in companies under the guidance of qualified in-company trainers. Teaching and learning materials are developed with the involvement of industry representatives. Employers are also engaged in competency assessment.

> **Box 12.2: Lessons Learned from ADB Projects for Industry Engagement in Technical and Vocational Education and Training**
>
> - **Industry engagement in occupational/competency standards needs to be intensified.** Occupational/competency standards and derived curricula should reflect the needs of the employers, not only with respect to technical skills, but to a broader set that includes core work skills/transversal skills. Strengthening industry engagement in this process is therefore crucial to increase the relevance and quality of technical and vocational education and training (TVET). To ensure regular and timely updates following changing requirements that result from technological developments, occupational/competency standard development needs to shift from a lengthy process and detailed format reflecting narrow and job-specific skills to a more flexible approach allowing for quick adaptations of broad skill sets.
>
> - **Competency assessment involving employers enhances trust in the TVET system.** Assessing students and workers and providing them with a recognized certificate documenting their skills are important measures to ensure TVET quality. Occupational/competency standards defined by industry need to be the basis for the assessment. Employers value certificates only if they are convinced of the quality that the certificates guarantee. To ensure this, industry representatives should be involved in assessments. This requires the development of relevant assessment tools and methods as well as training of assessors.
>
> - **Learning at the future workplace enhances practical skills and core work skills/transversal skills of the students.** For relevant, structured work-based training, qualified in-company trainers are crucial. A standard training program for in-company trainers needs to be developed; master trainers trained; and a system for the sustainable, regular implementation of these trainings established.
>
> - **TVET institutes should be embedded in local and regional industry clusters** not only to better fulfill their core mandate of training youth for the world of work, but also to support enterprises in product and business innovation, technology transfer, upskilling of staff, and facilitation of cooperation between companies in an economic sector or along supply chains.
>
> - **Industry/sector associations or chambers can take over a coordination role** bringing together member companies and initiating and organizing TVET activities. Some industry associations already have a person or department in charge of training or human resources development that takes over this coordination role; however, most associations require initial capacity development and support.
>
> - **Establishing strong industry linkages requires not only policy support but also capacity development.** The capacities of teachers and managers of TVET institutes as well as representatives of companies and associations need to be strengthened. They need to be able to speak each other's language, understand each other's needs and constraints, and develop the tools and processes to build and maintain strong partnerships. Long-term support is needed to create this kind of understanding and trust for a well-functioning collaboration. Favorable policies and incentives help facilitate TVET-industry cooperation, but will only lead to more industry engagement if mutually beneficial and combined with capacity development.
>
> Source: Authors.

---

[165] Ministry of Skill Development and Entrepreneurship. 2016. *Report of the Committee for Rationalization & Optimization of the Functioning of the Sector Skill Councils.* New Delhi.

Continually Adjust for Lifelong Learning

Narrow technical skills that are associated with a specific qualification are no longer sufficient on their own.[166] Instead, a broader set, including core work skills/transversal skills such as problem-solving, communication, and learning to learn, is required to perform effectively in an ever-changing labor market (Box 12.4). Close collaboration between industry and TVET providers can ensure the supply of these skills. These core work skills are a key factor for employability and a prerequisite for continuous learning (Box 12.3). They prepare graduates to take on more challenging and demanding positions in the future, at the same time enabling employers to adopt new technologies and enter new markets to meet the challenges of the Fourth Industrial Revolution and beyond.[167]

When multiple pathways to certification are recognized, assessment and certification centers for recognition of prior learning can be established and assessors and managers trained. The establishment of coherent pathways and transitions from secondary education to TVET, within the TVET system, and from TVET to higher education and to the labor market with career guidance at all levels, is a key factor contributing to the image and acceptance of TVET. Advanced degree programs are introduced to bridge the gap between TVET and higher education. A system of recognition of prior learning is important to allow for the certification of skills acquired outside of the formal TVET system, e.g., from work experience, informal learning, or a combination.

Strengthening public or private career advice and employment services can facilitate the transition from TVET to the labor market and promote options for lifelong learning for employees and unemployed persons. This includes via job centers, which provide advice for jobseekers and connects them with job offers, employers, and training or study options—in many DMCs, employment opportunities might not be sufficient to absorb all graduates. In addition to broad economic reforms and active labor market policies to expand employment opportunities and improve matching between jobs and job seekers, TVET can play an important role in developing entrepreneurship skills in graduates so they are able to leverage their gained skills into creating businesses.

Box 12.3: Incentives for Working Adults to Expand Occupational Skills in New Areas

Singapore's *FutureSkills* programs are designed to ensure workers are prepared for the digitalization of their respective industries. In some cases, workers have decided to change their fields entirely and develop new skills. Each citizen has a training account, which he or she can utilize for this purpose. There are road shows and fairs to encourage reskilling and upgrading to enable workers and job seekers to benefit from emerging opportunities and prevent them from being left behind. An Institute of Adult Learning has been established to provide research, training, and accreditation for adult education.

Source: SkillsFuture. n.d. https://www.skillsfuture.sg/.

---

[166] ADB. 2019. *Realizing Education for All in the Digital Age.* Manila.
[167] United Nations Educational, Scientific, and Cultural Organization (UNESCO). 2015. *Transversal Skills in TVET: Policy Implications.* Asia-Pacific Education System Review Series, Issue 8. Bangkok.

> Box 12.4: **Lessons Learned from ADB Projects on Lifelong Learning**
>
> As new occupations emerge and existing ones are transformed, workers' flexibility to adapt and continuously upgrade their skills makes imperative a technical and vocational education and training (TVET) emphasis on lifelong learning.
>
> - **A broader skill set which goes beyond narrow technical skills for a specific job and includes core work skills/transversal skills**, such as problem-solving and communication, needs to be reflected in occupational/competency standards and derived curricula. These core work skills or transversal skills are becoming a priority for employers. Strengthening industry engagement in this process is therefore crucial to increase the relevance and quality of TVET. Core work skills/transversal skills and solid basic/foundation skills are a prerequisite for lifelong learning to keep up with the changes in today's rapidly changing labor market and therefore need to play a prominent role in TVET.
>
> - **Coherent pathways from secondary education to TVET, within the TVET system and from TVET to higher education** with various entry and exit options, need to be created to establish a system of lifelong learning. This requires a joint effort by various stakeholders in TVET, general education, higher education, other government agencies, and industry.
>
> - **Career guidance and employment services can help facilitate the transition** from TVET to employment and to promote options for upskilling and reskilling. Capacities of staff providing advice for students or jobseekers in employment centers or at schools or TVET institutes need to be strengthened. They need to have a close connection to potential employers and be well informed about training or study options.
>
> - **Entrepreneurship skills need to be part of TVET courses** to enable graduates to leverage their gained skills into creating businesses. Fostering creativity, innovation, and business skills; exposing students to the world of work, as well as providing support for start-ups can be elements of a TVET program.
>
> - **Harmonizing the recognition of TVET qualifications across more than one country** and linking labor market information systems can help encourage labor mobility and ensure that workers moving across borders have recognized qualifications. Regional cooperation in TVET can lead to raised standards for qualifications and their adaptation to local TVET systems, increased movement of students and skilled workers, more efficient labor markets; and enhanced sharing of knowledge and experiences.
>
> Source: Authors.

Ensure Accessibility and Inclusion

TVET emphasis is shifting from training of youth for a specific occupation to the provision of learning opportunities for various target groups, and through different training platforms. Target groups range from secondary school students to working adults or unemployed persons with the desire to reskill themselves. A key factor for an accessible TVET system which promotes lifelong learning is the establishment of coherent pathways and transitions from secondary education to TVET, and from TVET to higher education and to the labor market with career guidance at all levels (Box 12.6). The line between general education, TVET, higher education, on-the-job training, etc., is becoming less distinct. Meanwhile, traditional paradigms of training delivery are being increasingly disrupted by online learning, informal learning, and new perspectives of skills development. The traditional structures of age-based cohorts moving uniformly together in tight synchronicity is no longer necessary. With access to online materials, makerspaces, and social media, individuals can approach experts, seniors, and peers easily to learn on a just-in-time basis.

A key element for improved access is ICT. ADB helps DMCs use digital solutions in TVET by integrating digital skills as a transversal skill in the curriculum and by introducing digital learning tools and methods to improve access to TVET, for example, in poor and remote areas (Box 12.5). Integrating digitalization in materials and also in course delivery, particularly through distance learning, can provide options for making TVET programs more cost-efficient and widely available. A few advanced applications have the potential to benefit special learners, for example, voice recognition apps for visually impaired learners.

Box 12.5: Digital Technical and Vocational Education and Training Delivery in Hunan

The Hunan Technical and Vocational Education and Training Demonstration Project in the People's Republic of China promotes inclusive technical and vocational education and training (TVET) through digital course delivery. Online courses for TVET institutions in poor and remote areas are developed in priority skills areas based on competency-based curricula developed under the project and uploaded onto the online platform of the province. Guidelines for online TVET courses ensure the utilization of the content in line with best international practice for using information and communication technology for TVET. By allowing non-project TVET institutions to access the online courses, the project improves access to high-quality online TVET courses in poor and remote areas in order to maximize resource sharing among TVET institutions.

Source: Authors.

Box 12.6: Lessons Learned from ADB Projects around Access and Inclusion

To deliver students with the right set of skills needed to benefit from changing employment opportunities enabled by Industry 4.0 equitable access to modern and relevant learning environments that act as hubs for innovation is crucial.

- **An increased standardization of workshop layouts and equipment specifications based on international standards** improves quality and cost-effectiveness. Moving toward international standards while considering local needs helps create modern and safe teaching and learning environments, which reflect authentic industry settings and requirements. International standards also include sustainability principles, such as features for energy and water efficiency or reducing, reusing, and recycling resources, and the selection of training equipment with low energy consumption. These standards can be incorporated not only in buildings and equipment, but also in campus management and teaching.

- **Investment in facilities and equipment needs to be combined with capacity building of teachers, institutional management, administrators, and policy makers.** Raising capacities of teachers to adequately utilize the facilities and equipment ensures that the students acquire the required theoretical and practical skills. Capacity building on maintenance, workshop management, and occupational safety and health for teachers and management is necessary to ensure the correct and safe utilization and maintenance of buildings, equipment, and tools, and to embed these practices into the teaching. Decision makers need to be aware of the operational and maintenance costs of facilities and equipment and need to be able to allocate budgets or explore additional income sources to cover these costs.

- **Partnerships with industry or private training providers for the establishment and operation of technical and vocational education and training (TVET) institutes,** in the form of public–private partnerships or others, are a mechanism for cost sharing and transfer of technology, knowledge, and innovation. Early engagement with companies and a close coordination between civil work and operation teams is needed to create a successful partnership. Understanding terms and conditions that work for industry or a private training provider helps to set up and maintain the collaboration. The government often provides support to operators at the initial stage of operation, for example, guidance on curricula, teaching and learning materials, and delivery of training.

Box 12.6: *continued*

- **Centers of excellence with specific functions can act as a regional or functional hub** and support the improvement of the overall TVET system. Centers of excellence need to have qualified teachers; innovative management; a close relationship with industry, outstanding equipment, and facilities; as well as financial stability to fulfill additional functions for the TVET system, such as the provision of TVET teacher training. Establishing a center of excellence, which fulfills its functions sustainably, requires intensive, long-term support in all defined areas.

- **Integrating digital solutions in TVET requires facilities and equipment, as well as capacities.** Facilities need to be adaptable to new technologies, devices need to be provided, and internet connectivity ensured. Further prerequisites include computer literacy and appropriate design of digital solutions. School management and teachers should be provided with continuous professional development opportunities to keep up with the latest technological developments. Collaboration with industry and tertiary institutions can bring in additional technical and management expertise, as well as financial resources. Public–private partnerships combine the strengths of both sides to ensure the sustainability and scalability of digitalization in TVET.

Source: Authors.

Invest in TVET Teacher Training

In many countries, the lack of trained teachers is a major constraint on effective TVET delivery. Improving the professional skills and competencies of TVET teachers, including pedagogical skills, domain-specific theoretical and practical skills, and industry experience, is a crucial factor for increasing the quality and relevance of TVET.[168] This becomes even more urgent given the increasing importance of lifelong learning. Yet, unknown skill demands of future workplaces will increasingly require core work skills, such as problem-solving, teamwork, and self-learning capacity, resulting in the need for TVET teachers to not only maintain a high level of knowledge and skills, but also to apply new teaching and learning methods. Furthermore, TVET teachers increasingly need to contribute to the development of TVET institutes regarding strategic direction, organization, and curricula and need to be able to interact with industry with confidence and strong subject knowledge.[169]

In-service training enables TVET teachers to keep abreast of new technologies and industry developments and to effectively prepare students for constantly evolving roles.[170] Besides continuously improving the professional skills and competences of TVET teachers, creating a well-designed system of selection, compensation, working conditions, recognition, and career prospects is necessary to increase quality and teacher motivation. Professional development can help identify candidates for positions in TVET research and management.

---

[168] Organisation for Economic Co-operation and Development (OECD). 2014. *Skills Beyond School: Synthesis Report, OECD Reviews of Vocational Education and Training.* Paris.
[169] G. Spöttll. 2009. Teacher Education for TVET in Europe and Asia: The Comprehensive Requirements. *Journal of Technical Education and Training* 1(1): 1–16.
[170] D. Dymock and M. A. Tyler. 2018. Towards a More Systematic Approach to Continuing Professional Development in Vocational Education and Training. *Studies in Continuing Education* 40(2): 198–211.

Management staff of TVET institutions need to have a vision for improving the quality and relevance of training. This includes setting directions concerning students, teacher development, and allocation of resources. Managers of institutes can positively contribute to effectiveness when they are prepared and able to solve complex problems, and to build collaborative relationships with staff, parents, students, and the community and industry.[171] Effective management staff designs and implements institutional development plans to guide their work, creates new revenue streams, provides incentives to staff, and holds staff accountable.[172] Understanding the needs of the industry and that of the community is crucial for managers of TVET institutions to organize learning around these needs. In order to respond to market needs, they need sufficient flexibility and freedom to act.

Work-based learning in companies is globally recognized as a best practice to provide students and apprentices with technical knowledge and practical skills. Yet, this also relies on in-company trainers with the right competencies to train students, apprentices, and other employees. Education and labor policies need to support in-company trainers in their important role as TVET staff. This is recognized, for example by the Association of Southeast Asian Nations (ASEAN), which has defined a benchmark for the essential competencies of trainers engaged in TVET delivery at the workplace and defined the standard for in-company trainers in ASEAN Countries.[173]

Support Governance, Management, and Quality Assurance

ADB supports governments in strengthening their TVET sector management and coordination capacity, for example, through supporting the establishment of inter-ministerial committees or a national TVET authority, fostering research on emerging priority sectors and needs, capacity building and developing monitoring systems,

---

Box 12.7: Qualified Technical and Vocational Education and Training Teachers in Indonesia

In Indonesia, many teacher training institutions and universities lack adequate programs, facilities, and industry linkages. These institutions are not adequately prepared to meet the demands of employers and to integrate new technologies that would help teachers address the changing demand for technical education. New and existing technical and vocational education and training (TVET) teachers lack the practical skills and industry experience needed for the technical subjects they teach, and the teaching and learning is characterized by traditional lectures and limited knowledge and use of more interactive, inquiry-based teaching methods. The Asian Development Bank (ADB) is supporting the government in transforming the Indonesia University of Education into a center of excellence for education of TVET teachers. The project is upgrading the infrastructure, strengthening the teaching capacity of the university staff in line with the new teacher education programs (e.g., artificial intelligence and robotics, renewable energy engineering), and supporting the university's TVET research in developing and applying new and contextualized models. Indonesia University of Education is also developing and offering in-service training to teachers and managers, as well as in-company trainers from the industry, and will establish itself as a professional certification body, equipped with centers for competency testing. Success factors include strong and sustained industry involvement in teacher training, continuous professional development of trainers, and recruitment of TVET teachers with industry experience.

Source: ADB. 2018c. *Advanced Knowledge and Skills for Sustainable Growth Project: Report and Recommendation of the President.* Manila.

---

[171] V. M.J Robinson. 2010. From Instructional Leadership to Leadership Capabilities: Empirical Findings and Methodological Challenges. *Leadership and Policy in Schools* 9(1): 1–26.
[172] K. E. Fernandez. 2011. Evaluating School Improvement Plans and their Effect on Academic Performance. *Educational Policy* 25(2): 338–67.
[173] Association of South East Asian Nations (ASEAN). 2020. *Standard for In-company Trainers.* Bangkok: Deutsche Gesellschaft für Internationale Zusammenarbeit (GIZ) GmbH.

Box 12.8: **Lessons Learned from ADB Projects on Technical and Vocational Education and Training Teacher Training**

As technological change continues to transform the task content of occupations, ensuring technical and vocational education and training (TVET) staff are up to date with new workplace realities is essential to ensure they impart students with adequate skills and capabilities.

- **A holistic approach in reforming TVET teacher training is needed** that aims to ensure interconnectivity between pre- and in-service training, and integration of pedagogical and domain-specific training components. Moving away from a donor-driven implementation of mostly ad hoc, short-term training courses for TVET teachers, the Asian Development Bank (ADB) puts the focus on supporting its developing member countries (DMCs) in establishing sustainable systems for high-quality, relevant pre- and in-service training for teachers.

- **Strong institutions for TVET teacher training are the basis for a sustainable system;** therefore, ADB supports the establishment and improvement of universities, TVET teacher training institutes, or centers of excellence that provide pre- and in-service TVET teacher training. This includes developing or improving TVET teacher training programs, facilities, and equipment; strengthening the teaching capacity of the teaching staff; and establishing a pool of master trainers in line with the training programs.

- **Selected institutions are transformed into centers of excellence for TVET teacher training,** providing not only relevant, high-quality pedagogical and domain-specific theoretical and practical pre- and in-service training, but also training for TVET teachers and managers on topics including industry linkages, technology use, curriculum, and learning materials development. ADB also helps these centers of excellence to provide coaching and mentoring by experienced master trainers to ensure the successful implementation of the gained skills in the daily teaching practice. Furthermore, TVET research on new models, vocational pedagogy, teaching and learning outcomes, industry collaboration, and other issues conducted by the centers of excellence contributes to the reform of the overall system.

- **Industry exposure during pre- and in-service training is a key factor** for obtaining relevant, up-to-date experience and skills. An in-depth understanding of the future workplaces of their students helps TVET teachers design and implement training that is linked more closely to the needs of the industry. Attracting people with previous industry experience to become TVET teachers and promoting the recruitment of part-time or temporary teachers from the industry are further intervention areas that contribute to an increased relevance of TVET.

- **Strong leadership at the institutional level is crucial for TVET teachers' continuous capacity development**, as a clear vision and mission, autonomy of faculties, and learning environment enable TVET teachers to continuously upgrade their skills and make use of their improved competencies. Therefore, ADB supports the training of institutional management and helps to ensure that trained leaders and teachers are given the financial means, infrastructure, and equipment to implement what they have been trained to do.

- **Policies and incentives supporting the capacity development of TVET teachers need to be in place** to create a framework which defines the regulations, structure, and resources for a successful TVET teacher training system. DMCs are supported in creating a framework that includes pre- and in-service training for TVET teachers, increased industry exposure, and employment rules that allow people with industry background to become TVET teachers. Policies can also incentivize TVET teachers to participate in training offers, for example, by making training a requirement for recruitment of new teachers and promotion of existing teachers or by increasing the salary of trained TVET teachers. Sufficient resources need to be allocated for a TVET teacher training system to function after the completion of a project.

- **Industry partnerships allow TVET teacher training institutes to enhance synergies with companies** for teacher professional development by aligning TVET teacher training closely with the needs of industry. Supporting policies and incentives, e.g., tax incentives, will facilitate TVET–industry linkages. Industry involvement in the development of TVET teacher training programs and the delivery of training ensures that teachers obtain relevant skills and up-to-date knowledge of the labor market requirements. Building the capacity of TVET teachers and managers to initiate and maintain industry linkages, e.g., for apprenticeships of students, remains one of the core elements of a demand-oriented training system.

Source: Authors.

> **Box 12.9: Lessons Learned from ADB Experience in Supporting Governance, Management, and Quality Assurance**
>
> In the context of rapidly changing technology developments and related employers' needs, well-functioning governance and management becomes increasingly important to ensure relevance and quality of technical and vocational education and training (TVET).
>
> - **Data collection and analysis as well as research capacities** need to be strengthened to create robust information on the performance of the TVET system, which supports evidence-based decision-making at the policy and institute levels. Collaboration between various government agencies, TVET institutes, and other stakeholders is required to obtain relevant data and information.
>
> - **Tracer studies need to be expanded and complemented by enterprise surveys,** which provide information on initial skill requirements and expectations and on the actual skills and performance of graduates. This gives TVET institutes and policy makers valuable information on the match or mismatch of the demand and supply side and areas for improvement.
>
> - **Systems for quality assurance and accreditation** ensure that standards are met and standardized procedures followed. Assessment criteria need to be output-oriented focusing on quality, relevance, and access to training, instead of on training inputs, and need to allow the flexibility required to respond to local needs and conditions. Assessors need to be independent and qualified.
>
> - **Sustainable financing of TVET ensures not only initial investments, but also operational and maintenance costs**. As major beneficiaries of a well-functioning TVET system, employers need to shoulder a larger part of funding. More diversified funding mechanisms are needed in many DMCs for sustainable development of TVET systems. This can include options for TVET institutes to generate income and offer services to a wider target group.
>
> Source: Authors.

and tools to support decision-making and policy making as well as sector management (Boxes 12.7 and 12.8). This includes the development and enhancement of labor market information systems, including labor force and employer surveys, as well as tracer studies, which provide information on skills demand and supply and on the destination and performance of graduates and form a basis for more focused and targeted policy making.

ADB also supports the establishment and enhancement of quality assurance systems which ensure that standards are met, and standardized procedures are followed. Supporting strong mechanisms for accreditation of training providers, programs, and assessment centers are important tools in ensuring and recognizing quality in TVET. ADB supports DMCs in developing, piloting, and establishing suitable financing mechanisms and plans, such as skills development funds, and advises on demand-driven performance-based financing options (Box 12.9). Financing can be an instrument to increase efficiency and the alignment of TVET with the requirements of the labor market. ADB generally supports the establishment of more demand-driven and less regulated models.

Conclusion

In the age of Industry 4.0, TVET systems must reform and redefine their roles in order to equip various target groups with skills that meet the rapidly evolving needs of the labor market. Governments across Asia and the Pacific are increasingly recognizing the importance of skills for the continuation of the region's economic and developmental success. Improving TVET systems have high priority, and the strategies toward, and key characteristics of, successful TVET systems discussed are clearly reflected in recent projects supported by ADB. This chapter drew from international experiences, including literature and the ADB's experience on projects, to help inform the design of successful TVET systems.

Lessons learned from ADB-supported projects reinforce many of the international findings of what works in TVET systems. These include: that qualified TVET teachers and managers are fundamental pillars of high-quality TVET, a strong link between public and private actors is fundamental for demand-driven TVET, and mutually beneficial partnerships need to be facilitated and capacities strengthened. Further, that successful TVET goes beyond narrow technical skills for a specific job and takes a lifelong learning approach that includes transversal and entrepreneurial skills; coherent pathways between various education levels are needed and transitions must be supported by career guidance and employment services; and standardization of workshops, equipment, and digital solutions based on international norms improve quality and cost-effectiveness. Data collection and analysis, as well as research capacities, are critical elements to obtain relevant TVET and labor market information. Finally, more diversified funding mechanisms are needed for sustainable development of TVET.

In sum, TVET systems must transform into agile, flexible, and truly demand-driven systems to support economic development, expansion of business, and employment opportunities. Now is the right moment in time for the Philippines to accelerate the efforts to prepare the country's workforce for the Fourth Industrial Revolution.

13. Conclusions and Recommendations

Rapid economic growth has not been accompanied by large-scale employment creation in the Philippines. The structure of employment has significantly changed, resulting in some progress in terms of the quality of work. Some important decent work shortages remain, however. Furthermore, benefits of growth have not been equitably distributed. The process of structural transformation underway has led to major changes in labor demand reflected in the occupational structure.

Industry 4.0 is likely to accelerate changes in occupational demand and affect the task content of occupations. Some occupations would become redundant, others significantly changed, and new occupations can emerge. In such a rapidly changing environment, workers need to be equipped to move across jobs and occupations. Those with skills that complement technology and those with transferable skills are poised to benefit, while low-skilled workers and those with largely routine skills, which can be easily substituted by technology, risk falling further behind.

The COVID-19 pandemic has heightened the importance of Industry 4.0 preparedness, all the while putting a strain on government resources. It has precipitated automation and the shift toward digital and technological solutions in many fields, and at the same time, has exacerbated inequalities, particularly among workers at different ends of the skills spectrum, and in different forms of employment. The pandemic has also demonstrated that TESDA can respond swiftly and relevantly to the country's massive economic and social challenges. TESDA must continue to strive to meet its objectives with respect to Industry 4.0, during and beyond the recovery period, while also answering to emerging priorities like reskilling workers displaced by the pandemic. Nonetheless, the intensified shift toward digital platforms for learning presents opportunities for TESDA's online programs to expand its reach and relevance in the country. The surge in the uptake of TESDA's online programs amid the pandemic shows them to be a cost-effective means to deliver TVET—reaching many learners with minimal investment in education infrastructure.

The centrality of skills in determining the impact of technological change implies a key role for TESDA in ensuring a sustainable and inclusive development path for the country. This impact is taking place at the worker level—benefiting those skilled workers with technology compatible skills and transversal skills—but also at the country level, as a skilled workforce is an increasingly important determinant of competitiveness.

Industry 4.0 and its associated challenges have been on the policy agenda in the Philippines, including with respect to TVET. This awareness of the challenges and opportunities involved is reflected in various government strategies, including through the selection of key industries to be priorities for Industry 4.0 technology adoption. In TESDA's National Technical Education and Skills Development Plan (NTESDP) 2018–2022, Industry 4.0 preparedness is explicitly stated as a main objective, along with strategies set out to achieve it. The challenge will be with regards to implementation. Despite widespread awareness of Industry 4.0 among TVET stakeholders in the Philippines, an apparent gap in terms of implementation underscores the need to enhance and support TVI preparedness.

This TVET sector study has provided an overview of TVET provision in the Philippine context, identifying trends, qualitatively assessing challenges, and empirically assessing various aspects of TVET performance. The process has resulted in a set of recommendations, which are consolidated and presented under four broad subheadings or categories, generally in line with international best practices and lessons learned from ADB's TVET projects as described in chapter 12. The recommendations are grouped and discussed as follows based on governance, management, and quality assurance; meeting rapidly changing industry demand; continually adjusting toward lifelong learning; and access and inclusion. The recommendations also incorporate the results from the overall review of the national system of TVET in the Philippines undertaken in 2018;[174] and an unpublished report "Future Perspectives, Next Steps: TVET of Tomorrow" (ADB, forthcoming).

Governance, Management, and Quality Assurance

The shift to K to 12 and the strengthened implementation of the Philippines Qualifications Framework (PQF) have far-reaching implications for TVET governance. Given the relatively fast rollout of the K to 12 program, together with changes being brought about by the PQF, it is important for TESDA to take stock of the implications of these developments for TVET and TVET-related program frameworks, design, and institutional arrangements. This would allow determining how to better rationalize the implementation and regulation of these activities given the changing education and training context in the country (Recommendation 1). Furthermore, given the huge impact that the technical–vocational–livelihood (TVL) track program has on the TVET sector, a more active role in the program would both consolidate TESDA's regulatory and quality assurance functions and enhance program offerings. For instance, an area where synergy between TESDA and the Department of Education (DepEd) can contribute to better outcomes in the senior high school TVL track program is in industry engagement, particularly at the regional and provincial/city/schools division levels. The representation of industry in policy making and standard setting had been a hallmark of TESDA's operations. Rather than DepEd having to develop its own mechanism, it could explore a partnership arrangement with TESDA as a means to align senior high school TVL offerings with sectors that have high growth and high value addition, as well as high prospects of employment.

> Recommendation 1: **Enhance institutional arrangements and implementation in light of the K to 12 reform and the Philippine Qualifications Framework**
>
> - **Revisit TVET and TVET-related program frameworks, institutional arrangements, and implementation in light of the K to 12 reform and the Philippine Qualifications Framework (PQF).** There is a need to determine how the government, through TESDA, can better rationalize the implementation and regulation of TVET and TVET-related activities, including those of other government agencies outside the education sector (e.g., Department of Agriculture), given the changing education and training context in the country.
>
> - **Strengthen and support TESDA's role in quality assurance in the senior high school TVL education program.** A more active role for TESDA in the TVL track program would enable the continuous enhancement of the program offerings by providing the metrics for improvement, better planning, evaluation, and generating objective bases for resource allocation.

---

[174] Report on the proposed "Future Perspectives, Next Steps: TVET of Tomorrow" submitted to ADB by the National TVET Specialist and Deputy Team Leader Clifford Paragua. 2018.

A key implication of the implementation of K to 12 implementation and adoption of the PQF is the renewed significance of interagency coordination among CHED, DepEd, and TESDA. Following these developments, it has become imperative to strengthen institutional mechanisms for policy setting and coordination, and reconsider proposals to put in place a coordinating body for this purpose (Recommendation 2). Past attempts at achieving this coordination and establishment of a coordinating body (e.g., based on the proposal to establish a National Council for Education [NCE], see Chapter 6) largely failed because of a time lag in acting upon proposals, and political dynamics whereby the institutionalization of such a body by law was not considered a priority and eventually fell off the policy agenda following changes in leadership. The current momentum afforded by recent reforms must be acted upon to achieve the institutionalization of such a coordination mechanism, specifically through legislation, such as to secure compliance and lessen the impact of political fluctuations that have hampered the full implementation of such reforms through the years.

In particular, it is crucial for DepEd and TESDA to clarify their distinct roles in the aftermath of the K to 12 law, including the reaffirmation of TESDA as TVET authority, so that both agencies can effectively exercise their respective mandates. Renewed efforts to establish a coordinating body, comprised of the three agencies are important, to avoid duplication of programs and offerings and improve the efficiency of resource allocation. Furthermore, better coordination between the three education subsectors could enable a sector-wide communications strategy, which would address the timeless issue of the "TVET image," i.e., help counter negative perceptions of TVET relative to college education through advocacy. The need to remove the low perceptions of TVET has always been part of recommendations, and has been duly pursued by TESDA. However, doing so in coordination with the other two subsectors of basic education and higher education may be more effective, particularly by fostering an understanding of how learners can navigate through equivalency pathways for seamless education transfer and/or progression between education levels in accordance with the PQF (Recommendation 10).

Recommendation 2: Improve communication and coordination across CHED, DepEd, and TESDA

- **Strengthen institutional mechanisms between DepEd and TESDA for coordination and policy setting.** Examples of such mechanisms include the establishment of a *DepEd-TESDA Joint Working Group on the TVL Track in the K to 12 Program*.[175] Similar mechanisms at the local level could help clarify the distinct roles of the of DepEd and TESDA with respect to the TVL program at various levels of governance.

- **Revive efforts to create a coordinating body comprised of CHED, DepEd, and TESDA.** The establishment of such a body would enable agencies to act strategically and address cross-cutting concerns, facilitate collaborative and complementary sectoral approaches, for example, in targeting the poor and disadvantaged and adopting holistic and integrated approaches to interventions. In particular, it would allow for a much-desired interface in setting policy and priorities, planning, budgeting, and program implementation and review.

- **Develop and implement a sector-wide communications strategy to promote better appreciation of TVET and its distinct niche in the education sector and in national development.** In collaboration with CHED and DepEd, TESDA can improve understanding of senior high school curriculum exits (i.e., employment, entrepreneurship, middle-level skills development, higher education) and of existing equivalency pathways that facilitate progression between education levels in accordance with the PQF. This would also help address negative perceptions of TVET.

---

[175] Department of Education. 2019. *DepEd, TESDA Formalize Agreements on TVL Education*. July 12. https://www.deped.gov.ph/2019/07/12/deped-tesda-formalize-agreements-on-tvl-education/.

Recommendation 3: Resolve the devolution debate as a priority

- **Refer to the study on devolution of TESDA's training function to make a definitive decision on the best course of action for TESDA.** The National Institute for Technical Education and Skills Development (TESD) study on TESDA's devolution and decentralization efforts is a valuable resource providing recommendations for completing devolution.[176]

- **If devolution is to take place, the TESDA budget for training services should be handed down to the appropriate local government units (LGUs).** Noting also that the devolution recommended in the Philippine Education Sector Study (PESS) (Box 6.1) is not only to LGUs, but also to nongovernment organizations and private providers, this requires a comprehensive and robust study to underscore the benefits and avoid pitfalls of devolution of functions.[177] In any case, there must also be a transition and phasing in the devolution process.

- **It is essential to clarify existing options given the current direction of TESDA to build provincial training centers across the country.** The various field offices are directed to strengthen accessibility of TVET programs by establishing provincial training centers in all provinces nationwide in line with the agency's slogan, TESDA *Abot Lahat*. This would imply the need for significant infusion of infrastructure funding, tools and equipment, operating budget, and additional staffing for the new facilities. However, it may be the case that rather than through direct training provision, the same objectives may be achieved through other means such as financing (e.g., the provision of vouchers to trainees). Different options need to be studies and weighed in terms of their effectiveness and efficiency.

Shifting from sector-wide issues, there are also important challenges to address with respect to TESDA's organizational structure and capacity. Although TESDA has made major achievements over the years, questions around its appropriate role, endemic resource constraints, and organizational capacity weigh on its ability to respond to Industry 4.0. In particular, the unsettled issue of devolution of its direct training function has important implications for its access to funding and resources and to provide up-to-date services. While previous studies have taken a position in favor of devolution, this TVET sector study recognizes it as a complex yet critical issue, and argues that, while there are pros and cons to each position, settling this issue should be a priority (Recommendation 3) to remove some of the obstacles hindering TESDA's ability to fulfill its objectives.

Beyond settling the issue of devolution, however, specific initiatives can help strengthen TESDA's organizational structure and capacity. For instance, establishing an office to perform the function of organization development, including taking charge of change management, quality management, and strategic planning; enhancing organizational development interventions; and building capacity for *adaptive change,* which involves the task of adjusting norms and behaviors to new ways of doing business as an organization (Recommendation 4).[178]

Improving financial management is another key issue that can help TESDA improve its organizational capacity. This can be done for instance through the establishment of a public financial management system, and conducting a review of the entire financial system of TESDA (Recommendation 5).

---

[176] The study by TESDA's planning office, TESDA (forthcoming), entitled "Assessment of Devolved TESDA Technology Institutes: Successes, Challenges, and Opportunities" is also expected to provide insights around devolution.

[177] For instance, experience from the devolution of hospitals in the health sector in the Philippines highlights the importance of ensuring that LGUs have the required technical and financial capacity.

[178] R.A. Heifetz, A. Grashow, and M. Linsky. 2009. Leadership in a (Permanent) Crisis. *Harvard Business Review* 87(7-8): 62–69.

Recommendation 4: Strengthen TESDA's organizational structure and capacity

- **Establish an office that would perform the function of organization development to take charge of change management, quality management, and strategic planning efforts.** This could be assigned to an existing office at the start, such as the Corporate Planning unit of the Policy and Planning office, which is already in charge of the strategic performance management system, and eventually create a new office if deemed necessary in the future.

- **Enhance capacity building and organizational development interventions.** The Workforce Training and Development Plan for 2018–2020 is already a comprehensive document that covers the training activities for all levels of staff for the next 3 years based on a thorough training needs analysis. This includes a list of proposed capacity-building activities for individuals, officers, and staff of the organization to upgrade their competencies and improve individual performance, along with proposed organization development interventions to further strengthen the organization.

- **Develop an environment for adaptive change that involves the task of adjusting norms and behaviors to new ways of doing business as an organization.** This is based on Heifetz, Grashow, and Linsky (2009). It is recommended for the organization to face the challenge of redefining its role as TVET authority in the context of a rapidly changing environment and given the realities of its own limited organizational resources. This includes developing and rigorously evaluating alternative models of TVET delivery.

Recommendation 5: Establish a public financial management system

- **Establish a PFM system in TESDA that integrates all financial aspects of government, from planning to budgeting, procurement, cash management, accounting, and auditing.** The PFM is a holistic system that mediates the relationship between objectives, policies, strategies, programs and projects, and outcomes. In such a system, there is a need for collaboration among the PFM functional practitioners in the organization that includes the budget analysts, accountants, auditors, staff from cash management, treasury, procurement, and planning office.

- **Conduct a study to review the whole financial system of TESDA to address key issues.** Such issues include a limited maintenance and other operating expenses budget for efficient operations of the personnel in the field offices and TESDA technical institutions (TTIs), and difficulties raised in procurement that requires capital outlay. TESDA receives a sizeable budget allocation for 2020, and it is important to ensure that these issues are sufficiently addressed.

In the short term, TESDA can take some actions to address its financial issues and resource constraints. Possible actions include rationalizing the use of funds and methods of attracting funding (Recommendation 6).

TESDA has generally maintained quality assurance in the organization as evidenced in the ISO 9001 certification and Philippine Quality Awards recognition of TESDA's commitment to quality. Nevertheless, a continuous pursuit of improvement building on existing initiatives within TESDA's Quality Management System will ensure sustained quality assurance in the face of future changes and challenges (Recommendation 7).

Recommendation 6: Identify short-term solutions for financial and staffing issues

- **Focus TESD centers and schools on Distinctive Areas of Competency program offerings to help address limited resources of TTIs.** This strategy proposes that the regional training centers will conduct pilot testing of new programs or new technology needed by industries, while schools can be laboratories for technical education. The TTIs should be available for trial runs of emerging technologies for simulation and research, which will be of use to the TVET sector.

- **Consider merging TESD centers and TESDA schools, with fiscal independence from the corporate TESDA budget.** The TTIs could maximize resources through sharing and cooperation with each other in an organizational structure with a centralized governance system to cover different campuses in a given area. The TTIs could then have more flexibility in determining their course of action if they have an independent budget separate from the TESDA corporate budget. Further study is needed, though, if this option is considered.

- **The TTIs should pursue awards or recognition from award-winning bodies and accreditation from reputable organizations like the Asia Pacific Accreditation and Certification Commission to raise their prestige and attract funding.** Furthermore, capacity-building activities for administrators and key staff of TTIs would help strengthen their performance to address challenges and opportunities in the short term and equip them in their future endeavors.

Recommendation 7: Pursue continuous improvement for sustained quality assurance

- **The Quality Management System already established in TESDA should be further strengthened along with other existing mechanisms and processes already in place.** TESDA can already enroll additional processes for ISO accreditation, to include even the registration of the Recognized Industry Boards (RIBs) and other key organizational processes. Another challenge is to go beyond level 1 or commitment to quality in the Philippine Quality Awards system.

- **In pursuit of continuous improvement, TESDA should encourage more process improvement teams (PITs).** There are actually some process improvement teams, as part of TESDA's Quality Management System, to improve selected processes in the organization. However, to improve the functioning and effectiveness, there should be mechanisms to mobilize these teams, incorporating team assignment as part of their duties and responsibilities, and providing incentives for innovative ideas to improve processes for optimal organizational performance.

Meeting Rapidly Changing Industry Demand

Although the most-availed TVET programs in recent years reflect growth sectors of the Philippine economy, TVET outputs may not be as aligned with market demand, as they seem to be. Many of the expected post-training occupations of TVET graduates are in low-productivity, nonroutine manual jobs; training–job mismatches are widespread, along with anecdotal evidence of skill shortages and limited employability of TVET graduates; and a slight decline in employers' satisfaction as measured in recent rounds of TESDA's employer surveys. This study did not find strong evidence of TVET improving employment outcomes for Filipino youth. These findings point to an important disconnect between skills supply and demand.

The primary means of ensuring demand-driven TVET, however, remains solid engagement of industry at all stages of the process. TESDA must continue to push for sustained industry involvement in training provision and in other areas of TVET including assessment and certification, and continuous identification of the changing needs and requirements in the Industry 4.0 context (with respect to skills, but also equipment, processes, etc.) TESDA can achieve greater industry involvement for instance by empowering RIBs to take on additional functions, and expand the number of existing RIBs by supporting the development of more industry boards of priority industries (Recommendation 8). This is not a straightforward solution, due to the limited number of existing RIBs, and requirement to develop mechanisms to ensure common standards and processes across industries with regards to their expanded functions.

Regarding industry involvement, a concerning trend in the context of Industry 4.0 is the decline in national enterprise-based training (EBT), and its complete absence in certain regions. EBT already accounted for a limited share of TVET and has further declined to only 3%–4% of enrollment since 2013. At the same time, the advantages of this modality are likely to be enhanced with Industry 4.0. TESDA must therefore intensify its efforts to expand EBT including through a review of the Dual Training System Act of 1994 (DTS Law) and the Apprenticeship Bill—both of which are already on its legislative agenda as per the NTESDP 2018–2022—and seek new and innovative means of incentivizing private sector participation to reverse the downward trend. Specifically, the underlying reasons (e.g., difficult bureaucratic processes or inadequate incentives, etc.) for the limited EBT take-up need to be understood so as find effective levers. Furthermore, efforts to engage with industry must not be done at the policy level only, but also at the level of TVIs and other providers across the country. Because of the regional clustering of industries, there is a need to enhance EBT in a way that will not exacerbate disparities across groups and regions. This will necessitate a great amount of political will, coordination, and resources.

In the rapidly changing Industry 4.0 environment, another issue for TESDA is the lengthy processes for developing standards and assessment tools. This is exacerbated by resource constraints. One potential solution would be the transfer of these functions to the RIBs (Recommendation 9).

Recommendation 8: Intensify push for greater industry involvement

- **Further expand the role and responsibility of RIBs for the development and delivery of services related to TVET.** Matured organizations that are already established RIBs could be empowered to assume some of the important functions of TESDA (e.g., assessment and certification functions, Recommendation 10). While there is already a risk management component in the Quality Management System of TESDA, there is a need to further improve the current model to emphasize compliance and consistency in the registration and management control of RIBs.

- **Support the development of more industry boards of priority industries identified as key economic generators to increase the current number of RIBs.** The *Partnerships and Linkages office* at the central office, which is in charge of engaging the industry boards, should work in tandem with the field offices in applying practical concepts and skills of organization development for industry boards to grow and mature as an organized body in their involvement with TVET and eventually become RIBs. Furthermore, it would be beneficial to also tap the local TESD committees to provide direction and assistance in the engagement of stakeholders from various industry sectors so that there is coherence of programs and activities at the local level with the NTESDP.

- **Intensify efforts to expand EBT. TESDA should prioritize efforts to expand EBT, including through a review of the Dual Training System Act of 1994 (DTS Law) and the Apprenticeship Bill.** Both of which are already on its legislative agenda as per the NTESDP 2018–2022.

Recommendation 9: Transfer certification functions to industry bodies

- **Any transfer of assessment and certification functions to industry requires that the proposed enhanced functions of the RIBs should also implement a quality management system and acquire ISO accreditation.** This means that TESDA must support the accreditation process of these RIBs, especially since the ISO accreditation and certification process entails cost, training, documentation, and a lot of time and effort.

- **Building up the RIBs as a key partner in TVET governance would require an internal review of the organizational arrangements of TESDA.** For instance, some of the processes under the Policy and Planning office, i.e., training standards development of the Qualifications and Standards office, as well as capacity building for TVET trainers and assessors by the National TVET Trainers Academy, will need to be streamlined in consideration of the proposed transfer of its major processes and functions to the RIBs.

Among the key challenges linked to TESDA's resource constraints is a shortage of technology competency assessors. This situation has been aggravated by the K to 12 reform, with several assessors shifting to the general education sector. TESDA must find alternative solutions, such as allowing RIBs to conduct the industry competency assessments (Recommendation 10).

Finally, another component of limiting mismatch and ensuring better targeting of TVET programs is through anticipating skills demand, to the extent possible, and through the assessment and evaluation of existing programs. Understanding industry demand requires stronger and more effective collaborations and partnerships among key stakeholders across industry, government, academe, and civil society. It also requires the availability of high-quality labor market information. Expanding and continually improving data collection techniques (Recommendation 11) can help in anticipating skills needs, and also evaluating programs. For instance, tracer surveys

Recommendation 10: Find alternative solutions to address shortages in assessors

- **Review the incentives and working conditions of assessors to combat the declining number of assessors and migration of assessors to the education sector.** TESDA has the option to recruit qualified assessors to fill up vacant *plantilla* positions that have recently been approved by the Department of Budget and Management; however, there is need to review the incentives and work conditions of assessors. The minimal assessor's fee, as well as their work schedule, and other requirements need to be reviewed. There should also be allocation for scholarships on training methodologies that will qualify candidates for accreditation to become assessors.

- **Explore alternatives to industry competency assessments.** In the face of declining assessor numbers, an option is to allow RIBs to conduct industry competency assessments. Industry vendor own-assessments could be further replicated in other industry sectors with TESDA providing oversight of the assessment process. There is, however, still a need for continued support in strengthening the accreditation of assessors from the industry (i.e., training for private sector practitioners as assessors/accredited trainers), particularly those from the RIBS.

Recommendation 11: Improve capacity for skills anticipation and program evaluation through expanded and improved data collection methods

- **Engage, support, and cooperate with stakeholders and partners for improved availability of labor market and TVET-related data.** Although labor market information in the Philippines is widely available, it can be further improved, for instance through the inclusion of additional TVET-related variables in the labor force survey (LFS), which would expand the range of analysis that can be undertaken with the data.

do not include information on those who have dropped out of TVET, and not all rounds of LFS contain information on the basic characteristics (i.e., public or private, type, and level) of the TVET course taken and completed of the individual. Such data would have provided important insights on specific program characteristics and its employment correlates. The inclusion of the year the individual completed his or her TVET program, if possible, would resolve the timing issue that arises when using the LFS as the primary source of data for this type of analysis.

Continually Adjusting toward Lifelong Learning

In an Industry 4.0 environment, where change is the only constant, workers must be able to move across industries and occupations, along career paths that may be nonlinear. In that regard, all levels of the education and skills supply system need to work in tandem to ensure that flexible pathways exist between different levels of formal education and for the recognition and development of skills acquired outside formal education (lifelong learning). In the Philippines, substantial gains in this respect have been achieved since 2012, culminating with the passage of the Philippine Qualifications Framework (PQF) Act in 2018 and the designation of a permanent governance mechanism mandated by law (i.e., the Philippine Qualification Framework National Coordinating Council [PQF-NCC]). The urgent task for the PQF-NCC is the formulation of an action plan that would operationalize what to many may still seem to be an abstract framework of qualifications and recognitions (Recommendation 12). The critical work on the development of a Philippine Credit Transfer System to establish pathways between TVET and higher education should be sustained and finalized. TESDA should seek opportunities for increased collaboration with CHED and DepEd in promoting understanding of the senior high school curriculum exits (i.e., employment, entrepreneurship, middle-level skills development, higher education) among various stakeholders, and how a learner can navigate through equivalency pathways for seamless education transfer and/or progression between education levels in accordance with the PQF qualification levels. A recent law, Republic Act No. 11206 (Secondary School Career Guidance and Counseling Act) that came into effect in 2019 should provide added impetus in pursuing this, as it mandates CHED and TESDA, among other agencies, to work with DepEd in the development and implementation of a career guidance and counselling program in secondary education.

The growing importance of transferable skills suggests a shift away from narrowly defined competencies. Vocational streams and clusters should be used to impart transferable skills and prepare students not only for an entry-level job, but for careers during which they may transition between jobs with similar skill requirements. Furthermore, although foundational and transversal skills need to be instilled early in the education process, emphasis on these skills must continue through to post-secondary and tertiary education. In particular, even "generic" skills like problem-solving can be highly context-specific and need to be further developed alongside specialized training in TVET or higher education.[179]

Access and Inclusion

Because of the potential distributive effects of technological change, in particular its potential to exacerbate existing inequalities, skills policy has a key role to play in building inclusive societies. TESDA is well aware of this, as is evident in its various documents and strategies. Nevertheless, large discrepancies remain in terms of access to skills acquisition in the Philippines, across regions and across sociodemographic groups.

---

[179] J. Buchanan, L. Wheelahan, and S. Yu. 2018. Increasing Young People's Adaptability and Mobility: From Competency Approach and Twenty-First Century Skills To Capabilities and Vocational Streams. In *Skills and the Future of Work: Strategies for inclusive growth in Asia and the Pacific*, edited by Akiko Sakamoto and Johnny Sung, 125–159. Bangkok: ILO.

Recommendation 12: Strengthen equivalency pathways and facilitate transfer across education levels in line with lifelong learning

- **Fast-track operationalizing the PQF.** It is important to support the PQF-NCC in the formulation of a strategic action plan to operationalize the PQF, which should include effective communications and advocacy to promote meaningful understanding of the PQF among the various education and training institutions, stakeholders in the public and private sectors, and the general public.

- **Sustain and finalize the development of a Philippine Credit Transfer System to establish pathways between TVET and higher education.** This important component of the work of the PQF-NCC must be supported.

- **Impart transferable, including foundational and transversal skills at all levels of the education process, including TVET.** Vocational streams and clusters should be used to impart transferable skills, which suggests a shift away from narrowly defined competencies.

- **Develop and implement a career guidance and counselling program in secondary education, pursuant to Republic Act No. 11206 (Secondary School Career Guidance and Counselling Act) that came into effect in 2019.**

To meet its objective of social equity and workforce inclusion, TESDA must actively encourage enrollment of youth, females, and disadvantaged groups in courses and programs conducive to decent work in manufacturing and services, through scholarships and other incentives, and partnerships with industry and other stakeholders. Although the gender gap in TVET enrollment has been reversed, enrollment remains highly segregated, with female students clustering in courses geared toward sales and services occupations, involving involve mainly nonroutine manual tasks and less pay, in lower-productivity services sectors like retail trade and tourism. TVET offers a promising means of labor market inclusion for women and female enrollment in TVET is high, even in regions with low female labor force participation rates (LFPRs).

Publicly provided TVET in the Philippines accounts for more than half of TVET enrollment, and targets the poor and vulnerable. However, while public TVET targets disadvantaged segments of the population, enrollment shares in public institutions are not necessarily higher in the poorer regions. Public TVET provision in poor regions and remote areas must be focused on local needs, including agriculture and sectors of rural economies.

Attracting youth to the agriculture sector will remain difficult as long as agriculture wages and productivity remain low. Despite the ongoing structural transformation underway in the Philippines, the agriculture sector remains important for the livelihoods of many, particularly in poorer regions outside the urban and industrial centers. TESDA must promote enrollment in agriculture programs and courses that can prepare workers for employment along agricultural supply chains. This also is a challenge recognized in the NTESDP 2018–2022. Thus, TESDA must join efforts with other initiatives aimed at boosting agricultural growth, and develop partnerships with investors in agribusiness and agro-processing ventures.

More generally, although improving the outputs of TVET is critical, there is also a need to expand and improve available opportunities, particularly for disadvantaged groups and remote regions. In that respect, skills policy must complement other policies, including sector policies and other active labor market policies.

Recommendation 13: Expand access to technical and vocational education and training to females and disadvantaged groups in poor and rural regions

- **Promote the enrollment of females and disadvantaged groups in courses leading to high-productivity employment.** TVET enrollment remains highly segregated, with females clustering in programs leading to lower-productivity work.

- **Expand public TVET provision in poor regions and remote areas, with a focus on local needs, including agriculture and sectors of rural economies.**

- **Promote enrollment in agriculture programs and courses that can prepare workers for employment along agricultural supply chains.** TESDA must join efforts with other initiatives aimed at boosting agricultural growth, and develop partnerships with investors in agribusiness and agro-processing ventures.

- **Equitable access to TVET can be facilitated through ICT and digital or alternative training delivery methods (refer to section 12.4 on ADB experience).** Distance and flexible learning options can make TVET programs more cost-effective and widely accessible, including for women who need to balance household responsibilities, employment, and skills acquisition.

- **Expanding access and promoting TVET enrollment, by addressing the TVET image problem, can be achieved through information provision, using innovative approaches.** For instance, recent pilot projects for promoting TVET to target groups in Viet Nam included organizing information sessions to potential students, as well as organizing visits of high school teachers to vocational training colleges to familiarize them with the facilities and learning environments, and help them promote TVET as not only viable but desirable options among their students.[180]

- **Increasing awareness among education sector stakeholders and the wider population of pathways and transitions from secondary education to TVET, and from TVET to higher education and to the labor market with career guidance at all levels (Recommendation 12), should also go a long way in promoting access to TVET for target groups.**

---

[180] Trained in Vietnam. 2017. Experimenting New Tools to Promote Vocational Training for Specific Target Groups: Efforts to Change the Society's Prejudice about Vocational Education" 30 September. https://www.tvet-vietnam.org/en/article/1357.experimenting-new-tools-to-promotevocational-training-for-specific-target-groups-efforts-to-change-the-society-s-prejudice-about-vocational-education.html.

Background Papers

Cabalfin, Michael R. (forthcoming, 2021). "Returns to Technical & Vocational Education & Training in the Philippines." Southeast Asia Department (SERD) Working Paper. Manila: Asian Development Bank.

———. (forthcoming, 2021). "Impact of Scholarships on TVET Outcomes in the Philippines." Southeast Asia Department (SERD) Working Paper. Manila: Asian Development Bank.

Generalao, Ian Nicole A. (forthcoming, 2021). "Measuring the Youth Employment Effects of TVET in the Philippines." Southeast Asia Department (SERD) Working Paper. Manila: Asian Development Bank.

———. (forthcoming, 2021). "Measuring Training-Job Mismatch Among TVET Graduates: An Application of the Task-Based Framework." Southeast Asia Department (SERD) Working Paper. Manila: Asian Development Bank.

Khatiwada, Sameer, Souleima El Achkar, Ian Nicole A. Generalao, and Rosa Mia Arao. (forthcoming, 2021). "Impact of COVID-19 on Labor Markets in Southeast Asia." Southeast Asia Department (SERD) Working Paper. Manila: Asian Development Bank.

References

Abrigo, Michael R.M., Rachel H. Racelis, J.M. Ian Salas, Alejandro N. Herrin, Danica A.P. Ortiz, and Zhandra C. Tam. 2018. "Are We Missing Out on the Demographic Dividend? Trends and Prospects." PIDS Discussion Paper Series No. 2018-23. Quezon City: Philippine Institute for Development Studies.

Acemoglu, Daron. 1999. "Changes in Unemployment and Wage Inequality: An Alternative Theory and Some Evidence." *The American Economic Review* 89(5): 1259–78.

Acemoglu, Daron and David H. Autor. 2011. "Skills, Tasks and Technologies: Implications for Employment and Earnings." *Handbook of Labor Economics* 4b: 1043–1171.

Acemoglu, Daron and Pascual Restrepo. 2016. "The Race Between Machine and Man: Implications of Technology for Growth, Factor Shares and Employment." National Bureau of Economic Research (NBER) Working Paper No. 22252. Cambridge, MA: NBER.

Acosta, Pablo, Takiko Igarashi, Rosechin Olfindo, and Jan Rutkowski. 2017. *Developing Socioemotional Skills for the Philippines' Labor Market*. Directions in Development Series. Washington, DC: World Bank.

Aleman-Castilla, Benjamin. 2006. "The Effect of Trade Liberalization on Informality and Wages: Evidence from Mexico." CEP Discussion Papers No. 763. London: London School of Economics and Political Science, Centre for Economic Performance.

Ali, Ifzal and Juzhong Zhuang. 2007. "Inclusive Growth toward a Prosperous Asia: Policy Implications." Economics and Research RD Working Paper No. 97. Manila: Asian Development Bank.

Angrist, Joshua and Alan B. Krueger. 1991. "Does Compulsory School Attendance Affect Schooling and Earnings?" *The Quarterly Journal of Economics* 106(4): 979–1014.

Aquino, Benigno III. 2010. "10 Ways to Fix Philippine Basic Education." *Philippine Daily Inquirer*. February. https://www.scribd.com/document/26541154/POLICY-NOTE-10-Ways-to-Fix-Philippine-Basic-Education.

Arayata, Ma. Cristina. 2020. "Filipinos Can Expect More from TESDA amid Pandemic: Lapeña." *Philippine News Agency*. 15 September. https://www.pna.gov.ph/articles/1115538.

Asian Development Bank (ADB). 2018a. *Economic Indicators for Southeastern Asia and the Pacific: Input-Output Tables*. Manila: ADB.

———. 2018b. *Asian Development Outlook 2018: How Technology Affects Jobs*. Manila: ADB.

———. 2018c. *Advanced Knowledge and Skills for Sustainable Growth Project: Report and Recommendation of the President.* Manila: ADB.

———. 2019. *Realizing Education for All in the Digital Age.* Manila: ADB.

———. 2021. *Reaping Benefits of Industry 4.0 through Skills Development in High-Growth Industries in Southeast Asia: Insights from Cambodia, Indonesia, the Philippines, and Viet Nam.* Manila: ADB.

Asian Development Bank Senior High School Support Program (ADB-SHSSP). 2019. *Field Visit Findings: Senior High School Support Program Review Mission Aide Memoire.* Manila: ADB.

Asian Development Bank (ADB) and World Bank. 1999. *Philippine Education for the 21st Century. The 1998 Philippines Education Sector Study.* Manila: ADB.

Association of South East Asian Nations (ASEAN). 2020. *Standard for In-company Trainers.* Bangkok: Deutsche Gesellschaft für Internationale Zusammenarbeit (GIZ) GmbH.

Attanasio, Orazio, Adriana Kugler, and Costas Meghir. 2011. "Subsidizing Vocational Training for Disadvantaged Youth in Columbia: Evidence from a Randomized Trial." *American Economic Journal: Applied Economics* 3(3): 188–220.

Autor, David H. 2015. "Why Are There Still So Many Jobs? The History and Future of Workplace Automation." *Journal of Economic Perspectives* 29(3): 3–30.

Autor, David H. and David Dorn. 2013. "The Growth of Low-Skill Service Jobs and the Polarization of the US Labor Market." *American Economic Review* 103(5): 1553–1597.

Autor, David H., Frank Levy, and Richard J. Murnane. 2003. "The Skill Content of Recent Technological Change: An Empirical Exploration." *Quarterly Journal of Economics* 118(4): 1279–1333.

Balakrishnan, Ravi, Chad Steinberg, and Murtaza Syed. 2013. "The Elusive Quest for Inclusive Growth: Growth, Poverty and Inequality in Asia." IMF Working Papers 13/152. Washington, DC: International Monetary Fund.

Bamber, Penny, Stacey Frederick, and Gary Gereffi. 2016. *The Philippines in the Aerospace Global Value Chain: Opportunities for Upgrading.* Durham, NC: Duke University Centre on Globalization, Governance and Competitiveness.

Bandura, Romina, and Paul Grainger. 2019. "Rethinking Pathways to Employment: Technical and Vocational Training for the Digital Age." Policy Brief. University College London: Center for Strategic and International Studies.

Baum, Christopher F. 2006. *An Introduction to Modern Econometrics Using Stata.* College Station, Texas: Stata Press.

Bayan Academy. Forthcoming. "2018–2022 NTESDP [National Technical Education and Skills Development Plan] Action Programming." Quezon City: Bayan Academy for Social Entrepreneurship and Human Resource Development (BASE-HRD or Bayan Academy).

Betcherman, Gordon, Martin Godfrey, Susana Puerto, Friederike Rother, and Antoneta Stavreska. 2007. "A Review of Interventions to Support Young Workers: Findings of the Youth Employment Inventory." World Bank Social Protection Discussion Paper No.0715. Washington, DC: World Bank.

Bidani, Benu, Niels-Hugo Blunch, Chor-Ching Goh, and Christopher O'Leary. 2009. "Evaluating Job Training in Two Chinese Cities." *Journal of Chinese Economic and Business Studies* 7(1): 77–94.

Buchanan, John, Leesa, Wheelahan, and Serena Yu. 2018. "Increasing Young People's Adaptability and Mobility: From Competency Approach and Twenty-First Century Skills To Capabilities and Vocational Streams" In *Skills and the Future of Work: Strategies for inclusive growth in Asia and the Pacific*, edited by Akiko Sakamoto and Johnny Sung, 125–159. Bangkok: International Labour Organization.

Bureau of Local Employment - Department of Labor and Employment (BLE-DOLE). 2012. "Job-Skill Mismatch: Is there an Effective and Quick Solution?" Presentation. https://www.britishcouncil.ph/sites/default/files/ruth_r_rodriguez_skills_job_mismartch.pdf.

Card, David. 1993. "Using Geographic Variation in College Proximity to Estimate the Return to Schooling." NBER Working Paper Series No. 4483. Cambridge, MA: National Bureau of Economic Research.

———. 1999. "The Causal Effect of Education on Earnings." *Handbook of Labor Economics* 3: 1801–1863.

———. 2001. "Estimating the Return to Schooling: Progress on Some Econometric Problems." *Econometrica* 69(5): 1127–1160.

Card, David, Jochen Kluve, and Andrea Weber. 2010. "Active Labour Market Policy Evaluations: A Meta-Analysis." *The Economic Journal* 120 (November): F452–F477.

Cattaneo, Matias D. 2010. "Efficient Semiparametric Estimation of Multi-Valued Treatment Effects Under Ignorability." *Journal of Econometrics* 155: 138–54.

Commission on Adult Vocational Teaching and Learning (CAVTL). 2013. *It's About Work... Excellent Adult Vocational Teaching and Learning.* England: Learning and Skills Improvement Service (LSIS).

Commission on Higher Education (CHED), A.A. Arcelo, and Educational Capital Corporation [mimeo]. "CHED Graduate Tracer Study." http://www.ched.gov.ph/wp-content/uploads/2013/05/CHED-00000016.pdf. Accessed 20 April 2019.

Congressional Budget Office. 2018. *Factors Affecting the Labor Force Participation of People Ages 25 to 54.* Washington, DC: Congress of the United States.

Cooperrider, David L., Peter F. Sorenson Jr., Therese F. Yaegar, and Diana Whitney. 2005. *Appreciative Inquiry: Foundations in Positive Organization Development.* Champaign, IL: Stipes Pub LLC.

Cooperrider, David L., and Lindsey N. Godwin. 2012. "Positive Organization Development: Innovation-inspired Change in an Economy and Ecology of Strengths." In *The Oxford Handbook of Positive Organizational Scholarship*, edited by Gretchen M. Spreitzer and Kim S. Cameron. Oxford: Oxford University Press.

CNN Philippines. 2020. "TESDA Lacks Equipment for Blended Learning." 9 September. https://cnnphilippines.com/news/2020/9/9/TESDA-lacks-equipment-blended-learning.html.

de Vries, Gaaitzen, Marcel Timmer, and Klaas de Vries. 2015. "Structural Transformation in Africa: Static Gains, Dynamic Losses." *The Journal of Development Studies* 51(6): 674–88.

Department of Education (DepEd). 2019. "DepEd, TESDA Formalize Agreements on TVL Education." July 12. https://www.deped.gov.ph/2019/07/12/deped-tesda-formalize-agreements-on-tvl-education/.

Department of Education (DepEd) Order No. 21. 2019. *Policy Guidelines on the K to 12 Basic Education Program.* Pasig: DepEd.

Department of Education (DepEd) Order No. 68. 2017. *Guidelines on the Implementation of the Joint Delivery Voucher Program for Senior High School Technical-Vocational-Livelihood Specializations (JDVP-TVL) for School Year (SY) 2017–2018.* Pasig: DepEd.

Dumaua-Cabautan, Madeline, Sylwyn C. Calizo, Francis Mark A. Quimba, and Lachmi C. Pacio. 2018. "E-Education in the Philippines: The Case of Technical Education and Skills Development Authority Online Program." Discussion Paper Series No. 2018-08. Quezon City: Philippine Institute for Development Studies.

Dymock, Darryl and Mark A. Tyler. 2018. "Towards a More Systematic Approach To Continuing Professional Development in Vocational Education and Training." *Studies in Continuing Education* 40(2): 198–211.

El Achkar Hilal, Souleima. 2018. "Creative destruction? Technological Progress, Employment Growth, and Skills for the Future in Indonesia, the Philippines, Thailand and Vietnam." In *Skills and the Future of Work: Strategies for Inclusive Growth in Asia and the Pacific*, edited by Akiko Sakamoto and Johnny Sung, 182–255. Bangkok: International Labour Organization.

Epetia, Maria Christina F. 2018. "College Graduates in Non-College Jobs: Measuring Overeducation in the Philippine Labor Market." PhD dissertation. Diliman, Quezon City: University of the Philippines School of Economics.

———. 2019. "Explaining the Gender Gap in Labor Force Participation in the Philippines." *Japan Labor Issues* 3(17): 30–38.

Esguerra, Jude H., Makoto Ogawa, and Milan Vodopivec. 2002. "Options of Public Income Support for the Unemployed in the Philippines and Social Protection." Social Protection Discussion Paper Series No. SP 0204. Washington, DC: World Bank.

European Centre for Development Policy Management (ECDPM). 2008. "Capacity, Change and Performance Insights and Implications for Development Cooperation." Policy Management Brief. No. 21. Maastricht: ECDPM.

Executive Order No. 5. 2016. Approving and Adopting the Twenty-Five-Year Long Term Vision Entitled Ambisyon Natin 2040 as Guide for Development Planning. Philippines.

Executive Order No. 67. 2018. Rationalizing the Office of the President through the Consolidation of its Core Mandates and Strengthening the Democratic and Institutional Framework of the Executive Department. Philippines.

Executive Order No. 83. 2012. Institutionalization of the Philippine Qualifications Framework. Philippines.

Executive Order No. 273. 2000. Institutionalizing the System of National Coordination, Assessment, Planning and Monitoring of the Entire Educational System. Philippines.

Executive Order No. 632. 2007. Amending Executive Order No. 273 (Series of 2000) and Mandating a Presidential Assistant to Assess, Plan and Monitor the Entire Educational System. Philippines.

Executive Order No. 652. 2007. Creating the Presidential Task Force to Assess, Plan and Monitor the Entire Educational System. Philippines.

Federal Institute for Vocational Education and Training (BIBB). 2018. "Metal Working and Electrical Occupations Structured in a Future-Proof Way." 19 June. https://www.bibb.de/en/pressemitteilung_81176.php.

Fernandez, Kenneth E. 2011. "Evaluating School Improvement Plans and their Effect on Academic Performance." *Educational Policy* 25(2): 338–67.

Fernandez-Stark, Karina and Penny Bamber. 2018. "Skills Development for Economic and Social Upgrading: The Case of Asian Developing Countries in the Global Value Chains." In *Skills and the Future of Work: Strategies for Inclusive Growth in Asia and the Pacific*, edited by Akiko Sakamoto and Johnny Sung, 62–97. Bangkok: International Labour Organization.

Generalao, Ian Nicole A. 2019a. "Skill Transferability and Mismatch Among Post-Training Graduates: An Application of the Task-Based Approach." Master's thesis. Diliman, Quezon City: University of the Philippines School of Economics.

———. 2019b. "Mapping Tasks to Occupations Using Philippine Data." University of the Philippines School of Economics Discussion Paper No. 2019-04. Diliman, Quezon City: University of the Philippines School of Economics.

———. 2020. "Distance between Occupations in the Task Complexity Space." University of the Philippines School of Economics Discussion Paper No. 2020-08. Diliman, Quezon City: University of the Philippines School of Economics.

Gertler, Paul, Sebastian Martinez, Patrick Premand, Laura Rawlings, and Christel Vermeersch. 2016. *Impact Evaluation in Practice*. Washington, DC: The World Bank.

Goldberg, Pinelopi Koujianou and Nina Pavcnik. 2007. "Distributional Effects of Globalization in Developing Countries." *Journal of Economic Literature* 45(1): 39–82.

Goos, Maarten, Alan Manning, and Anna Salomons. 2014. "Explaining Job Polarization: Routine-Biased Technological Change and Offshoring." *American Economic Review* 104(8): 2509–26.

Government of the Philippines. Undated. Philippine Qualifications Framework. https://pqf.gov.ph.

Griliches, Zvi. 1977. "Estimating the Returns to Schooling: Some Econometrics Problems." *Econometrica* 45(1): 1–22.

Gujarati, D.N. 2003. *Basic Econometrics*. New York: McGraw Hill Book Co.

Gutierrez, Catalina, Carlo Orecchia, Pierella Paci, and Pieter Serneels. 2007. "Does Employment Generation Really Matter for Poverty Reduction?" Policy Research Working Paper No. 4432. Washington, DC: World Bank.

Handel, Michael. 2017a. *Predictors and Consequences of Mismatch in Developing Countries: Results from the World Bank STEP Survey*. Geneva: International Labour Organization. https://www.ilo.org/skills/pubs/WCMS_726816/lang--en/index.htm.

———. 2017b. "Education and Skills Mismatch in Developing Countries, Magnitudes, Explanations and Impacts." Presentation. International Conference on Jobs and Skills Mismatch 11–12 May. http://www.ilo.org/skills/events/WCMS_538198/lang--en/index.htm.

Heckman, James. 1979. "Sample Selection Bias as a Specification Error." *Econometrica* (The Econometric Society) 47(1): 153–61.

Heifetz, Ronald A., Alexander Grashow, and Marty Linsky. 2009. "Leadership in a (Permanent) Crisis." *Harvard Business Review* 87(7-8): 62–69.

Herrendorf, Berthold, Richard Rogerson, and Ákos Valentinyi. 2013. "Growth and Structural Transformation." NBER Working Paper No. 18996. Cambridge, MA: National Bureau of Economic Research.

Hicks, Joan Hamory, Michael Kremer, Isaac Mbiti, and Edward Miguel. 2011. "Evaluating the Impact of Vocational Education Vouchers on Out-of-School Youth in Kenya." 3ie Impact Evaluation Report 37. New Delhi: International Initiative for Impact Evaluation (3ie).

Inter-Agency Task Force for the Management of Emerging Infectious Diseases – Technical Working Group for Anticipatory and Forward Planning (IATF-TWG for AFP). 2020. *We Recover as One*. https://www.neda.gov.ph/wp-content/uploads/2020/05/We-Recover-As-One.pdf.

International Labour Organization (ILO). 2012. *International Standard Classification of Occupations (ISCO-08), Volume 1. Structure, Group Definitions and Correspondence Tables*. Geneva: ILO.

———. 2013. *Global Employment Trends for Youth 2013: A Generation at Risk*. Geneva: ILO.

———. 2015. *World Employment and Social Outlook: Trends 2015*. Geneva: ILO.

———. 2017. *Decent Work Country Diagnostics: Philippines 2017*. Geneva: ILO.

International Labour Organization (ILO) and Asian and Development Bank (ADB). 2020. *Tackling the COVID-19 Youth Employment Crisis in Asia and the Pacific*. Bangkok: ILO, and Manila: ADB.

Kapsos, Steven. 2005. "The Employment Intensity of Growth: Trends and Macroeconomic Determinants." ILO Employment Strategy Papers 2005/12. Geneva: International Labour Office.

Khan, Azizur Rahman. 2001. Employment policies for poverty reduction. *Issues in Employment and Poverty Discussion Paper (IEPDP) 1*. Geneva: International Labour Organisation.

Kluve, Jochen, Susana Puerto, David Robalino, Jose Manuel Romero, Friederike Rother, Jonathan Stoterau, Felix Weidenkaff, and Marc Witte. 2016. "Do Youth Employment Programs Improve Labor Market Outcomes? A Systematic Review." Institute for the Study of Labor IZA Discussion Paper, No. 10263. Bonn: Institute for the Study of Labor (IZA).

Kluve, Jochen and Christoph M. Schmidt. 2002. "Can Training and Employment Subsidies Combat European Unemployment?" *Economic Policy* 17(35): 409–48.

Kopelman, Jason L. and Harvey S. Rosen. 2014. "Are Public Sector Jobs Recession-Proof? Were They Ever?" NBER Working Paper No. 20692. Cambridge, MA: National Bureau of Economic Research.

Kupets, Olga. 2017. "Educational Mismatch Among Young Workers in Low- and Middle-Income Countries: Analysis of the SWTS Data." In *Skills and Jobs Mismatches in Low- and Middle-Income Countries,* edited by Paul Comyn and Olga Strietska-Ilina, 89–148. Geneva: International Labour Office.

Leuven, Edwin and Barbara Sianesi. 2003. "PSMATCH2: Stata Module to Perform Full Mahalanobis and Propensity Score Matching, Common Support Graphing, and Covariate Imbalance Testing." *Statistical Software Components.*

Lewis, W. Arthur. 1954. "Economic Development with Unlimited Supplies of Labour." *The Manchester School* 22(2): 139–91.

Malindog-Uy, Anna. 2020. "'Build Build Build' Program Amid a Pandemic." *The ASEAN Post.* 13 September. https://theaseanpost.com/article/build-build-build-program-amid-pandemic.

Manpower Group. 2015. *2015 Talent Shortage Survey.* Milwaukee: Manpower Group.

Mapa, Dennis S. 2015. *Demographic Sweet Spot and Dividend in the Philippines: The Window of Opportunity is Closing Fast.* Pasig: National Economic and Development Authority.

McGuinness, Seamus, Konstantinos Pouliakas, and Paul Redmond. 2017. "How Useful Is the Concept of Skills Mismatch?" In *Skills and Jobs Mismatches in Low- and Middle-Income Countries,* edited by Paul Comyn and Olga Strietska-Ilina, 5–34. Geneva: International Labour Office.

McKenzie, David. 2017. "How Effective are Active Labor Market Policies in Developing Countries? A Critical Review of Recent Evidence." World Bank Policy Research Working Paper 8011. Washington, DC: World Bank.

McMillian, Margaret S. and Dani Rodrik. 2011. "Globalization, Structural Change and Productivity Growth." NBER Working Paper No. 17143. Cambridge, MA: National Bureau of Economic Research.

Mehta, Aashish, Jesus Felipe, Pilipinas Quising, and Sheila Camingue. 2011. "Overeducation in Developing Economies: How Can We Test for It, and What Does It Mean?" *Economics of Education Review* 30(6): 1334–47.

Mincer, Jacob. 1974. *Schooling, Experience, and Earnings* (Human Behavior and Social Institutions 2). Cambridge, MA: National Bureau of Economic Research.

Ministry of Skill Development and Entrepreneurship. 2016. *Report of the Committee for Rationalization & Optimization of the Functioning of the Sector Skill Councils.* New Delhi: Ministry of Skill Development and Entrepreneurship.

National Economic and Development Authority (NEDA). 2004. *Medium-term Philippine Development Plan 2004–2010.* Pasig City: NEDA.

———. 2017. *Philippine Development Plan 2017–2022.* Pasig: NEDA.

———. 2019a. "Out-migration in Agriculture: An Analysis of the Loss of Labor in Agriculture Sector in the Philippines." R&D Policy Note 1(1). Pasig: NEDA.

———. 2019b. "Joint Statement on the 176th DBCC Meeting: Review of the Macroeconomic Assumptions and Fiscal Program for the 2020 President's Budget." 18 July. https://www.neda.gov.ph/joint-statement-on-the-176th-dbcc-meeting-review-of-the-macroeconomic-assumptions-and-fiscal-program-for-the-2020-presidents-budget/.

———. 2020. "Innovative and Flexible Training Needed to Retool and Upskill Labor Force –NEDA." 16 June. http://www.neda.gov.ph/innovative-and-flexible-training-needed-to-retool-and-upskill-labor-force-neda/.

Nazario, Dhel. 2020. "TESDA Partners with Mobile App Developer to Assist Graduates." *Manila Bulletin.* 29 September. https://mb.com.ph/2020/09/29/tesda-partners-with-mobile-app-developer-to-assist-graduates/.

Nübler, Irmgard. 2016. "New Technologies: A Jobless Future or Golden Age of Job Creation?" ILO Working Paper 13. Geneva: International Labour Office.

Orbeta, Aniceto C. Jr. and Emmanuel F. Esguerra. 2016. "The National System of Technical Vocational Education and Training in the Philippines: Review and Reform Ideas." PIDS Discussion Paper Series, No. 2016-07. Quezon City: Philippine Institute for Development Studies.

Organisation for Economic Co-operation and Development (OECD). 2014. *Skills Beyond School: Synthesis Report, OECD Reviews of Vocational Education and Training.* Paris: OECD Publishing.

———. 2018. *Multi-dimensional Review of Thailand: Volume 2. In-depth Analysis and Recommendations.* Paris: OECD Publishing.

Palmer, Robert. 2018. *Job and Skills Mismatch in the Informal Economy.* Geneva: International Labor Office.

Perlman, Daniel H. 1978. "Higher Education in The Philippines: An Overview and Current Problems." *Peabody Journal of Education* 55(2): 119–26.

Philippine Statistics Authority (PSA). 2012. Technical Notes on the Labor Force Survey (LFS). Quezon City: PSA.

———. 2014. *2012 Philippine Standard Occupational Classification.* Quezon City: PSA.

Presidential Commission on Educational Reform (PCER). (2000). *Philippine Agenda for Educational Reform: The PCER Report.* Manila: Presidential Commission on Educational Reform.

Psacharopoulos, George. 1985. "Returns to Education: A Further International Update and Implications." *Journal of Human Resources* 20(4): 583–604.

Psacharopoulos, George and Harry Anthony Patrinos. 1993. "Secondary Vocational Education and Earnings in Latin America." *The Vocational Aspect of Education* 45(3): 229–38.

———. 2018. "Returns to Investment in Education: A Decennial Review of Global Literature." Policy Research Working Paper 8402. Washington, DC: The World Bank.

Psacharopolous, George and Ying Chu Ng. 1992. *Earnings and Education in Latin America: Assessing Priorities for Schooling Investments.* Washington, DC: World Bank.

PwC. 2017. Megatrends: 5 global shifts changing the way we live and do business. Available at: https://www.pwc.co.uk/issues/megatrends.html (Accessed 03.12.2020).

Republic Act (RA) No. 7796. 1994a. An act creating the Technical Education and Skills Development Authority, providing for its powers, structure and for other purposes. Philippines.

———. 1994b. Rules and Regulations Implementing the TESDA Act of 1994. Philippines.

Republic Act (RA) No. 10533. 2013. An act enhancing the Philippine basic education system by strengthening its curriculum and increasing the number of years for basic education, appropriating funds therefor and for other purposes. Philippines.

Republic Act (RA) No. 10647. 2014. An act strengthening the ladderized interface between technical-vocational education and training and higher education. Philippines.

Republic Act (RA) No. 10968. 2017a. An act institutionalizing the Philippine Qualifications Framework (PQF), establishing the PQF-National Coordinating Council (NCC) and appropriating funds therefor. Philippines.

———. 2017b. Implementing Rules and Regulations of Republic Act No. 10968: An act institutionalizing the Philippine Qualifications Framework (PQF), establishing the PQF-National Coordinating Council (NCC) and appropriating funds therefor. Philippines.

Republic Act (RA) No. 11206. 2018. An act establishing a career guidance and counseling program for all secondary schools and appropriating funds therefor. Philippines.

Resolution No. 2014-03. 2014. Adopting the Amendments of the Philippine Qualifications Framework and Descriptors. Taguig: TESDA.

Rivas, Ralf. 2020. "Farmers Trash Spoiled Vegetables While Poor Go Hungry." *Rappler.* 6 April. https://www.rappler.com/newsbreak/in-depth/farmers-trash-spoiled-vegetables-urban-poor-hungry-coronavirus-lockdown.

Robinson, Chris. 2018. "Occupational Mobility, Occupation Distance, and Specific Human Capital." *The Journal of Human Resources* 53(2): 513–51.

Robinson, Viviane M.J. 2010. "From Instructional Leadership to Leadership Capabilities: Empirical Findings and Methodological Challenges." *Leadership and Policy in Schools* 9(1): 1–26.

Rubin, Donald B. 1974. "Estimating Causal Effects of Treatments in Randomized and Nonrandomized Studies." *Journal of Educational Psychology* 66(5): 688–701.

Sakellariou, Chris. 2006. "Benefits of General Vs Vocational/Technical Education in Singapore Using Quantile Regressions." *International Journal of Manpower* (Emerald Group Publishing Limited) 27(4): 358–76.

Schwab, Klaus. 2016. *The Fourth Industrial Revolution.* Geneva: World Economic Forum. SkillsFuture. n.d. https://www.skillsfuture.sg/.

Smith, Peter C. and Lita J. Domingo. 1977. "The Social Structure of Underutilized Labor in the Philippines: An Application of Hauser's Labor Utilization Framework." *Philippine Review of Economics* 14(2): 29–63.

Spöttll, Georg. 2009. "Teacher Education for TVET in Europe and Asia: The Comprehensive Requirements." *Journal of Technical Education and Training* 1(1): 1–16.

StataCorp. 2015. *Stata 14 Base Reference Manual*. College Station, TX: Stata Press.

Sugiyarto, Guntur. 2007. "Measuring Underemployment: Establishing the Cut-Off Point." ERD Working Paper Series No. 92. Manila: Asian Development Bank.

Sung, Johnny. 2018. "Business Model, Skills Intensity and Job Quality for Inclusive Society." In *Skills and the Future of Work: Strategies for Inclusive Growth in Asia and the Pacific*, edited by Akiko Sakamoto and Johnny Sung, 24–40. Bangkok: International Labour Organization.

Tan, Jee-Peng and Yoo-Jeung Joy Nam. 2012. *Pre-Employment Technical and Vocation Training: Fostering Relevance, Effectiveness and Efficiency*. Washington, DC: The World Bank.

Technical Education and Skills Development Authority (TESDA). TESDA Trainee Management Information System (T2MIS). Taguig: TESDA.

———. (forthcoming). "Assessment of Devolved TESDA Technology Institutes: Successes, Challenges, and Opportunities" Taguig: TESDA.

———. 2012a. "The Philippine Qualifications Framework." TESDA Policy Brief, Issue 2. Taguig: TESDA.

———. 2012b. "Employer Satisfaction Survey." Taguig: TESDA.

———. 2014. "2014 Employers' Satisfaction Survey." Taguig: TESDA.

———. 2018a. *National Technical Education and Skills Development Plan (NTESDP) 2018–2022*. Taguig: TESDA.

———. 2018b. "Strategic Direction." In *National Technical Education and Skills Development Plan 2018–2022*. Taguig: Technical Education and Skills Development Authority.

———. 2018c. *2017 TESDA Annual Report*. Taguig: TESDA.

———. 2018d. *List of Promulgated TRs as of June 2018*. Taguig: Qualifications and Standards Office (QSO) of TESDA.

———. 2019a. *2020 Revised Planning Guidelines*. Taguig: TESDA. https://www.tesda.gov.ph/Uploads/File/Planning%20Guidelines/2020%20Revised%20Planning%20Guidelines.pdf.

———. 2019b. *2018 TESDA Annual Report*. Taguig: TESDA.

———. 2019c. *2018 Study on the Employment of TVET Graduates Full Report*. Taguig: TESDA

———. 2020a. "Globe/TM Customers Get Free Data Access to TESDA Online Courses." 21 August. https://www.tesda.gov.ph/News/Details/18965.

———. 2020b. "TESDA Encourages Public to Make Washable Face Masks." 10 April. https://pia.gov.ph/news/articles/1038559.

———. 2020c. "TESDA Commemorates 26th Founding Anniversary with the Theme "TESDA@26: Bringing Hope in Times of Crisis." 25 August. https://www.tesda.gov.ph/News/Details/18969.

———.2020d. *2019 TESDA Annual Report*. Taguig: TESDA.

TESDA Circular No. 3. 2018. Omnibus Guidelines for 2018 Training for Work Scholarship Program (TWSP) and Special Training for Employment Program (STEP). Taguig City: TESDA.

TESDA Circular No. 6. 2018. 2018 Special Training for Employment Program (STEP) TVET Programs Coverage and Schedule of Cost. Taguig: TESDA.

TESDA Circular No. 18. 2019. Revised Process Cycle Time for Program Registration and Assessment and Certification. Taguig City: TESDA.

TESDA Circular No. 28. 2018. Implementing Guidelines for 2018 Private Education Student Assistance (PESFA). Taguig City: TESDA.

TESDA Circular No. 49. 2019. Implementing Guidelines on the New TVET Governance Ecosystem: Creation of the TESDA Technology Institution (TTI) Advisory Council. Taguig: TESDA.

TESDA Circular No. 62. 2020. Guidelines in Implementing Flexible Learning in TVET. Taguig: TESDA.

The Congressional Commission on Education (EDCOM). 1993. *Governance and Management,* v.4. *Areas of Concern in Philippine Education,* Book One. Making Education Work. Quezon City: Congressional Oversight Committee on Education.

Trained in Vietnam. 2017. "Experimenting new tools to promote vocational training for specific target groups: Efforts to change the society's prejudice about vocational education." 30 September. https://www.tvet-vietnam.org/en/article/1357.experimenting-new-tools-to-promote-vocational-training-for-specific-target-groups-efforts-to-change-the-society-s-prejudice-about-vocational-education.html.

Tripney, Janice S. and Jorge G. Hombrados. 2013. "Technical and Vocational Education and Training (TVET) for Young People in Low- and Middle-Income Countries: A Systematic Review and Meta-Analysis." *Empirical Research in Vocational Education & Training* 5:3.

United Nations. 1990. *International Standard Industrial Classification of All Economic Activities Revision 3*. New York: United Nations.

———. 2010. *Manual on Statistics of International Trade in Services 2010 (MSITS 2010)*. New York: United Nations.

United Nations Educational, Scientific, and Cultural Organization (UNESCO). 2015. *Transversal Skills in TVET: Policy Implications*. Asia-Pacific Education System Review Series, Issue 8. Bangkok: UNESCO.

United Nations Educational, Scientific, and Cultural Organization - International Centre for Technical and Vocational Education and Training (UNESCO-UNEVOC). 2016. *Measuring the Return on Investment in TVET.* Bonn: UNESCO-UNEVOC.

———. 2019. TVET Country Profile: Philippines. Bonn: UNESCO-UNEVOC.

Vandenberg, Paul and Jade Laranjo. (forthcoming). Effective or Irrelevant? The Impact of TVET on Employment in the Philippines. ADB Working Paper Series. Manila: ADB.

Vivarelli, Marco. 2007. "Innovation and Employment: A Survey." IZA Discussion Paper No. 2621. Bonn: Institute for the Study of Labor.

von Gaudecker, Hans-Martin, Radost Holler, Lena Janys, Bettina Siflinger, Christian Zimpelmann. 2020. "Labour Supply in the Early Stages of the COVID-19 Pandemic: Empirical Evidence on Hours, Home Office, and Expectations." IZA DP No. 13158. http://ftp.iza.org/dp13158.pdf.

Wooldridge, Jeffrey M. 2010. *Econometric Analysis of Cross Section and Panel Data.* 2nd ed. Cambridge, MA: MIT Press.

World Bank. Poverty and Equity Database. (Accessed 23 October 2020). https://databank.worldbank.org/source/poverty-and-equity.

———. 2004. "Philippines - Education Policy Reforms in Action: A Review of Progress Since PESS and PCER." World Bank Other Operational Studies 14367. Washington, DC: The World Bank.

Yamazaki, Ken. 2018. "Network-Based Business Models and Employment Adjustments: Implications for Skills in Japan." In *Skills and the Future of Work: Strategies for inclusive growth in Asia and the Pacific,* edited by Akiko Sakamoto and Johnny Sung, 41–61. Bangkok: International Labour Organization.

www.ingramcontent.com/pod-product-compliance
Lightning Source LLC
Chambersburg PA
CBHW061935290426
44113CB00025B/2918